TOLSTOY'S AESTHETICS AND HIS ART

TOLSTOY'S AESTHETICS AND HIS ART

Rimvydas Šilbajoris

Slavica Publishers, Inc.

Slavica publishes a wide variety of scholarly books and textbooks on the languages, peoples, literatures, cultures, history, etc. of the USSR and Eastern Europe. For a complete catalog of books and journals from Slavica, with prices and ordering information, write to:

>Slavica Publishers, Inc.
>PO Box 14388
>Columbus, Ohio 43214

ISBN: 0-89357-216-0.

Copyright © 1990 by Rimvydas Šilbajoris. All rights reserved.

This book was published in 1991.

All statements of fact or opinion are those of the authors and do not necessarily agree with those of the publisher, which takes no responsibility for them.

Printed in the United States of America.

CONTENTS

Preface 6

Introduction 7

Chapter 1 *Beginning of the Quest* 13

Chapter 2 *The Lessons of Yasnaya Polyana* 41

Chapter 3 *The Conscience of the Artist* 68

Chapter 4 *What is Art?* 97

Chapter 5 *Theory and Practice* 134

Chapter 6 *The Legacy at Home* 179

Chapter 7 *The Legacy Abroad* 225

Chapter 8 *Conclusions* 250

Notes 269

Selected Bibliography 309

PREFACE

This publication was prepared under a grant from the Woodrow Wilson International Center for Scholars, Washington, D.C. The statements and views expressed herein are those of the author and are not necessarily those of the Wilson Center.

The 1984 Fellowship from the Kennan Institute of the Woodrow Wilson Center made it possible to complete the final stages of research for the present monograph. The first tentative explorations of the topic were begun at Moscow University, under the sponsorship of IREX.

I am deeply grateful to Dr. Youngjoong Seog, presently at the University of Korea, Seoul, for extensive research assistance and for perceptive, patient and supportive critique of the manuscript at various stages of its development.

The College of Humanities and the Slavic Department at the Ohio State University have been helpful in various ways while this monograph was taking its shape.

Lastly, I thank my wife Milda for encouraging me to continue and to endure during the many long hours spent at the writing desk.

INTRODUCTION

Russia in the nineteenth century did not have a systematically developed body of scholarly thought on the discipline of esthetics. Previously, there were some formal statements, such as *De arte poetica* by Feofan Prokopovich (1681-1736), but these amounted practically to direct copies of West European, particularly Jesuit, treatises on art and rhetoric. The versification reforms introduced by Vasiliy Trediakovsky (1703-69), Mikhailo Lomonosov (1711-65) and Antiokh Kantemir (1709-44) did represent systems of scholarly reasoning in esthetics, but for the most part they also followed West European models. Moreover, the discipline of esthetics in itself was to them secondary to their concerns with "correct," artistically effective prosody for the Russian verse. The famous nineteenth-century "radical critics" Vissarion Belinsky (1811-48), Nikolai Chernyshevsky (1828-89) and Nikolai Dobrolyubov (1836-61) were not primarily philosophers or theoreticians on art, but rather practical critics and social commentators working in an essayistic medium close to journalism. The major nineteenth-century Russian writers, such as Pushkin, Gogol', Dostoevsky or Turgenev, have left little more than marginal theoretical remarks on art, although they did engage in some practical criticism.

Lev Tolstoy was the only one who put forward a major effort to elaborate a treatise on esthetics called *What Is Art?* (1898).

In it, he raised a systematic and comprehensive set of questions: what is art, how is it distinguished from mere imitations, counterfeits of art, what is the function and place of art in the life of an individual, of society, and even where does art stand in its relationship to science and religion. As is proper in a scholarly discourse, Tolstoy also placed his own ideas in perspective against the body of esthetics that had developed in Western Europe as he was able to know it at the time. Tolstoy's opinions, of course, also carried the authority of a world-famous writer, a grand master of the word.

With all that, the essay itself never gained much of a place in the public mind. The scholarly community could not seriously consider a treatise which set itself flatly against the entire accumulated body of esthetic thought, most particularly by rejecting the concept of beauty as central to art, and then proceeded to further iconoclastic statements, including the notion that there is no such thing as literary criticism. The general reader, for his part, did not know what to make of Tolstoy's judgments that dismissed out of hand all the: "rude, savage, and, for us, often meaningless works of the ancient Greeks: Sophocles, Euripides, Aeschylus, and especially Aristophanes; or, of modern writers, Dante, Tasso, Milton, Shakespeare; in painting, all of Raphael, all of Michelangelo, including his absurd 'Last Judgment'; in music, the whole of Bach and the whole of Beethoven, including his last period ...the Ibsens, Maeterlincks, Verlaines, Mallarmés, Puvis de Chavannes, Klingers, Bücklins, Stucks, Schneiders; in music the Wagners, Liszts, Berliozes, Brahmses, and Richard Strausses, etc., and all that immense mass of good-for-nothing imitators of these imitators." [1] This whole list of worthless artists was then topped off with the name of Tolstoy himself, who counted his own works "in the category of bad art."

It was then that some readers thought they began to understand: Tolstoy was not really speaking about art, or critics, or world-famous authors -- he was flagellating himself and the entire Western civilization for amorality, hedonism, social injustice and oppression, and lack of any meaningful faith in God. *What Is Art?* really belonged together with those works of the early eighties, particularly *Confession* and *What, Then, Are We to Do?* (both 1882) which conveyed the tremendous moral crisis in Tolstoy's life, after which he increasingly turned away from art and toward treatises on morality, religion, and social justice. Tolstoy's esthetics, then, was no more interesting than his morality, indeed, less so, because the moral stance of Tolstoy found many admirers who still liked their Shakespeare. Some were also ready to follow Tolstoy's religious ideas, even if these led him to excommunication by the Russian Orthodox Church.

This change in Tolstoy from literary genius to literary moralist seemed to have engendered in him many complex contradictions and extreme positions, among which, it was thought, was the rejection of art. At this point, most readers simply turned to the enjoyment of Tolstoy's fiction and left his esthetics alone, having decided that his creative achievement and his thoughts on art were but minimally relevant to each other. The working hypothesis of the present study is that, on the contrary, Tolstoy's art and his esthetics are very intimately related; that, contradictions notwithstanding, his entire life, entire opus, are distinguished by a singular kind of internal unity and consistency, and that the nature of this internal unity of mind and heart, once understood, will lead to a much fuller appreciation of his genius.

If we read Tolstoy's fiction from this perspective, not as a detached body but as an integral function of his total personality, we can see how over the course of time Tolstoy's fictional characters generally express views on art, or have experiences related to art that are similar to his own, as these developed at various stages of his life. In this respect, Tolstoy might not be very different from many other writers whose life and work could be read as an ongoing discourse with the Muses. There are but few, however, for whom such a communion also included a systematic theoretical argument. Even fewer perceived their own thoughts on art as a sort of spiritual journey toward some particular point of understanding that represented the Truth, always distantly visible to the mind's eye, like the star that led the Magi to their Epiphany. Tolstoy was one such writer. A man of troubled wisdom, he committed both his life and art to one lifelong quest for the kind of knowledge that would give him peace -- a sense of belonging with everyone else in a universe which has meaning.

Like the Epiphany, of course, such knowledge must bring forgiveness and salvation, that is, it must exist on the moral plane. It is clear from the evidence of Tolstoy's works that they encode an ongoing effort to understand and define art in general while the power of his own art in particular was emerging from what his works could accomplish in the moral dimension. In this process, Tolstoy's personal quest for moral value invariably extends to the very act of writing fiction, of breathing life into people who must then seek answers to the questions that plague their own creator. As these answers emerge, they become a kind of metalanguage about art itself and can ultimately be articulated also in theoretical terms, as Tolstoy finally did in his essay.

In the Conclusion to *What Is Art?*, Tolstoy wrote that the subject had occupied him for fifteen years (that is, more or less from

1882, the time he wrote *What, Then, Are We to Do?*). He thought he could finish his work soon, but found that his "views on the matter then were so far from clear that I could not arrange them in a way that satisfied me." [2] Actually, he had been trying to "arrange," articulate his thoughts on art a great deal longer, in fact, from the very beginning of his writing career. His diaries, starting with the earliest years, are full of special notes, observations, opinions, questions, all pertaining to the nature and function of art. In his fiction, characters are shown exchanging ideas about art and responding to pictures, music and *belles lettres* not only in order to fill in the background of their lives but also to help shape the plots and define the moral-ideological issues being confronted in a given text.

In the present volume, an attempt will be made to trace the sometimes parallel, sometimes intertwining lines of Tolstoy's art and his thought on art. After reviewing some of his early works in conjunction with notes from his diaries, public statements and the like, we shall dwell on the very interesting "Yasnaya Polyana" period, in the early 1860s, when Tolstoy embarked upon an experiment in children's education in preference to being an artist. As his powerful, charismatic spirit descended upon the peasant children of his own estate, it filled them with an inspiration that, in Tolstoy's insistent claim, made them, the children, the true teachers of how one should write and be an artist. The particular qualities of the children's written work, strangely, do rather resemble Tolstoy's own in a variety of important ways. In discussing what his pupils wrote in his *Yasnaya Polyana Journal*, Tolstoy gradually developed a systematic view on art that was in every sense a preliminary version of the ideas brought forth in *What Is Art?*.

As the Yasnaya Polyana period can thus truly be said to be the beginning of Tolstoy's theories on art, so the period opening in the 1880's constitutes the final stage before the writing of the essay. In surveying the moral-autobiographical writings of this time, we will see how the effort of producing and describing art in such a way that one would also learn how to live led Tolstoy through a number of crucibles, periods of crisis, reevaluations of basic assumptions, and repeated resolutions to live quite differently from the way he lived before. The common feature of all these crises is that all changes that followed from them ultimately only reinforced what his basic moral instinct had always been telling him. Tolstoy's literary essays of the time, such as his introduction to a Russian translation of Guy de Maupassant, clearly reflect the last stages of Tolstoy's thoughts on art before the writing of the essay in question.

The essay itself is then presented in an analytical discussion that tries to touch upon its main points and elucidate some of the peculiarities of Tolstoy's position, with a view to revealing how they nevertheless fit logically into his entire body of thought and art.

The main part of the book turns to relationships between Tolstoy's esthetics and his art in a more focused way than the other sections. Among other things, questions are raised about the particular qualities of Tolstoy's art that made it impossible for him to endure, for instance, the French Symbolist poets, or to countenance modern painting. The role of music in Tolstoy's works is examined in the light of his views in the essay, revealing consistencies that are sometimes astonishing. For instance, Natasha's feelings of estrangement at the opera in Book Eight of *War and Peace* resemble almost perfectly Tolstoy's own description at the beginning of the essay of an opera rehearsal he saw and was disgusted by. The point emerges from such comparisons that while in reading the essay we are expected to confront the argument itself, in the fiction we need not judge that argument but are free to respond to the characters' human experiences in the context of their depicted lives. This may help us understand why it is that the art of Tolstoy seems so powerful, and the essay often so unacceptable. The deepest experience of all slowly emerges from our expanding understanding just how thoroughly the awesome body of Tolstoy's art is permeated with the same thoughts, feelings, attitudes, ways of perceiving things, that inform his essay. One may almost reach the point of believing even some of the most esoteric opinions on art expressed by Tolstoy precisely because we are so deeply affected by the experiences of the people we have followed through his works.

The final segment of this study presents a discussion of how Tolstoy's essay and his entire thinking on esthetics were received by his Russian and West European contemporaries and then later, by the scholarly establishment in the Soviet Union and in recent decades by some writers and critics in the West. Due to the time lag that is inevitable in protracted research, the samples of Soviet and Western reactions to Tolstoy's essay for the most part reach only to the seventies. A different study is needed to comprise the most recent developments, particularly in view of the political changes that may stimulate new intellectual challenges and opportunities in the still ongoing process of "glasnost" and "perestroika." The attitudes presented range from serious scholarly attention to mere articulations of personal feelings, perhaps even prejudices by some who, instead of confronting Tolstoy's arguments, preferred to dwell on his "gloomy and barbaric Slavic soul."

Those who rejected or ignored Tolstoy's insistently repeated ideas on esthetics, or forgave him because of his greatness as a writer, may, after all, be right if the premise of the present essay does not hold and there are no significant, nor intimate organic ties between his art and his thought on art. On the other hand, if there is a meaningful connection between the two, one might profitably study Tolstoy's essay not in order to judge whether he is "right" or "wrong," but for the insight his ideas may provide into the mystery of his tremendous creative achievement.

CHAPTER ONE

THE QUEST BEGINS

The deep roots of Tolstoy's commitment to the aesthetics ultimately articulated in *What Is Art?* become strikingly evident when we realize that, although written late in his life, in 1898, the essay is consistent in its basic propositions with everything that Tolstoy had always either consciously believed or instinctively felt about art. His ideas, set down in his early diaries or recorded in his correspondence, or presented as attitudes toward art in the views and feelings of his characters, or, again, implicit in the overall designs of his fiction, show a remarkable continuity of his basic thinking throughout the years. On the other hand, all through this time Tolstoy also kept reconsidering and renouncing his previous convictions on practically everything under the sun, including the nature and function of art. Over time, the tension between radical changes of outlook and persevering consistency of mind produced a continuing fluid relationship between change and permanence in Tolstoy's thought. Indeed, one might say that this relationship itself, more than any particular formulations adhered to or abandoned at various times, reveals the flexible but enduring underlying pattern of his convictions all through the quarrel with himself which Tolstoy would not appease to his dying day.

The first period of Tolstoy's concern with literary matters may be measured from approximately 1847, when he first began putting down his thoughts on art in his diaries, to the time he established the Yasnaya Polyana school, in early 1860's, when he made the first of his recurrent decisions to give up literature for some other, more useful and meaningful activity, in this case, the education of peasant children.

From the very beginning, one of Tolstoy's paramount concerns in art was the relationship between reality and imagination. It is, of course, a concern generally shared by all writers, but in Tolstoy we can see an effort to work this question through in his own particular way, irrespective of any consensus built upon shared experience in literary tradition. His approach was to seek out and focus upon the essential quality of this relationship as he could personally perceive it. It was to be an enduring governing principle rather than a variable of the creative process itself or something to be constantly structured and restructured while pondering other people's ideas. This desire for a valid, clearly stated point of departure, achieved through an independent effort of the mind, continued to be the basic structuring force of his entire argument on aesthetics including the essay *What Is Art?*.

The particular mode of interplay between reality and imagination Tolstoy always aspired to was to make it seem that this fiction is a faithful imitation of life itself in its natural course while it actually depicted something else, namely his own individual experience of the process by which life becomes art. In other words, the structures of art, however personal, were not to appear hermetic unto themselves, as mere verbal curtains of illusions between the world and the mind. Instead, these structures were to function like windows made of words, open wide to reality outside of language, so that this reality could enter and give meaning and purpose to the artistic text. Thus, in the relationship between imagination and reality, imagination was to be not an inventive but an imitative faculty of the mind, and artistic language is in principle not creative but significatory. An early formulation of this can be found in an entry in Tolstoy's diary made in 1851:

> L'imagination est le miroir [de la] nature, miroir, que nous portons en nous et dans lequel elle se peint. La plus belle imagination est le miroir le plus clair et le plus vrai, celui que nous appelons le genie.
> Le genie ne crée, il retrace (*PSS*, 46, 69).

In such a context, the conventional notion of "creation" would really signify an interference that obscures the clear reflection of reality in the mind. Inventions which do not correspond to anything that actually exists must appear lacking in universality, must even be hermetical and artificial to the degree that they represent only a set of social conventions shared by an elite imposing itself upon both art and society. On the other hand, the true quality of genius informs a consciousness commensurate with the infinitudes always implicit in nature itself in its entirety and capable of retracing them most clearly and truthfully. There is, consequently, a special reciprocity between nature and the spacious mind. The idea of such reciprocity later embodies itself as one of the cardinal principles of Tolstoy's art, and the process of this embodiment can be observed as a transition from art for its own sake to art as a necessary function of living because it gives a purpose, that is, a moral value to our lives.

The first step toward this transition led Tolstoy away from the notion that artistic language is a set of devices evolved in literary craftsmanship to which the imagination must address itself. The inevitable next question, however, is: what, then, does constitute artistic language? Can it dispense with figurative means of expression, or must it find some new way to use them? Looking at Tolstoy's early works, we can see how he searched for approaches to this new way and how the process of this search extended from himself to the characters in his fiction.

One such character is young Irtenyev in the trilogy *Childhood*, (1851-2) *Boyhood*, (1852-41) *Youth* (1855-6; 1857), the quasi-autobiographical hero whom we might now regard as a sort of canvas of the imagination upon which Tolstoy "se peint." Irtenyev is one of his first fictional heroes to confront the fact that the creation of a new artistic language means rejection of traditional usages of figurative speech in which something real is depicted through comparisons with something that represents an artifice instead of reality. In the second draft of *Childhood*, for instance, Irtenyev takes note of the "strange habit of the French to convey their impressions by means of images":

> In order to describe a beautiful face, they say "it resembled this or that statue," or nature — "it was reminiscent of this or that picture," — a group — "it reminded one of a scene from a ballet or opera." They even try to convey feelings by an image. A beautiful face, nature, an actual group of people, are better than any possible statues, panoramas, pictures and decorations (*PSS, 1,* 177-8).

Irtenyev seems to be saying that in trying to express feelings by an image, the mind paints itself on the wrong canvas and becomes distorted. This attitude is further elaborated in Irtenyev's comments upon the "great Lamartin," to whom he extends a heavy, sarcastic hand:

> The great Lamartin, whose exalted soul became known to the whole world since the publication of his "confidence" (by this publication the great genius *a fait d'une pierre deux coups* — revealed to the whole world the innermost secrets of his great soul and acquired an estate which he had so much wanted to buy), the great Lamartin, describing his impressions on a boat in the middle of the sea, when just one board separated him from death, says, in order to describe how nice were the drops of water falling from the oars to the sea — *comme les perles tombants dans un bassin d'argent.* Having read this phrase, my imagination immediately transferred itself to the maids' room, and I imagined a chamber maid with rolled-up sleeves who is washing her mistress' pearl necklace over a basin and has accidentally dropped several pearls — *des perles tombants dans un bassin de l'argent*, but about the sea and the picture which my imagination has been painting at that moment, with the help of the poet, I forgot already.[1]

It is rather amusing to see that in order to make his point about describing reality, Irtenyev himself concocts an awkwardly artificial scene with the maid and the silver basin, hardly plausible anywhere but in "Arabian Nights." What we get is artificiality laughing at artifice, in effect, a comic inversion of an image where nature and genius trace their outlines upon the canvas of imagination. The crux of the matter, however, is Irtenyev's deliberate refusal to picture to himself a dimension where the description is not really of the sea nor of the water, but of an experience in which perception becomes image and thus acquires a reality of its own, in the community of other images known to us as the world of literary conventions. And yet, someone who wishes to be an artist and thinks like Tolstoy is faced with a basic dilemma — how do you then depict reality and convey your own experience in the process? Even at the early stages of his career, Tolstoy himself was sharply aware of this difficulty. In 1851 he wrote in his diary:

> I was relaxing behind the camp a minute ago. A marvelous night! The moon had just come up from behind the hill and shed its light on two small, thin, low clouds; a cricket behind me was singing his un-

> ceasing, melancholy tune; a frog was heard in the distance, and near the aul [a mountaineer village] dogs barked, tartars yelled; then again all would be quiet, and again all you heard was the chirping of the cricket, and the light, transparent cloud was floating past the close and the distant stars.
> I thought: let me go and describe what I saw. But how do you write this down? You have to sit behind an ink-stained table, take a gray piece of paper, ink; smear your fingers and write letters on the paper. The letters will make words, the words — phrases, but how can you transmit feeling? Isn't there some way to transfer to someone else the look in one's own eyes at the sight of nature? Description is not enough. Why is prose and poetry, happiness and misfortune bound up so closely? How is one to live? (*PSS*, 46, 65).

In retrospect, this little note in the diary, written when Tolstoy was still a soldier in the Caucasus acquires a considerable, perhaps pivotal, significance in his development as an artist and thinker about art. Two themes that were always present with Tolstoy later, are stated here for the first time: the theme that art is the communication of emotion, of the "look in one's own eyes," more than of the beauty of nature as such (or, rather, that this beauty, transferred to the medium of art *becomes* that look in one's eyes), and the theme that the only answer Tolstoy will accept on how to be an artist must also tell him "how is one to live." Certainly, *What Is Art?* asks again these two basic questions, and gives answers which at this early date Tolstoy was not yet prepared to formulate very clearly.[2]

With respect to artistic communication, one idea that occurred to Tolstoy was that the gap between the world "out there" and the feelings of the artist might be bridged by an appeal to the reader's own imagination:

> Words are quite inadequate to convey the imaginary, but it is even more difficult to express reality. The true communication of reality is the stumbling block of language. One can only hope that the reader's imagination will supplement the insufficient expressiveness of an author. How cheap and colorless

would all descriptions be without such cooperation? (*PSS*, *3*, 216).

Here we are brought back to the question of relationship between reality and imagination, but with one very significant addition: the reader. If a genius does not create but retraces, the mirror of nature which is his imagination must now be further reflected in the imagination of the reader before it can communicate reality. The implications of this idea indicate that Tolstoy was about to grasp the principle of "co-creation," known in our day as "creative reading," or, some would say, "Perzeptionsästhetik." At the very least, Tolstoy's statement does appear to be a preliminary version of his ultimate notion that true art must infect the recipient with the artist's own emotion. The central idea, as in the essay later, is not focused upon expression, but upon communication; art is not something that *is* but something that *happens* between the artist and his audience.[3] For this, it is necessary to achieve a blending of fact and feeling so that, somehow, fact would *become* feeling, or, as the Soviet scholar E. N. Kupreyanova puts it, a dividing line would be removed "between the 'depiction' of the external and the 'expression' of the internal."[4] In other words, an image cannot be merely a servant of fact — it must also attend upon the soul.

The question, however, which troubled Tolstoy all his creative life, and which he formulated in a number of different ways, was this: how to achieve it that the expression of the internal would still permit the imagination to function as a "perfect mirror" of external reality, and would at the same time also accomplish an act of communication with another person? In depicting the world, a writer depicts his way of feeling its existence, thus really himself. Tolstoy was aware of this already in 1851, when he wrote in his diary: "In reading a work, especially fiction, the main interest lies in the character of the author which expresses itself in the work" (*PSS*, *46*, 182). This means that any depiction of reality will be modified by the factor of the author's personality, and the question becomes not only how to write but also who will understand it. If that personality is but minimally different from others, communication may be possible, but we all are indeed unique, and our solitude may stand facing a number of different walls. To understand this means to accept the principle of exclusiveness in art; Tolstoy struggled against this principle almost all of his life. In his rationalistic moments he thought that it may be our ideas that separate us;

but if we reason together, will the result still be art rather than, say, philosophy? If, on the other hand, we are somehow to feel our different ideas together, how can we achieve this without modifying our language, without charging it with some special electricity of emotion? Most commonly, this is achieved by making language figurative, establishing oblique meanings, creating metaphors — and yet, will that in itself not be a barrier? All such and similar questions very early grew to be fundamental issues of Tolstoy's aesthetics, and his attempts to resolve them read like a description of his entire development as an artist from the early works to his essay on art.

In a preliminary form, these issues were posed by Tolstoy in a series of diary notes in 1851 which in effect add up to a brief essay, one of his earliest theoretical statements on art and, as one might expect, generally on the meaning of life in conjunction with art. Among the points made, Tolstoy notes first of all that he is not speaking of books written with the express purpose of "gaining many readers," since these represent nothing but an author's professional know-how, nor is he speaking of scholarly works, since these do not enter the sphere of poetics. Real art, says Tolstoy in his diary, must "sing out of one's soul" (*PSS*, *46*, 70-71). The notion of a soul singing itself out to the world comes, of course, from the artistic vocabulary of the sentimental and romantic traditions, and as such it presupposes other special souls, so attuned that they can respond to that song of the artist with a resonance of their own. Not surprisingly, therefore, his own interests as an artist at the early stages remained with the educated, "developed" and sensitive people — his own kind. They were the Russian intelligentsia: writers, public figures, intellectuals with whom he became acquainted after returning from the Crimean War, bringing with him not only the fame of a war hero, but also a quickly rising reputation as a writer, after the success of his *Childhood* trilogy. Tolstoy had never met any established Russian writers before, and had corresponded extensively only with Nekrasov, the publisher of his early works. Now, with the enthusiastic assistance of Turgenev, he met Nekrasov personally, as well as the whole circle of writers centered around the public-minded progressive journal *The Contemporary*, including V. P. Botkin, A. V. Druzhinin, I. I. Panaev, and others. Among Tolstoy's earliest new acquaintances was the poet A. A. Fet, who did not really belong to any particular grouping but shared with Tolstoy an individualistic, fairly conservative bent and a fine sensitivity to art, including poetry.[5] The two maintained a very interesting correspondence for a long time in which they exchanged highly original ideas about poetry and about philosophy. A short while later, in Moscow, Tolstoy met the "right wing" of Russian letters, the Slavophiles, among whom was S. T. Aksakov and D. V. Druzhinin.[6]

Tolstoy was lionized as a war hero and highly appreciated for his *Childhood* and the early Caucasus stories, and thus it was no wonder that for a time he did seem inclined to believe that true and meaningful civilization amounted to the activities of small educated circles, and that the dilemma of communication between the artist and his public was to be addressed in those terms. There were other factors, too, which may have contributed to Tolstoy's desire to turn more intensely toward art and other intellectual pursuits that were separate from the uneducated masses. One of them may have been his unsuccessful attempt at social reform in his own estate at Yasnaya Polyana in 1856.[7] The serfs would not understand or accept the scheme he had proposed for their eventual liberation. Another factor was the trip abroad at the end of 1856 during which acquaintance with the arts and letters of France and Germany, and with the remnants of classical grandeur in Italy was most shockingly combined with the experience of man's inhumanity to man clothed in the garb of law and public justice. This was a public execution he witnessed in Paris.[8] The contrast between the elemental cruelty and stupidity of the vulgar crowds, be they serfs or burghers, with the noble monuments of Western civilization must have made devotion to art seem to Tolstoy like the only refuge. Such feelings found their explicit expression in 1857, in a letter to A. Tolstaya, after Tolstoy had returned from abroad only to be struck again with the spectacle of man's primitive inhumanity:

> In Russia it is awful, awful, awful... If you had seen, as I did within a week how a lady on the street beat her servant with a stick, how the policeman ordered that I be told to send him a cart of hay, for otherwise he will not give my serf his documents, how in front of my eyes an official beat a seventy-year old man with a stick half to death because their vehicles had hooked together, how my bailiff, wanting to please

me, punished the drunken gardener by beating him and then sending him barefoot through freshly cut stubble to herd the cattle, and how happy he was to see that the gardener's feet were all in wounds — if you had seen all this and much, much more, then you would have believed me that in Russia life is a constant, eternal work and struggle with one's own feelings. The only blessing is that there is salvation — the moral world, the world of arts, of poetry and of personal attachments. Here no one, neither the policeman nor the bailiff, bothers me. I sit alone, the wind blows, dirt, cold, and I play Beethoven terribly, with stiff fingers and shed tears of sentiment, or read "The Iliad," or invent people myself, women, live with them, mark up the paper, or think, as now, of people whom I love...[9]

In this complex early stage of Tolstoy's development, his indignation against barbarity did not as yet turn him against the upper classes whom he later accused of maintaining a social order that made barbarity possible, indeed, inevitable. An escape into the domain of the arts then seemed a natural thing and not, as later, an irresponsible retreat from confrontation with the evils of the world. Led by his aesthetic sentiments, Tolstoy even proposed to V. Botkin, an erudite, cultivated member of the Moscow circle of writers and critics, to issue a publication devoted exclusively to the arts. In a January, 1858 letter to Botkin, Tolstoy says in part:

What would you say at the present time, when the dirty stream of politics wishes to gather unto itself absolutely everything and to spoil, if not destroy, art, what would you say of people who, believing in the independence and eternal nature of art, would come together and by their deeds (that is, by art itself as a written word) and by their words (criticism) would prove this truth and would save the eternal and the independent from the incidental, biased and predatory political influence? Could not we ourselves be such people? That is, Turgenev, you, Fet, myself and all who share and *will* share our convictions? The means for this, of course, is a journal, an almanac, or whatever. Everything that has and will ap-

> pear of purely artistic work must be drawn into this journal. Everything Russian and foreign that belongs to art, must be discussed. The journal will have only one aim: artistic pleasure, to cry and to laugh, The journal does not pretend to prove anything, or to know anything. Its only standard is educated taste.[10]

The idea of a journal devoted to the arts had been preceded several years earlier by an opposite notion — a journal for the dissemination of morally uplifting works. On December 20, 1853, Tolstoy wrote in his diary:

> Here is a noble purpose within my power — to publish a journal the aim of which would be only the dissemination of useful (moral) works. It would accept contributions only on condition that they contain moral instruction, and it would publish them or not, according to the discretion of the author (*PSS, 46,* 214).

If the aims of these two journals (neither was ever published) seem to be dramatically opposed, there is still that inner connection between them that both express Tolstoy's striving for something of value, something radically different from what he perceived to be the prevailing corruption of society. One could see these youthful projects as preliminary statements of the cultural messages sent to us by morality and by the arts, both aiming at something of essence to the meaning of life, yet also carrying between them the great dichotomy as to the nature, place and function of each force in our society. Ultimately, *What Is Art?* became one of Tolstoy's extraordinary efforts to achieve a resolution in favor of the moral principle.

At the time, however, in late 1850s, it was the aesthetic principle which prevailed. Tolstoy's "Speech at the Society of Friends of Russian Literature," made in 1859, in essence presents the same viewpoint as the letter to Botkin, and again proposes adherence to "pure art" which, however, is understood as something much more than mere aestheticism, namely, also as a means of uniting all people together. Tolstoy took the position that, whereas until recently "the majority of the public began to think that the task of all literature consists only in the exposure of evil, in its discussion and correction, in a word, in the development of the civic feeling in general," now it is again important to develop a literature which "reflects in itself all the eternal, common human interests, the most valuable, the innermost consciousness of the people, a literature which is accessible to people of any nation and any time." [11] We can see Tolstoy working his way out of a confusing tangle of ideas. The eternal, common human interests referred to in his speech, implying though they do a commitment to pure art, are in essence the same as the moral values proposed for dissemination earlier in the diary, but it was difficult not to perceive them as standing in conflict with one another. What Tolstoy lacked at this stage was the unifying idea of religious consciousness which underlies his thinking in the essay on art.

Tolstoy's speech was misplaced in the specific context of the time, because the "social school" of literature, dominated by the triumvirate of Belinsky, Chernyshevsky and Dobrolyubov, still held its sway. As a writer, however, Tolstoy could choose to address himself to those who can understand him, even if such were very few, finding justification for this in an earlier, Sentimentalist tradition represented in Russia most prominently by the poet and translator V. Zhukovsky who had devoted the first book of his verse to a select few, "für wenige," as he put it, significantly, in German, thereby clearly indicating where his Sentimentalism had its roots. Similarly, in the second draft of his preface to the readers of *Childhood* Tolstoy attempted to formulate for himself a clear idea of who his intended readers are to be. "To be accepted among my readers," wrote Tolstoy:

> I ask for very little: that you should be sensitive, that is, could at times take pity from the heart and even shed a few tears on account of an invented person whom you have grown to love, and be glad from the heart for his sake, and be not ashamed of this... The main thing is that you should be an *understanding* person, one of those people with whom, upon first acquaintance, you see no need to explain your own feelings and inclinations, because you can see that he understands you, that every note in your soul creates an echo in his. It is difficult, it even seems to me impossible to divide people into wise, stupid, good or evil, but the distinction between *those who understand* and *those who do not* is for me such a sharp

line that I draw it involuntarily among all the people whom I know.[12]

Considering the tremendous complexity of Tolstoy's talent, it is not at all "little to ask" that his readers should understand him inwardly at the slightest hint, should share completely his feelings as these emerge from the written page. In a sense, this might be called elitism, a call for an aristocracy of the spirit. Although later Tolstoy expended a great deal of energy in opposing such a view, there is also a continuing underlying idea: the contact with another soul through art is a special moment, which can be shared only in the condition of readiness. The difference is that in this early stage readiness seemed to Tolstoy accessible only to the sensitive, delicately-tuned members of the educated classes, while in the essay on art it became the attribute of the simple people toiling on the soil.

Two stories, called *Lucerne* and *Albert*, written in 1857 and 1858, respectively, seem to be quite remarkable in their aestheticism, sentimentality and even, in the case of *Albert*, dream textures and fantasy. In some, though by no means all, respects they have a touch of "decadent art" about them, especially in their assumption of the uniqueness and solitude of the artist, whose inner life is like a special dimension, a code, indecipherable to ordinary mortals. While writing *Albert*, Tolstoy thought that it was "not a descriptive, but an exceptional story, which in its meaning must stand entirely on its lyrical and psychological passages and therefore must not and cannot please the majority, there is no doubt about that." [13] The "majority" referred to, however, did not pertain to peasants in the field of whom Tolstoy at that time expected nothing in the way of literary appreciation; we are dealing with "profanum vulgus" within the educated and aristocratic readership itself. For the first time, it became possible to think that the entire cultured layer of society was corrupt by its very nature.

As if to test this possibility, the central point, the issue around which *Albert* and *Lucerne* are built, has to do with one special moment, when the power of art touches the soul. *Lucerne* depicts an episode in Switzerland with a poor street singer, a spontaneous and gifted artist who can, for a moment, communicate his own magic to the "Englishmen" — rich idlers who have forbidden themselves any expression of true emotion. Similarly, in *Albert*, there is a mad musician who can, with his music, transfigure briefly a bored and listless crowd of aristocrats. In this sense, the stories do become relevant to the definition given in *What Is Art?* which deals with the transmission of emotion. Moreover, just like the essay, both stories show an awareness of social evils directly related to the issue of art. When the song in *Lucerne* is ended, hearts freeze over once more, and the singer is treated with contempt. In *Albert*, the musician eventually freezes to death on the threshold of the palace where he had played and transformed everyone with his music before. In both stories, there is a sensitive, indignant observer (Nekhlyudov[14] in *Lucerne* and Delesov in *Albert*, both aristocrats not unlike Tolstoy himself) who tries to reach out to the poor and despised artist, and in failing to do so, recoils in bitterness against himself for his own lack of understanding, and against the privileged world to which he belongs and which has crippled his soul.

Without elaborating on any reasons, Tolstoy did later express a dislike for both stories. It could be that the autobiographical nature of *Lucerne*[15] and its general appeal to the refined sensibilities of a few exceptional persons reduced the story in his eyes to an inconsequential toy — a toy, moreover, tainted by its maker's hidden self-admiration for being so much more sensitive than the rest of the aristocratic world which was despising the person of the street singer. It could also be that the moment of communication, as depicted, held in it nothing of value, conveying no more than mere aesthetic experience which in itself was not a reality, but rather a mannerism taken from the romantic and sentimental traditions.

The sentiments of disgust with at least some segments of the educated upper classes must have contributed to Tolstoy's disillusionment with the idea that the opportunities he had in Moscow and Petersburg circles to exchange feelings and thoughts with people on his own intellectual level might resolve most of his questions about the purpose, nature and function of art. Many years later, in his *Confession*, Tolstoy recalled with bitterness these early days among the literary and intellectual elite which, by then, seemed to him a total waste, precisely because he felt neither they nor he himself had anything of real value to contribute at the time.[16]

In opposition to the empty pastimes of corrupt sophisticates, Tolstoy began to feel more and more clearly that the work of an artist was first and foremost a matter of some special quality of the feeling transmitted to his audience by the artist. At one point, he likened this quality to an inner fire: "Poetry is fire which starts in the soul of man. This fire burns, warms and illuminates. ... the true poet, in suffering and against his will, does burn himself and sets others on fire. And this is all that counts." (diary entry for April 4, 1870, *L.N. Tolstoj o literature*, p. 133.) The fire metaphor has long been known in literature as a name for inspiration, but for Tolstoy what mattered was not the image as such but the emotion behind it that led eventually to the concept of "feeling" in his ultimate definition of art in the 1898 treatise.

In a rather short time Tolstoy found himself in disagreement with both the conservative and the liberal sides of the Russian literary establishment. True, it was always difficult for him to accept a system of values if the system was not his own but there was also something else wrong, something which the ideas current in the writers' circles did not address. The Slavophiles, he found, were making too much of a solemn, reproachful ideology of their basically healthy instincts of promoting Russian national character and civilization. He saw that at the base of their beliefs there were "serious truths, such as family life, commune, the orthodoxy," but he was troubled by the manner in which these beliefs were promoted, particularly the orthodoxy:

> Especially what concerns Orthodoxy, first of all because acknowledging the correctness of their opinion about the importance of its participating fully in the life of the nation, one must also acknowledge, from a higher point of view, the perverted ugliness of the manner in which it manifests itself and its kind of historical validity; and secondly, because the censorship closes the mouths of all who oppose it (*PSS*, 47, 70).[17]

Much has been made by any number of Soviet critics of Tolstoy's supposed spiritual linkage to the progressive circles, to people like the publicist-philosopher Herzen, to Nekrasov, and through them to the earlier heritage of Belinsky but the fact seems to be that some aspects of the Westernizers' position were also alien to Tolstoy. Most particularly, it was their tendency toward abstract ideological constructs — the "convictions" for which Tolstoy attacked Turgenev in their personal arguments. Tolstoy disliked the Westernizers' desire to subordinate art to such rhetorical notions as "serving the causes of progress and justice," customarily resorted to by intellectuals who use words to address other words rather than any significant reality. The distinction between life, a set of instinctive and emotional responses to concrete experience, and civilization — a universe of words, may have begun around this time in Tolstoy's mind. Later it penetrated to the roots of Tolstoy's every conviction, but at this early stage he seems to have mostly felt a frustration that was hard to define, but seemed like the lack of a focus in his system of values. He was then still seeking within himself for a "center", as K. Aksakov put it,[18] for a spiritual commitment to some basic force of truth revealed to him independently of anyone's systems of beliefs.

Some as yet not quite distinct intimations of what outline this truth may take can already be seen emerging from the twilight of Tolstoy's early works. In the *Childhood, Boyhood, Youth* trilogy, Irtenyev's feelings as a child and an adolescent are refracted through the memory of the grown-up narrator where they acquire a hue of moral anguish and solitude centered upon the profoundly personal questions: what is life? what is art? how shall I live? — the same questions, of course, that echoed all through Tolstoy's life. One of the most moving, crucial moments of this anguish is described in *Childhood* in the episode "Grisha," about a religious pilgrim who stopped to spend the night at Irtenyevs' estate. Led by curiosity, the children watch him secretly as he prepares to go to sleep in the barn. Expecting nothing but idle amusement, Irtenyev underwent instead a shattering experience that stayed with him for life:

> For a long time Grisha continued in this state of religious ecstasy, improvising prayers. Now he would repeat several times in succession *Lord have mercy* but each time with renewed force and expression. Then he prayed *Forgive me, O Lord, teach me how to live... teach me how to live, O Lord* so feelingly that he might be expecting an immediate answer to his petition. Then piteous sobs were all that we could hear... He rose to his knees, folded his hands on his breast and was silent. I poked my head softly round the door and held my breath. Grisha was not moving; heavy sighs escaped his chest; a tear ... stood in the dim pupil of his blind eye which was lit up by the moon.

"Thy will be done!" he exclaimed suddenly in an inimitable tone, sank with his forehead on the floor and sobbed like a child.
Much water has flowed under the bridges since then, many memories of the past have lost their meaning for me and become dim recollections; even the pilgrim Grisha has long ago completed his last journey; but the impression he made on me and the feeling he evoked will never fade from my memory. [19]

In a special but very real sense, Tolstoy, the man who wrote *What Is Art?*, was still the same Grisha, asking how to live, just as he was Grisha on the brink of total despair in *Confession*, and Grisha, named Pierre, in French captivity, learning that God is life, and Grisha in *Anna Karenina*, now called Levin, who saw, his eyes widening in horror, that life is actually death.

At the same time, Tolstoy's emerging hostility to members of his own class is also reflected in *Childhood* in passages that show the inception and growth of the idea that the prevalent social structure can corrupt an artist's judgment by implanting in him an acquiescence to untruth. To take but one example, young Irtenyev, having cited the naive but heartfelt verses by his tutor Karl Ivanych, describes his own poem, written to honor his grandmother's name-day. The last two lines:

To comfort thee we shall endeavor,
And love thee like our own dear /mother.

were made to rhyme quite nicely, but only at the cost of a patent untruth, the pretense that loving one's mother and grandmother is the same thing: "all right, so I love my grandmother and respect her, but still, she's not the same thing... Why did I write this, why did I lie?" (Penguin, 56; *PSS*, *1*, 47). Embarrassed and ashamed of himself, Irtenyev waited to be reproached by the grownups, but what came instead was applause and the French compliment: "charmant." Surprised and confused, Irtenyev then simply sidestepped the issue, surrendering to what he felt was a falsity: "oh, well, so be it! I said impatiently, quite upset, and ran off to try on my Moscow clothes." Thus a sacred distinction between love for mother and for everybody else became obliterated somewhere between verses that rhyme and a fashionable Moscow outfit. Worse yet, this surrender also carried with it the implication that art, as far as society is concerned, is a matter of skillful and charming lies.

Whatever Irtenyev may have learned from this episode, Tolstoy never forgot the lesson and returned to it with a vengeance in *What Is Art?*.

On the other hand, young Irtenyev, being the child of Tolstoy's imagination, was inevitably also a true artist who could indeed describe his love for mother to make it seem unique. Here is Irtenyev's description of his mother from the special perspective of a grownup imagining himself back into childhood, in a kind of lovetime continuum that constitutes a grownup's memory:

> So many memories of the past arise when one tries to recall the features of somebody we love that one sees those features dimly through the memories, as though through tears. They are the tears of imagination. When I try to recall my mother as she was at the time I can only picture her brown eyes which always held the same expression of goodness and love, the mole on her neck just below the place where the short hairs grow, her embroidered white collar, and the delicate dry hand which so often caressed me and which I so often kissed; but the complete image escapes me (*Childhood,* Penguin, pp. 17-18).

The point is, of course, that the image *is* complete, for our own emotion, reaching out and blending with Irtenyev's, fills in all the gaps with finely shaded nuances of love: we recognize that the distance between the eyes and the mole on her neck — the two spots of brown in the dim light of memory — has been traversed many times by a boy's admiring heart as in her short, evanescent life mother moved about, turned her head, bent over work, smiled, leaned wearily on her arm: each such journey told a story of its own. We see how the goodness and love of those eyes are echoed back in, as it were, the metaphor of the white collar, we can feel the calm, the security in love of the dry caressing hand, so wax-like later, in death. All these unsaid things are indeed "tears of imagination," and the gently, carefully placed physical features function, one might say, as an emotional synecdoche, expressing the whole of the soul by a part of the body. We recognize here Tolstoy's signature as an artist; when, as a speaker on art, he tells us that art is infection by feeling, we know what he means.

The next paragraph, about a music lesson, stands in such full contrast of mood from the preceding one that the two passages taken together seem to contain in themselves almost the entire argument in *What Is Art?* on the differences between its genuine and counterfeit varieties:

> To the left of the sofa stood an old English grand piano at which sat my rather sallow-skinned sister, Lyuba, her rosy fingers just washed in cold water playing Clementi's studies with evident effort. Lyuba was eleven. She wore a short gingham frock and white lace-trimmed drawers, and could only manage an octave as an arpeggio. Beside and half turned towards her sat Marya Ivanovna, wearing a cap with pink ribbons and a short blue jacket; her face was red and cross, and assumed a still more forbidding expression as soon as Karl Ivanych came in. She looked severely at him and without returning his bow went on tapping the floor with her foot and counting "*un, deux, trois; un, deux, trois*" more loudly and imperatively than before (*ibid.*; incidentally, these same Clementi's *Roulades* are heard again in *The Resurrection*, as a counterpoint to the desperate shouts of prisoners and their visitors in jail. See *The Resurrection*, pp. 171-2).

Right before our eyes, there is the opera rehearsal with which the ultimate essay on art begins: the angry conductor tapping out time with his baton, the strange clothing of the actors who "omit to raise their hands from time to time in sign of animation," just as poor Lyuba, in her lace-trimmed drawers, can only manage an arpeggio. Her hands, "washed in cold water," are also very reminiscent of the pitiable little fingers of deformed young children Tolstoy talks about in his essay, who are taught to move them with extraordinary rapidity by piano teachers no less terrifying than Marya Ivanovna. In any event, it is pleasing to the imagination, tearful or not, to perceive the outlines of Tolstoy's culminating statement on art in such early passages of his fiction as these.

It is quite evident that Tolstoy implicitly proposes the principle of simplicity and sincerity, of singing from the soul, in place of piano exercises played with hands washed in cold water. At this early date, however, Tolstoy had not yet arrived at the conviction that anything truly sincere, deeply felt will be immediately understandable to every simple heart. There was still the question of education, of the ability to respond to and articulate the complex achievements of civilization which could not be shared with the common people. On the other hand, Tolstoy also felt that the people — the largely illiterate masses working the soil — were there, in the background, and seemed themselves to know something Tolstoy did not and could not learn from his intellectual acquaintances in Petersburg and Moscow. Even as he was sadly contemplating the difficulties of communication with people below one's own level of development, Tolstoy began to feel something like a moral obligation to elevate them, at least in terms of his own moral principles. The result was a strangely ambivalent attitude, recorded in his diary in 1853 in the following way:

> The simple people stand so much higher than we do because of their life, filled with work and suffering, that somehow it seems wrong for one of us to seek and describe the bad things about them. They are there, but it is better to speak of these people (as of the dead) only what is good (*PSS,46*, 184).

Obviously, such a funereal affection for the common people was inadequate — to be at peace with himself, Tolstoy had to find a reason to admire them for their own living virtues. Yet, paradoxically, one of those virtues was precisely the peasants' ability to stand calmly in the face of death. In a story called "Three Deaths" (1858) an aristocratic woman dies in fear and trembling, pleading with God to have mercy and prolong her worthless life, while a peasant calmly faces up to the fact that his end has come and recedes into the soil from whence he came with quiet, unconscious dignity. The most beautiful death is that of a tree put to the axe which descends majestically to the ground without even being corrupted by an awareness that it is dying. In a letter to A. A. Tolstaya, a distant relative, Tolstoy explained about his story:

> My thought was: three beings died — the lady, the peasant and the tree. The lady is pitiful and repulsive because she lied all her life and is lying in the face of death... The peasant dies peacefully precisely because he is not a Christian. His religion is different, although by habit, he performed the Christian duties; his religion is nature, with which he lived. He himself cut down trees, sowed the rye and harvested it, killed sheep, and sheep were born to him, and so

were children, and old people died, and he knows well this law from which he never turned his face, like the lady did, but looked simply, directly into its eyes (*L.N. Tolstoy o literature*, p. 47).

Ideas concerning nature and the natural order of things in conjunction with the life of plain working people have many answering echoes in all of Tolstoy's creative work. In one respect, however, the story *The Cossacks* (1852-1863) is particularly important for the development of Tolstoy's thoughts on society and the artist because it also subjects the "natural man" to a critical view. In a way, *The Cossacks* may be read as an extension and elaboration of the basic idea contained in "Three Deaths," since here, too, the calm acceptance of the cycles of life by the Cossacks is contrasted with the tense, restless questioning of Olenin, the hero, who hopes to find some "deep secret" salutary for him in the soul of the people, the Cossacks, children of nature, neighbors of Rousseau's noble savages whom, with his artificial aristocratic upbringing, he could never hope to resemble. In this sense, Olenin is really the same troubled observer of the failure of aristocratic values whom we saw in *Albert* and *Lucerne*, continuing his search among the woods and mountains of the Caucasus. The important difference is in the reasons for Olenin's failure. He tried to impose upon the Cossacks his own notions of what their values supposedly are, and what love and life mean to them. These notions were not derived from a clear-eyed observations of life's realities in the Cossack village but rather conceived as Olenin's own reaction against the meaningless mode of living in his own social circles. He failed to understand that the Cossacks themselves lived in a framework of values worked out in their own hermetic society which also was no longer true to the natural instincts of man.

The question of "natural instincts" and of the possible greater inherent nobility of people with minimal links to civilization, belongs to the complex of issues and problems pertaining to both civilization and art which relate to Tolstoy's encounters with Rousseau. The Soviet critic B. Bursov notes the affinity of Tolstoy's view of the Cossacks in his story with the general outlines of Rousseau's thought:

Tolstoy's story in some of its aspects touched upon the works of Rousseau; it undoubtedly has rousseauistic motifs. In the confrontation of a civilized person with a world untouched by civilization, the latter remains victorious.[20]

The Academician M.N. Rozanov, in his lecture "Rousseau and Tolstoy," given in 1928, quotes, among other things, from Tolstoy's interview with a French educator held as late as 1901 where Tolstoy is very emphatic about Rousseau's influence on him:

> People have been unjust to Rousseau, the greatness of his thought was not acknowledged, he was slandered in all sorts of ways. I read the whole of Rousseau, all the twenty volumes, including the "Dictionary of Music." I was more than enthused about him, I worshiped him. At the age of fifteen, I carried a medallion with a portrait of Rousseau around my neck. Many pages in Rousseau are so close to me that it seems as if I had written them myself.[21]

According to Rozanov, Rousseau had a crucial forming influence on Tolstoy in his youth, most particularly because:

> Spiritual affinities between them rested in one primeval, deep-rooted and essential aspect of both of their natures: some sort of elemental, subconscious nearness to the earth, to nature, some sort of instinctive pull toward the original sources of all life (Rozanov, *Russo...*, pp. 9-10).

Tolstoy however, did make the following distinction between himself and Rousseau:

> They compare me to Rousseau. I am much indebted to Rousseau and I like him, but there is a big difference. The difference is that Rousseau rejects all civilization, while I reject just the falsely Christian. That which is called civilization is the growth of humanity. That growth is necessary, and there is no point in considering whether it is a good thing or not (*PSS*, 55, 145).

Tolstoy himself spoke as late as 1903 of still wider affinities with certain kinds of French literature; affinities which in a sense embrace his principle of the universality of art:

> I think that each people in their own way expresses in art the universal human ideals; this is why we feel particular satisfaction when we meet our own ideals expressed in a way that is new and unexpected to us.

> Such an expression of something new I received from French literature when, in time past, I read for the first time Alfred de Vigny, Stendhal, Victor Hugo and especially Rousseau. (Letter to Sergeenko, 1903; Rozanov, pp. 7-8).

In Rozanov's opinion, Tolstoy's fascination with Rousseau was romantic in its emotional ambience:

> The cradle of the great realist was rounded with romantic dreams, through which one could see again and again the image of one and the same "strange sorcerer" — Rousseau (Rozanov, p. 4).

It is not clear whether Rozanov's "romantic dream" is the same as Romanticism in literature. If it is, then another Soviet critic, Boris Eikhenbaum, has a different, and more substantial idea which goes back to his general notion that literary change includes a process in which the new wave must look backward over the heads of the preceding generation, towards one's "grandparents." Describing what Tolstoy read in the early fifties, Eikhenbaum notes Sterne and Rousseau, and then continues:

> On the other hand, [Tolstoy] nowhere mentions the main gods of the generation preceding his — Shakespeare, Goethe and the German Romantics. One cannot help thinking that the young Tolstoy was more closely connected with his literary grandparents than with parents, as it often happens in the change of generations. The roots of his spiritual style, as expressed in the diaries of his youth, go back to the epoch of sentimentalism ... not for nothing did he return to the spiritual leaders of the time of Karamzin and young Zhukovsky — to Sterne and Rousseau. [22]

This interpretation helps us understand a good deal about relationships between Tolstoy's rationalism and his fine perceptions of feeling, since both do go back to the ambience of eighteenth-century France. Rozanov also notes this relationship as another element linking Tolstoy and Rousseau:

> Both writers possess a mind with a special emotional tint. The spheres of thought and feeling are not clearly divided in their minds. These are passionate minds, and therefore often biased. They have a

great tendency toward paradox; in Tolstoy this tendency is even greater than in Rousseau (Rozanov, pp. 11-12).

Since Tolstoy felt his spiritual affinities with Rousseau late in life as much as he did at the beginning, it seems clear that these affinities, this "emotional tint" are also present in Tolstoy's essay on art. Indeed, the "specter" of Rousseau may stand at the very center of Tolstoy's definition of art as infection with emotion. In trying to say that art must communicate some sort of essential value, unique to itself but also as necessary and organic a function of life as any other, Tolstoy may have come to the word "feeling" almost inevitably, almost as a kind of memory of what Rousseau and life have meant to him in his youth and through all his days — a sort of deep, "atavistic" perception somewhere at the center of being human that for him could only be encoded in that word. A number of critics thought Tolstoy should have made a distinction between feeling in art and feeling in life; others have tried to explain that by "feeling" Tolstoy must also have meant "thought," but the crux of the matter may well be that both terms could be better comprehended in such a language as that of the neo-Formalist Jurij Lotman, as "artistic information," in essence different from information of any other kind and thus not classifiable by means of concepts that by their nature reside outside of art.

Returning to *The Cossacks*, there is a tradition of criticism which repeats Olenin's error and oversimplifies Tolstoy's painful search for a class, a type of reader, or a segment of humanity which could fully respond to the artist because it does fully possess the quality of genius, described in the diary note he wrote in French in 1851 — the ability to "retrace" the infinitude of reality in its own soul. It may be true, as N. A. Semenova says, that:

> Tolstoy shows that these "simple people" among whom Olenin for the first time felt himself to be simply a person, and nature, constitute an inseparable whole, or, more precisely: only people who are close to nature can simply be people. In this way the story reveals the *motif* of naturalness as the main moral and aesthetic criterion of the human personality.[23]

The real point, however, is not this. It is that the only truly spontaneous man among the Cossacks was Erosha, the huge old hunter and former thief and brigand who, Olenin thought, had befriended him, and who was himself an outcast among his own people. Erosha is a separate individual, and not a part of any society. He does resemble the peasant in "Three Deaths" in that he is not "good" in the conventional Christian sense, nor in the sense of life as self-sacrifice, the lesson Olenin thought he learned from the gnats in the forest, namely, that "happiness lies in living for other people." [24] Erosha never did learn any such lessons from nature, and this is why he was always right. He has only immense age and immense strength — a pagan force that was there the first day the earth began. He is immortal because of his indifference to mortality.

The feeling that there is a fateful dichotomy between the simple nobility of ordinary people and the self-centered conventions of the privileged class is also present in Tolstoy's semi-fictional reports from the Crimean war called *Sevastopol' Tales*. There, particularly in the first segment, "Sevastopol' in August," Tolstoy contrasts the calm and altogether natural, unconquerable simplicity and courage of the common Russian soldiers — peasants who can die as the peasant did in "Three Deaths," or like the people who stood and died at Borodino — with the complex but in essence morally worthless experiences of the officer class as a whole. According to B. Bursov:

> From the point of view of Tolstoy's spiritual search, the story "Sevastopol' in August" is important precisely because it discloses one of the possible means of uniting one man with all the others — by standing in the face of war, forced upon the people, although in the given instance such a unity, through the fault of the "Napoleons" became impossible.[25]

In other words, the values of the petty self-seeking upper classes were found inadequate to the demands of Tolstoy's "main hero — truth" in the crucible of war. Preoccupations with prestige, social standing, with the insignificant questions of personal worth in the catastrophic events where the entire country was being judged by history contrasted too sharply with the deep devotion of ordinary soldiers to the land of their birth. Something that the soldiers knew could have saved the country, but the aristocratic officers could not begin to understand what it was.

As we noted before, the feeling that the simple people of the land knew something as a matter of course which the intellectualizing aristocrats could not really imagine, let alone comprehend kept growing inside Tolstoy's mind, and as it did so, became more and more pertinent to the issues of art. Gradually, the effort to find a place for the common folk in his developing views on aesthetics became one of the most important aspects of his thinking about them. At first, Tolstoy considered that perhaps one could think in terms of "two literatures" — both genuine in their own way — which do nevertheless represent the artistic imagination of two different sections of society. In 1851 he wrote in his diary that "the people have their own literature, beautiful and inimitable, "but it is not made literature — it comes from the people themselves" (*PSS*, 46, 71). Yet, at the time he was not able to explain very clearly even to himself what it was that made the peoples' literature so beautiful. The delicacy of sentiment combined with assured knowledge, in instantaneous comprehension, when a work of art is true remained for Tolstoy in the province of "the elect."

It was not until 1898, when he wrote his essay on art, that the "elect" became those who work with their hands in constant and intimate contact with nature and with other people who share their kind of life. Then he also knew that there really is only one true literature — that which either comes from the people or is written in the spirit and manner which is accessible to them and reflects the concerns of their lives. In the essay, Tolstoy was quite eloquent about the rich inner lives of the peasants and workers, about the variety of challenges they had to meet and the various stimuli for thought and feeling they received from their surrounding world, about the intensity of their love, heroism and self-sacrifice. The only thing the reader might ask for in retrospect is to experience all this for himself while reading Tolstoy's works — to get to feel from the inside, "from the soul" all the great and powerful, yet to him as well as to the peasants depicted, intimately personal emotions that emanate from the text.

Alas, this is difficult. When we look at Tolstoy's peasants in *War and Peace*, we see figures like Karataev, portrayed from the outside, through the eyes of Pierre, who may well be merely ascribing to Karataev all the wisdom of the soul he himself has begun to acquire, in part from the thoughts of his Masonic mentor Bazdeev, and, more importantly, from his experiences on the field of Borodino, where the peasants seemed to congeal into something he called "they" — an unconquerable, wise, simple, but impersonal, power that is the very essence of Russia. [26] In *Anna Karenina*, also, there are figures like the peasants with whom Levin mowed the meadow — skillful, wise but rather inarticulate people whose measure of personal inner life is hard to gauge in the novel. After all is said and done, it is Levin, the educated aristocrat, who in the most intimate nuances of his soul can hear what the wind-swept grass is saying on a sunny day and who can read messages from configurations in the clouds that pertain to his future hopes of life with Kitty. It takes a rich inner life, delicately balanced amidst complex ideas and sensations, impossible without a high degree of educated sophistication, to make nature, and life in nature, interesting. What Tolstoy really demands from the spiritual aristocrats of his early years as well as from the idealized peasants of late works, and from us, his present partners, is a talent for reading commensurate with his own talent as a writer.

One may say even more: Tolstoy's ideas on art, even at this early stage, tended to come together with his notions on what is moral and what is rational generally in life as well, [27] and these, in turn, reflected his own powerful thrust toward resolving the issue of himself — of that turbulent and puzzling force which he felt himself to be. [28] It is rather evident, for instance, that the theoretical premises of Tolstoy's early ideas on art, as well as those of his treatise in 1898, seem to be predicated on the underlying tacit assumption that the effectiveness of art depends primarily not on what an artist does, but on what he is. The recreation of the immense richness of reality in the end amounts to the communication of the artist himself to his readers, or to put it differently, to the total conquest of the reader by the artist. Art therefore is not a constructed thing, not a set of skills, not a system of technical devices, but as it were, a magnetic field, bending the reader's mind and his emotions to the outlines of the artist's own personality. That personality itself does not appear to Tolstoy as some enormous ego, self-centered and tyrannical, but rather as a medium, a level of existence called consciousness, which transmits a larger truth, be it the infinitude of being, or the voice of God.

One may indeed say that Tolstoy's religious thought developed in close relationship to his views on aesthetics. In 1855, we find the first statement by Tolstoy concerning religion which, like the succinct 1851 note "Why do People Write," contains the seed of the tremendous development of his later religious philosophy, an achievement comparable to his creative works and to his thoughts on aesthetics. On March 4, 1855, Tolstoy wrote in his diary:

> Yesterday, a conversation about the Divine and about faith led me to a great, tremendous thought, to the fulfillment of which I feel I am capable of devoting my life. This thought — the foundation of a new religion, which would correspond to the development of man, the religion of Christ, but cleansed from faith in mystery, a practical religion which would not promise future bliss, but would give bliss on earth — I understand that only generations, consciously working toward this purpose, can bring this thought to fulfillment (*PSS*, 47, 37).

When Tolstoy spoke of "religious consciousness" in his essay, this had nothing to do in his mind with church Christianity, but was related to what he meant by "the religion of Christ" at this early stage.[29]

Thus we come to the broad outlines of Tolstoy's developing thought on art during this first span of his career. We can see that his earliest concerns had to do with the relationship between reality and imagination — precisely the issue that is at the root of all concern with art. Already at this early stage Tolstoy took a turn in the direction of rejecting any traditional and conventionalized basis for artistic imagery, preferring instead to penetrate through to the poetics immanent in reality itself. The second great question for Tolstoy was the relationship between an artist and his public. On the one hand, he felt that only exceptional people, of superior mind, sensitivity and education, could truly partake of a writer's creativity. On the other, a closer look at the educated classes revealed to Tolstoy their lack of the quality of truth in life which is indispensable for art. This returned Tolstoy's attention to the masses to whom he had already been willing to relegate their own special artistic world containing true values, with the suspicion that these particular values may indeed be the only thing that is true in art as it is true in nature. In these early years, Tolstoy did not quite manage to establish a full relationship of interdependence between the concept of "the people" and that of morality and religious consciousness. Yet, there was a movement in that direction, an impetus which could quickly develop into conviction given an opportunity to test himself and his ideas when working on something together with representatives of the peasant class. He did create such an opportunity for himself when he undertook to be a teacher of peasant children on his own estate in Yasnaya Polyana.

Finally, we have seen that almost all of Tolstoy's early ideas were seminal to later developments and that underneath any given beliefs of Tolstoy at some given time there was always the same basic thrust, the same urge to seek the meaning of art in terms of the meaning of life itself.

CHAPTER TWO

THE LESSONS OF YASNAYA POLYANA

A brief period in Tolstoy's life, approximately between 1857 and 1862, is particularly significant in the development of his aesthetic views, paradoxically, in part because just then he considered abandoning altogether his career as a writer. During those years Tolstoy underwent his first truly major moral and intellectual crisis — a radical questioning of all his values with the intent of opening the door to a new and this time truly meaningful way of life. Embraced by the very roots of his ancestral estate on Yasnaya Polyana, he seemed to become an alien to himself as he lived through his spiritual crucible that included the issue of art. He'd had his ultimately disappointing experiences in Moscow's world of letters, but a new impetus for thinking about art grew, as it were, directly from the soil — from the lives of the common people all around him. Seeing that his peasants could live and work without the help of worldly *belles lettres*, he started questioning in principle the essence of art and its function in society. He did it with such seriousness that the consequences of his moral and intellectual quest extended far into his future as a writer and a thinker about human affairs.

One matter of particular interest is the striking basic similarity between Tolstoy's ideas and attitudes dawning on him as he struggled to understand where he stood with art and those he finally articulated late in life, when he wrote his essay. Another is the constant presence of these very ideas in his subsequent fiction as it expanded into the great novels. Tolstoy's thoughts about art at Yasnaya Polyana underwent various reincarnations to become the thoughts and feelings of his heroes, also a quality of his landscapes, cities, a motivating force for human conflicts and affections, and even part of the very fabric of history.

The particular factors that led Tolstoy to reconsider the nature and function of art seemed to acquire a cumulative force as they crowded around his life. To begin with, his two "artistic" stories, *Lucerne* and *Albert*, were coolly received by the critics, and Tolstoy himself was especially disappointed with his *Family Happiness*. This story, written from the perspective of a girl deeply in love with a handsome landowner, who bears a good deal of resemblance to Tolstoy himself, contains elements of his relationship with Valeriya Arsenyevna, a young woman whom he thought of marrying.[1] Tolstoy may have become ashamed of the self-admiration implicit in the girl's adoring thoughts of her beloved. In any event, Tolstoy's unhappiness about the story strengthened his feeling that literature could be a meaningless enterprise, at least for him. In 1859 he wrote to Druzhinin:

> As for now, I am completely useless as a writer. I don't write and have not written anything since *Family Happiness*, and it seems, will not be writing either. At least, I flatter myself with this hope. Why? It's a long story, and difficult to tell. The main point is that life is short and I am ashamed to waste it in my mature years writing the kind of stories that I have written. One can and one must, and I wish to do meaningful things.[2]

The idea of education came to his mind as one of such "meaningful things," and indeed, he established a school for peasant children on his estate after returning from his first trip of Europe, in 1859. This trip, as well as the second tour in 1860-61, left Tolstoy depressed by what he had seen of human misery and cruelty both at home and abroad to the point where he could question the very concept of civilization. While in Germany and France, he visited classrooms[3] and observed with great interest and sometimes indignation the educational practices in Western Europe, objecting particularly to the enforcement of strict and seemingly mindless academic discipline upon pupils who, in Tolstoy's view, could not have any real interest in the subject they were forced to study, that is, such things as rhetoric and dead languages.[4] He was determined to make his own school in Yasnaya Polyana the opposite of the tyrannical practices he had seen; freedom for the natural flow of human desire for learning and the rejection of any intellectual prejudices as to what constituted the proper subjects for study were to be his main principles.

Another significant factor may have been the pull of the earth, the native soil itself. Rather like Konstantin Levin in *Anna Karenina*, dejected after his refusal by Kitty, Tolstoy may also have attempted to transform his depression into the powerful, concrete physical activity of farming that was of itself meaningful beyond any dispute, unlike the rootless, brainspun specter of art.[5] If art is to remain a viable activity and idea, then it must draw its nourishment from the same soil under the farmer's feet. Before the possibility of a literature and civilization that grows directly and organically from contact with the everyday life of labor, and is always a matter of the present, the prevalent Western civilization, built in a cumulative process from books upon the foundation of other books, seemed to lose all relevance.

A. V. Chicherin, a Soviet critic, is of the opinion that Tolstoy's previous short-lived "aestheticism" which led him to deny social purpose in art stood in direct contradiction with the spirit of his early works and with his own nature as an artist:

> The parting of the ways with Chernyshevsky, to whom Tolstoy had been so warmly sympathetic at the time when he wrote his article about *Childhood* [1852] and produced his [Caucasian] war stories, his quarrel with the editors of *The Contemporary* and his coming together with the defenders of "pure art", such as Botkin, Annenkov, Fet ... all this stood in irreconcilable contradiction with the works Tolstoy had already written and with the entire personality of the artist himself. These opinions [about "pure art" — R.Š] led Tolstoy to a dead end.[6]

In the end, according to Chicherin, "In denying that art is capable of reconstructing man and his life, Tolstoy, with the inflexibility characteristic of him, went on to deny both art and life completely" (*ibid.*, p. 134). One could agree that such works as *Sevastopol' Tales* or even the *Childhood, Boyhood, Youth* trilogy, bear directly upon social issues and the moral meaning of life. Nevertheless, it is more accurate to say that Tolstoy during his "aesthetic" period, sought in art those higher spiritual values which he found lacking in the life around him in the social setup of Russia.

Tolstoy's words to Druzhinin that life is short came back at him with a special urgency with the death of his brother Nikolay from tuberculosis in 1861. Tolstoy's great sensitivity to the issue of death, his unceasing preoccupation with it, affected his art and thought throughout his career. One might perhaps say of Tolstoy that he felt the immeasurable void of death just because, and in the same degree, as he felt the equally immeasurable fullness and intensity of life. The consciousness of life, and the consciousness of death may have been for him but two different aspects of experiencing the ultimate confrontation with his hero, Truth. The question of how does art, which is always in some sense a "lie," relate to this final presence of truth was often tied in for Tolstoy with his thoughts and feelings about his talented older brother Nikolay, whom he at times considered superior to himself. Now, with Nikolay gone, how is one to write stories about imaginary lives, when life itself is an illusion? It is in this spirit that Tolstoy wrote a letter to Fet at around this time, testifying, perhaps unwittingly, as much to his great moral power and intensity as to his deep despair:

> Praise Allah, God, Brahma. Such a benefactor. "Take life as it is. You and not God, have put yourselves in this situation." To be sure! But I do take life as it is, as the most vulgar, repulsive and false condition. And the proof that I did not put myself into it is in the fact that we keep trying to believe as centuries go by that this condition is very good. But as soon as man reaches a higher state of development, he ceases to be stupid, and it is clear to him that everything is absurdity, deceit, and that truth, which he does, after all, love, this truth is terrible. And that when you see it well, clearly, you will wake up and say with horror: "Wait, brother, what is this?"
> Of course, as long as you want to eat, go ahead and eat, as long as there is this unconscious stupid desire to know and to speak the truth, one tries to know and to speak. This is the only thing from the moral dimension which has left to me, above which I could not rise, and this is the one thing I will do, but only not in the form of your art. Art is a lie, and I can no longer love a beautiful lie.[7]

If the bitter truth about everyday Russian life inclined Tolstoy to withdraw to the realm of pure art, then the terrible existential truth about death made him wish to renounce art altogether. In both experiences, however, he remained the same Tolstoy, a born artist, endowed, or burdened, with a great moral urgency. What he did not understand very well at that time was that his search for something meaningful to do instead of being a writer was really a search for the true understanding of art as something that remains important after it leaves the fancies of mere aesthetics. Perhaps, therefore, Tolstoy also failed to realize that, when he started the Yasnaya Polyana school in the Autumn of 1859, he inevitably was going to learn as much or more about art, about being a writer, as he taught the peasant children about life.

An extensive record of Tolstoy's experiences, activities and maturing thought about art during the entire period of the Yasnaya Polyana school is contained in twelve issues of a monthly magazine he published between February, 1862, and March, 1863, called *The Yasnaya Polyana Journal.* This journal contains a number of pedagogical articles discussing art and education in close relationship to each other. A running undercurrent of thought in these articles centers around the idea that there is an inner striving for truth in the broad masses of humanity — a striving which Tolstoy had personally felt in himself since his early years. One expression of this striving that he saw was the general desire for learning among the people which, paradoxically, runs counter to what the established order of society considers to be education and thrusts upon unwilling pupils in the public schools. In an article called "On Popular Education," Tolstoy's whole argument for a new and radically different approach to schoolwork proceeds from this dichotomy. Instead of a united educational enterprise, says Tolstoy, there is a constant struggle going on between the people and the educational establishment, as well as society at large:

> The need for education dwells in every man; the people love and seek education, as they love and seek the air for breathing; the government and society burn with the desire to educate the masses, and yet, notwithstanding all the force of cunning and the persistency of governments and societies, the masses constantly manifest their dissatisfaction with the education which is offered to them, and step by step submit only to force.[8]

The overall structure of Tolstoy's argument in the article "On Popular Education" resembles the manner in which the dichotomy between art and the people was presented in *What Is Art?*. There too art was seen to be as necessary to everyone as the food one eats, but everyone (that is, the great majority of mankind, which is what counts) resists the art of the educated classes, for the production of which the simple people are made to labor and suffer. Beyond this surface similarity of argument there is also a deeper resemblance of historical perspective. In the essay Tolstoy had said that in the Middle Ages the ruling classes and the people as a whole shared a common faith in Christianity as taught to them by the established Church, even if this teaching was already perverted. The real prostitution of art came when the rulers ceased to believe in such Christianity, but continued to encourage works of art which appeared to promote this non-existent faith. The history of education, as Tolstoy saw it during the Yasnaya Polyana period, presents a similar picture: in the Middle Ages it was clear to everybody what must be taught in schools, and why, even if it did not make any rational sense, but in modern times no one knows what the truth is anymore, yet, both the teachers and the society which they represent continue to force contradictory and useless information upon the pupils. "What is the position of the school in our day," asks Tolstoy:

> which has persevered in the same dogmatic principles, when, side by side with the class where the scholar learns by heart the truth about the immortality of the soul, they try to make it clear to him that the nerves, which are common to man and to a frog, are that which anciently used to be called a soul; when, after the story of Joshua, the son of Nun, which is transmitted to him without explanations, he finds out that the sun had never turned around the earth; when, after the beauties of Vergil have been explained to him, he finds the beauties in Alexandre Dumas, sold to him for five centimes, much greater; when the only faith of the teacher consists in the conviction that there is no truth, that everything existing is sensible, that progress is good and backwardness bad; when nobody knows in what this universal faith in progress consists? (Wiener, pp. 6-7; *PSS*, *8*, 7).

The implied conclusion from the arguments of 1898 and 1862 is that false art and false education are the means by which the ruling classes of society maintain themselves in their position. On this basis, just as he said in his essay on art that there is not, nor can there be, such a science as aesthetics, Tolstoy affirms in his article that there is no science of education, either:

> At the basis of our activity lies the conviction that we not only do not know, but we cannot know, wherein the education of the people is to consist; that not only does there not exist a science of education, — pedagogics — but that the first foundation of it has not yet been laid; that the definition of pedagogy and of its aims in a philosophical sense is impossible, useless, and injurious (Wiener, p. 29; *PSS, 8,* 24).

What actually happens is that the schoolchildren obtain their education on the streets and at home, from their parents and friends, and that they resist the artificial education foisted upon them just as, in the essay on art, people are said to resist any counterfeits.

Tolstoy's comment on Russian universities in the article "Education and Upbringing" bears essentially the same message. He accuses the social establishment of producing its servants at the universities instead of educating the people:

> No one has ever thought of establishing universities based on the needs of the people. That was impossible because the needs of the people have remained unknown. The universities were founded to answer certain needs, partly of the government and partly of higher society, and for the universities was established all that preparatory ladder of educational institutions which has nothing in common with the needs of the people. The government needed officials, doctors, jurists, teachers, and universities were founded in order to train these. Now higher society needs liberals of a certain pattern, and the universities train these. The only blunder is that the masses do not need these liberals at all.[9]

True education, like true art, is not to be conceived as an imposition of values, or attitudes, developed outside of the common consciousness of the people, but rather as an expression of that consciousness, changing and growing in harmony with the same laws that govern the nature and growth of a given society. "The school", says Tolstoy, "is good only when it has taken cognizance of the fundamental laws by which people live."[10] These laws, as Tolstoy saw them, were instinctive forces related to the basic organic needs of man, and not to any abstract legal structures. One such law is that people must communicate with each other by whatever means possible, including, most importantly, those of language. Real education, at its roots, takes place as a natural process growing out of a mother's efforts to communicate with her child:

> A mother teaches her child to speak only that they may understand each other; the mother instinctively tries to come down to the child's view of things, to his language, but the law of educational progress does not permit her to descend down to him but compels him to rise to her knowledge. The same relation exists between the author and the reader, between the state and society — the people (Wiener, p. 30, *PSS 8*, 25).

This kind of thinking eventually led Tolstoy to the conviction in *What Is Art?* that art is not something in essence different from any natural effort of communication, but only an aspect, one special form of it, which functions as the means for transmitting emotion rather than objective thought. As it does so, art remains "one of the conditions of human life," one "of the means of intercourse between man and man."[11]

Tolstoy's views on history articulated in the Yasnaya Polyana journal are relevant to our discussion to the extent that, in opposing the idea that there are any laws of history that could be offered as a systematic and rational description of the universal progress of humanity, he also denied educational "progress" toward greater and more abstract knowledge as well as the "progress" of the arts, of aesthetics, toward sophistication and complexity. In a polemical article called "Progress and the Definition of Education," arguing against the writer and educator E. V. Markov, who had objected to Tolstoy's first report form Yasnaya Polyana, Tolstoy said:

> I see no necessity of finding the common laws of history, even if this were possible. The common eternal law is written in the soul of each man. The law of

progress, of perfectibility, is written in the soul of each man, and it is a mistake to transfer it to the plane of history. As long as it remains personal, this law is fruitful and accessible to all; when it is transferred to history, it becomes an idle, empty prattle, leading to the justification of every insipidity and to fatalism. Progress in general in all humanity is an unproved fact, and does not exist for all the Eastern nations; therefore it is as unfounded to say that progress is the law of humanity as it is to say that all people are blond except the dark complexioned ones.[12]

Such a view of progress and history fits very well into the overall network of values holding together Tolstoy's entire philosophy throughout his life. His argument in the second epilogue of *War and Peace* about free will and determinism is constructed on the very same principle, namely, that each separate action is meaningful to the individual who wills it within the limits of his personal knowledge and consciousness, and that history — or "progress" — is shaped by the incalculable consequences of innumerable individual acts in their infinitely complex relationships with each other rather than by some abstractly conceivable "general laws" which can be superimposed upon events.

Therefore, as in art, pedagogical activity must be that type of communication between two people in which one person's inner drive toward perfection makes an impact upon the consciousness of another, exciting and stimulating his own striving and giving it fresh forms. Education is intense personal contact, an exciting emotional experience shared by the teacher and his students. It is this feeling of excitement, of infection with emotion, that makes Tolstoy's pedagogical activities relevant and important to his definition of art. As an educator, Tolstoy was effective without theories, through the magic of his enthusiasm, the force of his personality. There is a vibrant, intense and joyful excitement radiating from all of the Yasnaya Polyana articles describing his work with the children. Indeed, one could say that Tolstoy never ceased being an artist, even if it did seem so to him at the time. He merely worked in a different medium, consisting of living people, the schoolchildren of his estate, and he developed them almost as if they were characters from his fiction, figures in his dreams.

There are truly poetic moments in Tolstoy's reports from his school, where one feels not only the thinker's argument, but also the artist's skill. The first article, "Yasnaya Polyana in November and December," contains the description of an evening of Bible stories which is as carefully prepared as any passage in Tolstoy's fiction, and the only difference is that both the setting and the people are real. The underlying premise in this description is the belief that Bible stories have the power to touch and move the human heart irrespective of age and the level of education. Tolstoy does not attempt to argue this premise explicitly, but shifts instead to an evening mood, when the lessons "have a peculiar character of calm, dreaminess and poetry, different in this from the morning classes" (*PSS 8*, 40; Wiener 242). The building is almost quiet, says Tolstoy, and only some snow on the stairs, tracked in from outside, and a little urchin clambering up the steps, two at a time, show that the school is in session. Inside the room it is dark behind the frosted windows, and the pupils, crowded around he teacher, listen to his every word with rapt attention. In this twilight, standing alone, speaking of the Passion of Christ, the teacher himself seems to radiate a mysterious inner light which spreads amidst the silence like a hypnotic force:

> You would think all are dead: there is no stir, can they be asleep? You walk up to them in the semi-darkness and look into the face of some little fellow, — he is sitting, his eyes staring at the teacher, frowning from close attention, and for the tenth time brushing away the arm of his companion, which is pressing down on his shoulder. You tickle his neck, — he does not even smile; he only bends his head, as though to drive away a fly, and again abandons himself to the mysterious and poetical story, how the veil of the church was rent and it grew dark upon the earth, — and he has mingled sensation of dread and joy! (*PSS 8*, 40; Wiener 43).

Precisely this "mingled sensation of dread and joy," the magic movement of communion, is what Tolstoy himself managed to impart to his pupils, and this for him was education, and it was art as well — the infection with emotion of which he spoke years later, in *What Is Art?*. In that essay, Tolstoy returns to the Bible stories as examples of the highest form of good art:

That Joseph's brethern, being jealous of his father's affection, sell him to the merchants; that Potiphar's wife wishes to tempt the youth; that having attained to highest station he takes pity on his brothers, including Benjamin the favorite — these and all the rest are feelings accessible alike to a Russian peasant, a Chinese, an African, a child, or an old man, educated or uneducated (Maude, 244; *PSS*, *30*, 161).

It is important to understand that the significance of Tolstoy's statement does not necessarily lie in its validity as a general proposition; cultural differences among various groups may make the story not at all equally accessible or even comprehensible to them all. Tolstoy's argument is valid the way a work of art would be: as a strong and continuing personal experience from the days of the Yasnaya Polyana school to the end of the century when Tolstoy, himself now approaching Biblical age, is still as moved by the power of warm human feeling in the story as he was during that magical evening in his youth. In the second article of the Yasnaya Polyana Journal Tolstoy makes a remark which acquires great profundity when put in juxtaposition with certain moments in his works where the meaning of life and the meaning of death seem accessible only to children: "It seems to me that the book of the childhood of the human race [i.e., the Bible — R.Š] always will be the best book of the childhood of every single human being" (*PSS*, *8*, 86). If we add to this Tolstoy's thought in the essay that the corrupted members of the upper classes might, perhaps, have had true feelings once, "in their earliest childhood," it becomes quite impressive to see how in Tolstoy's work the beginning of an individual life and the book of all beginnings meet on a timeless plane where they illuminate both the meaning of life and the meaning of art.

At another lyrical moment of deep emotional communication the question of art itself, of its meaning and purpose, came up and was resolved together by Tolstoy and his young pupils. This passage, again from "Yasnaya Polyana in November and December," describes a spontaneous discussion about art among Tolstoy and three of his pupils as he was walking them home through the wintry wood. The conversation is so reported that it acquires a carefully designed structure, again, as if it were a passage from one of Tolstoy's novels. There is the proper emotional setting: a dark thicket, a sense of danger from unseen wolves, and a deep gladness of being together, man and boy, in the uncertain night. There is also a "cast of characters" so chosen as to represent three different approaches which, among them, constitute a comprehensive treatment of the topic of art. The restless, intense creative spirit of Fed'ka, one of the boys, stood closest to the wellspring of art, and was best able to understand instinctively the self-justified, unmotivated beauty of all existing things. Semka, a strong, clear-headed boy, provided the crucible of questioning reason through which all flights of fancy must pass (at least in Tolstoy's world-view) before they become meaningful either as ideas relevant to the human condition, or as works of art. Finally, Pronka, a sickly boy, contributed the element of compassion, of love for living things. The discussion began with tales of adventure and terror, evoked by the dark, menacing presence of the woods. One of those tales, interestingly enough, was that of Hadzhi Murat, the freedom fighter in the Caucasus, which was much later (1896-1904) written down by Tolstoy as one of his best short stories.[13] At this point Tolstoy introduces the topic of art just where it meets the most profound and catastrophic human experience: he tells the boys that "the abrek, being surrounded, he began to sing songs, and then threw himself on his dagger" (Wiener, p. 250; *PSS, 8,* 45). The boys' response, tersely recorded, shows how well they understood, albeit in their own terms, the full significance of this moment:

...All were silent.
"Why did he sing a song when he was surrounded?" asked Semka.
"Didn't you hear? He was getting ready to die!" Fed'ka replied sorrowfully.
"I think he sang a prayer," added Pronka (*ibid.*).

Here we have it: the meaning of a life, asserted at its climactic all-important moment, that of death, by means of a song which is art and is also a prayer, understood by the boys precisely as Tolstoy would have us understand his own aesthetics. It is no wonder, then, that after another gruesome story of death, that of the murder of Countess Tolstoy,[14] Fed'ka suddenly asked why is it that people learn to sing. At this point, Tolstoy makes a very important comment to the effect that no one, including him, was surprised at this abrupt change of topic, because all felt that there was a "vivid and lawful connection of this question with the preceding conversation". What was this connection? Tolstoy's best guess, that "the connection consisted in his feeling that now was the time for intimate conversation, and that now in his soul had arisen all the questions demanding a solution," establishes the place of art near the center of the boy's inner life, perhaps near the place in his own heart where Hadzhi Murat's song arose from his. Art thus becomes as important as the opening of one person to another, complete without defenses, just as it happened on that night, in the shadow of the woods, with Fed'ka holding on tightly to Tolstoy's hand. This moment of personal intimacy, of course, is not yet a theory of art, but it does presage the direction in which Tolstoy's thoughts were to develop, namely that art is an inward-looking, intimate communion of souls, entirely on the ordinary human scale and not an exalted service to abstract ideals, as, for instance, the theoretical principles of Classicism, or the aesthetics based on the notions of Truth, Goodness and Beauty would have it.

From this beginning, the discussion led to the general question what art is for. Tolstoy felt he had no answer, but the boys, each in his own fashion, provided the crucial explanations:

> And we began to speak of there not being only a usefulness of things, but also a beauty, and that art was beauty, and we understood each other, and Fed'ka comprehended well why a linden grew and what singing was for.
> Pronka agreed with us, but he had mostly in mind moral beauty — goodness.
> Semka understood it rightly with his big brain, but he did not recognize beauty without usefulness. He doubted, as people of great intelligence doubt, feeling that art is a force, but feeling in their souls no need of that force; he wanted, like them, to reach out for that art by means of reason and tried to start the fire in himself (Wiener, p. 252; *PSS, 8,* 46).

Just at this point, with his unerring artist's instinct, Tolstoy suddenly returned to the topic of the song:

> "Let us sing 'He who' to-morrow, — I remember my voice."

And so this discussion on art is set off by art itself, the performance, at moments of crucial human significance. In his essay, Tolstoy was very much against various devices "to make it interesting," and it is perhaps a moot point as to whether he was using just such a device here himself, or merely reproducing faithfully the seemingly disconnected fragments of feelings and thoughts that emerge at important times in our lives from somewhere deep in us where there is a logic to them. Perhaps, as happens in the best pages of his prose, Tolstoy, only half understanding this, but nevertheless in full control, just created the *impression* of unpredictable spontaneity that nevertheless is placed with extreme precision in the overall structure of the narrative.

Further on, the conversation on art focused upon a tree. The issue was now one of utility and beauty:

> Fed'ka comprehended completely that the linden was nice with its leafage and that it was nice to look at it in summer, and nothing else was needed. Pronka understood that it was a pity to cut it down, because it, too had life: "when we drink the sap of the linden, it is just the same as though we were drinking blood" (Wiener, p. 252; *PSS, 8,* 47).

The final comment by Tolstoy establishes this conversation as another "mini-essay" on art which contains in embryonic form much of what his later theory was able to develop:

> It feels strange to me to repeat what we spoke on that evening, but I remember we said everything, I think, that there was to be said on utility and on plastic and moral beauty (*ibid*).

Another matter of importance to Tolstoy's later views of art is the aura of authority and understanding with which Tolstoy surrounds the little boys discussing art with him on a winter evening in the woods. True knowledge, it seems, does not result from a wealth of factual information, or from its sophisticated analysis. It is a matter of being human, that is, natural, maintaining one's inborn integrity which is organic, like a body not yet poisoned by the effulgences of civilization. This attitude pertains to all those ideas in *What Is Art?* which stand opposed to the necessity of knowledge and training in the arts, and also, eventually, to the development of performing skills, which, for Tolstoy, really amounted to various methods of counterfeiting art.

One of the articles from the Yasnaya Polyana journal: "Are the Peasant Children to Learn to Write From Us, or Are We to Learn from the Peasant Children?" goes beyond the idea that no special education is needed to understand true art and suggests that writers whose skill and fame has come from the educated tradition of letters would do well to come back to the original sources of inspiration by watching untutored children who can write as well or better as any accepted authors. Ostensibly, the article concerns itself with pedagogics — it describes how Tolstoy finally succeeded in getting his pupils to write original compositions, that is, to learn the art of verbal expression, and "the charm of this art." His simple expedient (actually, in response to a challenge by his students) was to give the boys some topic based on a popular proverb and to let them write in competition with him, their teacher. It is interesting to see, in terms of Tolstoy's explicit insistence in *What Is Art?* that art only happens when there is strong feeling which communicates itself to others, how at first the work did not go very well, until both Tolstoy and the children became excited:

> ...I read to them what I had written. They did not like it, and nobody praised it. I felt ashamed, and, to soothe my literary ambition, I began to tell them the plan of what was to follow. In the proportion as I advanced in my story, I became enthusiastic, corrected myself, and they kept helping me out. ... All were exceedingly interested. It was evidently a new and exciting sensation for them to be present at the process of creation, and to take part in it (Wiener, pp. 193-4; *PSS*, 8, 303).

Precisely in this excitement resides the mystery of art. In truly inspired words that explain nobly and clearly just what he eventually meant in *What Is Art?* by "infection with emotion" Tolstoy wrote:

> He [the boy Fed'ka — R.Š.] was agitated for a long time and could not fall asleep, and I cannot express that feeling of agitation, joy, fear, and almost regret, which I experienced during that evening. I felt that with that day a new world of enjoyment and suffering was opened up to him — the world of art; I thought that I had received an insight in what no one has a right to see, — the germination of the mysterious flower of poetry.[15]
> I felt both dread and joy, like the seeker after the treasure who suddenly sees the flower of the fern, —

> I felt joy, because suddenly and quite unexpectedly there was revealed to me that stone of the philosophers which I had vainly been trying to find for two years, — the art of teaching the expression of thoughts; and dread, because this art called for a whole new world of desires, which stood in no relation to the surroundings of the pupils, as I thought in the first moment. There was no mistaking. It was not an accident, but a conscious creation (Wiener, pp. 197-8; *PSS*, *8*, 305-6).

Thus did someone who had renounced art finally arrive, through intense emotional experience, at the holy fount of its mystery in the soul of a child. From that point on it was no longer possible (if it had ever been) that Tolstoy should cease to be a writer for the sake of something "more useful."

The excitement of Tolstoy's discovery serves as the point of departure for the article, which describes in detail just how the pupils worked with such an unexpected mastery of the written word that they proved themselves much superior to Tolstoy himself, or anyone else in the accepted world of letters. A number of critics have thought that Tolstoy's praise of the children's work was in essence but a forensic device, aiming at a dramatic challenge to accepted notions in art. The Soviet critic E. Dosycheva wrote in 1922:

> The article leaves the impression of a sort of challenge not so much to educators as to artists and theoreticians of art. The device itself — the passing of the topic through the prism of a child's perception — has its roots in the philosophical-aesthetic views of Tolstoy which were developed in more detail in *What Is Art?*[16]

Dosycheva further notes that the best qualities of the children's writing, those which Tolstoy praised the most, are really the characteristics of Tolstoy's own style, namely the choice of significant detail, the sense of balance and measure, and a straightforward, unsentimental treatment of emotions. Other critics, for example, A. Chicherin, felt that Tolstoy may well have learned as much from the children as he taught them:

> It seemed to many that the great writer imbued the village children with the sparks of his own talent, and

thus they started writing so well. But this is not altogether true. The author of *War and Peace* did indeed learn no less from his pupils than they did from him; therein resides his greatness.[17]

Unfortunately, Chicherin does not point out what in particular are those characteristics of a work like *War and Peace* which Tolstoy may have acquired from his pupils. Even so, his statement is not entirely theoretical, because, in describing how he worked together with the children on the text, Tolstoy did dwell in considerable detail on the various corrections and improvements which the boy Fed'ka introduced in Tolstoy's own composition. The reason, as Tolstoy explained it, why he was wrong and Fed'ka was right has some bearing on those sections of *What Is Art?* where the most common methods of counterfeiting art are discussed. Basically, Tolstoy's own work was, he felt, inferior because he kept trying to write according to the generally accepted standards of literary composition:

> I was strongly possessed by the demands of a regular structure and of an exact correspondence of the idea of the proverb to the story; while they, on the contrary, were only concerned about the demands of artistic truth.[18]

In other words, artistic truth is not something that has been described by certain rules developed over a period of time that now compose the discipline of aesthetics. It is something else altogether, and is also the only thing that matters in art. And it cannot be learned, but those with true feelings know it from the beginning. The rest is mere counterfeit, as Tolstoy claimed later in the essay. If Tolstoy's experiences with the boys did indeed contribute to the ultimate development of his aesthetic thought, then B. Bursov is correct when he says:

> The important thing is not so much what Tolstoy found in one or another of his pupils, but what he found within himself in his relationships with them. And the stories written by the peasant children must be regarded, actually, not so much as something that belong to them, but more as a search by Tolstoy himself for a new artistic and aesthetic position.[19]

Tolstoy's search for these new artistic positions is most evident in his interpretative comments on the stories written by the boys with his participation. In them we can see the master artist whose talent for creation is but the other side of his talent for reading. At one point, for instance, we see Fed'ka, another boy, Semka, and Tolstoy himself writing together a story to illustrate the Russian proverb "He feeds you with the spoon and stabs you in the eye with its handle." The story is about a peasant who, while he feeds a poor beggar, also wants to make him feel guilty of being such a sponger. One of the characters is a gossipy fellow who, Fed'ka wrote, went out of the room having put on a woman's fur coat. Challenged to explain why should this man take a woman's and not a man's coat, Fed'ka cannot say much more than "a woman's fur coat is better," but Tolstoy has a full and exciting explanation:

> Every artistic word, whether it belongs to Goethe or to Fed'ka, differs from the inartistic in that it evokes an endless mass of thoughts, images and explanations. The gossip in a woman's fur coat involuntarily presents himself to us as a sickly, narrow-chested peasant, just such as he apparently ought to be. The woman's fur coat, carelessly thrown on the bench and the first to fall into his hands, in addition, presents to us a winter evening scene in the life of the peasant. The fur coat leads you to imagine the late evening, during which the peasant is sitting without his wraps near a torch, and the women, coming in and out to fetch water and attend to the cattle, and all that external disorder of the peasant life, where no person has his clearly defined clothes, and no one thing is in a definite place. With this one sentence, "He put on a woman's fur coat," the whole character of the surroundings, in which the action takes place, is clearly outlined, and this phrase is not used by accident, but consciously (Wiener, pp. 198-9; *PSS*, *8*, 306-7).

Tolstoy was equally responsive to a certain stark simplicity in the boys' style, their ability to convey complex information by minimal means. Upon Tolstoy's suggestion and with his assistance (which, Tolstoy says, only spoiled things) Fed'ka wrote a story called "A Soldier's Life," about a dissolute peasant who is taken into the army and comes back years later, reformed, but in the meantime his son dies. Fed'ka describes the event in the following

way:
> At midnight the mother for some reason began to weep. Grandmother arose and said "What is the matter? Christ be with you!" The mother said: "My son has died." Grandmother made a fire, washed the boy, put a shirt on him, girded him and placed him beneath the ikons (Wiener, p. 208).[20]

"There are in all five lines," says Tolstoy:
> and in these five lines there is painted for the reader the whole picture of that sad night, — a picture reflected in the imagination of a boy six or seven years old....
> You see the boy himself [another son — R.Š], awakened by the familiar tears of his mother, half-sleepy, under a kaftan somewhere on the hanging bed, with frightened and sparkling eyes watching the proceedings in the hut; you see the haggard soldier's widow, who the day before had said "How soon will this slavery come to an end?" repentant and crushed by the thought of the end of this slavery, to such an extent that she only says, "My son has died," and knows not what to do, and calls for the grandmother to help her; and you see the old woman, worn out by the sufferings of life, bent down, emaciated, with bony limbs, as she calmly takes hold of the work with her hands that are accustomed to labour; she lights a torch, brings the water, and washes the boy; she places everything in the right place, and sets the boy, washed and girt, under the images. And you see those images, and all that night without sleep, until daybreak, as though you yourself were living through it, as that boy lived through it, gazing at it from underneath the kaftan; that night arises before you with all its details and remains in your imagination (Wiener, pp. 208-9).

The emotional impact of the situation arises precisely because of the lack of surface emotion in the telling of it. Yet, it takes a reader like Tolstoy to respond with rich and powerful images in his own mind to fill in, indeed, perhaps to augment, enrich, everything that was implicit but unsaid in Fed'ka's lines. But the question is:

how would a coarse-grained, simple-minded peasant read these lines? Would he miss their impact completely, or would he — and here is the crux of the question — only seem indifferent because the situation depicted in the story, with all that it implies, is so well known to him from his own life that he no longer needs a lot of words, or emotional gestures, to comprehend it? Such a peasant may simply *live* the full tragic depth of his human condition, very much like the Homeric heroes stood with terrible simplicity in front of their inexorable fate.[21] We may, from this perspective, gain an insight into what Tolstoy meant in his essay when he spoke of instant and universal communicability of true art. Tolstoy is really saying that a given quality of human life is also the quality of art, that the "text" of human existence is the same thing as the text of a work of art, and that is indeed simply a natural function of living. We should also take note that the elements in the boys' stories Tolstoy could most sensitively respond to are also characteristic of his own writing. Whatever Fed'ka's talents may have been, both, the evocative usage of detail and the vast simplicity of an utterance full of unstated complexities are found over and over again in all Tolstoy's prose. For an example, we might look at Book Seven, Chapter Ten, of *War and Peace*. Sonya is dressed as a mummer at Christmas time in the costume of a Circassian, with black charcoal mustache and eyebrows that are "extraordinarily becoming" to her. During the enchanting, magical sleigh ride to the house of Pelageya Melyukova, a neighbor, young Nikolay Rostov is sitting next to Sonya:

> Nicholas glanced round at Sonya, and bent down to see her face closer. Quite a new, sweet face with black eyebrows and mustache peeped up at him from her sable furs — so close and yet so distant — in the moonlight. "That used to be Sonya," thought he, and looked at her closer and smiled. "What is it, Nicholas?"
>
> "Nothing," said he and turned again to the horses.[22]

Nikolay's smile, fleeting and unexplained, is a typical Tolstoyan detail. Nikolay is basically still a boy who nevertheless is also a hussar; he had seen battle, riding together with his immediate superior and best friend, Denisov, a reckless fellow with an enormous black mustache and the ferociously cheerful soul of a Circassian brigand. The pretty little kitten, Sonya, is funny now, looking at Nikolay like a warm and distant echo of Denisov's face. Something blends strangely together: a boy and a man, a man and a woman, a presence and a memory, and finally, friendship and love — two feelings which Nikolay, at his age, had not yet learned to separate very clearly. He has been telling himself that he was in love with Sonya, and everyone else assumed the same, and now, there they were: two young people who grew up under the same roof, who knew and loved each other, and who were somebody else as well, totally unfamiliar to each other — she a Circassian, he an old woman in a hoop skirt, and it was all funny and touching somehow, and all part of the inexplicable magic of that impossible, enchanted moonlit evening. Nikolay smiles at himself, at his friendship with Denisov, at his joy that he is now at home and all is well, and yet, he cannot begin to comprehend, or analyze, let alone explain, his smile which contains it all. Actually, it contains even more — something that is not altogether a matter of happiness. Denisov had been unjustly punished, and Nikolay had failed to help him with his petition to the Tsar, his adored Tsar. He may have forgotten all this at that magic moment, but it was there, somewhere in the shadowy regions of his smile, nevertheless. Further beyond Nikolay's knowledge looms the future fact that they shall never marry, and that Sonya will remain alone, a barren flower. One might say, now the author himself adds a bittersweet touch of irony to Nikolay's unknowing smile. Thus does a single moment's detail contain the inner world of Nikolay and Sonya, and implicitly the world in time in which they live, and beyond — the world of the novel in which they are "verbal constructs," configurations in the total design of the author.

An important difference between what Fed'ka wrote and what Tolstoy did is that Tolstoy's details absorb their meaning from the context of the whole, thus becoming increasingly more significant with our increasing comprehension of that whole, the endlessly complex interrelationships of all its elements. Fed'ka, on the other hand, wrote with the excitement of the moment, and it took Tolstoy himself, as a reader and interpreter, to create the context in which his little detail about the woman's fur coat became complex and meaningful beyond itself.

Writing together with the children at Yasnaya Polyana, Tolstoy may well have became aware of the stylistic principle of minimum realization in intellectual terms and thus could use it as one of the key concepts in his own aesthetics, when he eventually sat down to formulate it explicitly in *What Is Art?* In that essay we find the principle of the essential detail reaffirmed repeatedly as one of the trademarks of true art, as that magic ingredient, the "wee bit" which transforms an inert material into living piece of art. During the intervening period between the essay and the Yasnaya Polyana school, Tolstoy wrote his great novels, employing sophisticated artistic techniques which he thought were much more "literary" in the traditional sense than those he praised in the boys' writing. Therefore it is less surprising that he eventually dismissed most of his own works as base art. In spite of the full blossoming of his genius, the memory of the Yasnaya Polyana experience, of the insight gained there, must have remained inside him, made him feel that his great novels might, after all, be a fraud. The tendency toward self-rejection as an artist is already implicit in some of Tolstoy's reactions to the work of the peasant boys. At one point in the article Tolstoy writes:

> It seemed so strange to me that a peasant boy, with the bare knowledge of reading, should suddenly manifest a conscious artistic power, such as Goethe, in all his immeasurable height of development, had been unable to equal. It seemed so strange and offensive to me that I, the author of *Childhood*, who had certain success and had earned recognition for artistic talent from a cultivated Russian public, — that I, in the matter of art, not only should be unable to teach anything to them, but that I only with difficulty and in a happy moment of excitement should be able to follow and understand them (Wiener, p. 201; *PSS*, *8*, 308).

The question naturally arises, as it did in the 1898 essay as well, namely, why is it that the Tolstoys and Goethes of this world are world-famous immortals, while Fed'ka will never be heard of again, except in the pages of the Yasnaya Polyana journal. Tolstoy's answer is that great reputations are made in the process of alienation from true human values. According to Tolstoy, there is a process of acclimatizing people to the poisonous air of civilization, and it is called education, and in the arts it amounts to the perversion of the innate capacity in each individual to be moved by beauty. In the third report from Yasnaya Polyana Tolstoy cites a number of examples of art ordinarily meaningless to most people; many of these examples appear again in the essay *What Is Art?* The point made is that people can be trained to like such art, but then they must be considered to have become corrupt, rather than educated:

> Ivanov's painting will rouse in the people nothing but admiration for his technical mastery, but will not evoke any poetical, nor religious sensation, while this very poetical sentiment is evoked by a chap-book picture of John of Novgorod and the devil in the pictures. The Venus de Milo will rouse only a legitimate loathing for the nakedness and shamelessness of the woman. Beethoven's quartet of the latest epoch will appear only as a disagreeable sound, interesting perhaps because one plays on a big fiddle and the other on a small fiddle. The best production of our poetry, a lyrical composition by Pushkin, will seem only a collection of words, and its meaning the veriest nonsense. Introduce a child from the people into this world; you can do that and are doing that all the time by means of the hierarchy of the educational institutions, academies, and art classes: he will, and will sincerely feel, the beauty of Ivanov's painting, and of the Venus de Milo and of the quartet by Beethoven, and of Pushkin's lyrical poem. But, upon entering into this world, he will no longer be breathing with full lungs, — the fresh air, whenever he has to go into it, will affect him painfully and inimically (Wiener, p. 343, *PSS 8*, 113).

Beethoven's late music, his *Kreutzer Sonata*, became much more and much worse than mere disagreeable noise in Tolstoy's late short story of that name, for it led to jealousy and murder. There the basic metaphor of corruption is also a kind of intoxication, a poisoning of the soul, very reminiscent of the poisonous air in the Yasnaya Polyana article. Precisely this notion of corruption is held by Tolstoy as a counterbalancing argument against those who think of education in the arts as an arduous, demanding and ennobling process. *In What Is Art?* Tolstoy categorically denied that any training should be necessary in order to enable a person to enjoy true art, because such art is by definition accessible to all.

In the Yasnaya Polyana essay the same point is made:
> I convinced myself that a lyrical poem, for example, "I remember the charming moment," the musical productions, such as Beethoven's last symphony, were not as unconditionally and universally fine as the song of "Steward Van'ka", and the tune of "Down the Mother Volga"; that Pushkin and Beethoven please us, not because there is any absolute beauty in them, but because we are as much spoilt as Pushkin and Beethoven were, because Pushkin and Beethoven alike flatter our freaky irritability and our weakness. How common it is to hear the trite paradox that for the comprehension of what is beautiful there is needed a special preparation! Who said that? How has that been proved? It is only an excuse, a way out from a hopeless situation, into which we have been brought by the falseness of the direction, by our art's belonging exclusively to one class (Wiener, p. 345; *PSS 8*, 114).

These passages could easily have been written for the essay *What Is Art?*, for instance for chapter XII, where both Pushkin and Beethoven are cited again as examples of bad art that became famous through the corrupting labors of literary critics and schools of art. Tolstoy, so to speak "learned nothing" in the intervening years, during which he wrote his masterpieces, valued by these same literary critics on a par with Pushkin and Goethe. Not to see that great art, such as his own, must be measured in dimensions entirely different from those applicable to a peasant ditty is one of the most puzzling things in Tolstoy's entire system of aesthetics. He himself explained it, both in the essay and in the Yasnaya Polyana notes in terms of a certain "democracy of values":
> I shall be told: "Who said that the knowledge and the arts of our cultivated society are false? How can you conclude from the fact that the masses do not receive them that they are false?" All such questions are solved very simply: Because there are thousands of us and there are millions of them.[23]

Tolstoy's argument rests on an analogy: most people want to live in fresh air, therefore fresh air is best for people, and the physiologists must confirm this from their own evidence; in the same way the art liked by most people is, like fresh air, the best and the most meaningful. This explanation is obviously inadequate as it stands. It is quite easy to imagine, for instance, an isolated and lonely cultivated Roman patrician shuddering with horror at the bloody games in the Coliseum, while thousands of plain people cheer in ecstasy. It does not help to argue against such an example of failed "democracy of values" by saying that the masses were corrupted by patricians in the first place. The dark, atavistic thirst for blood in men's hearts has only too well been attested to over the centuries. Tolstoy's equation simply does not hold. But the point is that real thought is not founded on such naive arithmetic. "Majority" for Tolstoy actually means the true and natural condition of man.

Separation from the family of man in Tolstoy is separation from reality, a loss of true vision, a betrayal of human essence. The great majority of mankind is not "wiser" than the corrupt and powerful few in any sense of an intellectual comparison of values. It is simply closer to the reality, to the natural condition of life. This is why the art which great masses of people can respond to is true art; it is real in the same sense that the work around them and within them is real "Why", asks Tolstoy, "are the beauty of the sun, the beauty of the human face, the beauty of the sounds of a popular song, the beauty of an act of love and self-renunciation accessible to all, and why do they demand no preparation?" (Wiener, pp. 345-6; *PSS 8*, 114). Leaving aside agreement or disagreement with Tolstoy on this matter, but aiming instead to understand what he says, it is important to note how several different categories of phenomena are treated by him equally, as if they all were one and the same. The sun, a human face, a song, an act of moral nature compose a single sequence in this equation. This is how art, too, becomes a natural function of living, fully equivalent to physical enjoyment of the body's functions, or of a landscape, and equivalent in the same way to pleasurable moral experience. Art is not a product of the mind, conceived in detachment from organic being, and imposed upon reality. It is one more way in which a person physically exists. In *What Is Art?* Tolstoy compares the creation and enjoyment of art to the eating of food and to everyday communication by means of speech.

The mark of true art, then, is its "rich simplicity," and the richness of it does not come from an author's knowledge, craftsmanship or sophistication, but from feeling truly and profoundly. The little boy Fed'ka could feel like that, and this has made him the equal of Goethe. It has not, however — and this is crucial to Tolstoy's aesthetics — made him into a professional, a person who makes his living by writing, or who belongs to a distinct class called "writers." Fed'ka is one of millions of ordinary people, and, since these are the ones who have true feelings, art dwells among them and not among professional practitioners. Indeed, the matter of true feeling, the central issue in Tolstoy's definition of art, best sums up the meaning of his pedagogical experiences in Yasnaya Polyana as they relate to his aesthetics. All the significant moments at the school, during which the question of art comes up, are moments when intense emotional experiences are shared by Tolstoy and his pupils. The art of teaching, in Tolstoy's school, came down to the art of learning how to communicate one's feelings — the essence of one's personality. The inner laws of human relationships operate on this level, and, for Tolstoy, the whole notion of progress is meaningful only on these terms — that is, mankind shall progress and develop to the degree that people learn to share with each other their own humanity, instead of building mechanical superstructures of civilization. If art is to be one of these super-structures, then it is indeed a lie, perhaps not even a beautiful one. What Tolstoy may have learned ultimately from his work in pedagogics is that art is not a lie after all. Consciously or not, this may have contributed to his eventual return to literature. The Yasnaya Polyana period started out with a state of mind akin to despair and ended with the discovery that there is a way to think of life as being meaningful. Tolstoy's marriage, which followed shortly after this pedagogical episode, certainly contributed to the resurgence of his creative powers. A long period followed, during which Tolstoy developed his own perfection as an artist, often forgetting the lessons taught him by the children of Yasnaya Polyana. Indeed, as early as 1963, just before setting out to write his *War and Peace*, Tolstoy already felt miles away from the simplicity of the children and from his love for the common people, because he now felt an inner strength in him which needed an altogether different challenge:

> Whether this proves weakness of character, or strength — sometimes I think it proves both — but I must admit now that my views of *the people* and of

society are now quite different from what they were when we saw each other the last time. Nevertheless, I am glad that I went through that school; this last love of mine did a great deal to help determine my personality. I do love the children and pedagogics, but it is difficult for me to understand myself as I was a year ago. The children come to me in the evenings and bring me memories about the teacher there was in me, now no longer to be. Now I am a writer with *all* the strength of my soul, and I write and think like I have never yet thought or written...[24]

It seems quite clear from Tolstoy's letter that, as always, change and continuity were in him intertwined, were in themselves, in their conflict and ebb and flow, a particular continuing state, inwardly very consistent. The thread of continuity in his thought and instincts as an artist goes on unbroken — there are many elements in Tolstoy's major works which clearly echo his insights gained at the earlier periods and which are therefore relevant to the development of his position on aesthetics.

If the Yasnaya Polyana period helped Tolstoy through his crisis by building a bridge from the despairing thought that art is a lie to the insight that it is a natural function of living, then the second great crisis, the moral crucible of the 1880s, brought his the profound understanding of moral responsibility as the basis of true art. We may now turn to this period, from which *What Is Art?* directly grew out in a natural continuum.

CHAPTER THREE

THE CONSCIENCE OF THE ARTIST

Tolstoy's little schoolhouse in Yasnaya Polyana was also the place where he made his first major effort to lay down the foundations for an eventual theory of art, even if he did not at the time explicitly so describe his ideas and his experiments in creative writing with the children. He may not even have been aware that an edifice of aesthetics was beginning to grow in his mind; yet, the process was there, and ultimately it reached its completion in the 1898 essay on art.

The second major process of building Tolstoy's aesthetics continued throughout his creative life as an artist. His novels, short stories and plays are full of direct or indirect references to art, and the experiences of his characters quite often deal with interpersonal communication, the sharing of emotion, sincerity, artificiality and the awareness or ignorance of the moral dimension — all being issues which Tolstoy held close to the realm of aesthetics, so that his fiction itself was in an important way also a theory of art.

The relationship between Tolstoy's theory and practice as an artist is one of the main issues in the present study, but for now we shall sidestep it to discuss the third major turning point in the development of his aesthetics, namely his moral and philosophical crisis at the beginning of the 1880s. The two most powerful documents describing this particular crucible and its consequences are *Confession* (1879-81) and *What Then Must We Do?* (1882).

Confession is the record of Tolstoy's journey to the bottom of despair in search of a way to live which would remain meaningful even in the jaws of death. In the course of this journey, all the social norms and institutions and systems of beliefs founded on the proposition that life as it is lived by most of us has meaning turned out to be ephemeral, groundless and false. It seemed as if life itself had died, leaving a bleak expanse of empty space and time, because, as Ernest J. Simmons put it, there was no answer to the simple question "why?":

> Now he had to know *why* he did anything — why he built up his estate, bettered the lot of his peasants, educated his children, or wrote novels. He found no satisfactory answer. Life came to a standstill; it had become meaningless. There was nothing ahead, he wrote, but suffering and real death — complete annihilation.[1]

Tolstoy struggled upwards from this condition through two fundamental levels — the temporal, the lives we all must live, and the eternal, the realm of faith. Gradually, as he developed his confession, he came to the understanding that the cosmic silence of life, of God, did not signify that there was no answer, but rather that he had been asking the wrong question:

> ...my question, simple as it at first appeared, included a demand for an explanation of the finite in terms of the infinite, and vice versa. I asked: "What is the meaning of life beyond time, cause and space?" And I replied to quite another question: "What is the meaning of my life within time, cause and space?" With the result that, after long efforts of thought, the answer I reached was "None."[2]

The illuminating resolution was that instead of trying to extract from infinity a promise of meaning for one's brief visit among the living, one should conceive of personal existence itself as a significant relationship between the finite and the infinite, a relationship of faith understood not as some particular religion, but as a constant process of listening in one's own small heart for the great voice of God.

Within these terms, *Confession* resembles a traveler's diary describing the various deserts of the mind and the heart which Tolstoy had traversed up to that time in his search of this illumination, of that epiphany where the finite and the infinite would meet. Of special interest here are those of Tolstoy's ideas and experiences which have a bearing on the issue of art.

On the temporal plane, the ongoing process of living, the progression leading to despair touches all the basic landmarks we recognize from Tolstoy's aesthetics as well as from his fiction as the images of evil and decay depicting what faithless humanity considers to be civilization. As Tolstoy describes in *What Is Art?* how the history of our civilization degenerated from trivial indulgences in the comforts of evil to the moral catastrophe of our time as if it were the progress of a disease, we may immediately recall *Confession*, where his own moral disintegration to the point of despair is depicted in similar terms:

> ...then occurred what happens to everyone sickening with a mortal internal disease. At first trivial signs of indisposition appear to which the sick man pays no attention; then these signs reappear more and more often and merge into one uninterrupted period of suffering. The suffering increases and, before the sick man can look around, what he took for a mere indisposition has already become more important to him than anything else in the world — it is death (*Confession*, Maude, 16; *PSS*, 23, 11).

We can see an echo of this in Tolstoy's fiction, when the illness and death of Ivan Ilyich envelops him in precisely the same gradual manner until, railing against God for His cruelty and for His nonexistence, he is confronted no longer with the thought but with the palpable reality of death that simply stands there, in the room, and does not answer any questions. In *Anna Karenina*, the description of Levin's strange despair at the end of the novel, although functioning as a fully integrated structural element in the text, is exactly the same as Tolstoy's autobiographical, factual reminiscence of his own similar condition.[3] The same emotion, the same existential perception of one's own self in relation to the world, and therefore the same inner crisis, was already there, deep in Tolstoy's mind all the time, surfacing on different occasions as either artistic or expository word.

The very absurdity of imagining that an artist, by virtue of being one, is automatically endowed with some superior knowledge and authority, exposed with eloquent anger in *What Is Art?*, is also revealed in the *Confession* as a stage in Tolstoy's own personal experience:

> Our vocation is to teach mankind, and lest the simple question should suggest itself: What do I know, and what can I teach? it was explained in this theory that this need not be known, and that the artist and poet teach unconsciously. I was considered an admirable artist and poet, and therefore it was very

natural for me to adopt this theory. I, artist and poet, wrote and taught without myself knowing what. For this I was paid money; I had excellent food, lodging, women, and society; and I had fame, which showed that what I taught was very good (*Confession*, p. 9).

This is an exact description of the innumerable false artists, writers, musicians, dancers — all parasites upon society whom Tolstoy denounces in his essay with the same heavy-handed irony. We also meet them in the pages of *Anna Karenina* and see them gyrating stupidly, half naked, on the opera stage in *War and Peace*; the essay on art begins with a rehearsal of just such an opera.

The conventional practice of a religion, as Tolstoy saw it in his *Confession*, had nothing to do with what really mattered in relation to either life or God. People went to church without really asking themselves what they believe and were content not to see that the irrelevance of professed faith to living God made their actions pointless and grotesque. They merely clung to the outward forms and habits of religion in order to sustain their social status or to maintain themselves in their positions of power. In the essay on art, this describes exactly the relationship between religion and the coming of the Renaissance. The faith which is described in *Confession* as the answer to Tolstoy's agonized doubts, as the one factor capable of relating meaningfully the finite with the infinite, was the faith of the simple people, the working masses, for whom the existence of God was not an issue to be resolved but simply a way of life which by its own processes of daily work, tilling the land together with others, in the common struggle with nature, fully answers the question of its meaning. In *What Is Art?*, such a faith is like the soil from which religious consciousness arises and grows to become an attribute of the highest forms of true art. This faith overcomes both the despair of existential solitude and the solitude of intellectual despair. Instead of cosmic aloneness, what Tolstoy arrived at in his confession and elaborated into a theory of aesthetics was a sense of cosmic wholeness, of belonging together, resulting from the expansion of a personal identity to encompass the whole world — a blending of the self with the sea of life. This, in *War and Peace*, is Pierre Bezukhov's highest insight into the meaning of his existence.

The essay *What Then Must We Do?*, written in 1882, also contains elements of personal confession. In it Tolstoy explains how he tried and failed to help Moscow's poor by appealing to the philanthropic sentiments of the rich. He soon realized it was a naive mistake to think that the wealthy merchants and aristocrats would be moved by the plight of the hungry poor in their filthy apartments and flophouses. They only agreed to pretend they were helping because they were embarrassed by having to humor the famous man Tolstoy who undertook to plead such a useless cause. Tolstoy saw how they were "ashamed to look in the eyes of a good and decent man who is saying foolish things."[4] Then it turned out that these heartless people were in their own way right. Alms did not help the poor because they could work no permanent change in their condition. Some, the lower class people, often peasants who came to the city seeking work, needed no artificial assistance, because their work sustained them, and they lived humbly but decently, with a sense of pride and goodwill for all. Others, often landowners and aristocrats who fell upon hard times, did not want to work but only somehow to regain their former status of the idle rich living from the labor of others. The money Tolstoy gave them helped for a while, but then they sank again into their stupor of false hopes for the future. Indeed, Tolstoy understood that even if they did again become rich, and even if they still had money, they could never be happy: "their misfortune cannot be helped by outside means, they cannot be happy in any condition if their view of life will remain the same (*ibid.*, p. 207)," that is, if they will always think that they were special, higher people who deserved to work less and use others' labor more.

And so, visiting the poor and watching them, drunken men and women, prostitutes and brigands wallowing in filth together, Tolstoy began to feel that his efforts at charity made him:
> like a doctor who came to the sick man with his medicines, opened up his wound, poked inside it and had to admit to himself that he did all that for nothing, that his medicines are no good (*ibid.*, p. 220).

Even worse, Tolstoy's finely-tuned conscience, always alert for opportunities of self-accusation, revealed that even his own efforts to help the poor may in the end be motivated by the desire to maintain his privileged status in life:
> ...not only the success of this undertaking, but even just the activity itself gave me the possibility of continuing to live the same way I always have. If I were

to fail, however, then I would be faced with the necessity to renounce my present way of life and seek another. And unconsciously, I was afraid of this (*ibid.*, p. 195).

Eventually Tolstoy did confront the necessity to reconsider all his premises about life, and it led him to a new, personal vision of society as a vicious system of slavery and exploitation which yet bears the name of "civilization." Civilization is based on money; as a means of exchange, money could be functional and harmless enough, but the fact is that it serves as a means of achieving power over others, of making others work for you. Civilization is based on distribution of labor. Some serve society's material needs, others attend to matters of the spirit. The problem is that the ruling, educated classes have failed to keep up their end of the bargain:

> We prepared, as a repayment to the people for feeding us, something that is only suitable, as it seems to us, for science and for art but is unsuitable, totally incomprehensible and repulsive, like Limburger cheese, to the very people whose labor we devour under the excuse that we are providing them with spiritual nourishment (*ibid.*, p. 351).

The significance of this argument for *What Is Art?* is that it provides a broad conceptual base for the specific rejection of accumulated intellectual and artistic tradition as a determinant of values in art. In the light of Tolstoy's ideas, such a tradition is worthless because it is the end product of our civilization, itself a malignant outgrowth of the system of exploitation, the perverted principle of division of labor.[5] What we have in the arts is a sort of self-enclosed artistic "industry" which has nothing to do with the true, simple needs of the people:

> We have elevated enormous numbers of people to the status of great writers, we have analyzed these writers down to their fingernails, we have written mountains of criticism, and criticism of criticism, and criticism of criticism of criticism; we have built up picture galleries and studied various schools in the arts to the finest detail; our symphonies and operas have become such that it is hard even for ourselves to listen to them. But what did we add to the people's *Bylinas* [folk epics — R.Š.], legends, tales,

songs, what pictures have we given to the people, what music? In the Nikol'skaya books and pictures are produced for the people; in Tula — accordions, but we have had no part in either the one or the other (*ibid.*, p. 358).

Modern science is equally pernicious, because it is focused upon itself and pursues such aims as studying organic cells, or counting stars, or calculating planetary orbits, instead of reaching out for spiritual truths by which we could learn to live righteously, or else solving practical tasks in order to make the people's labor easier and more productive. Both science and the arts have become hermetic, exclusive enterprises totally unable to provide spiritual nourishment to the working masses in return for their daily bread. Just as he did later in the essay on art, Tolstoy here emphasizes the tremendous costs of these exclusive, useless arts and sciences which must be borne by the the people whom they do not serve. In contrast to all this, says Tolstoy:

True science and true art can be recognized by two sure signs. The first is internal — that the servant of science and the arts will fulfill his calling not to his own advantage, but with self-abnegation, and the second is an outward sign — that his works will be understandable to all those whose well-being he has in mind (*ibid.*, p. 374).

In *What Is Art?* this external criterion of accessibility is at the core of the definition of art as the transmission of and infection with feeling and it constitutes a large part of Tolstoy's entire argument. The point about self-abnegation is elaborated further in *What Is Art?* and becomes a denial of professionalism in the arts. At the conclusion of this essay, speaking of the art of the future, Tolstoy says:

The artist of the future will live the common life of man, earning his subsistence by some kind of labor. The fruits of the highest spiritual strength that passes through him he will try to share with the greatest possible number of people, for in such transmission to others of the feelings that have arisen in him he will find his happiness and reward. The artist of the future will be unable to understand how an artist, whose chief delight is in the wide diffusion of his works could give them only in exchange for a certain payment (Maude, 271; *PSS*, *30*, 182).

In both treatises, the amateur status of the artist (in the original sense, as lover of the arts) is in principle a consequence of refusal to live by the labor of others. Thus Tolstoy's economic argument about the division of labor becomes a moral plea in the tradition of self sacrifice and joy of sharing in love that has long existed in Christianity and in other religions. In such a theory of aesthetics we have, in effect, an example of what Tolstoy means by a "science," a study of the question of how is one to live. In this sense, his own efforts to avoid living by the toil of others, the insistence on making his own boots, working in the fields, sewing his famous Tolstoyan shirts, and so on, really amount to an extension to real life of the theoretical principles of aesthetics and of science.

In both essays, the transferral of artistic activity to the amateur sphere reduces the arts to a marginal popular activity. In *What Then Must We Do?* we read:

> Tell the painter that he should work without a studio, without live models and should make five-kopeck drawings instead,[6] and he will say that this means the renunciation of art as he understands it. Tell the musician to play the accordion and to teach peasant women how to sing songs; tell the poet, the writer, to forget about his poems and novels and to compose little songs or tales that are understood by illiterate people — they will say that you have lost your mind (p. 362).

In *What Is Art?*, the language is almost identical:

> The artist of the future will understand that to compose a fairytale, a touching little song, a lullaby, an entertaining riddle, an amusing jest, or to draw a sketch which will delight dozens of generations or millions of children and adults, is incomparably more important and more fruitful than to compose a novel or a symphony, or paint a picture, which will divert some members of the wealthy classes for a short time and then for ever be forgotten. The region of this art of the simple feelings accessible to all is enormous and it is as yet almost untouched (Maude, 273; *PSS*, *30*, 183-4).

Here we reach an issue which was implicit, but not so stated, in Tolstoy's basic understanding of art, namely, what does "simplicity" mean? Critics have asked about the nature of the "feeling" that is transmitted in art, whether it is just an ordinary feeling, or an aesthetic feeling of some sort, or again a feeling that resembles thought, or something like a combined thought and feeling. The other question, however, is what it really means to say that the commonly accessible feelings are "simple." Must it be that complex and profound feelings, such as may be generated by the contemplation of the entire edifice of human civilization, say, in relation to both human nature and the nature of God are not the kind to be accessible to the masses, and thus true art cannot deal with them? If so, then "religious consciousness," supposedly the highest goal of art, is actually outside of its sphere. On the other hand, we may be talking about a special kind of simplicity which, however easily accessible to the ordinary mind, is in reality extraordinarily complex. Tolstoy once said that everything truly great is simple, like, for instance "Lord have mercy." The mercy of the Lord, however, is not a simple matter at all, and in the manner in which an artist would need to describe it would require a system of devices, of signs, sufficiently complex to be commensurate with all the innumerable dimensions of that issue. The feelings that such a system may evoke, or transmit, however "simple" and accessible they might appear on the surface, would be equally complex, and such would also be the measure of an ordinary soul. It seems evident that Tolstoy did understand "simplicity" in this complex way, for only then could he claim that "the region of this art of the simple feelings accessible to all is enormous." Certainly, Tolstoy's own art is at its greatest when an infinite variety of feelings and ideas becomes focused together in a single glance or in a seemingly inconsequential movement, or gesture, or a fleeting moment of special awareness. These passages remind one of that single and infinitely small point now postulated by the astronomers which, they say, exploded in a "big bang" to become our universe.

In view of this, it is interesting to remember that Tolstoy denounced his own works in *What Is Art?*, speaking in the context of what he called bad art and counterfeits of art, and therefore in effect accusing himself and his works of having merely an artificial, surface complexity, based on a writer's tricks and not upon any moral purpose.[7] This may very well point to some very deep roots of self-hatred in this man of genius, against his genius, from which all his moral and aesthetic teaching may have grown. Indeed, both, *Confession* and the essay *What Then Must We Do?* seem to be built upon this context of self-condemnation. While the reasons for this would surely be accessible to a psychological analysis, for the moment it may suffice to think that there is something in his and all our natures that requires a counterforce to our will to be. The almost infinitely powerful act of self-assertion which is Tolstoy in his art may bring about, somehow, a similar effort of self-destruction.

An observation on Tolstoy's conception of the relationship between art and science may also be in order. In *What Then Must We Do?* and later in his essay on art he emphasizes that true science must not be concerned with matters of idle curiosity (like, for instance, the measurement of light waves from the Milky Way) or with systems of thought that justify the present unjust social order (developed by perverse professors of "theology, jurisprudence, political economy, financial science, etc.")[8] but with things of practical necessity for the working people — how to make a better saw or an axe — and with issues that touch upon the meaning of life, that is, knowledge of the difference between good and evil. This is how Tolstoy states his position in *What Is Art?*:

> We need only look around us to perceive that the activity proper to real science is not the study of whatever happens to interest us, but the study of those questions of religion, morality, and social life, without the solution of which all our knowledge of nature will be harmful or insignificant (Maude, 281; *PSS, 30*, 189).

And on the relationship between science and art:

> Art is not a pleasure, a solace, or an amusement; art is a great matter. Art is an organ of human life transmitting man's reasonable perception into feeling. In our age the common religious perception of men is the consciousness of the brotherhood of man — we know that the well-being of man lies in union with his fellow-men. True science should indicate the various methods of applying this consciousness to life. Art should transform this perception into feeling (Maude, 286; *PSS, 30*, 189).

In *What Then Must We Do?* Tolstoy maintains almost exactly the same position and also provides us with examples of what he understands to be science and art:

> Whatever people were to consider their purpose and their well-being, science will be the teaching about this purpose, and art — the expression of this teaching. The laws of Confucius are science; the teaching of Moses and of Christ — science; the buildings in Athens are art, the Psalms of David also art; the Vespers service is art; but the study of bodies in four dimensions and the tables of chemical compounds, and then all our poems and symphonies and pictures have never been and will never be either science or art (p. 374).

All these unorthodox, apparently confused, explanations really convey a sense of unity, as art and religion would, rather than a sense of distinction, as befits a scientific discipline. What is "science," as Tolstoy understands it, in the teachings of Confucius, Moses, and Christ is their affective aspect: we learn to be better people not in consequence of reasoned arguments supported by repeatable experiments but because we are awe-struck by God's Law from the top of the mountain, delighted by the practical wit and style of Confucius' maxims and touched by the great love pouring into our hearts from the parables of Christ. In this sense, the Psalms of David and the Vespers can also be as much science as they are art, for they, too, teach us how to be better by the means of infecting us with emotion. The works of Sakya Muni (Buddha) are referred to in *What Is Art?* as among the highest, most immortal kinds of art, and Buddha was a teacher no different from those Tolstoy implicitly designates as "scientists" by his definition. It would seem fairly evident that Tolstoy is not really talking about science and art as the rest of us know them, even if he does use these terms, but rather that his concern is a kind of sacred thrust upwards by the entire moral and emotional force of a human being — something like a prayer, a confession and a rebellion all at once. It is here, in this wondrous, heady turbulence of the mind and the soul, that Tolstoy most closely approaches the same sort of emotional drive we find in Dostoevsky. Any comparison in depth between these two writers should probably begin from this point.

The Conscience of the Artist 79

The primary purpose of *Confession* and *What Then Must We Do?* was to present the readers with the troubled and urgent concerns, first of all, of an individual who felt that he had misplaced his values in life and, secondly, of society which had structured itself in a manner demeaning to human dignity, happiness and truth. Because Tolstoy was and remained even in this trying period above all an artist, the question of art itself had to be a significant aspect of both issues. In that sense, it is true indeed that his specific and intense inquiry into the nature and function of art began at this time, as Tolstoy said, fifteen years before the publication of his essay. From then on, things began to appear in print which reflected various stages in Tolstoy's search for a definition and description of art, leading to the final formulations in the essay itself. Tolstoy's first attempt to work out a theory of art based on moral values is contained in his open letter, dated 1882, to N.A. Aleksandrov, editor of the *Fine Arts Journal*. It immediately sets out thematic markers which also exist at the beginning of *What Is Art?* As art is generally understood, says Tolstoy, it includes the concepts of truth, goodness and beauty, it is supposedly the expression of the finite in the infinite, an so on. All this is very beautiful and exalted "but very misty and diffuse, so that in the end it comes out that art is whatever pleases people."[9] Consequently:

> Girls with naked legs are dancing about — a useless thing, but there are those who like to look at them, and so — art.[10] To collect many sounds and titillate the ear with them — art. To depict naked women, or a forest — is art. To gather up some rhymes and to describe how gentlemen debauch themselves — is also art (to Aleksandrov, p. 211).

Tolstoy comes to the point here much quicker and more ruthlessly than he did in his essay, but the point itself is the same: without a proper definition of art, our very sins and stupidities will acquire the patina of aesthetics.[11] As for the process of arriving at a proper definition, one of the drafts of the letter calls for the sort of simple and radical approach that typifies Tolstoy's thinking on such matters:

> The whole thing became all mixed-up a long time ago; for a long time now aesthetics has been grinding grains of rye and ergot together into one poisonous flour, and in order to understand this matter proper-

> ly it is necessary either to forget or at least put aside for a time all the methodology and devices of aesthetics and start thinking anew from the beginning. We should forget and set aside words like "the infinite in the finite," "the embodiment of ideals," "fine arts," and so on, and begin to consider straightforwardly that which is there, checking what there is against what there was (*PSS, 30*, 429).

We can see now that the long survey of various authorities on aesthetics given in *What Is Art?* was probably deliberately intended to lead us nowhere, to serve as an example of the poisonous mixture of grain and ergot served up by traditional philosophical and theoretical thought on art. The root of the problem is crisply stated in the letter to Aleksandrov as follows:

> And not one wiseacre German aesthetician can show me the dividing line between Raphael and a naked woman by Titian, and between Titian's naked woman and a pornographic stereoscope (to Aleksandrov, p. 210).

Since the letter was written in 1882, at the very time when Tolstoy experienced and described his great moral shock upon contact with the thousands of hopeless poor in Moscow, it may be easier to understand its tone of great disgust with the pleasures of the rich, particularly their lust, with their idle pretense at having some sort of high conception of life, of art, and most particularly, Tolstoy's disgust with himself, even more intense than in *Confession*. Here, in the letter, Tolstoy accuses himself directly:

> I did what all other so-called artists were doing: I learned a useless skill, but such a skill that I could titillate people's lust with it, and I wrote books [Tolstoy, the author of *War and Peace*, says: "booklets" — "knizhki" — R.Š] about whatever wandered into my head, but only I shaped these books in such a manner that they would titillate people's lust and that I would receive money for this (to Aleksandrov, p. 211).

Tolstoy's rage against "lust" continues years later in the essay, but the topic of the worthlessness of his own art is relegated to a passing footnote. Another idea that faded, possibly because it did not work very well as a definition of art, was the notion of "uselessness." It came from German idealism, where it designated disinterestedness as a criterion of art, and Tolstoy, in the letter, seemed trying to treat it in terms of two contrasting aspects. One represented the useless and repulsive enterprise some called "art," and the other — a "uselessness" in the sense that no material gain was sought by an artist, whose work, however, was therefore very useful in that it "tried to make people better," as he put it in one of the drafts for the letter:

> And in all this enormous quantity of items from history, philosophy, religion we shall also find a proverb, a story, a *bylina*, and a picture which has the purpose of making people better. And it is this part, i.e. the stories, pictures, music, if there is any such, which has the purpose of making people better — this is what I do call art (*PSS, 25,* 428).

The topic of popular stories comes up again in Tolstoy's preface to a collection of fairy tales and fantasies called *The Flower Garden* (1886). There Tolstoy makes a very important observation pertaining to truth and fancy in art. "Truth," says Tolstoy:

> is a path. Christ said "I am the path, truth and life." And for this reason it is not those that know the truth who look down at what's at their feet, but those who can tell by the sun where they are to go.[12]

Somewhere in this poetic statement there must be a thought, unspoken but present also in the essay on art, that nothing which is true in life is an entity, but it is rather a movement, a transition, a relationship (as indeed modern semiotics also seems to have understood). Christ is how we walk to our salvation. As soon as He ceases to be a path and becomes a "thing" — a statue, crucifix, or an institution, there is no more truth, nor faith, in that. In a similar sense, when Tolstoy arrived at his definition of art, it turned out to be not an institutional concept, but a process, an act of communication, something that is happening and not something that is. From this, Tolstoy also derived an attitude to what may be called "realism" in art, regarding it from the perspective of fancy:

> Whatever miracles were to be described, whatever beasts were to talk human language, whatever flying carpets were to carry people here and there — the legends, and the parables, and the fairy tales shall be truth, if they shall contain the truth of the Kingdom

of God (*ibid.*, 190).

This seems like a brief, elegant and truly poetic statement that was later elaborated upon in the essay in terms of religious consciousness as the highest aim of art. From this perspective, what was conventionally understood as "realism" became in the essay just one of the methods of implanting a semblance of art, which Tolstoy called "imitation":

> The essence of this method consists in supplying details accompanying the thing described or depicted. In literary art this method consists in describing in minutest detail the external appearance, the faces, the clothes, the gestures, tones, and the habitations, of the characters represented, with all the occurrences met with in life (Maude, 183; *PSS, 30*, 114).

If this is so, then, from Tolstoy's perspective, realism is not a necessary mode for the communication of feeling, and in fact only hinders feeling because it clutters up the heart with dead things. There is more poetry and truth in sitting on a flying carpet, looking at the sun.

The "Preface to Amiel's Diary,"[13] 1890, makes the point that whatever the text produced, artistic or not, the inner striving of the soul that is new, original, and not one already accomplished before by someone else, is the only important thing in art:

> For a writer is dear and necessary to us only to the extent that he reveals to us the inner striving of his soul, of course, if that labor is new, and not already done before. ... Only this inner striving of the soul is dear to us in the work written by an author, and not that architectural structure of the text within which he confines his thoughts and feelings, for the most part, indeed, I think, always distorting them in the process ("Predislovie k dnevniku Amielja," *Polnoe sobranie...*, p. 209).

Looking backwards, the expression "inner striving of the soul" takes us again to the Yasnaya Polyana diaries, where the literary efforts of the peasant boy Fed'ka were described in the same way. Looking forward, we can see here one of the earlier articulations of the criterion of originality applied to the definition of art. In this way, much of Tolstoy's preliminary work toward *What Is Art?* is focused upon the elaboration of some basic criteria for the definition of art. Tolstoy's problem in all this was that the strong feeling, the emotional thrust of art, does not yield very easily to the metalanguage of explication, definition and analysis. Consequently, it was a painful struggle for him to move from one draft statement to another toward a logical articulation of this feeling so that it could become a valid definition of art. At one turn of the road, he developed a version of the three basic criteria by which we are to recognize art:

> Only that will be a perfect work of art in which the content is significant and new, its expression perfectly beautiful and the artist's attitude toward his work completely truly felt and therefore completely truthful ("Ob iskusstve," *PSS, 30*, 214).

The requirement for significant content was later replaced by the notion of originality, meaning, of course, that the two were related in Tolstoy's mind. Tolstoy was not speaking of a content that was already claimed or acknowledged to be significant, but rather of the moment when an artist realizes the importance of his unique vision. Beauty became clarity, and we can see how this leads to Tolstoy's idea of instant and universal accessibility (i.e., clarity) as the criterion of art — the lucid and the beautiful, at least at this stage seemed to be one and the same thing. Truthfulness became sincerity, leading to the notion that sincerity gives an artist the power to know what is true.

The fragment "On Art" (1889) also contains the notion of sincerity perceived as a particular relationship between feeling and form, namely, the relationship of spontaneity. Having said that in order for a work of art to be perfect, the artist must say something "altogether new and important" for humanity, Tolstoy then continues:

> In order that what the artist has to say be expressed well, it is necessary that he should master his skill to the degree that, in working, he would think as little about the rules of this skill as a pedestrian thinks about the rules of mechanics when he is walking.
>
> And in order to achieve that, an artist must never look back upon his work, savor it, make his skill his purpose, just as a pedestrian should not think about his gait and savor it (*PSS, 30*, 213).

Here it seems like Tolstoy is talking across the years to the Formalist Viktor Shklovsky who defined art as a "walk, constructed to be felt" and saw Tolstoy's achievement precisely in deautomatization, in making conscious and strange that which is no longer perceptible because of familiarity. The point is not here, however. Instead of Shklovsky, we might remember Konstantin Levin mowing his meadow together with the peasants and doing it better and better to the degree that he managed to forget himself and not think about how he is, or should be, accomplishing the job. For that matter, we could also think of Vronsky who went into the horse race feeling that somehow something was wrong in his relations with Anna, and made a false move on the horse, and broke its back. Above all, we could think of what Tolstoy said in his introduction to the work of G.M. Bondarev (*Polnoe sobranie sochinenij, 19,* 197) to the effect that whoever believes in the teaching of Christ will know what to do just as a spring welling up from the ground will naturally spread its life-giving waters upon earth, man and beast. At issue here is spontaneity which is the mark of a feeling so intense that the artist simply knows he is right and what he does must be so, just as the peasant boy Fed'ka in Yasnaya Polyana knew it.

Another effort came in 1889 and was called: "On What Is Art and What It Is Not, and on When Is Art an Important Thing, and When It is an Empty Matter." [14] There Tolstoy set himself, first of all, two tasks: a) to distinguish genuine art from its counterfeits and b) within genuine art, to distinguish good from bad and/or insignificant art. This is already the basic scheme in *What Is Art?*. Now, the essence of that genuine art consists in: "truthful, concrete depiction of reality; in order that art should be true, it must depict real life as it is." This sounds like a programmatic statement of realism in art.[15] In "On Art," however, Tolstoy called "realistic" that school of criticism which demanded sincerity in art. It seems, then, that the notion of what is even objectively, not just personally, true and the notion of what is sincere were coalescing in Tolstoy's mind. Actually, the key statement was made much earlier, in 1862, still during the Yasnaya Polyana period, in the article called "Progress and the Definition of Education," where Tolstoy said that the important thing is not to write history, but to "speak the word on which reality could be built."[16] If so, then reality itself must already be immanent in such a word, and perhaps vice versa as well as, for instance, Mandel'shtam believed that poetry is immanent in stone. Such a relationship between word and thing is indeed the essence of art, certainly as Tolstoy practiced it, saying the words on which entire universes were built. It is also essential to his eventual definition of art, if we accept it that intense feeling shared together produces a a primary reality, life itself, and not just secondary, a world of verbal semblances. Thus ultimately in the essay itself, the three criteria became defined as factors determining the intensity of infection with feeling:

> And the degree of the infectiousness of art depends on three conditions: (1) On the greater or lesser individuality of the feeling transmitted; (2) on the greater or lesser clearness with which the feeling is transmitted; (3) on the sincerity of the artist, that is, on the greater or lesser force with which the artist himself feels the emotion he transmits (Maude, 228; *PSS, 30,* 149).

The "inner striving of the soul" mentioned in the Amiel preface might then be a progress from "individuality" to sincerity, because the product of the soul's labor is like a mirror of the artist's personality as well as of the intensity of his experience. Later in the essay, Tolstoy came to perceive both things as one and admitted that all his criteria can actually be reduced to just one — that of sincerity.

Beyond the issue of art criteria as such, Tolstoy also laid out a preliminary approach toward the discussion of various "false" directions in the theory of aesthetics. The three aspects of art, as defined by the appropriate criteria, must all be present in equal degree in a perfect work of art. Yet, if we regard any one of them in isolation from others, we produce wrong theories:

> The three main false theories of art are divided along the lines of these three aspects of art.... One such theory holds that the worth of a work of art depends most of all upon the content, even if the work were not to possess either beauty or sincerity. This is the so- called tendentious theory. The other holds that the worth of a work of art depends on the beauty of form, even if the content were unworthy and the artist's attitude without sincerity; this is the theory of art for art. The third holds that everything is in

> the sincerity and truthfulness; however poor the content and imperfect the form, if the artist only loves what he is expressing, the work will have artistic quality. This theory is called the theory of realism (*ibid.*, "Ob iskusstve," *PSS*, *30*, 214).

Having described his three wrong theories, Tolstoy then developed a link between them and what he called "counterfeit art":

> The most important thing is that according to all three of these theories anyone who desires to be an artist could produce pieces of so-called art continuously, just like any handicraft. This is how it's actually done ("O tom, chto est' i chto ne est' iskusstvo..., *PSS*, *30*, 218).

This, of course, opens the entire repulsive panorama of fake, harmful art we see in the essay: opera rehearsals, deformed dancers, Beethoven, Wagner and so on.

In the essay itself, these wrong theories were no longer discussed, false directions in art were reclassified according to different criteria — borrowing, imitation, being striking and interesting — and literary theory or criticism were dismissed altogether.

Stubbornly sustaining his focus on the main question: what is, after all, art? Tolstoy reached the stage where the nature of art could not be explained without also considering the nature of science. At this point, his three criteria again appear to blend together into a single notion, but, with science present, the clarity of a work becomes the main element:

> What is scientific and artistic work? Scientific and artistic work is a spiritual activity which takes a dimly seen thought or feeling and brings it to such clarity that the thought is assimilated by other people, and the feeling is also communicated to others (*ibid.*, p. 218).

This is basically the same definition as Tolstoy gives in the essay to art alone. At this stage, however, Tolstoy was still troubled with it, because, unless we expand the notions of art and science to include all modes of effective clarification and communication, this definition does not have the required discrete precision, and if we do exclude those other modes, the definition becomes moot, because whatever it says, there still is clarification and communication going on outside of it. Rhetoric, for instance, may not be strictly speaking either art or science, but it may well clarify and communicate. As far as science was concerned, Tolstoy tried to firm up his definition by introducing the main commonly accepted element of scientific validity: predictability. Science then turned out to have its own three criteria of definition, both resembling and not resembling those of art:

> A work of science is all new knowledge, brought to such clarity of proof that the consequences of applying this knowledge could be unfailingly foretold. And therefore, the qualities of a scientific work are: 1) newness of thought, 2) clarity of its presentation and 3) its indubitability, confirmed by tested prediction (*ibid.*, p. 221).

What, then, of cell structures and wavelengths from the Milky Way? The above criteria certainly are applicable to the work of a biologist or an astronomer, and yet, Tolstoy rejected that as pseudo-science. Now, if both the "true" and the "false" science meet the same criteria, how shall we distinguish between them? Inevitably, Tolstoy could only do it by using a criterion which by its nature stood outside the realm of science or art, namely, the moral criterion. If a science meets his definitions but contributes nothing to the question how is one to live, then it is not science, but a mere counterfeit, like there also exists counterfeit art. The validity of such a distinction, unfortunately, is not supported by any objective logic. What we have, therefore, is not an objective statement of fact but the encoding of an attitude, an assertion of self.

The impression of a painfully heaving and laboring enormous mind that one gets from reading these pages is perhaps most of all due to the fact that Tolstoy could not let anything drop, any part of his burden, for the burden itself would then become something else and something of no account — it would no longer be a totality of universal insight. As long as the *answer* itself could be postponed, or allowed to become an irrelevance, one could divide and classify, and define with a precision suitable for some partial purpose. This is how some of us keep our sanity. But what, then, *is* art? What *is* science? One of the most touching, helpless, and probably for that reason effective, answers Tolstoy could give in this particular essay again came down to what he had always known, to the word upon which reality could be built:

> The process of creation, accessible to each person and for this reason known to everyone from inner experience takes place as follows: a person supposes, or feels dimly something entirely new for himself, something he had never heard of from anyone. ... That which he has clearly [dimly? — R.Š] understood remains incomprehensible for others. And the question arises whether he supposes and feels something that does not exist, or is it that others do not see or feel that which really does exist? And, in order to resolve this doubt, the person applies all his strength in order to clarify for himself this something in such a way that there could no longer be even the slightest doubt about the reality of existence of that which he sees. And as soon as this clarification is brought to completion, and the person himself no longer doubts the existence of what he sees, then also the others immediately see, understand and feel the same as he does. And this desire to make for oneself doubtless and clear that which appears to oneself and to others dim and unclear, — that is the wellspring from which arises the activity of science and of art (*ibid.*, p. 220).

In Tolstoy's works, we can observe how the process described here actually takes place, and as we come to understand it, we also gain an insight into his art. As a definition, however, it is troubled, convoluted and reveals most of all Tolstoy's uncertainty and anxiety in trying to formulate as aesthetics what has really been his quintessential personal and moral position and experience throughout his life. Yet, this experience, however touchingly described, does not really define either art or science, because it does not permit any meaningful analysis of itself. Any attempts at a definition of art that are not subject to formal categories and logical distinctions can only speak of it as a single, indivisible entity. Tolstoy himself understood this in one of the variants to his essay when he said that the divisions of human spiritual activity into philosophy, religion or science, or art, do not in fact exist and are made only for convenience of observation.

Being himself, however, Tolstoy could not help analyzing literary phenomena, could not, in fact, stop being the critic, even if criticism was supposed to make no sense. One of his best pieces of literary criticism is the "Introduction to the Works of Guy de Maupassant" (1893-4). This is a complex and interesting, persuasively written essay that has great bearing on his views on art, soon to be formulated in their final shape. The editors of the Jubilee (*PSS*) edition of Tolstoy's works note that the Maupassant article amounts mainly to a supplement to the treatise because it contains:

> ...ideas and statements not found in the treatise on art, for instance, the remarks about views on art held by the Egyptians and Hebrews and also the Indians "who do not even understand what beauty means in our sense," as well as considerations on the relativity of the concept of beauty...[17]

On the other hand, E. Nuralov in his 1979 study quotes N. Afanasyeva to the effect that the Maupassant piece is much more than mere supplement, that it "it gives immeasurably more valuable and reliable material for the understanding of the aesthetic views of Tolstoy as realist than his famous treatise 'What Is Art?'."[18] Other, scarce, comments on the Maupassant introduction, at least in Soviet scholarship, are on the whole not very illuminating.[19] Be that as it may, we need to look at the piece a little more closely, for it does indeed help elucidate some aspects of Tolstoy's troubled thoughts on art.

The most significant contribution of the Introduction to Maupassant is basically twofold. First of all, it adds the dimension of a developed analysis of particular texts to Tolstoy's general considerations on art. This is different from the few negative remarks made in the essay about the French Decadent poets, or the parodic summary of Wagner's "Nibelungen Ring" in Chapter XIII. Later, in 1903-4, Tolstoy wrote another piece of what may be called textual literary criticism — his famous attack on Shakespeare in "On Shakespeare and on Drama" which stands in a special relationship with the Maupassant article in that Tolstoy's ultimate reproach against both writers is for their lack moral commitment. On the other hand, Maupassant is acknowledged to be a talented writer, while Shakespeare is called at best a mediocre hack.

Secondly, while engaged in practical literary criticism, Tolstoy also continues to think through various approaches toward the definition of art. Here his earlier insight that a sufficiently clear elucidation of a new and personal perception can communicate itself as a new reality is applied to considerations about the nature of talent. The three criteria defining art again change their emphasis and to some extent their components, to the point where one begins to think that this particular line of thought did not lead Tolstoy to any resolution satisfactory to him.

One of the first impressions of Tolstoy as a literary critic is his keen interest, personal frankness and readiness for both enthusiasm and denunciation. Addressing the broad reading public with the disarming assumption that everyone out there also belongs to the intimate circle where Tolstoy and Turgenev are household words, he tells how Turgenev gave him some stories by Maupassant to read, what were his motivations, and how he, Tolstoy, did not at first like them at all. Then he confesses that just at that time — 1881 — he was going through "a period of most ardent inner reconstruction of my whole outlook on life," during which literature had become actually "obnoxious" to him. The first work he liked was the novel *Une Vie*, and here Tolstoy speaks warmly, writing in a mode of criticism some might call "impressionistic" or "affective." Leaving aside all analytical tools, he simply sweeps across the novel, as if with a wide brush dipped in the light of affection, and the text comes alive before our eyes:

> The form, which was beautiful in the first stories, is here brought to such a pitch of perfection as, in my opinion, has been attained by no other French writer of prose.... That is why all the events and characters of this novel are so lifelike and memorable. The weak, kindly, debilitated mother; the upright, weak, attractive father; the daughter, still more attractive in her simplicity, artlessness, and sympathy with all that is good; their mutual relations, their first journey, their servants and neighbors; the calculating, grossly sensual, mean, petty, insolent suitor, who as usual deceives the innocent girl by the customary empty idealization of the foulest instincts; the marriage, Corsica with the beautiful descriptions of nature, and then village life, the husband's coarse faithlessness, his seizure of power over the property, his quarrel with his father-in-law, the yielding of the good people and the victory of insolence; the relati-

ons with the neighbors — all this is life itself in its complexity and variety. And not only is all this vividly and finely described, but the sincere pathetic tone of it all involuntarily infects the reader. One feels that the author loves this woman, and loves her not for her external form but for her soul, for the goodness there is in her; that he pities her and suffers on her account, and this feeling is involuntarily communicated to the reader. And the questions: Why, for what end, is this fine creature ruined? Ought it indeed to be so? arise of themselves in the reader's soul and compel him to reflect on the meaning of human life.[20]

This is Tolstoy infected with emotion, precisely as he had required this of a work of art. The other level of criticism may be called "structural," not in the sense of modern Structuralist methodology, but because of Tolstoy's ability to give a structure, namely, an overall review of Maupassant's works establishing a hierarchy of values representing a declining curve of the writer's accomplishments and governed by a "dominanta" — a clear and firmly held moral position consistent with all of Tolstoy's views about art and life. Thus, *Bel-Ami*, "a very dirty book," "still has at its base a serious idea and sentiment," because it does demonstrate that all that is pure and good must perish in our society because it is "depraved, senseless and horrible." In *Mont-Oriol,* the themes and plots of the first two novels are repeated, but now "the writer's inner estimate of wrong and right begins to get confused," because the scoundrel, Paul, seems to have the author's sympathy. Further, *Pierre et Jean, Fort comme la Mort* and *Notre Coeur* all "bear the stamp of indifference, haste, unreality, and, above all, again that same absence of a correct moral relation to life which was present in his first writings." *Notre Coeur,* in particular, has no heart in it at all, but just "various kinds of sex-love," and therefore it "excites only disgust." In *Une Vie* the question is why a good creature is sacrificed to a monster; in *Bel-Ami* it is not quite so harsh: "why do wealth and fame go to the unworthy?"; in *Mont-Oriol* such questions are no longer asked, and it is "tacitly admitted that it should be so." *Pierre et Jean* and *Fort comme la Mort* are "built on debauchery, deceit and falsehood," and in *Notre Coeur* "the position of the author is monstrous, wild and immoral."[21] The degeneration of Maupassant, in short, is that he lost the moral perspective without losing his artistic ability:

> ...and though he continues to elaborate the form of his work as well as or sometimes even better than before, and even though he is fond of what he describes, yet he no longer loves it because it is good or moral and lovable to all, or hates it because it is evil and hateful to all, but only because one thing pleases and another thing happens to displease him (Maude, p. 29; *PSS*, *30*, 11).

The moralistic point of view sustained through this broad sweep across Maupassant's novels is then restated in terms relevant to literary theory in general, pertaining to what really holds together the structure of a work:

> People of little artistic sensibility often think that a work of art possesses unity when the same people act in it throughout, or when it is all constructed on one plot, or describes the life of one man. That is a mistake. It only appears so to a superficial observer. The cement which binds any artistic production into one whole and therefore produces the illusion of being a reflection of life, is not the unity of persons or situation, but the unity of the author's independent moral relation to his subject.... Whatever the artist depicts — saints, robbers, kings, or lackeys — we seek and see only the artist's own soul (Maude, p. 38; *PSS*, *30*, 18-19).

Whether or not the notion of "morality" belongs any longer (if it ever did) in the vocabulary of literary theory, the point Tolstoy is making seems quite valid; one may speak of "soul," or of "dominanta," or of "the algorithm for establishing coefficients of structural relationships," it still is so that some inner force in the mind must fuse a work together, and the greater that force, the larger the sweep of life it can transform into a literary text.

Tolstoy finds his explanation for the decline of moral values in Maupassant in the corrupting spirit of the times which makes a fashionable writer liable to the temptations of commercialism, of money and fame:

> In the first place, the success of his first novels, the praise of the press and the flattery of society, espe-

cially of women; in the second, the ever increasing amount of remuneration ... in the third the impertinence of editors outbidding one another, flattering, begging, and no longer judging the works the author offers, but enthusiastically accepting everything signed by a name now established with the public — all these temptations are so great that they evidently turn his head, and he succumbs to them (Maude, 29; *PSS*, *30*, 11).

One of the drafts to the Maupassant article expands on this theme in general considerations that call to mind Tolstoy's attacks against the Renaissance in *What Is Art?*, where a similar curve is drawn from the early Christian faith shared by all to its perverted image produced by greed for power and lust for sex.

Christianity, says Tolstoy, explained the meaning of life "simply, clearly assuredly and joyfully," (*PSS*, *30*, 286) but then this message was reinterpreted in such a way that it lost all meaning, and people started living without any real standards, "giving in to their desires, most of all to the strongest one — sexual sensuality." Whatever the truth of the matter, it is interesting to see how the Rousseauistic perception of humanity's progress from noble innocence to refined depravity has continued to define the Tolstoyan model of any social, religious or literary commentary he ever made. This parabola of argument even extends to some of his fiction, as, for instance in the *Death of Ivan Ilyich*, where we see the hero proceeding from a child full of innocent life, through the processes of corruption, toward a terrified solitude, looking at death.

The denial of beauty as a valid criterion of art is also closely linked with this line of argument. In *What Is Art?* Tolstoy rejected the notion of beauty because it did not permit a clear and binding definition, but in the essay on Maupassant he also draws upon the factor of time. Beauty, particularly of the sensual sort, is not a timeless ideal, but a process subject to the ravages of time:

> Then is this beauty indeed beauty? And why is all this so? It would be all very well if one could arrest life, but life goes on. And what does that mean? "Life goes on" means that the hair falls out, turns gray, the teeth decay, and there are wrinkles and offensive breath. Even before all is finished, every-

thing becomes dreadful, disgusting: the rouge, the powder, the sweat, the smell, and the repulsiveness, are evident. Where then is that which I serve? Where is beauty? But she is all! And if she is not, there is nothing left. There is no life! (Maude, pp. 44-5; *PSS, 30,* 24)

In this way, according to Tolstoy, the concept of beauty has itself degenerated in time. For the ancient Greeks, it represented the highest aim of human aspirations, but this concept became obsolete in time as was replaced by one of moral goodness, until "people of our time," having abandoned that ideal:

> thought up for themselves a renewed Greek theory of the beautiful and under the cover of it are ossifying in their coarse moral vulgarity, pretending that this vulgarity is the radiance of enlightenment (*PSS, 30,* p. 287).

In *What Is Art?* this is stated more clearly, naming the Renaissance as the time when these false theories and wrong revivals of Greek concepts of beauty were created with the aim of protecting the privileges of power. In any case, when Maupassant surrendered to this false theory of beauty, particularly to the idea that representation of feminine beauty and sex-love is *"grand art,"* his novels themselves were art no more. The irony of it is that even that beauty, for the sake of which Maupassant surrendered his art, was called by him nothing more than "une convention humaine."

The Introduction to Maupassant still attempts to operate with three main criteria of some sort for judging a work of art. Again, as before, the main difficulty for Tolstoy is the first, the main and ultimately, in the essay, the only criterion: the special compelling vision which turns the author's experience into the reader's reality. This time Tolstoy tried to separate one's ability to have such a vision by creating, as it were, a fourth category called "talent":

> He [Maupassant] possessed that particular gift called talent, which consists in the capacity to direct intense concentrated attention, according to the author's tastes, on this or that subject, in consequence of which the man endowed with this capacity sees in the things to which he directs his attention some new aspect which others have overlooked; and this gift of seeing what others have not seen Maupassant evi-

dently possessed (Maude, p. 21; *PSS*, *30*, 4).

This special gift was earlier called "individuality," then "sincerity," then the ability to perceive something unknown but necessary to the people. This last concept is now developed to the notion of "morality" and replaces the "first criterion" and is then separated from the special vision, or gift:

> ...he [Maupassant] unfortunately lacked the chief of the three conditions, beside talent, essential to a true work of art. These are: (1) a correct, that is, a moral relation of the author to his subject; (2) clearness of expression, or beauty of form, — the two are identical; and (3) sincerity, that is, a sincere feeling of love or hatred of what the artist depicts (*ibid.*).

Again, the pressure in the mind is simply to combine all of these: talent, moral relation to the subject, clarity and sincerity into just one thing which, however, cannot become a concept, or "truth," but only truth as a process, or a path — really, art itself can in the end, for Tolstoy, best be defined in the words of Christ, as the path, truth and life.

Another unfinished sketch, "On What Is Called Art?," was written in 1896, just before the final essay. In it Tolstoy denounces Wagner's *Nibelungen Ring* and modern poetry in terms quite similar to those in the essay. He is particularly vehement about the concept of "beauty" brought into play by Western aesthetics to justify, in Tolstoy's opinion, the obscene power of the upper classes:

> And who are these "we," who supposedly possess that unusual beauty? These are our well-known parasites, living their lives in gluttony, idleness and drunkenness. This is a tiny group of people, of parasites who came to think that there is no God, no meaning in life, that one must destroy oneself, and, while still alive, seek out any pleasures one can find. And it is this little group which is going to teach the entire masses what is true art, and we, who know how to enjoy healthy, understandable, universal art — we are supposed to come to you for lessons!! ("O tom, chto nazyvajut iskusstvom," *PSS*, *30*, 248).

The sketch goes on to denounce "art for art's sake," as well as science for the sake of science, i.e., idle curiosity, and to reject the Baumgartenian triad of goodness, truth and beauty, just as Tolstoy had done before and again in his final essay. It is interesting, and perhaps paradoxical, to note a parallel between this "triad" and the "three criteria," however unsettled, which Tolstoy tried to use for judging what is true art. When he says in this sketch: "there exists only goodness; truth and beauty are conditions of life, one of them needed for the manifestation of goodness, and the other arbitrary, having no connection with goodness" ("O tom, chto nazyvajut iskusstvom," p. 264), this becomes reminiscent of his saying that the three conditions of contagion in art — individuality, clarity and sincerity — may all be summed up into one: sincerity. Sincerity, then, and goodness, and the very special perception of something that no one else had known before, and the effort of communicating that something with compelling force, all become essentially the same thing, and in the end define art as a very noble game indeed. By the same token, as Tolstoy points out, "the distinctions and definitions of morality, science and art as separate things are altogether wrong."

Nevertheless, Tolstoy is careful to place a distance between his convictions and those who demand "social significance" of art. The distinction, if not very easily made, seems valid:

> It is true, one hears voices rejecting art for art's sake, that is, rejecting service to beauty and demanding a social content to art. These voices will remain without influence on the activity of art because what they say is not possible for art. An artist, if he is an artist, cannot do anything else except to transmit in his art his own feelings (*ibid.*).

The issue here is not whether art is to serve goodness understood in one way or another by various interests and ideologies — it is a question of the kind of goodness that is an individual's inspired vision. The rest is counterfeit.

Perhaps the best summary of Tolstoy's troublesome search for the essence of art, and of his insights just before the final essay, is contained in the following summary on the function of art:

> The whole business of art is only that it should be understandable, that it should make the incomprehensible comprehensible, or the half-understood understood by this special, direct means of infecting with emotion which constitutes the peculiarity of the activity of art (*ibid.*, p. 267).

CHAPTER FOUR

WHAT IS ART?

In the light of Tolstoy's explorations preceding the essay *What Is Art?*, we can see that the need for a definition of art arose for him on the moral plane. During the process culminating in the dramatic encounters with his own conscience and the conscience of society in *Confession* and in *What Then Must We Do?*, Tolstoy convinced himself that the social convention called "art" is actually one of the most powerful instruments of enslavement of one class of people by another and that it was particularly dangerous because of its power to pervert and stunt human nature itself. Not surprisingly, this very conviction became the starting point of *What Is Art?*. As the essay opens, Tolstoy speaks of hundreds of thousands of workmen — carpenters, masons, painters, joiners, paperhangers, tailors, hairdressers, jewelers, moulders, type-setters, who spend their whole lives in hard labor to satisfy the demands of art, so that hardly any other sphere of human activity, the military excepted, consumes so much energy:

> Not only is enormous labour spent on this activity, but in it, as in war, the very lives of men are sacrificed. Hundreds of thousands of people devote their lives from childhood to learning to twirl their legs rapidly (dancers), or to touch notes and strings very rapidly (musicians), or to sketch with paint and represent what they see (artists), or to turn every phrase inside out and find a rhyme to every word. And these people, often very kind and clever and capable of all sorts of useful labour, grow savage over their specialized and stupefying occupations and become one-sided and self-complacent specialists, dull to all the serious phenomena of life and skillful only at rapidly twisting their legs, their tongues, or their fingers (Maude, 74; *PSS, 30,* 28).

Once laid down at the very beginning, the premise of Tolstoy's opening gambit will permit him to speak in the essay against exclusiveness and professionalism in art and to describe the works of art produced by specially trained performers, writers and painters as inherently worthless — a counterfeit coin. As a result, the claims artistic activity makes on human and material resources are made to seem out of all proportion to its importance in society, and indeed, that activity itself appears for the most part to be grotesquely meaningless. This manner of arguing is really quite consistent with Tolstoy's artistic method in his own fiction, only there one speaks of it as the device of "making strange": something is presented either entirely without the context which usually gives it meaning or after such context has been discredited. If art is adequately defined in this manner, then there would seem to be no further point in asking what it is. But Tolstoy, having been a committed artist all his life, obviously either had to persist in asking this question, or abandon all his work and thus all meaning of his life up to that point. The issue was crucial: if art is not the monstrosity he had made it out to be by defining it as a corrupt pastime of the ruling classes, then what other definitions are there to be found, and what is their validity? As it was with the question of religion in *Confession*, so here, in art, the first thing Tolstoy saw on the outside of his own circle of thoughts was a great confusion of contradictory claims. The artists of various sects, like the theologians of various faiths, mutually exclude and destroy one another:

> Listen to the artists of the schools of our times, and in all branches you will find each set of artists disowning others. In poetry the old romanticists deny the parnassians and the decadents; the parnassians disown the romanticists and the decadents; the decadents disown all their predecessors and the symbolists; the symbolists disown all their predecessors and *les mages*; and *les mages* disown all, all their predecessors. Among novelists we have naturalists, psychologists and "nature-ists," all rejecting each other. And it is the same in dramatic art, in painting, and in music (Maude, 79-80; *PSS, 30*, 32).

Whatever the case may be with religion, in art it is possible to view the literary scene, this clamorous market place of ideas, in quite a different way. Instead of a confused "happening," this ongoing debate could be seen as a as legitimate historical process in which art continues to define itself by means of this very dialectic of mutual and universal oppositions. Tolstoy, however, whose hero was truth and whose heart was aching over the condition of the poor, could not regard aesthetics as an exercise in relativity. For him it was a matter of moral and philosophical commitment that called for a single governing definition of art which would not only prescribe a judgment in aesthetics but also set a moral standard in life. Such a definition had to be scientific in the sense of being acceptable on its logic to all reasonable minds and, even more important, it also had to be emotionally compelling — its reasons were supposed to be found in the wisdom of the heart.

The issue, as Tolstoy states it is this:
> It is necessary for a society in which works of art arise and are supported, to find out whether all that professes to be art is really art; whether (as is presupposed in our society) all that is art is good, and whether it is important and worth the sacrifices which it necessitates (Maude, 82; *PSS*, *30*, 33).

The rest of the essay revolves around these three questions. Tolstoy's first step is to mark the boundaries within which one may seek approaches to the definition of art.
> Art in all its forms is bounded on one side by the practically useful, and on the other by unsuccessful attempts at art. How is art to be marked off from each of these? The ordinary educated man of our circle, and even the artist who has not occupied himself specially with aesthetics, will not hesitate at this question either. He thinks the solution was found long ago and is well known to everyone.
> 'Art is an activity that produces beauty,' says such a man (Maude, 82-3; *PSS*, *30*, 34).

In contemporary aesthetics, "practically useful" is really practically a useless distinction, because what actually exists is a continuous set of essentially limitless modulations of the relationship between the practical and the aesthetic function of any object produced, or perceived, by society, according to the degree to which the function of beauty (i.e., of aesthetics) is thought to be subordinate or dominant. Obviously, then, one must first of all find the proper definition of beauty. Both Tolstoy and the traditional aesthetics of his time connected the idea of beauty, in the manner of Kant, with disinterested pleasure; the difference was that Tolstoy further connected such pleasure with the corrupt amusements of the idle rich who failed to honor their part of the social contract understood as "division of labor." Consequently, the first thing Tolstoy now tried to do was to separate the idea of beauty from the "pleasure principle" and to place the activity of art on the solid basis of scientific logic and objectivity:

> In order to define any human activity, it is necessary to understand its sense and importance; and in order to do this it is primarily necessary to examine that activity in itself, in its dependence on its cause and in connexion with its effects, and not merely in relation to the pleasure we can get from it (Maude, 116; *PSS*, *30*, 60).

As it stands, the statement seems clear enough. Its implications, however, become rather curious when Tolstoy goes on to a supporting example:

> Now if we consider the food question, it will not occur to any one to affirm that the importance of food consists in the pleasure we receive when eating it. Everybody understands that the satisfaction of our taste cannot serve as a basis for our definition of the merits of food, and that we have therefore no right to presuppose that dinners with cayenne pepper, Limburg cheese, alcohol, and so on, to which we are accustomed and which please us, form the very best human food. (*ibid.*, 60-61).

To accept Tolstoy's argument here is like agreeing to live in some dreadful world of "nutritional units" consumed by us as "digestive entities." But what then about art? In using his example, Tolstoy in effect chooses the trek of barren logic among God's many mysterious ways for he cannot help implying that our acceptance or rejection of art must depend on the same kind of "clinical" analysis. If on the basis of science we "have no right to presuppose" that pleasure is relevant to food then neither can we so judge about art, and it is the question of "having a right" which brings the moral dimension into the context of scientific thought.

The chill of Tolstoy's reasoned argument in the essay and the warmth of bodily desire, grace, sorrow and hope in his fiction do, however, seem interwoven at various points of contact into a single thrust — that of a human conscience seeking a just and meaningful way to live. It is not so strange, therefore, that however scientific in intent, the essay does ultimately arrive at a definition of art in terms of our emotions and then develops it around the issue of our personal and universal moral responsibility.

In this moralistic Tolstoyan world, beauty, coupled with the principle of pleasure for its own sake, and attended by the discipline of aesthetics, gives birth to a monstrosity called "art." Rejecting such a progeny, Tolstoy set out to find a different, more valid notion of art that could be formulated in a new definition. In the process, the idea of beauty as a criterion of art had to be put to the test, together with those prevalent theories of aesthetics which supported it. Chapter two of the essay begins a survey of various authorities whom Tolstoy discusses briefly and then dismisses each in turn, like so many highschool seniors at their final examinations.[1] In essence, his procedure amounts to a rhetorical gambit designed to make us feel, in view of all this evidence, that there is indeed no reasonable alternative to Tolstoy's own eventual definition.

The basic method is first to survey those reputed authorities who build their aesthetics on the concept of beauty, and then look at those who rely on some other principle. Having noted that the definition of art can lose focus by becoming so broad as to include all sorts of human activities, Tolstoy first of all dismisses authors like "Professor Kralik" (Richard Ritter von Meyrswalden, 1852-1934), who extends the concept of art to various applications of aesthetics to the pleasures of the senses and Jean-Marie Guyau (1854-1888) who holds to a similar idea: "Chacun de nous probablement avec un peu d'attention se rapellera des jouissances du goût, qui ont été de veritables jouissances esthétiques" (Maude, 85; *PSS*, *30*, 36).[2]

From there Tolstoy proceeds to set the very concept of "beauty" in the frame of its proper grammatical usage in Russian — namely, that it should indicate only that which is visually pleasing, but should not extend to such ideas as "beauty of the soul," and so on.[3] In this framework, Tolstoy looks at Baumgarten (1714-1762), thought to be the founder of modern aesthetics, and finds that beauty for him is "the Perfect (the Absolute), recognized through the senses; Truth is the Perfect perceived through reason; Goodness is the Perfect reached by moral will" (Maude, 92; *PSS*, *30*, 41). Other aestheticians say that Beauty is an experience which evokes and educates moral feeling, or that its ideal is a beautiful soul in a beautiful body; thus they wipe out Baumgarten's categories by substituting those of physical and emotional interrelationships. Johann Winckelman (1717-1767) distinguishes beauty of form, of idea, as it expresses itself in plastic arts, and beauty of expression, attainable only when form and idea are present. For Hemsterhuis (1720-1790) beauty is that which gives us pleasure, that is, the greatest number of perceptions in the shortest time, and for the philosopher Kant, the basis of aesthetic feeling is the judgmental capacity "which forms judgments without reasoning and produces pleasure without desire" (Maude, 97; *PSS*, *30*, 45). The German idealist Fichte (1762-1814) speaks of beauty as existing not in the world but in the "beautiful soul" while Schelling (1775-1845) thinks beauty is the perception of the infinite in the finite based on contemplation of things in themselves as they "exist in the prototype (*in den Urbildern*)" (Maude, 99: *PSS*, *30*, 47). Hegel, again, thinks beauty is the shining of the Idea through matter, while for Schopenhauer beauty is the Will objectivizing itself. All these disparate notions do not converge toward a single reasonable definition of art and create nothing but confusion in the mind. The French followers of the German idealists are still worse, for it is even harder to make out what they are saying. Among the English, beauty seems to be a matter of taste, and of breeding. For Lord Kames Home (1996-1782) beauty is that which is pleasant, what is pleasant being in turn defined by one's taste. Burke (1729-1797) thinks it (beauty) is a matter of self-preservation in its aspect of social intercourse which keeps any given society together and helps it sustain itself. Herbert Spencer (1820-1903) identifies the origin of art with play; for the mathematician Isaac Todhunter (1820-1884) there is no criterion for beauty except socially conditioned taste, while to Thomas Sully (1783-872) there is no beauty at all as a concept in art — art is something that gives us enjoyment.

In Tolstoy's opinion, this confusion is further compounded by the addition to the undefined term "Beauty" two still less understood notions, namely Goodness and Truth, as Baumgartner did in his definition, although for Winckelman beauty is separate from and independent of goodness. Thus again, there is no clear agreement. According to the Italian aesthetician Pagano, "beauty commingles with goodness, so that beauty is goodness made visible, and goodness is inner beauty" (Maude, 96; *PSS*, *30*, 44). Hegel's Idea through which Beauty shines is Truth, and thus truth and beauty are the same thing. To others again, beauty is the Idea in the form of a finite phenomenon, or something like that. None of this, for Tolstoy, achieves any coherence in the mind and thus cannot be used as any sort of criterion, or criteria, defining art. The main reason why these quasi-philosophical abstractions — Goodness, Truth and Beauty — cannot be defined in any objective universally valid way is that they either rest on the assumption that our palpable reality is but a symbol of another — a notion of no particular substance — or, worst of all, that they require the arbitration of taste, that is, in Tolstoy's view, the preferences of those who wield power in society.

It is certainly true that the question of taste is at least in part also a question of social norm, a fact widely recognized in twentieth-century aesthetics and literary theory. Some of the earliest lucid statements on that issue have been made by the Prague circle theoreticians, particularly Jan Mukařovsky. To a certain extent, Mukařovsky's argument does appear to give credit to Tolstoy's position that aesthetic taste is a class phenomenon:

> It may seem that the hierarchy of aesthetic canon is directly related to the hierarchy of social strata. The latest norm, occupying the summit, seems to correspond to the highest social stratum, and in like manner further gradations of both hierarchies seem to have a mutual correspondence, so that lower social categories seem to correspond to older canons.[4]

Such a recognition does help to legitimize Tolstoy as a genuine presence in aesthetics, instead of being an intruder from some quasi-religious realm of morality. Yet, Mukařovsky regards the social factor with some reservations: "As a rough outline this idea is not without some justification, but it should not be dogmatically understood as a valid blueprint of reality" (ibid.). His reservations take cognizance of the fact that the issue of hierarchy in aesthetics is much more complex in reality than mere division into "upper" and "lower" social strata since there are also many different "horizontal" subdivisions, such as by sex, profession, generation, politics and so on. Nevertheless, Mukařovsky agrees that: "the existence of a bond between aesthetic and social hierarchies is undeniable" (*ibid.*, p. 47), so that the aesthetic norm, or canon, may well be, to that extent, a class phenomenon.

The divergence between Tolstoy and the Prague aestheticians becomes evident when we understand that, while Mukařovsky thought that a socially prevalent aesthetic norm is a value constantly changing in time, to Tolstoy it seemed basically static, established more or less with the coming of the Renaissance, and since that time sustaining its dominance over the entire history of art:

> There exists an art-canon according to which certain productions favoured by our circle [by "our circle" Tolstoy, of course means himself as Count Tolstoy, an educated aristocrat, and others like him — R.Š.] are acknowledged as being art, — the works of Phidias, Sophocles, Homer, Titian, Raphael, Bach, Beethoven, Dante, Shakespeare, Goethe, and others, — and the aesthetic laws must be such as to embrace all these productions. In aesthetic literature you will constantly meet with opinions on the merit and importance of art, founded not on any certain laws by which this or that is held to be good or bad, but merely on consideration as to whether this art tallies with the art-canon we have drawn up (Maude, 114-5; *PSS, 30*, 59).

In this context, Tolstoy's views may be regarded as basically anti-historical, and in that sense conservative, because he not only does not see the relationship between creativity and aesthetic norm as a constantly developing process, but also requires that the entire question of what art is and is not be shifted from the plane of existing, or changing, norms to that of a "law," an objective, governing definition to which all social and aesthetic processes in time must remain permanently subordinate. "Instead of giving a definition of true art," complains Tolstoy:

> and then deciding what is and what is not good art by judging whether a work conforms of does not conform to this definition, a certain class of works which for some reason pleases a certain circle of people is accepted as being art, and a definition of art is then devised to cover all these productions (Maude, 115; *PSS, 30*, 59).

From the perspective of the Prague circle, however, Tolstoy himself is a participant in the constantly evolving tension between norm and art. Tolstoy's demand for an objective law above all particulars was understood by them simply as a given position inside the arena where "particulars" were fighting it out for dominance in the hierarchy of norms:

> let us recall that L.N. Tolstoy in *What Is Art?* also sought, with the aim of social equalization, the unification of the aesthetic canon, but in such a way that the upper levels of the aesthetic hierarchy would be rejected. He advocated the universalization of the canons of folk art (Mukařovsky, fn., p. 48)

Eventually, Tolstoy's final verdict on all theories of art based on the concept of beauty is that they are simply fraudulent:

> the theory of art founded on beauty, expounded by esthetics and in dim outline professed by the public, is nothing but the setting up as good of that which has pleased and pleases us, that is, pleases a certain class of people (Maude, 116; *PSS, 30,* 60).

What remains are definitions of art not based on the notion of Beauty. In Chapter Five Tolstoy summarizes these as follows:

> The latest and most comprehensible definitions of art, apart from the conception of beauty, are the following: — (I) *a*, art is an activity arising even in the animal kingdom, and springing from sexual desire and the propensity to play (Schiller, Darwin, Spencer), and *b*, accompanied by a pleasurable excitement of the nervous system (Grant Allen). This is the psychological-evolutionary definition. (2) Art is the external manifestation, by means of lines, colours, movements, sounds, or words, of emotions felt by man (Veron). This is the experimental definition. According to the very latest definition (Sully), (3) art is "the production of some permanent object or passing action which is fitted not only to supply an active enjoyment to the producer, but to convey a pleasurable impression to a number of spectators or listeners, quite apart from any personal advantage to be derived from it" (Maude, 119; *PSS, 30,* 62).

Among all these definitions, only that of Eugene Veron (1825-1889) is held worthy of some favor, because he considers art to be an external manifestation of feelings. Veron's idea is as follows:

> We may say then, by way of general definition, that art is the manifestation of emotion, obtaining external interpretation, now by expressive arrangements of line, form or color, now by a series of gestures, sounds, or words governed by particular rhythmical cadence. If our definition is exact, we must conclude, from it, that the merit of a work of art, whatever it may be, can be finally measured by the power with which it manifests or interprets the emotion that was its determining cause, and that, for a like reason, must constitute its innermost and supreme unity.[5]

Veron's criterion of value is in a way reminiscent of Tolstoy's own notions embracing his "three criteria," because both measure the worth of a work of art by its emotional power, or impact. After his troubled search for the description of these three criteria in the preliminary discussions of art, Tolstoy settled in the essay on the following:

> (1) On the greater or lesser individuality of the feeling transmitted; (2) on the greater or lesser clearness with which the feeling is transmitted; (3) on the sincerity of the artist, that is, on the greater or lesser force with which the artist himself feels the emotion he transmits (Maude, 228; *PSS*, *30*, 149).

Immediately thereupon, however, Tolstoy realized that these three factors "may all be summed up into one, the last, sincerity; that is, that the artist should be impelled by an inner need to express feeling" (*ibid.*). At this point, Veron and Tolstoy would seem to be unanimous, but there is one important difference: Veron spoke of nothing more than expression, whereas for Tolstoy this power of expression only acquires the properties of art when it can also infect the recipient, make him feel exactly the same thing, and as strongly as the artist himself.

Furthermore, this communication of feeling is for Tolstoy not a matter of pleasure but "one of the conditions of human life," that is, "one of the means of intercourse between man and man" (Maude, 120; *PSS*, *30*, 63-4). From here, his central definition:

> To evoke in oneself a feeling one has once experienced and having evoked it in oneself then by means of movements, lines, colours, sounds, or forms expressed in words, so to transmit that feeling that others experience the same feeling — this is the activity of art. Art is a human activity consisting in this, that one man consciously by means of certain external signs, hands on to others feelings he has lived through, and that others are infected by these feelings and also experience them (Maude, 123; *PSS 30*, 65).[6]

As we can see, by calling art an "activity," Tolstoy does not really say what art is, but rather describes what it does.[7]

Art is thus not some static concept or entity, but a dynamic process, an event that is continuously happening between the object of art and the beholder. That this process is also a constant, a "law" that does not change along with unstable social values, gives it the sort of dynamic flexibility that may be observed in Nature itself; in that sense, Tolstoy's definition is also organic. It is also related in great depth to the dynamics of Christian religious feeling. We may at this point recall Tolstoy's comments in 1886, in his preface to the collection "The Flower Garden," where, speaking of the relationship between truth and fancy, he said that truth is not some "thing," but a path — in other words, again, a process, and activity. In that same context, he then referred to the words of Christ: "I am the path, the truth and the life." It becomes clear that for Tolstoy truth, morality and art are based on the same premise, as things that are happening in the human heart and mind. Art, then, is not to be understood and described in and of itself, as a "Ding an sich" of some sort, but as an ongoing evolution of relationships with factors outside the realm of art, particularly with moral norms and realities. These in the end constitute the standard by which art shall be judged. And the most significant moral reality is that of the feeling of unity in love of all humanity:

> Art is not, as the metaphysicians say, the manifestation of some mysterious Idea of beauty or God; it is not as the aesthetic physiologists say, a game in which man lets off his excess of stored-up energy; it is not the expression of man's emotions by external signs; it is not the production of pleasing objects;

and, above all, it is not pleasure; but it is a means of union among men joining them together in the same feelings, and indispensable for the life and progress towards well-being of individuals and of humanity (Maude, *ibid.*).

For that reason, art does not really use feeling to convey some emotionally unmarked "content" but makes that content itself a feeling — an emotion that comprehends the same dimensions as may be measured by the yardsticks of moral, social or philosophical ideas. Emotion, then, as contemporary structuralists might say, is the message; indeed, it may be considered even in the Jakobsonian sense as "meaning," since it amounts to a total act of communication, comprising all the factors considered by Jakobson, in their relationship, to constitute a speech event.[8] In some ways, one might even consider Tolstoy to be instinctively a structuralist thinker, for both in his fiction and in his thought on art, a given relationship does in itself also represent the substance.

Emotional communication, infection with emotion, by its very nature is most easily understood as an instantaneous thing, an infinitesimal fraction of a second, in some figurative sense perhaps even similar to that mathematical point in space-time in which, as astronomers are now inclined to think, the entire universe was "conceived" and predetermined to its most distant events. If so, then this infection with emotion Tolstoy speaks of should be timeless and immeasurable — an unanalyzable event in the realm of the spirit. Indeed the entire essay points to the idea that the difference between real art and its counterfeit is exactly this indefinable something, the "wee bit," as Tolstoy put it:

> the feeling of infection by the art of music, which seems so simple and so easily obtained, is a thing we receive only when the performer finds those infinitely minute degrees which are necessary to perfection in music. It is the same in all arts: a wee bit lighter, a wee bit darker, a wee bit higher, lower, to the right or the left — in painting; a wee bit weaker or stronger in intonation, a wee bit sooner or later — in dramatic art; a wee bit omitted, overemphasized, or exaggerated — in poetry, and there is no contagion (Maude, 200; *PSS*, *30*, 128).

Tolstoy then continues with the assertion that only this sort of detail can carry the emotional impact and it is, consequently, not subject to any sort of methodical critical analysis or instruction:

> Infection is only obtained when an artist finds those infinitely minute degrees of which a work of art consists, and only to the extent to which he finds them. And it is quite impossible to teach people by external means to find these minute degrees: they can only be found when a man yields to his feeling (Maude, 201, *PSS*,128).

Detail in art, in this sense, is actually the very moment of creation itself, thus the ultimate reality, because everything that comes after it is but a consequence of that moment. As Tolstoy well understood and demonstrated in his works, such use of detail as a focal point so that it becomes evocative of many possible meanings makes all the difference. The secret of his power as a writer often resides in his ability to use an artistic language in which each single semiotic sign reveals itself upon observation as a microcosm of the whole text.

In opposition to this, the kind of details that Tolstoy objected to in art are details which merely fill out a picture but do not encompass and signify it as a whole and therefore carry no emotional impact. In Tolstoy's work, this is a crucial distinction between a microcosm which can, does expand in the imagination to signify the macrocosm of which it is but one part, and a superfluous detail that merely clutters up the text. Tolstoy's idea in *What Is Art?* was that this latter type of detail actually represents one of the types of devices, gimmicks, that go into the counterfeiting of emotion, that is, also counterfeiting of art:

> The second method of imparting a semblance of art is that which I have called imitation. The essence of this method consists in supplying details accompanying the thing described or depicted. In literary art this method consists in describing in minutest detail the external appearance, the faces, the clothes, the gestures, the tones, and the habitations, of the characters represented, with all the occurrences met with in life. For instance in novels and stories, when one of the characters speaks we are told in what voice he spoke and what he was doing at the time. And the

things said are not given so that they should have as much sense as possible, but as they are in life, disconnectedly and with interruptions and omissions (Maude, 183-4; *PSS 30*,114).

Yet, the instant of shared emotion that contains the essence of art and is in that sense a universal aesthetic sign, meaningfully relevant to everything in the world, cannot help being, implicitly and in its essence, at least as complex as that world itself, and so, it must consist of "parts," and be analyzable, and such analysis belongs to the discipline of literary theory and scholarship. Tolstoy's own fiction abounds in examples of extraordinarily complex and powerful inner events, not measurable in any actual time, yet determining, as if it were a space-time continuum, the very shape of the reality in which a text exists. Even in the definition itself, the idea that an artist hands his feelings over to others "consciously," by means of "certain external signs," can best be understood in contemporary terms as "encoding" — a process requiring subtle and complex encounters, decisions, relations, ordering and the establishment of hierarchies in the verbal material to be transformed into art, and it does not matter that all this may seem to the artist to have come in an instantaneous flash of inspiration. Furthermore, the difference between a mere instantaneous transmission of emotion and art is that in art the author *recalls* a feeling he has had, however recently, with the *purpose* of transmitting it to others, that is, this purpose for an encoding of the feeling in a particular manner.

It is also true that we really cannot step twice into the same river; a feeling once experienced is irretrievably gone. Only a new feeling is possible even in all our efforts to recall the old. It follows that the recollection itself is a complex relationship of two "texts" — the feeling the author has had, and the one he acquires in the effort of recollecting the first.

All this, of course, speaks for the legitimacy of analytical reading. Tolstoy, however attacked literary scholarship, criticism and schools of art basically on the grounds that, since true art is unteachable, there is nothing to teach, and since true art communicates itself directly and instantaneously to an uncorrupted person, there is nothing to analyze. On the other hand, moral and intellectual corruption, in Tolstoy's view, does need schools and literary criticism, because art built upon systems of counterfeit devices has a particular surface complexity — a collection of puzzles, tricks, conceits which can, indeed must be analyzed, "puzzled out," before they can be brought to any sort of coherence, even if it has nothing to do with what is meaningful or important in life and by the same token in true art. What Tolstoy is basically against could also be described as the general principle that art is an encoding of reality perceived not in its "natural" aspect but as a superstructure upon our civilization which in turn already consists of sign systems as these accumulate in the course of history. In his essay, Tolstoy lists the basic types of such counterfeit art under the headings of: 1) "borrowing" — "taking whole subjects, or merely separate features, from former works recognized by everyone as being poetic"; 2) "imitation" — "describing in minutest detail the external appearance, the faces, the clothes..." and so on; perhaps, then, "realism" or "verism"; 3) being "striking" — bringing together strongly contrasting things in the hope of a dramatic effect, and 4) being "interesting" — having intricate, suspenseful plots, or giving fascinating exotic details, and things of that nature (Maude, 182-185; *PSS, 30*, 111-116).

This leads to another major issue, that of the recipients of art, the "addressees," as today's terminology has it. Are they some specially attuned group, learned in recognizing and operating with these artifices, or must the appeal of art be indeed universal? The answer seems obvious: of course it must be that. According to Tolstoy, the communication, infection with emotion in art which must be immediate, total and universal cannot be contingent upon one's level of education or general cultural background:

> Art is differentiated from activity of the understanding, which demands preparation and a certain sequence of knowledge (so that one cannot learn trigonometry before knowing geometry) by the fact that it acts on people independently of their state of development and education, that the charm of a picture, sounds, or of forms, infects any man whatever his plane of development (Maude, 178, *PSS, 30*, 109-10).

Nevertheless, as the essay develops, it becomes gradually evident that Tolstoy is thinking in terms of two different kinds of people: those who always instantaneously, assuredly have recognized true art, and those who have lost their human capacity, in some ways similar to an animal's natural instinct, to do so. The dividing line, as one might expect, follows the boundaries of class distinctions:

> For a country peasant of unperverted taste this is as easy as it is for an animal of unspoilt scent to follow the trace he needs among a thousand others in wood or forest. The animal unerringly finds what he needs. So also the man, if only his natural qualities have not been perverted, will without fail select from among thousands of objects the real work of art he requires — that which infects him with the feeling experienced by the artist. But it is not so with those whose taste has been perverted by their education and life. The receptive feeling of these people is atrophied, and in valuing artistic productions they must be guided by discussion and study, which discussion and study completely confuse them. So that most people in our [upper class — R.Š.] society are quite unable to distinguish a work of art from the grossest counterfeits (Maude, 221; *PSS*, *30*, 143).

The choice of "uncorrupted" peasantry as the class capable of perceiving true art brings with it consequences beyond that issue alone. Since art, for Tolstoy, is inextricably tied in with morality, the "natural" ability to appreciate it also implies an equally natural, unerring understanding of what is true and false, right and wrong in one's life as well. Religion itself becomes, by this token, subject to judgment by a "class criterion." The unspoiled masses have not perverted, therefore have not lost, God's gift of knowing what is true, and they have preserved that gift largely because they sustain themselves by honest labor, in the surroundings of nature. Originality, depth and rich variety of feelings can exist only among simple people who must every day confront the challenges of nature for their survival. Only out of this soil, tilled by those who work with their hands, can eventually grow that wisdom of the ages, the religious consciousness, the oceanic feeling of harmony with the deepest mysteries of life, to which the only key is love: love of God, of humanity, of every living thing.

Tolstoy's argument, if accepted today, would to a large extent eliminate the entire theoretical approach to art known as "typology of cultures," where the very essence of art emerges from interrelationships with various different social classes and numerous other systems of knowledge and values, the consequence being that there are many different, culture-conditioned and culture specific ways of "truly" and "naturally" responding to art. Once such an approach is rejected, the understanding of art as something that develops in the stream of history as an accumulating aesthetic-social process, or entity, must also be dismissed and with it, of course, the assumption that the appreciation of art requires some special knowledge.[9] Complex encodings which involve this special knowledge and are tied to some artistic tradition, lack the necessary universality and are in effect not art. Indeed, this is one of the most significant ideas permeating the entire essay: that true art, like any other true human activity, deals with life itself, and not with the recorded traditions of its own development. That, too, was noted by Tolstoy as early as 1871, when he made an emphatic distinction between "life" and the universes of concepts which accrue, like barnacles, around all true concerns of living:

> There is a literature of literature — when the subject of literature is not life itself, but the literature of life, and this literature of literature comprises 999/1000 of all that is written. There is a politics of politics — when the subject of politics is not the body of the state but the previously dominant politics, and this, the previously prevailing politics comprises 999/1000 of all the activity of parliaments. There is a poetry of poetry, and so also in music, and in painting, and in sculpture — when the subject of poetry is not life but the poetry that existed before, and that, too, comprises 999/1000 of everything that is being created. There is a science of science, when the subject is not life, but the previous formulations of science — Lynneus, Cuvée, Darwin. Are there species or not? Is there a concept of justice or not? Is there gravity or not? There is a philosophy of philosophy, when the subject is not thought, but systems. The first is easy and unlimited, the second — difficult and rarely seen. (See *L.N. Tolstoy o literature*, p. 136.) [10]

There is, according to Tolstoy, something that all schools of art, literary critics and specialists in aesthetics do perpetrate, and it is that they pervert and corrupt our natural, unerring taste. Thanks to them, we learn to think that we like worthless and counterfeit art and, having learned that, we then further deceive ourselves into thinking that we have achieved the condition of civilization. Here is a list of famous authors who, in Tolstoy's view, are of little or no merit:

> It is solely due to the critics who in our times still praise rude, savage, and, for us, often meaningless works of the ancient Greeks: Sophocles, Euripides, Aeschylus, and especially Aristophanes; or, of modern writers, Dante, Tasso, Milton, Shakespeare; in painting all of Raphael [11], all of Michelangelo including his absurd "Last Judgment"; in music, the whole of Bach, and the whole of Beethoven, including his last period, — thanks only to them, have the Ibsens, Maeterlincks, Verlaines, Mallarmés, Puvis de Chavannes, Klingers, Böcklins, Stucks, Schneiders; in music, the Wagners, Liszts, Berliozes, Brahmses, and Richard Strausses, etc., and all that immense mass of good-for-nothing imitators of these imitators, become possible in our day (Maude, 197; *PSS, 30*, 125).

It is pleasing to see that Tolstoy did not exempt himself from this illustrious company, saying in a footnote (Chapter XVI): "I consign my own productions to the category of bad art, excepting the story *God Sees the Truth but Waits*, which seeks a place in the first class and *A Prisoner of the Caucasus* which belongs to the second" (*PSS 30*, 163; Maude, 246). The two "classes" of art distinguish, first, good art that also exemplifies and transmits religious consciousness, and, second, good art which merely transmits ordinary positive feelings. Both kinds must, of course, be instantly and universally understood. We might understand better Tolstoy's feeling about these two stories in the context of his attitude toward such works as *Don Quixote*, or Molière's comedies, or *David Copperfield* and *The Pickwick Papers*:

> these works for the most part — owing to the exceptional nature of the feelings they transmit, and the superfluity of special details of time and locality, and above all on account of the poverty of their subject matter in comparison with examples of universal ancient art (such, for instance, as the story of Joseph)

— are comprehensible only to people of their own circle (Maude, 243, *PSS, 30,* 161).

Tolstoy then goes on to summarize the story of Joseph, himself evidently still moved by it, and it may just be that certain pivotal points of similarity between the Biblical tale and Tolstoy's two stories caused to him to remember them now as the only acceptable examples of his own works as good art. The main point is that, although imprisoned, sold into slavery by his brothers, Joseph does take pity and forgives them later, having himself attained a station of power. The *motif* of imprisonment is treated much the same in *God Sees the Truth But Waits*, where the merchant Aksenov is sent to Siberia for a murder he did not commit and, years later, forgives the real murderer thus moving him as well to repentance. In *Prisoner of the Caucasus* the hero is captured by the Tartars and held for ransom, but with determined effort eventually makes his escape. Enduring faith in the grip of bondage is the element uniting both stories with the story of Joseph. In *God Sees the Truth*, however, Aksenov acquires "religious perception" in that he abandons himself totally to the universal love of God at the point of his deepest despair, when he is condemned by everyone. On the other hand, Zhilin, the hero of *Prisoner*, only endures in his commitment to his personal human dignity: he will not permit anyone to set a monetary measure upon his freedom. This may be the reason why Tolstoy relegated the *Prisoner* to the second category of good art, one that transmits basic human feelings which do not extend to the highest moral-religious dimension.

At this point, readers of *War and Peace* and *Anna Karenina* and perhaps most particularly, of *The Resurrection*, may well wonder how could Tolstoy believe his works have not moved anyone either with their depth of universal feeling of sonship to God and brotherhood of men, or certainly with their decent and loving humanity. Surely, he must have often been moved by these feelings himself while he worked at his desk, creating Pierre's dream of the universal globe, Andrey's lingering and illuminating death, Konstantin Levin's liberating insight that one must have God in his heart, or the character of Simonson, yes, even of Nekhljudov in *The Resurrection*. Perhaps the deep-rooted need for self-punishment, so evident in *Confession*, has prompted him to turn to his creation on this seventieth decade of his days and find it not good. Perhaps also, Tolstoy became increasingly and irritably aware that his works are full of all sorts of devices, writer's tricks just like those employed in counterfeit art as defined in his own essay. He thus may have become impatient with all that we have learned to admire in prose: infinite nuances of the tremendous complexities of human mind inscribed in a universe which itself is as awesomely complete as the mind of God; momentary glances, tremors of the heart, flashes of insight, acts of will, accumulating to an irresistible force which is that of history; rich and spacious worlds of description where every single detail of nature, of things, colors, sounds reveals itself to be an encoding of the minutest and the most powerful movements of the soul — all this has now been banished by the artist himself to the dead realm of bad, counterfeit art. But the works remain, and the loss is his, not ours.

Tolstoy's modesty about his own accomplishments may also reflect his opposition to the crippling moral confusion that ensues from the hero-worship accorded to famous artists, even though no person of sane mind can understand what their merits are. Thus, Tolstoy says, a simple peasant can understand physical strength, or military power, like that of Napoleon or Alexander the Great, or spiritual strength, like that of Christ or Buddha, but he is totally perplexed upon hearing that monuments are erected to the memory of poets like Pushkin, or Baudelaire, or Verlaine. Here, according to Tolstoy, is how a simple peasant would react to the worship of Pushkin:

> He tries to learn who Pushkin was, and having discovered that Pushkin was neither a hero, nor a general, but a private person and a writer, he comes to the conclusion that Pushkin must have been a holy man and a teacher of goodness, and he hastens to read or to hear his life and works. But what must be his perplexity when he learns that Pushkin was a man of more than easy morals, who was killed in a duel when attempting to kill another man, and that all his service consisted in writing verses about love, which were often very indecent (Maude, 256; *PSS*, *30*, 171).[12]

In Tolstoy's view, the universal accessibility of true art is an attribute originating not from the realm of aesthetics, but from that of religious feeling. He believed that everyone must have the same capacity to appreciate art because everyone's relationship to God is the same. Consequently, there is no special talent needed for responding to music, or any art without help from the critics. Some who believed in such talent, like L. William Flaccus, thought they could explain Tolstoy's hostility to so many of the world's most admired artists by saying that his own ability to appreciate art was limited:

> Limited in range his feeling for art certainly is, for he could not enjoy verse and its music, and so misjudged the Symbolists utterly. When he tests King Lear by means of retelling the plot in the baldest possible prose, he overlooks the meaning of poetic pitch of character and incident. Highly complex forms of art he could not appreciate, but within this range and its racial, personal and cultural limits his appreciation of art is genuine and in the main convincing and sound; and what is true of his art holds also of his judgment of art: it is truest when nearest the soil.[13]

Within Flaccus' own "personal, racial and cultural limits," especially considering with charity his total ignorance of Tolstoy's wonderfully perceptive comments on many Russian poets, and his well-known acute sensitivity to music, we may concede that there is some point to what Flaccus says. Even then, before agreeing that the author of *War and Peace* and *Anna Karenina* could not appreciate "highly complex forms of art," we should learn to think of "complexity" the way Tolstoy did, as an accumulation of ingenious artifices, and not as the fullness of the world we perceive in his novels.

Some of Tolstoy's specific objections to modern art, particularly to the French Symbolists, will merit closer attention at a later point, because they may provide clues to some qualities of Tolstoy's own mode of writing. His uncomfortable relationship with Shakespeare could also be illuminating in this way. Finally, we might also consider that perhaps there is, as Tolstoy maintained, a special kind of complexity in the simplicity of a peasant's life "close to the soil" which is essentially moral in nature and reflects both the infinite simplicity and the infinite complexity of God, at least in the implications of Tolstoy's view of the matter.

Tolstoy's argument that art is instantly recognized by any person without experience in the intellectual dimension and that consequently there should not be any literature of literature, or philosophy of philosophy, leads to the conclusion that there also should not be any metalanguage of art, and that the understanding of it should not be a rational construct but itself an emotion. Thus the concepts of universal moral relevance and immediate personal communicability tend to run together and become in turn synonymous with the intense feeling which represents what we call greatness in art and which itself is a luminous and spacious clarity, containing and transcending the full range and depth of important human feelings that are not dependent upon experience or learning. This is why, as Tolstoy puts it:

> ...the stories of Isaac, Jacob, and Joseph; the Hebrew prophets, the psalms, the Gospel parables; the story of Sakya Muni and the hymns of the Vedas, all transmit very exalted feelings and are nevertheless quite comprehensible now to us, educated or uneducated, just as they were comprehensible to the men of those times, long ago, who were even less educated than our labourers (Maude, 178; *PSS*, *30*, 109-10).[14]

We may note that the particular examples of great and timeless art chosen here by Tolstoy all have to do with the religious experience. This is how aesthetic and moral concepts and values meet again; at this point in the essay Tolstoy speaks of art as "the transmission of feelings flowing from man's religious consciousness" and of art as being "founded on man's relation to God." This religious consciousness, "nothing else than an indication of a new creative relation of a human being to the world" (*PSS*, *30*, 86) is also defined as the highest standard by which all other feelings are measured:

> In every period of history and in every human society there exists an understanding of the meaning of life which represents the highest level to which men of that society have attained — an understanding indicating the highest good at which that society aims. This understanding is the religious perception of the given time and society (Maude, 232; *PSS*, *30*, 153).

In his essay, Tolstoy describes organized religion as the legend, custom and ritual accruing around the memory of an outstanding person who, in his time and for his time, understood the meaning of life most clearly and most universally. This understanding, then, and not the person, custom or ritual, constitutes religious consciousness. It represents the highest human achievement of each given epoch, and it alone can illuminate the meaning of art in that epoch. Our own time, according to Tolstoy, has achieved its highest understanding of the meaning of life in the specifically Christian religious perception, which is defined as follows:

> The essence of the Christian perception consists in the recognition by every man of his sonship to God and of the consequent union of men with God and with one another, as is said in the Gospel. (Maude, 238; *PSS*, *30*, 157).

In the perspective of religious consciousness, then, art is defined as a process commensurate with the history of human moral (or "sacral") culture, versus the lay history of culture which comprises the corruption of the Renaissance and all that follows from it to this day. Tolstoy also attempts to postulate historical stages of "religious consciousness," but since the meaning of life can only be one for all time, his historical approach fails — Tolstoy is not a historical, but a religious thinker. Progress for him is an increasingly perfect understanding of what the highest good must ultimately be for all humanity, and, in the dimension of feelings, art has the role of furthering this.

In addition to this highest form of art which communicates religious consciousness, Tolstoy does accept as good the art which is based on everyday human relationships, or even on our ordinary responses to our surroundings, and allows it a place in a hierarchy based upon the quality of the transmitted feeling. Thus we get two basic categories of good Christian art:

> first, art transmitting feelings flowing from a religious perception of man's position in the world in relation to God and to his neighbor — religious art in the limited meaning of the term; and secondly, art transmitting the simplest feelings of common life, but such always as are accessible to all men in the whole world — the art of common life — the art of the people — universal art. Only these two kinds of art can be considered good art in our time (Maude, 241; *PSS*, *30*, 159).

In the essay, there is also a further subdivision, pertaining to that art which is still genuine, that is, infects with emotion, but is also bad, because the emotions transmitted tend toward isolating one group of people from another, toward imbuing us with hatred, pride and so on. Here again, the more important the context of such feelings, the more dangerous are the consequences of this evil art.

To the degree that Tolstoy's rejection of what he calls false art extends to the modern, post-Renaissance history and civilization as a whole, the position taken in the essay in fact stands at the pivotal point of Tolstoy's entire philosophy of life, where it meets his moral, religious and political thought. The new era in Western Europe that began with the Renaissance is, in Tolstoy's view, an aberration outside of the true mainstream of history. At that time, according to Tolstoy's reasoning in the essay, humanity underwent something like a rite of passage from sacral to secular systems of values, and so it was "born again" into a world without God, or, more precisely, without faith, and it was all the fault of the ruling classes:

> No longer able to believe in the Church religion whose falsehood they had detected, and incapable of accepting true Christian teaching which denounced their whole manner of life, these rich and powerful people, stranded with no religious conception of life, involuntarily returned to the pagan view of things which places life's meaning in personal enjoyment. And then took place among the upper classes what is called the Renaissance of science and art, which was really not only a denial of every religion, but also an assertion that religion is unnecessary (Maude, 133; *PSS*, *30*, 73).

Images of God without faith produced profane art with religious subject matter but without religious consciousness. According to Tolstoy, religious subject matter was continued in art because it still represented the symbols of faith to the masses of simple working people who were still believers and could therefore be more easily oppressed and exploited.[15] This art then continued to spread through the centuries like an enormous amoeba in the mind, engulfing and perverting time, space and civilization until the present day.[16] Now, after many surface changes which did not affect the godless void within, the Renaissance tradition has developed into a way of life, and contemporary art is still fulfilling the same function as art did when Renaissance began, namely, to be a means by which the ruling classes can maintain themselves in power.

In this context of worldly power, the Renaissance, in Tolstoy's view, was much more than a mere aberration in history and an interruption in the flow of developing religious consciousness. It was, rather, a unique and catastrophic event which upset the stable condition of an essential knowledge that underlies all truly historical civilizations, namely, the knowledge of God as infinitely the greatest Idea and eternally the ultimate reality.

The ideal of lay humanism, which has sustained so many cultural and academic institutions is, in Tolstoy's mind, not a fitting substitute for faith, because humanity, when it replaces God, becomes nothing but an abstraction, a common denominator without substance or meaning. There simply is no Anthropos in the way that there is God, and so, the center does not hold, and humanity loses its focus as an Idea. All the meaning life can have then relates only to isolated, particular individuals; to things that are meaningful merely to them and hardly anyone else. Thus, according to Tolstoy, what is today conventionally thought of as civilization is in essence nothing but a monstrous fraud perpetrated upon the working masses of the people.

In art, the instruments of deception were the corpulent graces of what some might call today "atheistic humanism," offering the apple of sensual delight in the counterfeit landscape of an imaginary "golden age." The paintings of Raphael or Titian, later of Rubens, and the plays of Shakespeare, were among the earlier offshoots of this malignant growth of Renaissance which then branched out through time into the music of Beethoven, and into various trends in literature and the arts to blossom forth, finally, in the mystic-barbaric stupidities of Wagner and of Symbolism.

In this modern art, esoteric, counterfeit emotions that are bought and sold among the upper classes substitute for true feeling, pointless obscurities take the place of thought, and meaningless complexities of form, inaccessible to reason, pretend to be a means of communication. Lacking a basic idea and a universally valid definition, modern art loses all historicity and must substitute for it a continued process of self-definition in terms of its own hermetic norms and references, running perpetually around in its own vicious circle, far from the real concerns of life.

Tolstoy was not the first nor altogether alone in his attacks upon the Renaissance. For example, almost half a century earlier, in 1853, the famous English art critic and social theorist John Ruskin (1819 - 1900) published his major work *The Stones of Venice* in which he maintained that "the Gothic architecture of Venice reflected national and domestic virtue, while Venetian Renaissance architecture mirrored corruption."[17] Ruskin felt that in Renaissance architecture:

> There is indeed an expression of aristocracy in its worst character; coldness, perfectedness of training, incapability of emotion, want of sympathy with the weakness of lower men, blank, hopeless, haughty self-sufficiency. All these characters are written in the Renaissance architecture as plainly as if they were graven on it in words.[18]

Tolstoy's own reaction to the architectural perfections of the Renaissance was indeed rather similar:

> I would rather live in Mamadoshi [a small Russian village, not far from Kazan' — R.Š.] than in Venice, Rome or Naples; upon these cities, and upon life in them, there weighs such an artificial, always one and the same grandeur and refinement that it stifles me just to think of it (*PSS*, 62, 259).

Ruskin also shared Tolstoy's idea that the Middle Ages was an epoch of faith and that therefore its art was meaningful. Ruskin's comparison of the organic architecture of the Middle Ages with the dead comforts of the Renaissance could have been acceptable to Tolstoy:

> It is to be noted also that it [the Renaissance architecture] ministered as much to luxury as to pride. Not to luxury of the eye, that is a holy luxury [at this point one may remember Tolstoy's insistence in the essay that, at least in Russian, the word "beautiful" properly describes only things seen by the eye]; Nature ministers to that in her painted meadows and sculptured forests, and gilded heavens; the Gothic builder ministered to that in his twisted traceries, and deep- wrought foliage, and burning casements. The dead Renaissance draws back into its earthli-

ness, out of all that was warm and heavenly; back into its pride, out of all that was simple and kind; back into its stateliness, out of all that was impulsive, reverent, and gay (*The Stones of Venice*, p. 61).

Chapters IX through XIV of the essay are dedicated to an elaborate discussion of the sins of modern art as it serves the self-indulgence of the ruling classes, offsprings of the Renaissance. Their lack of religious faith makes it impossible for them to seek the realization of religious consciousness in art, and this means the weakening and near-destruction of art itself:

> The first great result was that art was deprived of the infinite, varied, and profound, religious subject-matter proper to it. The second result was that, having only a small circle of people in view, it lost its beauty of form and became affected and obscure; and the third and chief result was that it ceased to be natural or even sincere and became thoroughly artificial and brain-spun (Maude, 149; *PSS*, *30*, 85).

Consequently, the only feelings which such artificial art could convey are those of the upper classes: pride, sexual desire and a discontent with life; all three are usually combined in modern art. Perhaps for the reason that Tolstoy was more familiar with the French literature of his time than with any other, the French Decadent and Symbolist poets and prose writers are singled out for particular blame because of their incomprehensibility, nihilism, absence of taste and pornographic tendencies. Baudelaire and Verlaine seem especially noxious to Tolstoy for their cult of obscurity and moral depravity:

> The philosophy of life of one of them, Baudelaire, consisted in elevating gross egotism into a theory and replacing morality by a cloudy conception of beauty — especially artificial beauty. ... The conception of life of the other, Verlaine, consisted in weak profligacy, in confession of moral impotence, and as an antidote to that impotence, in the grossest Roman Catholic idolatry. Both moreover were quite lacking in naïveté, sincerity, and simplicity, and both overflowed with artificiality, forced originality, and self-assurance (Maude, 166; *PSS*, *30*, 99).

Mallarmé and Maeterlinck are similarly denounced, and particular works of all three, including those of some others, are quoted for all to see, along with Tolstoy's disparaging comments. In the essay we also learn what painting is not, or should not be, in view of what the French Impressionists have done to it. Here Tolstoy entrusts his daughter, Tatjana Sukhotina, to report on the Paris exhibitions in 1894, and she writes very much as Tolstoy might have if he had seen the pictures himself. The problem with Pissarro, Suxotina says, is that he cannot draw and uses most improbable colors; someone else splashes just one color all over the picture, including the face of a girl he is painting. One of the symbolists had a *haut-relief*, "wretchedly executed, representing a woman (naked) who with both hands is squeezing from her two breasts streams of blood." There was also a picture of yellow sea in which "something swims which is neither a ship nor a heart." Another picture showed a man's profile, "before him a flame and black stripes — leeches, as I was afterwards told." Just as Levin in *Anna Karenina* inquired of an "expert" about music, so here Mme Suxotina finally asked someone who looked like he understood all this and was told that the *haut-relief* was a symbol, and represented "*La Terre*." The heart swimming in a yellow sea was "*Illusion perdue*," and the gentleman with the leeches was "*Le Mal*" (Maude, 171-2; *PSS*, *30*, 104). In short, the same charges of promoting sexual lust, of obscurity and of sheer nonsense as were leveled against the modern French poetry applied as well to the art of the Impressionists.

What Is Art? contains three fairly extensive references to music. The first is to the rehearsal of an unnamed opera — it serves as a rhetorical device at the beginning of the essay, to set up the question what is art and why is it important if such great sacrifices as the physical and moral crippling of the unfortunate cast and orchestra, etc., must be made for it.

The second reference is to Beethoven's music of the later period which, Tolstoy notes, has an "obscure, almost unhealthy excitement," perhaps not unlike the disquieting magnetism of the French Decadents. The contrast there is with a happy peasant song celebrating his daughter's birthday, a song which had "such a definite feeling of joy, cheerfulness, and energy" that Tolstoy was infected by its mood the same way he would be by good art. The point of the comparison is to contrast this women's song with the music of Beethoven, in particular his sonata Opus 101, of course, to the latter's disadvantage in terms of his search for the nature and meaning of art. An even stronger condemnation of Beethoven is directed against his Ninth Symphony:

> "What! the Ninth Symphony not a good work of art!" I hear exclaimed by indignant voices. And I reply: Most certainly it is not. All that I have written I have written with the sole purpose of finding a clear and reasonable criterion by which to judge the merits of works of art. And this criterion, coinciding with the indications of plain and sane sense, indubitably shows me that that symphony of Beethoven's is not a good work of art (Maude, 248; *PSS*, *30*, 165).

In other words, Beethoven is not a good musician because he cannot accomplish the infection with feeling needed in true art, nor can he therefore fulfill the highest aim of true art — to embody religious consciousness. Considering Beethoven's reputation as a dramatic and philosophical composer concerned with the deepest issues of the human condition, Tolstoy's opinion seems unorthodox indeed.

The other composer singled out for harsh treatment is Richard Wagner to whose *Nibelungen Ring* Tolstoy devotes an entire chapter of heavy sarcasm. His main objection to Wagner is that he tried to unify music, poetry and drama into a single aesthetic entity, quite forgetting that each has its own requirements and, so to speak, semiotics, incompatible with the other. On the whole, Wagner's music seems put together from incoherent bits whose unity is to be maintained by the merely mechanical device of *leitmotifs*. Not only do words or phrases in Wagner have their own musical motifs, tunes, but so do his characters, objects, institutions and even ideas. All these *leitmotifs* can then be juxtaposed and manipulated in various ways to make up a musical artifice, a structure conveying some semblance of the mythological artifices we see on the stage, which in turn try to construct a semblance of life as divorced from all true human affairs.

One of the worst sins of modernistic and generally all counterfeit art pertains to the thematics of love. What Tolstoy meant by "love" at this late hour of his life was not romance, nor, in his aesthetics, the great brotherly, sisterly love of religious consciousness, but simply sex — in modern art, the depictions of lust that arises from hedonistic idleness of the ruling classes. The issue of lust at the time was a very painful matter in his own life as well, and it was reflected in his art. The three strong "anti-sex" works, *The Resurrection*, the *Kreutzer Sonata* and *The Devil* were all written between 1887 and 1899 — just when Tolstoy was putting the finishing touches on *What Is Art?*.[19]

The presence of sexuality (to Tolstoy, pornography) in art was also a consequence of putting beauty — "that which pleases us" — at the center of aesthetics. This pornographic sexuality is the main mark of decadence, one of the monsters produced by the sleep of reason; another is the racist (in modern terms, perhaps even fascist) philosophy of power, glorifying the superior individual and proclaiming the survival of the fittest; among such philosophers the worst and the best known is Nietzsche.[20]

In his essay, Tolstoy balances his discussion of art with a brief consideration of science. Throughout the essay, Tolstoy makes a consistent effort to assign different aspects of human activity, on the one hand, to science, and, on the other — to art. Sometimes it seems as if the basic means for such a division are derived from an opposition that Tolstoy sets up between articulation, that is, the verbal mode of communication, and what may be called a gesture: art as a sign. Before giving his definition of art, for instance, Tolstoy builds a distinction and a parallel between art and what he calls "speech transmitting thoughts and experiences," given that both serve as means of union among people:

> The peculiarity of this latter means of intercourse, [i.e., art], distinguishing it from intercourse by means of words, consists in this, that whereas by words a man transmits his thoughts to another, by art he transmits his feelings (Maude, 121; *PSS*, 30, 64).

Crisply clear though Tolstoy attempts to be, there is a vagueness misting over his statement. For one thing, it is difficult to perceive how any thought, particularly if coupled with experience, could be separated from emotion neatly enough to validate the distinction.[21] Conversely, it is hard to feel any emotion, especially if it needs to be transmitted by some system of signs, that would not also involve at least some kernel of an argument or a conviction. Thus, in blurring his own distinctions, Tolstoy may well have surrendered to an inner voice which told him that feeling is ultimately the basic means of comprehending reality, because an emotion which seeks to become knowledge must of necessity also represent an idea. In our day, Tolstoy's distinction is generally rephrased to describe the difference between expository and artistic discourse in any semiotic system, although that does not help much if one is not sure that these two types of discourse are clearly separable at all. In the general structure of the essay, Tolstoy's attempted distinction between "art" and "word" is not intended to make these notions mutually exclusive, but rather to have them lead to distinctions between art and science as separate but equally essential functions of living. Both are justified by moral purpose, and therefore both reach their highest meaning in religious consciousness:

> And the degree of importance both of the feelings transmitted by art and of the information transmitted by science, is decided by the religious perception of the given time and society, that is, by the common understanding of the purpose of their lives possessed by the people of that time or society (Maude, 277; *PSS*, *30*, 186).

This line of thought had been developing during the years of exploratory and preparatory discussions of the relationships between science and art. It did not reach the point of complete clarity either before or in the essay itself. In one attempt to achieve a unified understanding of science and art, Tolstoy relates these two activities on the basis of human evolution:

> And as the evolution of knowledge proceeds by truer and more necessary knowledge dislodging and replacing what was mistaken and unnecessary, so the evolution of feeling proceeds by means of art — feelings less kind and less necessary for the well-being of mankind being replaced by others kinder and more needful for that end (Maude, 231; *PSS*, *30*, 151).

The problem is that, while we can very well decide which feelings are more important to us than others, we cannot judge the importance of some particular knowledge until we have acquired it. In essence, science is the search for truth, not the propagation of it, and it is not possible to decide a priori but on scientific basis what truths are to be sought. Tolstoy, however, demands that these decisions be made, on the same grounds of religious consciousness as in art, although any such knowledge of what life means obviates the need for science as generally understood. In Tolstoyan terms, the only science possible is one that studies, as he puts it "how people should live in order to fulfill their mission in life": theology, philosophy, social sciences and the like. All the "hard" experimental, quantifying sciences Tolstoy dismisses as either idle pastimes, satisfying pointless curiosity about things like "n-dimensional geometry, spectrum analysis of the Milky way, the form of atoms, dimensions of human skulls of the Stone Age, and similar trifles" (Maude, 280; *PSS, 30,* 188-9), or as decidedly harmful, since they draw our attention away from the important task of studying how we should live. What we are expected to do, then, is to substitute an attitude, a stance, for understanding. For Tolstoy, science must not investigate what *is*, but what is felt to be important; its significance lies not in objective inquiry into the laws of nature but in its sense of human values. Tolstoy says:

> ...real science lies in knowing what we should and what we should not believe, in knowing how the associated life of man should, and should not, be constituted: how to treat sexual relations, how to educate children, how to use the land, how to cultivate it oneself without oppressing other people, how to treat foreigners, how to treat animals, and much more that is important for the life of man (*PSS, 30*; Maude, 281-2).

Viewed from this angle, Tolstoy's ideas on science may seem, indeed they are, quite irrelevant to a serious professional scientist, but their import lies in their affinity with his views on art. The essence of science, as of art, is to be sought in the moral dimension:

> True science investigates and brings to human perception such truths and such knowledge as the people of a given time and society consider most important. Art transmits these truths from the region of perception to the region of emotion. If therefore the path chosen by science be false, so also will be the path taken by art (*PSS, 30,* 186; Maude, 277).

In the end, it seems evident that for Tolstoy neither art nor science had any value in and of themselves as discrete human activities. Just like the life of an individual, a Karataev, let us say, is only significant as one among many possible configurations of the basic, omnipresent moral life-force, so is the work of art, the insight of the scientist, only true and valuable when they are part of the context of eternal moral verities. Furthermore, unlike the present-day Structuralists, Tolstoy regarded art not as an autonomous sign, but as an event in the universe of feeling shared by the artist and his audience; thus art is communication the same way as life itself is even in its nonaesthetic dimension, and the only difference lies in what is being shared — information, as in the sciences, or feelings, as in art.

The art of the future, according to Tolstoy, unfolds a vision of universal brotherhood and love among all peoples no longer divided into hostile nations or ideologies, and also no longer classified as to who among them is an artist and who is not. There will be no special schools of art to teach how to make complicated counterfeits, and all will be open to all. Here Tolstoy makes a point that really pertains also to his own efforts to abandon the complex and highly sophisticated manner of his great novels in favor of maximum simplicity and clarity of the moral point in later writings:

> People think that if there are no special art-schools the technique of art will deteriorate. Undoubtedly it will deteriorate if by technique we understand those *complexities* of art which are now considered an excellence; but if by technique is understood clearness, beauty, simplicity, and compression, in works of art, then even if the elements of drawing and music were not to be taught in the national schools not only will the technique not deteriorate but, as shown by all peasant art, it will be a hundred times better (*PSS*, 30, 181; Maude, 270).

To insist that peasant art has a technique superior to the most sophisticated achievements in cultural and artistic tradition is really to speak on the level of rhetoric and not of a scholarly discourse. While maintaining the appearance of a reasoned argument, the essay communicates on the level of personal confession by an artist at war with his own Muse, and thus it invites the language of imagery, along with that of scholarship, to describe it. One might say, we see the swelling of a tide — ideas and emotions which have gathered strength during long years of troubled encounters with a restless conscience, now cannot not be held back any longer; they demand to be stated with an intensity that simply sweeps aside any just or unjust objections by specialists in the discipline of aesthetics whose scholarly minds may have grown either large of small by virtue of their own conventional rationality.

What Tolstoy achieves in the end is the communication of emotion, much as an artist should according to his definition. This justifies the reading of the essay itself as at least marginally an artistic text in which one may recognize the devices of rhetoric and fiction. An example of the large rhetorical gesture passing beyond particular arguments to become an integral part of the entire structure of the essay can be seen right at the beginning. After preliminary remarks on the high price exacted by the activities of art in both material resources and stunted lives of performing artists, Tolstoy switches to a concrete illustration, a visit to an opera rehearsal. Although ostensibly factual, the description reads like an episode worthy of any of Tolstoy's novels where the governing device is that of estrangement. Tolstoy "makes it strange" in two opposite ways: first, by coloring potentially neutral reality with negative emotional connotations, and, second, by taking away from the scene feelings engendered by our acceptance of artistic conventions, so that what we see immediately becomes both factual and absurd. The first approach becomes manifest when we enter the rehearsal room "by dark entrances and passages" through "gloom and dust" where "pale and haggard" workmen "with dirty, work-worn hands and cramped fingers, evidently tired and out of humor" pass by scolding each other like so many shades out of a Dantesque limbo.[22] The second kind of estrangement is accomplished when, after "ascending by a dark stair," we come upon the stage with "dozens, if not hundreds of painted and dressed-up men in costumes fitting tight to their thighs and calves, and also women, who are as usual, as nearly nude as might be." These people are then tortured for hours on end by the producer-director who sits in an armchair like some Satan in charge of his hellish proceedings and makes the actors repeat the same motions or musical phrases endlessly, cursing them all the while, to the point where the birth pangs of an opera become a meaningless spectacle of total alienation (the opera, based on a standard quid pro quo device, has to do with the marriage of an Indian king):

> That there never were or could be such Indians, and that they were not only unlike Indians but that what they were doing was unlike anything on earth except other operas, was beyond all manner of doubt; that people do not converse in such a way as recitative,

and do not place themselves at fixed distances, in a quartet, waving their arms to express their emotion; that nowhere except in theatres do people walk about in such a manner, in pairs, with tinfoil halberds and in slippers; that no one ever gets angry in such a way, or cries in such a way; and that no one on earth can be moved by such performances — all this is beyond the possibility of doubt (*PSS, 30* 33; Maude, 78).

The question waiting in the wings is, of course: "What is this art which is considered so important and necessary for humanity that for its sake these sacrifices of labour, of human life, and even of goodness, may be made?" (*PSS, 30,* 33; Maude, 82). A morally neutral, scholarly answer to the question so phrased is now not possible: no definition of art will be valid unless it is also an apology and a justification.

The description of a performance of Wagner's *Nibelungen Ring* is similarly colored. Tolstoy says:

> When I arrived, an actor sat on the stage amid decorations intended to represent [but not representing! — R.Š.] a cave and before something which was meant to represent a smith's forge. He was dressed in tricot tights, with a cloak of skins, wore a wig and an artificial beard, and with white, weak, genteel hands (his easy movements and especially the shape of his stomach and his lack of muscle revealed the actor) beat an impossible sword with an unnatural hammer [here the estrangement device almost reaches the comic level of decadent poetry — R.Š.] in a way in which no one ever uses a hammer; and at the same time, opening his mouth in a strange way, he sang something incomprehensible (*PSS, 30,* 133; Maude, 207).

These devices of alienation are then structurally reinforced by sets of systematic repetitions hammering in the same points over and over again. Just for one example, the description of the opera rehearsal in Chapter I is complemented in Chapter XVII with images of children who grow up crippled because they must learn the meaningless skills of counterfeit art:

> It is often said that it is horrible and pitiful to see little acrobats putting their legs over their necks, but it is not less pitiful to see children of ten giving concerts, and it is still worse to see schoolboys of ten who as a preparation for literary work have learnt by heart the exceptions to the Latin grammar.[23] These people not only grow physically and mentally, but also morally, deformed, and they become incapable of doing anything really needed by man (*PSS*, *30*, 168-9; Maude, 253).

The opposite device is to "make familiar": to infuse strange and distant things with a warm glow of recognition thus creating a euphoric aura from which Tolstoy's argument itself draws emotional and therefore also rational, validity. Perhaps the best known example of this device is the description of a deer hunt, as re-enacted by members of the Siberian Vogul tribe. It was something that Tolstoy himself did not even see, but only read about. Yet, his report has all the immediacy of a tense personal experience from which comes all art:

> The huntsman gains more and more on the pursued. The little deer is tired and presses against its mother; the doe stops to draw breath. The hunter comes up with them and draws his bow. But just then the bird sounds its note warning the deer of their danger. They escape. Again there is a chase and again the hunter gains on them, and lets fly his arrow. The arrow strikes the young deer. Unable to run, the little one presses against its mother. The mother licks its wound. The hunter draws another arrow. The audience, as the eye-witness describes them, are paralyzed with suspense; deep groans and even weeping are heard among them. And from the mere description I felt that this was a true work of art (*PSS*, *30*, 147; Maude, 225-6).

Again, such an imaginative description is calculated to strike us with the force of a reasoned argument. The important thing to realize, however is that exactly through this interrelationship between the intellectual and personal dimensions thought in Tolstoy becomes feeling, and feeling becomes life. We begin to grasp that the essay, just like Tolstoy's own fiction, is in reality about Tolstoy before it is about anything else; that it is an intense and powerful statement of self-realization and that in this sense it functions in the same way as his art.

Appearances to the contrary, Tolstoy's position in the essay is not a matter of stubborn adherence to some highly idiosyncratic point of view. The very breadth and catholicity of his sweeping, unorthodox pronouncements against most of modern art, as well as against the modern conception of science and its purposes, distinguishes him from mere narrow-minded traditionalists of some particular creed, conservatives resentful of change and of intellectual challenge. What Tolstoy does is defend with revolutionary fervor what he perceives as the most ancient and timeless moral foundations of human existence against the hollow specter of a modern civilization that has betrayed and abandoned the categorical imperative of quest for meaning. The pattern of ideas in Tolstoy, in spite of occasional internal contradictions, redundancies and even argumentative irrelevancies, does constitute a highly unified structure where almost every statement repeatedly reaffirms and illuminates every other from multiple perspectives. As we follow Tolstoy perusing learned books on aesthetics, making pointed criticisms of modern poetry and opera, arguing from a high moral platform, God at his right-hand side, about Art, Morality and Meaning, a feeling of unity emerges from the midst of all this; we perceive it at first as Tolstoy's sense of astonishment at the decadence of contemporary art, at the worthlessness of most of the conventional ideas in aesthetics, and as a sense of astonished understanding how really simple everything is when seen from the perspective of a compelling feeling which, in true art, embraces both the artist and his audience. What emerges later is the force of Tolstoy's personality — a powerful thrust of moral commitment, involving all his spiritual resources to shape a universe of personal Tolstoyan truth out of the suffering and strength of that world's own being.

CHAPTER FIVE

THEORY AND PRACTICE

In *The Resurrection* (1889 - 1899) there is a convict in Siberia named Simonson. This is how Tolstoy describes him:

> All men rule their lives and deeds partly by their own ideas, partly by the ideas of others. The extent to which they do the one or the other is one of the chief things that differentiate men. Some people only play at thinking: their minds are like a driving wheel without a load; their acts are determined by laws, by traditions, by the ideas of other men. Some, on the contrary, base their acts on their own ideas, follow their own reasoning and bow to public opinion only on occasion, after much careful thought. Simonson belonged to the second of these types. He made up his own mind about the truth of a matter and then acted by his decisions.[1]

Simonson is Tolstoy: from all his fiction and all his teachings Tolstoy emerges stubbornly alone, concentrated in purpose, painting a universal self-portrait to convey the image of truth as he felt it in his heart. He did not pretend always to be right, as some have accused him; his desire was to be sincere and speak from the innermost core of his own being and with a total personal commitment to what he said.[2] In a 1889 draft of *What Is Art?* Tolstoy describes this commitment — he calls it love — as a necessary condition for sincerity in art:

> In order for the artist to express the innermost needs of his soul and thus to speak fully from the heart, he must, first of all, not waste his time on all sorts of trifles which get in the way of loving that which one should and, secondly, to love by himself, with one's own heart, not with that of another, and not to pretend to love something which others deem, or admit,

to be worthy of love. And in order to achieve this, the artist must do as Valaam did when messengers came to him and he withdrew, waiting for God, so as to say only that which God shall command (*PSS, 30,* 213).

The notion that truly original thinking is but thinking along with the design of God underlies at the deepest level all that Tolstoy ever wrote or said. And it is not really a matter of being "godlike," as some have called him; on the contrary, perhaps the figure of a lowly pilgrim listening for the voice of God in the words of simple people close to the earth was one of Tolstoy's most favored images of himself. In *The Resurrection* there is an old wanderer across Siberian towns, villages and prison camps who, as another self-portrait by Tolstoy, articulates both the ultimate aloneness and nothingness of man and his timeless universality:

...they can't do me any harm because I am a free man, "What's your name?" they ask. They think I'm going to call myself by my own name, but I'm not, I deny everything — I have no name, no place, no country, I have nothing, I am just my own self, "My name? A man " "And how old are you?" I reply, "I never count the years, it can't be done, I always was, and I always shall be " "Who are your father and mother?" "I have no father and no mother except God and Mother Earth"[3]

It may be possible to think of Tolstoy's aesthetics as something that came into being in his consciousness of standing alone between Father God and Mother Earth. Admittedly, the distance is large indeed, possibly even infinite, and yet, these are the ultimate points of reference for all of Tolstoy's work, In *What Is Art?* Tolstoy began with the gladness pouring from a village women's song and reached out from there toward religious consciousness — the highest fulfillment of art. In his fiction, together with his hero and alter-ego Levin, he listened intently to the sound of new grass pushing through dry leaves in the spring, until he thought he could hear the voice of the universe speaking through innumerable signs that the artist could devise, like keys, to unlock its secrets, not the least among which were the wonders of the human heart. Within this same great span of spiritual quest, then, it may also be possible to speak of Tolstoy's fiction itself as a mode of thinking about the principles of his aesthetics, for indeed, every artistic text is in some measure also its own theory of art. Points of relevance, connections, have already been noted between Tolstoy's early prose, his writings on education, and the ultimate ideas in *What Is Art?*, We may now look at his mature work, the great novels *War and Peace* and *Anna Karenina*, as well as later *The Resurrection*, *Kreutzer Sonata*, and others, to further explore our premise.[4]

On the simplest level, these works contain direct references to the various arts either in their themes, plots or ideas articulated by the narrator or by the characters. Music and painting among these seem especially prominent. Most of these references are structured to reflect an emotional response, or lack of it, vis a vis a particular work of art. Almost always, this relationship can be seen to portray in terms of fictional narration the point of principle, stated in *What Is Art?*, about communication of feelings. Already in the early story, *Albert*, a scrawny-looking musician appears at a ball and, after clumsily, ridiculously trying to dance "like everyone else" (almost like Dostoevsky's Golyadkin Sr.), takes up a violin and suddenly transforms everything into a magic moment of music as an enchanted emotion. In *The Cossacks*, rather unexpectedly, the music of Bach serves as a reference point for describing a cheap imitation of feeling as Olenin fails upon first encounter to perceive the awesome majesty of the Caucasus mountains:

> Mountains and clouds appeared alike to him, and he began to suspect that the special beauty of snowy peaks, of which he had so often been told, was as much a figment of the imagination as the music of Bach, or love, in neither of which did he believe — and so he gave up looking forward to the mountains.[5]

Olenin is, of course, an intense and troubled young man, anxious to free himself of the perceived falsehoods of his life. At the same time, he also seems faintly comical as a disillusioned youth, a pale romantic hero whose body is bursting with vigor and ruddy health. Because of that, his lack of faith in Bach and love do not seem all that terribly important for the reader. Yet, years later we read in *What Is Art?* that "all of Bach" belongs among worthless imitations of art made famous only through the efforts of critics whose job is to pervert all natural aesthetic feeling. It thus turns out that whatever Olenin was designed to be as the central figure in the story, the feelings about Bach attributed to him have always been Tolstoy's own, long lasting, and finally placed in the foundations of his essay on art. Remembering Tolstoy's demand for originality and sincerity of feeling, we may note that all three things: Bach, mountains and love appear at that moment to Olenin as second-hand, as something he has been "told" about and thus could only have loved "with the heart of another," which means not at all. In the essay, such hand-me-down feelings are the only ones possible in counterfeit art, or among the corrupted aristocratic types which Olenin in part represents. Olenin does learn in the course of the story what it is to be overwhelmed by the beauty and majesty of the mountains, to be smitten by love and to respond to music — this time a simple Cossack tune sung by Uncle Erosha, who is Tolstoy's early image of man as a natural force, perhaps less "noble" and more "sauvage" than Rousseau's, but containing in himself the potential of becoming the serene wanderer we ultimately see in *The Resurrection*, standing free between Earth and God. Just to make the contrast between the two kinds of music clear, Tolstoy has Erosha begin with little city tunes, with words like "I fell in love on Monday,/ I suffered all day Tuesday, / I popped the question Wednesday/ and waited all day Thursday," followed by the refrain: "Ah did-dee, did-dee, did-dee/ When you saw him where was he?" Then comes the explanation:

> Songs like *Ah did-dee* — "gentlemen's songs," he called them — he sang for Olenin's benefit but three or four more glasses of *chikhir* brought back the old days and he began singing real Cossack and Tartar songs.... There was one Tartar song which moved him especially. It had few words and its charm lay in its melancholy refrain: "Ay, dy, dalalay!"... "Alone like thee, alone am I left! Ay, dy dalalay!" And old Yeroshka repeated the wailing, heart-rending refrain several times, Then he suddenly snatched a gun from the wall, rushed out into the yard and fired both barrels into the air. After that he began again, even more dolefully, "Ay dy, dalalay — ah, aa-h!" and relapsed into silence (*The Cossacks, op. cit.*, pp. 284).

As Eroshka sang, the night was full of stars, the young Cossack Lukashka was celebrating his betrothal with Maryanka, and Olenin with Eroshka, two outsiders, shared their solitude like that deep emotion which is transmitted in true art. From this perspective, watching Olenin learn something about having true feelings of his own, we might imagine him, too, as an early self-portrait by Tolstoy just starting out on a very long pilgrimage across a great many pages of stories and novels to become much later a Simonson who thinks for himself — an ancient, ageless free wanderer who, of course, ultimately wrote *What Is Art?* Precisely this point, the human sharing of sorrow or joy, is made again in *What Is Art?*, in Tolstoy's description of peasant women's song with its "cries and clanging of scythes," full of joy and energy, that was certainly better than Beethoven.

Simple songs that stir the blood and make people brothers and sisters together can also be heard in *War and Peace*, where the same contrasting device as in *The Cossacks* is used in the overall context to point up the degeneracy of the upper classes and their meaningless counterfeit art. There is, for instance, a moment in the novel, not long before the battle of Austerlitz, when marching Russian soldiers strike up a song:

> A drummer, their leader, turned round facing the singers, and flourishing his arm began a long drawn-out soldiers' song, commencing with the words: "*Morning dawned, the sun was rising,*" and concluding: "*On then, brothers, on to glory, led by Father Kamenski*" This song had been composed in the Turkish campaign and was now being sung in Austria, the only change being that the words "Father Kamenski" were replaced by "Father Kutuzov" (Norton, *War and Peace*, p. 126).

The artificial transplanting of the song from one context to another is a clear clue to the absence of true feeling in it, just as there was none in the "gentlemen's" ditties sung to Olenin by Erosha. By contrast, when the soldiers themselves wish to sing from their hearts, both the song and its leaders appear spontaneously, straight from the ranks:

> a lean and handsome soldier of forty — looked sternly at the singers and screwed up his eyes. Then having satisfied himself that all the eyes were fixed on him, he raised both arms as if carefully lifting some invisible but precious object above his head and holding it there for some seconds, suddenly

> flung it down and began:
> "*Oh, my bower, oh, my bower...!*"
> "*Oh my bower new...!*" chimed in twenty voices, and the castanet player, in spite of the burden of his equipment, rushed out to the front and, walking backwards before the company, jerked his shoulders and flourished his castanets as if threatening someone, The soldiers, swinging their arms and keeping time spontaneously, marched with long steps. Behind the company the sound of wheels, the creaking of springs, and the tramp of horses' hoofs were heard, Kutuzov and his suite were returning to the town. The commander in chief made a sign that the men should continue to march at ease, and he and all his suite showed pleasure at the sound of the singing and the sight of the dancing soldier and the gay and smartly marching men.

Tolstoy then adds a marvelous touch just a few lines later, when the horse of Zherkov, an officer in Kutuzov's retinue, gallops off in time to the beat of the song:

> Zherkov touched his horse with the spurs; it pranced excitedly from foot to foot uncertain with which to start, then settled down, galloped past the company, and overtook the carriage, still keeping time to the song. (*Ibid*, p. 127).

The interplay of truth and artifice in the entire passage is exceedingly complex and rich in associations, delightful to analyze. Just for one example, the three-tiered structural arrangement: artificial singing — true and natural feelings and song of the soldiers — instinctive, spontaneous rhythmic movement of the horse, is very reminiscent of the structural triad in *Three Deaths*, where an aristocratic lady from that artificial world is terrified of death, a peasant dies calmly, and a tree — magnificently. We see the same order of decreasing self-consciousness and increasing proximity to the ultimate truth of things. The added irony here is that Zherkov was an empty-headed society boy, particularly good at imitating other people's movements and facial expressions just for a joke, to make himself popular. He was, in a sense, a perfect example of counterfeit art, as Tolstoy describes it in his essay, in full contrast to his horse acting as naturally as the soldiers did.

A similar point emerges from another scene in *War and Peace*: Natasha's dance at "Uncle's" just after the hunting party and a good Russian country meal served by the bounteous Anisya. There the contrast between the formalities of aristocratic culture and the spontaneous, infectious communication of feeling that is essential to art is embodied in the actions of Natasha Rostova, which are then refracted through the narrator's comments to acquire the status of an idea underlying the entire novel. Here is what happens:

> Natasha threw off the shawl from her shoulders, ran forward to face "Uncle," and setting her arms akimbo attitude.
>
> Where, how, and when had this young countess, educated by an *emigrée* French governess, imbibed from the Russian air she breathed that spirit and obtained that manner which the *pas de châle* would, one would have supposed, long ago have effaced? But the spirit and the movements were those inimitable and unteachable Russian ones that "Uncle" had expected of her. As soon as she had struck her pose, and smiled triumphantly, proudly and with sly merriment, the fear that had at first seized Nicholas and the others that she might not do the right thing was at an end, and they were already admiring her. She did the right thing with such precision, such complete precision, that Anisya Fedorovna, who had at once handed her the handkerchief she needed for the dance, had tears in her eyes, though she laughed as she watched this slim, graceful countess, reared in silks and velvets and so different from herself, who yet was able to understand all that was in Anisya and in Anisya's father and mother and aunt, and in every Russian man and woman (Norton, *War and Peace*, p. 564).

Since these "right Russian moves" are "unteachable," the secret of executing them lies not in skill but in feeling. In this sense, Tolstoy here again is saying the same thing as he does much later in *What Is Art?* when he refers to the infinitesimally small differences which make for the enormous distinction. Natasha's quick gesture, throwing off her shawl, in conjunction with the narrator's remark about *pas de châle,* immediately places her dance in the symbolic context of genuine versus superficial and artificial values pertaining to culture and to art. Moreover, in the much larger context of approaching cataclysmic encounter between Russia and Napoleon, the *pas de châle* comes to represent everything that Napoleon stands for, and thus Natasha's small action becomes, structurally, the equivalent, the sign, of the epic Russian struggle as the whole country shook off the invader.

A much stronger indictment of high society and its rotten morals and false art, again developed through the carrier metaphor of music and dance, is made in Part Five, Chapters VIII to XI of *War and Peace*, where Natasha first becomes enchanted with the rake Kuragin during an opera performance. Tolstoy's basic device is to juxtapose Natasha's state of mind — she had just been coldly received by the Bolkonskys and is in shock, lonely and hungry for loving kindness — with the glitter of the opera and the audience, depicted in Tolstoy's best style of "estrangement"[6] as a totally incomprehensible, stupid and perverse world suffused by an all-pervading atmosphere of luxury and lust. The dynamics of the passage consist of Natasha's gradual intoxication with the poisonous glamour in the air, gradual acclimatization to the opera, while at the same time she becomes more and more receptive to Kuragin's advances, thus acting out precisely Tolstoy's idea, vigorously expressed again in the essay, that false art corrupts and destroys the soul. The descriptions of the opera performance, interwoven with Natasha's slow sinking into moral helplessness, could easily be transposed to the opening section of *What Is Art?*, where an opera rehearsal is depicted in just the same terms of estrangement. At first Natasha saw:

> only the painted cardboard and the queerly dressed men and women who moved, spoke, and sang so strangely in that brilliant light. She knew what it was all meant to represent, but it was so pretentiously false and unnatural that she first felt ashamed for the actors and then amused at them (*War and Peace*, Norton, 620).

Then she begins to enter a state of intoxication, and "the strangest fancies unexpectedly and disconnectedly passed through her mind." In the meantime, Kuragin appears, walking with "a restrained swagger which would have been ridiculous had he not been so good looking" and says: "charmante," so that the word reverberates in Natasha's ears, In the second act, the realization that Kuragin is talking about her "gave her pleasure," and then:

> She turned, and their eyes met. Almost smiling, he gazed straight into her eyes with such an enraptured, caressing look that it seemed strange to be so near him, to look at him like that, to be so sure he admired her, and not to be acquainted with him (*ibid.*).

In the meantime, the nonsensical proceedings on the opera stage go on, and Kuragin keeps looking at Natasha until she becomes "pleased to see that he was captivated by her," while Kuragin's sister, the beautiful, vicious and mindless Helen sits nearby "her whole bosom completely exposed." On stage, the dancer Duport "who received sixty thousand rubles a year for his art" was jumping up and down on his fat, bare legs, and "Natasha no longer thought this strange. She looked about with pleasure, smiling joyfully." Then "the nearly naked Hélène with her proud, calm smile" introduces Kuragin to Natasha, and the sordid affair begins to take its course, and we have Tolstoy's whole argument about high society, its ethics and aesthetics, acted out as life, in a performance no less nonsensical than that of Duport.

One of the references to music in *Anna Karenina* bears almost directly on Tolstoy's essay. In Part Seven, Chapter Five, Levin, already married to Kitty, in town on business, already beginning to feel the corruption of city life, goes to a matinée to hear a fantasia by Balakirev, "King Lear on the Heath," and a piece dedicated to Bach. Bach, as we have already seen, never quite won Tolstoy's heart, and Shakespeare's *King Lear* is mercilessly drawn and quartered in the essay *On Shakespeare and on Drama* which Tolstoy wrote later, in 1903, and where he confesses that, after having read Shakespeare in several languages, including English, for many long years, he cannot help thinking of him as a talentless hack.

Considering the enduring world-wide fame of Shakespeare, possibly rivaling Tolstoy's own, it may be useful at this moment to make a small digression and take a brief look at some salient points of his critique of the English bard.

Tolstoy's anti-Shakespearean tree of discontent, the seeds of which can be found as early as 1855,[7] grew to full blossom in the essay on Shakespeare first published in English in 1907.[8] This essay singles out *King Lear* for special unfavorable attention. Tolstoy points out the implausibility of the opening situation, where King Lear, who knew his daughter for many years, suddenly decides to divide his kingdom on the strength of a single profession of love that could well be false. He attacks the "barbaric cruelty" of the blinding of Gloster and ridicules the supposed "miracle" where Gloster, walking on an even stage, thinks he had just fallen, unhurt, several hundred feet. Turning to Hamlet, Tolstoy notes the total lack of any particular character in the melancholy prince and says that just this feature — no character — was declared to be Hamlet's greatest virtue by pedantic German critics. Most seriously, Tolstoy attacked Shakespeare's ideological position, as he understood it, namely, that one should always aim at the golden mean, neither seeking goodness to the point of harming oneself, nor avoiding evil excessively. This, Tolstoy complained, showed that Shakespeare had no ideals and no commitment to humanity, wishing only to please the crowds and to enrich himself by doing so. To Tolstoy, Shakespeare was basically a Falstaff, the only character in his plays who comes through as natural and convincing.

These and similar objections to Shakespeare couched by Tolstoy in terms of both morality and stagecraft, may well have their origins in the two writers' different perceptions of the relationship between reality and language. What in Tolstoy's view matters for Shakespeare is not what a person suffers, believes, or whom he loves, but how well one can speak of such things — how clever, grandiloquent, playful, poetic is the author himself. Thus any issue in Shakespeare, however serious, draws its substance from little else than a game of words, where, as Tolstoy says, thoughts arise either from sound repetitions or from verbal contrasts, and thus the artistically important relationship exists not between reality and language, but between a word and its shadow grinning foolishly at each other, as they do at the very beginning of *King Lear*, where Kent, not understanding Gloster's explanation that Edmund is his bastard son and that there was "good sport" at his making, says: "I cannot conceive you," and Gloster answers: "Sir, this young fellow's mother could: whereupon she grew round-wombed and had indeed, sir, a son for her cradle ere she had a husband for her bed" (Act I, Scene I). Thus begun, the entire tragedy mocks itself; as Tolstoy might have said, it means no more than the good sport at its making.

Believing that the ornamental word in Shakespeare is only a message about itself, Tolstoy speaks of the naked Edgar, the Fool and Kent as examples of how Shakespeare has insulted the suffering of humanity by turning it into a foolish pretense of madness, as in the heath, where these characters spout pompous or nonsensical verbiage often at the very times when anything human in us should become speechless with pity and fear. In Tolstoy's view, this deprives the characters not only of all individuality, but also of all humanity — they become mere demented forms of speech.[9] When Tolstoy himself does arrive at a certain surface similarity with Shakespeare, in his own noisy Bedlam-like scenes, he starts out from radically different premises. For instance, in the prisoners' visiting room in *The Resurrection*, the absurdity of the scene, where everyone in the crowded room shouts at the top of their voice in a hopeless effort to be hear by the loved one, is so outrageous that it even reaches the point of being comical, and then precisely because of that, pierces the heart with pity (see *The Resurrection*, Signet, 961, p. 142). The heart-piercing power of the Tolstoyan statement here comes not from the extravagant theatricality of the text, containing Shakespearean kings and madmen, long-winded speeches and spectacular winds — but from its matter-of-fact rationality in the prison setting: for security reasons, two wire mesh partitions separate the prisoners from the visitors by seven feet.

There are also radical differences in the two writers' use of language not only as a means of reproducing or deforming reality but also in its structuring function within a given text itself. When, for instance, Anna Karenina is prompted to say: "a bad omen" as her first meeting with Vronsky is marked by a railroad guard's death, we, having read the novel before, know something she does not — that she will die under the wheels of a train. For this reason, the meaning of her words goes far beyond the limits of her human knowledge and perception and strikes us, at least in retrospect, as a sort of dark force that will bend the novel to its conclusion not unlike the Shakespearean "destiny that shapes our ends" At times Shakespeare also gives a structuring function to individual utterances even over and above the immediate context they serve. That function, as in Tolstoy, has the effect of predicting future configurations of the entire text. Let us, for instance, listen to Goneril lying about how much she loves her father:

> Sir, I love you more than words can wield the matter;
> Dearer than eyesight, space and liberty,
> Beyond what can be valued rich or rare;
> As much as child ever lov'd or father found;
> A love that makes breath poor and speech unable;
> Beyond all manner of so much I love you.
> (Act I, scene I)

In view of the future events, this passage becomes as strangely frightening as Anna's premonition and as bitterly ironic in the counterpoint between what eventually happens and what Goneril now says. Her "I love you more than words can wield the matter" sounds like a mocking echo of the helplessness of Lear's own words when his daughters throw him out: "I will do such things, — / What they are yet I know not; but they shall be/ The terrors of the earth." When Goneril says she loves Lear "dearer than eyesight, space and liberty," her choice of words becomes bitterly prophetic when we think of the blinding of Gloster, of the wide-open heath into which Lear is driven, and of Cordelia's death in jail. And, of course, the words: "No less than life, with grace, health, beauty, honor," later fall like stones upon Lear's dishonored head. As Tolstoy's Anna, so also Goneril could not possibly foresee what matter her words will wield, as there is certainly no possible causal or logical connection in the ordinary sense. The difference between Tolstoy and Shakespeare here is that Goneril has no personal feeling for the things she says and thus becomes merely a depository for words and a component in the playwright's design, while Anna Karenina speaks from a sudden depth of terror before the strange and troubled feelings of guilt and love that befell her, even unconsciously, just a moment ago when she saw Vronsky and are now crowding with the force of death into her soul. From such a perspective, an important difference between Tolstoy and Shakespeare appears to be that one of them, Tolstoy, imitates in the moral dimension the ongoing flow of the river of life itself, while the other merely constructs complex literary texts. To take a somewhat different example, Karataev's meandering speech, incoherent as it may seem or even be, does, in Tolstoy's intention, encode the meaning of human relationships with history and therefore has its source in the heart of God. The mock-insane speeches of Kent, Edgar and the Fool on the heath spring from the mind of Shakespeare and embody the verbal history of the English stage.

Humanity in Shakespeare is therefore a degree of eloquence, while humanity in Tolstoy is a matter of perception, an image of life. As this image strains to embody what Tolstoy called "religious consciousness," this very effort in itself becomes the process that in Tolstoy defines both the theory and practice of art.

Returning now to Levin at the concert, we can see how Tolstoy has stacked the deck pretty well ahead of time. Yet, this is not quite enough for him. Using similar devices as he did in the opera scene in *War and Peace*, Tolstoy now portrays the conductor and the audience in such a way that they become bothersome and ridiculous at once:

> He [Levin] tried not to let his mind wander nor to let his impression of the music be marred by looking at the white-tied conductor's arm-waving, which always so unpleasantly distracts one's attention from the music; nor by the ladies with their bonnets, the ribbons of which were so carefully tied over their ears for the concert; nor by all those other persons who were either not interested in anything or were interested in all sorts of things other than music (*Anna Karenina*, Norton, p. 619).

And so, as Levin stands behind a pillar (a classic outsider's pose in cheap novels, and also in Pushkin's *Eugene Onegin*, at the ball where Tatyana appears as a *grande dame*) watching the gesticulating clown, deaf ladies and indifferent city rabble, no one should be surprised at his reaction:

> the longer he listened to the *King Lear* fantasia, the further he felt from the possibility of forming any definite opinion. The musical expression of some emotion seemed perpetually on the point of beginning, when it suddenly broke into fragments of the expression of other emotions or even into unrelated sounds which, elaborate though they were, were only connected by the whim of the composer. Even these fragments of musical expression, though some of them were good, were unpleasing because they were quite unexpected and unprepared for. Mirth, sadness, despair, tenderness, triumph, came forth without any cause, like the thoughts of a madman. And, as in the mind of a madman, these emotions van-

ished just as unexpectedly (*ibid*).

To some other listeners than Tolstoy and his literary offspring Levin, such an impression of Balakirev's music may even seem very perceptive and complimentary, for the particular scene the fantasia refers to is the scene where King Lear is mad on the heath, wandering disconnectedly in his mind amidst the storming furies. Levin, however, is timidly perplexed and even fails to make any connection between the music and Shakespeare's play, until a critic, Pestsov makes it for him. The ensuing commentary could have come straight from *What Is Art?*:

> Levin maintained that the mistake of Wagner and of all his followers lay in trying to make music enter the domain of another art, and that poetry commits the same error when it depicts the features of a face, which should be done by painting, and, as an example of this kind of error, he mentioned a sculptor who carved in marble certain poetic phantasms arising round the pedestal of his statue of a poet (*ibid.*, p. 620).

Twenty-one years later, in the essay, we read:

> Wagner wishes to correct the opera by letting music submit to the demands of poetry and unite with it. But each art has its own definite realm which is not identical with the realm of other arts, but merely comes in contact with them; and therefore if the manifestations, I will not say of several but even of two arts — the dramatic and the musical — be united in one complete production, then the demands of the one art will make it impossible to fulfill the demands of the other (Maude, 203-4; *PSS, 30*, 130).

The kind of unity Tolstoy perceives in Wagner pertains not to reality but to the artifice. This is his main objection to Wagner who tried to unify music and poetry into a single aesthetic entity, quite forgetting that each has its own requirements and, so to speak, semiotics, incompatible with the other. Not only words or phrases in Wagner have their own musical motifs, tunes, but so do his characters, objects, institutions and even ideas. All these motifs can then be juxtaposed and manipulated in various ways to make up a musical artifice, a structure conveying some semblance of the mythological artifices we see on the stage, which in turn try to construct a semblance of life as divorced from all true human affairs. The result is known as modern art which, according to Tolstoy, it definitely is not.

> Tolstoy is particularly taken with Wagner's *leitmotifs*: there is one fixed combination of sounds, or *leitmotif,* for each character, and this *leitmotif* is repeated every time the person whom it represents appears; and when any one is mentioned the *motif* is heard which relates to that person. Moreover each article also has its own *leitmotif* or chord. There is a *motif* of the ring, a *motif* of the helmet, a *motif* of the apple, a *motif* of fire, spear sword, water, etc. (Maude, 208).

The basic *motif* in Tolstoy's criticism of Wagner is that music and theater cannot be brought together to make a new hybrid genre. To be fair to Wagner, he did seem to be aware of the "definite realm" of each art, of immanent nature, as he clearly said in his "Die Oper und das Wesen der Musik": "Jedes Ding lebt und besteht durch die innere Nothwendigkeit seines Wesens, durch das Bedürfniss seiner Natur." His point, however, was that the tremendous impact of the opera has been due to the fact that it overcame the natural separateness of the arts and brought about "true drama on the basis of absolute music."[10]

In the novel, at least, Tolstoy provides some faintly comic relief by having his opinionated phantasm, Levin, himself engage in a bit of counterfeit art:

> "The sculptor's phantasms so little resembled phantasms that they even clung to a ladder," said Levin.
> He liked this phrase, but could not remember whether he had not used it before, and to Pestsov himself, and after saying it he grew embarrassed.[11]

Levin's entire stay in Moscow at that point in the novel is described in a delicate interplay between truths and falsehoods, pertaining to ideas about art, education, or agriculture, as Levin makes his rounds talking to relatives, intellectuals, artists and other members of the Moscow society, including Vronsky, his old rival over Kitty, and finally Anna herself who is by then in a state of near-hysteria, desperately flirting with all sorts of men, including Levin, for reasons she cannot understand any more. All this is presented as a process of slow poisoning in the soul which in the end begins to strain even Levin's relationship with Kitty who accuses him of wanting to be unfaithful to her. The atmosphere of moral rot, seeping almost imperceptibly, but pleasantly, into the veins is in itself very similar to the world of false values described in the essay on art. As in *War and Peace*, so also here we are witnesses to the transformation of Tolstoy's deeply felt, albeit idiosyncratic, ideas into the fabric of fiction, only to have them return again to the status of expository statements in his writings on art.

No other work of Tolstoy is so full of music and hatred as *The Kreutzer Sonata* (1887-89). It is a story of tragic marital conflict in which Beethoven stands accused of murder together with Pozdnyshev, the killer of his unfaithful wife, In fact, Pozdnyshev himself is the accuser:

> Ugh! Ugh! It is a terrible thing, that sonata. And especially that part [the first presto]. And in general music is a dreadful thing! What is it? I don't understand it. What is music? What does it do? And why does it do what it does? They say music exalts the soul. Nonsense, it is not true! It has an effect, an awful effect — I am speaking of myself — but not of an exalting kind.[12]

Pozdnyshev is not exactly Tolstoy's alter ego, even if he does share many of the same opinions about art, love and marriage. He is more like a special gesture, an exaggerated polemical stance, a dramatization of certain ideas Tolstoy was anxious to promote. Therefore Pozdnyshev both speaks and acts with a dagger rather than with balance and reason, and unlike Tolstoy's expository prose, his style of argument against Beethoven and cultured music in general is one of a passionate outburst rather than of logical discourse. Yet, the question is exactly the same — what *is* music (or art) and what are its effects? The answer is also the same: that which cultivated society calls music is a false and dangerous thing, because it arouses passions which decorum requires us to suppress, forcing pretense and avoidance of choice between good and evil. Music, says Pozdnyshev:

> is a terrible instrument in the hands of any chance user! Take that *Kreutzer Sonata* for instance, how can that first presto be played in a drawing-room among ladies in low-necked dresses? To hear that played, to clap a little, and then to eat ices and talk

of the latest scandal? (*Kreutzer Sonata*, p. 220).

There is a strange sense of frustration in the story, of evil hypnosis, very similar to the atmosphere in *War and Peace* when Natasha is at the opera, or in *Anna Karenina* when Levin listens to Balakirev's "King Lear." If we compare the descriptions of music in these three scenes from *War and Peace*, *Anna Karenina* and *Kreutzer Sonata*, we can see the emergence of a single line of thought leading to a summary of insights gradually accumulated over the long years of creating art and thinking about it. Society is a construct of artifices, and enculturation consists of learning to perceive these artifices as things natural to our humanity, accumulated over the course of history in the hope of defending our existence and enhancing its quality. In *The Resurrection*, Tolstoy very effectively juxtaposes music as artifice with grotesque scenes of pitiful suffering to demonstrate how "natural" and rational may appear to us the horrors of what we have accustomed ourselves to call "civilization." First, there is a prison scene in the visiting room, with its abominable noise produced by the efforts of loved ones to speak to each other:

> Wives, husbands, fathers, mothers, and children pressed their faces close against the partitions in their efforts to see each other, and to say what they wanted. As each spoke so as to be heard by the one he was talking to, and his neighbors did the same, the result was that they did all they could to drown the voices of everyone else. (*The Resurrection*, p. 142)

When prince Nekhlyudov saw this, he "was astounded that this terrible thing, this outrage to human feelings, should apparently offend no one. The inspector, the soldiers, the visitors, and the prisoners acted as though all this was as it should be" (p. 142). A few pages later, this very device — noise that impedes communication — is transferred to the topic of music, and thus the horrors of society become also the horrors of its art. Nekhlyudov comes to the prison inspector's house and has trouble conversing with him because of his daughter's loud piano:

> "Markova?" asked the inspector, not hearing distinctly because of the music.
> "Maslova"
> "Oh, yes"

> The inspector rose and went to the door through which the torrent of Clementi's *roulades* came pouring in.
> "Stop a moment, Marusya! It is impossible to hear ourselves speak," he said in a voice that showed that this music was the bane of his life (pp. 171-2).

In all this, Tolstoy's point is that successive assimilation of a series of artifices called art and of mindless horrors called culture to the point where they seem normal will make it impossible, indeed unthinkable, to redeem and fulfill our humanity — by the force of love, to become united with the truth immanent in nature and in ourselves. This "liberation from solitude," the feeling of joyful unity with everyone evoked by emotional contact by means of art can be found over and over again in Tolstoy's novels and stories, from any period of his work as a thinker and artist.

In light of this, we can begin to see in what a great and tragic measure *Anna Karenina* is the story of catastrophic failure of human communication. Tolstoy is cruel enough to let us perceive this at the very moment when Vronsky and Anna make love for the first time. There Tolstoy steps in as narrator to explain that after the deed Vronsky must have felt just like a murderer watching the bloody corpse of his victim:

> The shame she felt at her spiritual nakedness communicated itself to him. But in spite of the murderer's horror of the body of his victim, that body must be cut in pieces and hidden away, and he must make use of what he has obtained by the murder.
> Then, as the murderer desperately throws himself on the body, as though with passion, and drags it and hacks it, so Vronsky covered her face and shoulder with kisses (Norton, *Anna Karenina*, pp. 135-6).

The cruel phrase "as though with passion," with its suggestion that murderous, possessive violence may function as an imitation, a counterfeit, of love permits us to transfer its terrible meaning unto the plane of art, for in his essay Tolstoy did describe the effects of false art in the very similar terms of maiming and crippling both the human body and spirit. From such a perspective, we may also see Anna's suicide at the railroad station as another "portrait" of Anna, where reality itself enacts, embodies the consequences of Vronsky's failure to love, just as he failed in his attempt to paint

Anna's portrait in competition with Mikhailov.

The episode with Mikhailov in Italy also has its specifically theoretical — aspect there is a sort of symposium in his studio during which Vronsky, Anna, Mikhailov, the false and fruitless intellectual Golenishchev, and indirectly the narrator, engage together in a discourse on art. The narrator, of course, is protected from entanglement in the threads of words, thoughts and feelings from which the characters' fate is being woven while they talk, so that what he explains to us in his running commentary amounts to a prototype essay on art. In many ways it closely resembles the ideas Tolstoy put down in his own name in *What Is Art?* There, for instance, he says that:

> The second condition [of the diffusion of false, counterfeit art] is the growth in recent times of art criticism, that is, the valuation of art not by everybody, and above all not by plain men, but by erudite, that is, by perverted and at the same time self-confident, individuals (*PSS, 30,* 122; Maude, 194).

And this is what Mikhailov in *Anna Karenina* thinks of Anna and Vronsky:

> Vronsky and Anna, according to Mikhailov's conception, were in all probability distinguished wealthy Russians, who like all these wealthy Russians comprehended nothing of art but pretended to be amateurs and critics. "Probably they've seen all the antiquities, and are now going the rounds of the modern painters, the German quack and the stupid English pre-Raphaelite, and to complete the series have come to see me too," he thought (Norton, *Anna Karenina*, p. 430).

Mikhailov also feels about technique in art just the same way as Tolstoy does in his essay, where he maintains that "technique" has meaning only in false art, bereft of feeling and thus concerned only with tricks and gimmicks that can be learned by anybody. In the novel, it is precisely Vronsky, the amateur painter, who brings the point up. The group has been looking at Mikhailov's picture "Christ Before the Pilate":

> "Yes, its mastery is wonderful! How those figures in the background stand out! This is technique," said Vronsky, addressing Golenishchev and alluding to a

conversation they had had about Vronsky's despair of attaining technical mastery.

"Yes, yes, wonderful!" chimed in Golenishchev and Anna. In spite of his elation, this remark about technique grated painfully on Mikhailov's heart, and, glancing angrily at Vronsky, he suddenly frowned. He often heard the word *technique* mentioned, and did not at all understand what was meant by it. He knew it meant a mechanical capacity to paint and draw, quite independent of the subject-matter. He had often noticed — as now when his picture was being praised — that technique was contrasted with inner quality, as if it were possible to paint well something that was bad (Norton, p. 431).

In Tolstoy's novels, people look at pictures and listen to music, but it is curious that hardly anyone is interested in literature. There is actually a kind of gradation, a hierarchy of response to art. First comes painting, where we not only see people experiencing various feelings when looking at the pictures, but in *Anna Karenina* there is also a true painter, Mikhailov, the creator of Anna's wonderful portrait, who thinks of his own art and responds in his mind to criticism by others. He even has a fake counterpart to himself, Vronsky, who also paints Anna's picture without any feeling or competence; thus the juxtaposition between true and counterfeit art that we see in the essay is built into the novel as well. Second is music; there are no composers, only performers who do elicit strong emotional responses from their audiences, even as they are affected themselves. Lastly, in literature, there are even no readers, except possibly for Anna Karenina struggling through her English novel on the train. With the exception of the fake "poet" Boris Drubetskoy in *War and Peace*, only essayists, scholars, judges, bureaucrats and priests are shown occupying themselves with the written word. It could be that the closer, more intimate, an artistic medium was to Tolstoy himself, the more constrained he felt about depicting it in his fiction, to avoid the potential absurdity of writing words about words. It could also be, of course, that the society described by Tolstoy did not read a great deal in fiction; certainly not in Russian.[13]

Though few in number, the literary references do have a significant function. Even in painting, art was used by Tolstoy not as a topic in itself, but rather to reveal, explore and relate to each other the varied spiritual and interpersonal experiences of the characters. In the case of Mikhailov, art was an instrument of exploring the question of how much Vronsky really loved Anna after all. In music, Pozdnyshev of *Kreutzer Sonata* and Natasha in *War and Peace* underwent traumatic and euphoric experiences that pertained to their own lives and in the case of Natasha, to the life of the entire country. From this perspective, literature, like music and painting, becomes a literary device intended to convey an image of life both inside and outside the domain of art. As such, its function is generally negative and sometimes only minor, as with Boris Drubetskoy, where the French verses helped him to reveal himself as the complete fool. He is, after all, the one poet in *War and Peace* and, next to another officer, Berg, he is one of the novel's blond and handsome cardboard cutouts. He writes verse in a melancholy vein, because he is then courting the rich heiress Julie, and the fashion of the time demands that lovers be sad. With Karamzin and all the Russian sentimentalists watching, this is what Drubetskoy writes:

> Aliment de poison d'une âme trop sensible,
> Toi, sans qui le bonheur me serait impossible,
> Tendre mélancholie, ah, viens me consoler,
> Viens calmer les tourments de ma sombre retraite,
> Et mêle une douceur secrète
> A ces pleurs que je sens couler.
> (Norton, *War and Peace*, p. 608)

Quite evidently, Tolstoy meant this as a parody of all city-bred sentimental poetry and the social customs that go with it. It is quite fascinating, however, to see Tolstoy in the essay, some twenty-nine years after Drubetskoy's immortal lines, quoting Baudelaire with exactly the same intention of demonstrating nonsensical verse that pretends to be an expression of lyrical sentiment:

> Je t'adore a l'égal de la voûte nocturne,
> O vase de tristesse, o grande taciturne,
> Et t'aime d'autant plus, belle, que tu me fuis,
> Et que tu me parais, ornement de mes nuits,
> Plus ironiquement accumuler les lieues
> Qui séparent mes bras des immensités bleues.
> (*PSS*, *30*, 93; Maude, p. 160)

Whether Baudelaire's talents are indeed no greater than Drubetskoy's is, of course, beside the point. What matters is Tolstoy's judgment, conveyed in *War and Peace* simply and quickly in the very next paragraph after the quote from Drubetskoy, to the effect that the two supposed lovers were obvious fakes:

> For Boris, Julie played most doleful nocturnes on her harp. Boris read *Poor Liza* aloud to her, and more than once interrupted the reading because of the emotions that choked him. Meeting at large gatherings Julie and Boris looked on one another as the only souls who understood one another in a world of indifferent people (Norton, *War and Peace*, p. 608).

It is amusing to note how Tolstoy is quite prepared to use literary allusions, that is, wade into the stream of the "continuum of culture," when it suits his purposes. Julie, after all, has her namesake in Rousseau's famous work, itself a new version of the medieval romance *Héloise et Abelard*, and *Poor Liza* is Karamzin's sad story of a young peasant girl loved and abandoned by a spineless young aristocrat. All this would hardly seem to suggest much promise for the future of Boris and Julie, but Tolstoy wants to show that neither of them knows or cares what literature really means, and that for them one sad story will do as well as another — exactly Tolstoy's point about counterfeit art. For us, however, it may also be instructive to remember that what Tolstoy is laughing at in *War and Peace* are his own attitudes of just a few years before:

> The main thing is that you should be an *understanding* person, one of those people with whom, upon first acquaintance, you see no need to explain your own feelings and inclinations, because you can see that he understands you, that every note in your soul creates an echo in his. It is difficult, it even seems to me impossible to divide people into wise, stupid, good or evil, but the distinction between *those who understand* and *those who do not* is for me such a sharp line that I draw it involuntarily among all the people whom I know.[14]

When Anna Karenina reads the English novel on the train, coming back to Petersburg, after her fateful encounter with Vronsky, there is a great snowstorm, a metaphor of her new passion, raging outside. Emotionally distraught, she acts in a way that will bring tragic consequences to her in the future: she imagines herself being in another place, away from her own life with its unresolvable stress:

> When she read how the heroine of the novel nursed a sick man, she wanted to move about the sick-room with noiseless footsteps; when she read of a member of Parliament making a speech, she wished to make that speech; when she read how Lady Mary rode to hounds, teased the bride and astonished everybody by her boldness — she wanted to do it herself. But there was nothing to be done, so she forced herself to read, while her little hand toyed with the smooth paper knife.
> The hero of the novel had nearly attained to his English happiness of a baronetcy and an estate, and Anna wanted to go to the estate with him, when she suddenly felt that he must have been ashamed and that she was ashamed of the same thing, — but what was she ashamed of? (Norton, *Anna Karenina*, p. 92).

There is no sympathy on Tolstoy's part with either the novel or its hero's "English happiness"; both seem equally stupid.[15] But he uses this passage as an encoding of prophecy, as a forecasting of Anna's fate. To understand this, we need only recall how she attained her "English happiness" on Vronsky's estate in the country, just as she told herself she would, and what a bitter taste this happiness left in her mouth.[16] Just like Tolstoy's encounters in the novel with painting and music in terms of their narrative function, here we also have an oblique device intended to give additional resonance to the plot, to add to our perception of the underlying structural necessity of Anna's approaching tragedy. At a deeper level, one could, figuratively speaking, envisage even a third literary text, in addition to the English novel and Vronsky's anglophile Arcadia. It would be Anna's own story about herself as the heroine of a tragic romance. David A. Sloane, in his report on Pushkin's legacy in *Anna Karenina*, asserts the following:

> Anna progressively subjugates reality to the tyranny of a literary model, and her misfortune in life results

largely from her insistence on writing life into a pre-existing text.... Like tragic author she transforms a chance occurrence (the death of the train watchman) into a sign [of] inevitability ("a bad omen"). The death of the watchman *can* indeed be a "bad omen" but only from a perspective that places events into an aesthetic framework and sees them as elements of myth. As the novel unfolds it becomes apparent that Anna is fashioning her own life into a tragedy with the semblance of fateful inevitability that the genre demands.[17]

Sloane further comments that Anna's very suicide" is an act of tragic authorship: she chooses her means of death [under the train] and she plots the location so as to fulfill the fantasy of her recurring nightmare — positioning herself in the vicinity of a "little peasant" working on the rails. If she does so deliberately, then it must be on a very deep unconscious level indeed, for there is no hint in the Tolstoy's text of her awareness of these matters at the time. Yet, Sloane's point is on the whole well taken. Anna does indeed follow some sort of irresistible self-destructive urge, like the most Dostoevskian of all of Tolstoy's heroines. She also seems to be shaping the parabola of her descent into death almost as if it were the curve of a literary plot. This becomes particularly clear in the last stages of her relationship with Vronsky, when she very deliberately excludes any possibility of mutual understanding and reconciliation, as if afraid that this might avert the approaching tragic dénouement.

We could then speak of a balanced arrangement in the novel between the references to visual arts and to literature that pertain to Anna. It is a pattern of deepening tragic irony. The counterfeit "fulfillment" of the English novel in the life on Vronsky's estate corresponds to his portrait of Anna: neither has any love,[18] and both are false, desolate and, in the end, inconsequential, in view of the growing mutual hatred and darkening shadow of death. On the other hand, Mikhailov's portrait, in which we see Anna in all her brilliance and beauty of body and soul, stands in bitter confrontation with the tragic text of Anna's destiny designed by herself. The growing gulf between Anna's wonderful portrait and the decomposing corpse of her happiness illustrates precisely Tolstoy's views on the relationship between true art and the privileged classes.[19]

Tolstoy carries the device of contrasting a woman and her portrait beyond *Anna Karenina*, to *The Resurrection*, for there we also see a portrait, of Nekhlyudov's mother. When Levin looked at Anna's portrait, he saw:

> not a picture, but a living, charming woman with curly black hair, bare shoulders and arms, and a dreamy half-smile on lips covered with elegant down, looking at him victoriously and tenderly with eyes that troubled him. The only thing that showed she was not alive was that she was more beautiful than a living woman could be (Norton, *Anna Karenina*, p. 630).

Levin was unable to understand at the time how much the real Anna was already a woman with a dead soul, for at the very moment she came and greeted him with such vitality and charm that he became totally enchanted. On the other hand, in *The Resurrection*, Nekhlyudov looks at his mother's portrait when she is already physically dead, and the contrast between feminine allure and the dread corruption of death is immediate, dramatic and bitter:

> Anxious to recall a pleasing memory of her, he looked at her portrait, for which he had paid five thousand rubles. It was the work of a famous artist. She was painted in a low-cut gown of black velvet. Evidently the artist had taken great pains over the neck, the shadow between the breasts, and the dazzling shoulders. This seemed shameful and disgusting to him now. There was something repellent and blasphemous in that picture of his mother painted as a half-naked beauty, hanging in the very room where three months ago she had lain emaciated and dry as a mummy, filling the room and indeed the whole house with a heavy, sickening smell which nothing could overpower (*The Resurrection*, op.cit., p. 101).

In a sense, the beautiful Helen of *War and Peace*, sitting nearly naked at the opera, is also a portrait, and the corruption is the same, only here, in *The Resurrection*, death is a malodorous reality, and not something hidden behind the perfumed and glittering mask of high society glamour. Moreover, by saying that the artist who painted Nekhlyudov's mother was famous, and by letting us know how much he was paid, Tolstoy in essence does the same thing as in Natasha's opera scene, where we are informed that Duport gets sixty thousand rubles per year for jumping up and down on the stage. The issue turns around the commercialization of feelings, around the substitution of conventions for reality in order more easily to pursue the promptings of one's lust or greed.

It is significant that in describing Mikhailov's portrait of Anna, Tolstoy desists from the sort of condemnatory language he used to refer to the painter in *The Resurrection* and even makes it quite clear that Mikhailov is a true and talented artist. In doing this, he transforms the difference between Vronsky's and Mikhailov's portraits into a plot device — an implicit dead space between Vronsky and Anna where their love should be. When Mikhailov paints the portrait, Vronsky is particularly struck by its quality:

> After the fifth sitting the portrait struck everyone, and especially Vronsky, not only by its likeness but also by its beauty. It was strange that Mikhailov had been able to discover that special beauty. "One needed to know and love her as I love her, to find just that sweetest spiritual expression of hers," thought Vronsky, though he himself had only learnt to know that "sweetest spiritual expression" through the portrait. But the expression was so true that it seemed both to him and to others that hey had always known it (Norton, *Anna Karenina*, pp. 433-4).

The point is precisely that Vronsky, the possessor of Anna's passion and of her body, had never known her soul before, and that even now, in thinking that one had to love her "as I did" he fails to understand that he is a stranger, for it was not he who captured Anna's magic in a work of true art. Tolstoy then reinforces his point by having Vronsky himself paint a portrait of Anna — an artificial piece without the power to communicate anything. In the Tolstoyan world, this is a clear enough indication of the true nature of Vronsky's feelings toward Anna, namely that, in spite of their seeming intensity, they are nothing but lust. Vronsky himself, of course, never had any organ for perceiving things like that, and so, Mikhailov's lesson brought him no understanding:

> Anna's portrait, the same subject painted from nature by both of them, should have shown him the difference between Mikhailov and himself; but Vronsky did not see it. He merely left off painting Anna,

deciding that it would be superfluous now (*Anna Karenina*, Norton, p. 435).

Another character with a literary bent is, not surprisingly, Anna's brother Stiva. Occasionally, he likes to refer to Pushkin, or quote from Heinrich Heine, in such a way that he condemns himself out of his own mouth without, of course, understanding this at all. At dinner with Levin early in the novel, the conversation turns to marital fidelity. Stiva, who happens to be in the doghouse at home because of his latest affair with the French governess of his children, speaks quite happily of stealing sweet rolls even after a good meal, simply because they are so "irresistible." Then Stiva turns literary and quotes from Heine to support his view:

Himmlisch ist's wenn ich bezwungen
Meine irdische Begier;
Aber doch wenn's nicht gelungen
Hatt' ich auch recht hübsch Plaisir [20]
(Norton, p. 37)

The context in "Heimkehr" in which this verse is set speaks with irony and passion of love, illicit and legitimate, of the virtues of domesticity and of the poet's inspiration, described as an agony of desire. Poem No. 7, to which Stiva does not refer, contains lines that seem like a mocking commentary, sophisticated beyond Stiva's ken, of his own condition as a husband engaged in illicit and inconsequential dalliance:

In den Küssen, welche Lüge!
Welche Wonne in dem Schein!
Ach, wie süss ist das Betrügen,
Süsser das Betrogensein!

Stiva has no idea how bitter for Dolly is her "Betrogensein" and how little he himself deserves to inflict such suffering. This in a restaurant, eating oysters with Levin, while Dolly is crying her eyes out at home. What Tolstoy thought of Stiva's philosophy of life is quite succinctly expressed in one of the drafts of his letter to N.A. Aleksandrov in 1882 — a letter which in effect constitutes one of the preliminary approaches to the essay itself, and where he quotes Heine in the same version as Stiva's. Having said that it is very important to understand what art is and what it is not, Tolstoy then tells why we usually treat this topic so lightly:

We speak so lightly of it only because of our myopia,
or because of moral obtuseness, that is, because

Himmlisch ist's wenn... etc.; that is, because we love filth (*PSS*, *30*, 429).

We can see here how Heine's poetry is used as a bridge between the plane of fiction, where it helps to define Stiva as a character and also to establish the framework of moral values in the novel, and the plane of expository discourse, where it illustrates Tolstoy's thought about linkages between morality and art. The same principle holds true in the other references to literature, painting or music in Tolstoy's fiction.

The essay, of course, makes numerous particular references to music, painting and literature, especially to the French Symbolist and Decadent poetry. If we now shift our perspective and try to look at Tolstoy's own fiction through the prism of these references, we may be able to see if there are not indeed significant differences, either in specific techniques of Tolstoy's art, or in the source of his artistic imagination, which could help us understand his hostility toward modernistic art. By the same token, we might then be able to cast some additional light on Tolstoy's own art from this particular angle of vision. Especially useful for our purposes are Chapters X and XIII of *What Is Art?*, focused on modern French poetry and on the music of Wagner. Tolstoy does not develop a systematic theoretical position against French modernism, but rather leafs through some poems, making incidental observations, the main thrust of which is that this poetry seems designed to prevent, not to establish, communication of the kind important to Tolstoy, namely a spontaneous and universal sharing of feeling. His starting argument is that "the so-called art of the Decadents" came about as an ultimate consequence of the Renaissance, because at that time:

> when an artist composed for a small circle of people placed in exceptional conditions, or even for a single individual and his courtiers — for popes, cardinals, kings, dukes, queens, or for a king's mistress — he naturally aimed only at influencing these people, who were well known to him and lived in exceptional conditions familiar to him (*PSS, 30*, 89; Maude, 156).

This produced an art full of obscurities to the uninitiated, because it was based on allusions to what this special world knew about and therefore even found a certain "charm in the cloudiness of such a manner of expression." This method "reached its outer limits in the so-called art of the Decadents," and these are for the most part French and Belgian contemporaries of Tolstoy, such as Baudelaire, Verlaine, Mallarmé, or Maeterlinck.[21]

There were also Russian authors with connections to Symbolism and Decadence who perceived affinities between Tolstoy and these movements. According to E. Nuralov (*Èstetika L'va Tolstogo v ocenke kritiki*, pp. 154-5), even Dmitry Merezhkovsky, one of the best-known contemporary critics of Tolstoy thought that the Russian Symbolists "in their art continue the traditions of Tolstoy." Valery Bryusov, one of the first and most famous among the Russian Decadents, was so struck by Tolstoy's essay that he noted in his diary:

> The most important event these days is the appearance of Count L. Tolstoy's article about art. Tolstoy's ideas so much coincide with mine that at first I became desperate, wanted to write "letters to the editor," wanted to protest — but now I have calmed down and was satisfied with just a letter to L. Tolstoy himself.[22]

In complaining that the works of these poets even lack ordinary common sense, Tolstoy implicitly raises the issue of which of two alternative realities should be chosen as a measuring frame to validate artistic language: the reality of "life" or that of its artistically developed reflection in our imagination. Tolstoy bases his poetics on the illusion of actual life, achieved by the means of structuring a narrative discourse with minimal figurative deformations. While being against the conventionalization of language, Tolstoy did understand that the process by which experience and language become literary convention also describes the birth of metaphor. Then the search for some way to develop a literary language not based on the history of its tradition must lead to a point of decision about the uses of metaphor. This question: did Tolstoy use metaphorical language or did he not still looms very large in the minds of Tolstoyan scholars. Let us, at least for the moment, go with those who say he did make use of metaphorical language, but in a manner peculiar to himself, that is, in such a way that the very concept of metaphor became different from what it was generally supposed to be. First of all, he rejected the so-called "pathetic fallacy,"[23] as one of the most common means of conventionalization of figurative language. He refused to allow a confu-

sion between what is human and what is not, even if such confusion has become an accepted habit in a society that perceives the language of human communication as a set of rhetorical inanities. Quite early, in 1851, we find a note in Tolstoy's diary that says:
> I don't know how others daydream, but from what I have read and heard, they do it quite differently from me. Some say that, looking at beautiful nature, thoughts come about the greatness of God and the insignificance of man. Others say that *mountains, it seemed were saying something* and *the leaves something else again* and that *the trees were calling somewhere.* How can such thoughts occur? You have to work at it to stuff your head with such nonsense (*PSS, 46,* 80-81).

The issue itself may well be quite serious, for it pertains to our human solitude in a world where the trees and the mountains do not even have a consciousness to be aware of our existence. The use of pathetic fallacy may be thought of as an attempt to break this barrier between us and "the outside world" by means of make-believe that this world has crossed over to our "semantic space" and the barrier no longer matters, or even exists, or at least that we can mask our solitude by painting it over with images of communion with nature taken from literary convention. What Tolstoy tried to accomplish instead was to go in the opposite direction: not to make believe that the "world" is "us," but to establish that "we" are the "world." In practice, this meant constructing an entirely different kind of metaphorical language. This has been described by the Soviet scholar L.N. Kupreyanova as follows:
> A scrupulously pursued and accurately produced dynamic of perception accomplishes, in Tolstoy, the function of a trope, without the artificiality of the latter, that is, the function of making objective the internal by means of the external and of giving a human quality to the external... Tolstoy does not by any means neglect metaphorical constructs belonging to both artistic and everyday language, but uses them in a new way, extracting from the verbal metaphor its psychological root, its true meaning in the psychological sense. As a result of this operation, the language metaphor is renewed, acquires the meaning of

an artistic metaphor but without any artifice. Because its second, figurative meaning, being in its sense related not to the object of perception, but to its subject, loses its figurative character, expressing directly and accurately the logic inherent in language itself, of direct perception and associative thought (Kupreyanova, p. 152).

It may be rather difficult to demonstrate what the "true meaning" of an artistic metaphor might be in its psychological, rather than image-making aspect. The issue does pertain, however, to the matter of communicating what an author perceives to be direct truth rather than some artistic device — pretense or artifice. One passage in *Childhood* attempts to approach this whole dilemma by way of narrating a child's experience at a troubled moment of his life. The setting is the aftermath of a hunting party. Young Irtenyev took part in it, but failed his father and fellow-hunters by letting a rabbit escape, in part because he was overly excited, and also because his attention had been distracted by observations on the curious life of a microcosm of ants.[24] At home in the evening, Irtenyev tries, as it were, to expiate his shame and guilt by recreating the hunting scene in a drawing:

> It was already getting dark when we came home. *Maman* sat down at the piano, and we children brought our papers, pencils, crayons and settled down to drawing around the round table. I only had a blue crayon; in spite of this, I got the idea of depicting the hunt. Having very vividly depicted a blue boy riding a blue horse and blue dogs, I did not really know if one can draw a blue hare and ran off to the study to consult father about this. Father was reading something, and to my question: "are there blue rabbits?" answered, without raising his head: "yes, my good boy, there are." Having returned to the round table, I drew a blue hare and then found it necessary to make a shrub from that blue hare. I did not like the shrub; I made it into a tree; from the tree I made a cloud, and finally the whole paper became so smeared all over with the blue crayon that I got mad, tore it up and went to dream in the Voltairean chair (*Childhood*, p. 40).

By giving Irtenyev only a blue crayon to depict the whole scene, Tolstoy creates a "psychological metaphor"; the crayon becomes a material counterpart to his feeling of personal inadequacy. Another fact — that mother is playing the piano — reinforces and complicates this feeling. First of all, Irtenyev loved his mother with great lyrical intensity for her beauty and devotion to him. Sitting at the piano, she becomes a structural counterpart to the distant figure of the father in another room; both figures become in effect metaphorical representations of the emotional span between intimacy and isolation. Secondly, mother's skill at playing the piano contrasts with Irtenyev's failure and intensifies his solitude as he attempts somehow to "relive" and "put right" the unfortunate afternoon with just the one color in his hand. Thus, by just the setting alone, Tolstoy evokes in us the subtle and complex emotions experienced by the boy, and the plain factual descriptions acquire for us the quality of poetic images, metaphors in Kupreyanova's use of the term. Furthermore, young Irtenyev can depict the whole scene "very vividly," except for the hare — precisely the object of his failure. The hare is for him the emotionally significant, the "true" reality which cannot be conveyed in a reduced, figurative manner, in just one color. He then turns to his father for reassurance that there are indeed blue hares, that is, his crayon has not forced him to lie. The blend of sensitivity and naiveté in the boy as he runs off to ask his father (the authority, the competent, cold figure, one who does not fail) about the hare increases the reader's commitment to this complex, fragile soul and enables him to perceive Irtenyev's "mute catastrophe" when the father, without even looking up, tells him yes, there are blue hares — something which the boy now knows cannot be true, not, of course, because of the color itself, but because of the negligent indifference, permitting no emotional contact, with which his father answered him. By making us feel this betrayal together with the boy, Tolstoy has committed our imagination to his art as a writer and has raised this brief scene to the level of poetry, of something conveyed beyond the words, yet through their mediation, the way a metaphor does. We know exactly what Irtenyev means when he destroys his picture, passing from hare to shrub, to tree, to cloud, to tatters but we cannot name or comprehend this multifaceted, painful complex of emotions any more than the boy can. The magnitude of Irtenyev's depression becomes multiplied for us to the extent that we ourselves had become caught up in the description of the hunt and surrounding nature as it had been pouring into the large open windows of the boy's consciousness, appearing like some great living beast, or great living soul: the baying of hounds, the tension, the busy life of ants — both the large and the minuscule world crowding in on the mind, filling it with wonder and tenderness just as the deep-lying hunter's instinct asserts itself. It was all this that they boy now feels he failed to communicate, and an entire world was thus destroyed. In Tolstoy's hands, every detail of the scene becomes symbolic of this feeling and communicates on the level of imagery as well as of straight description.

This manner of metaphorization is characteristic of all of Tolstoy's early works, from *Childhood* to *Sevastopol' Tales*, to *The Cossacks*. In fact, his later works continue the development of the same device even as the depth and complexity of issues increase tremendously. In essence, this sort of appeal to the reader's imagination communicates the author's own personality at least as much it does as the text in question, so that the reader experiences both the author and his created world as one. Thus the specific qualities of Tolstoy's art, even in the early period, make inevitable his ultimate definition of art as the transmission of and infection with feeling. What Tolstoy actually depicts is his way of feeling the existence of the world, thus really himself. Tolstoy was aware of this implication when he noted in his diary in 1851 that "In reading a work, especially fiction, the main interest lies in the character of the author which expresses itself in the work" (*PSS, 46,* 182).

The quoted fragments of French Symbolist poetry, as they are seen by Tolstoy in the essay, do not seek such an effect at all and are in fact highly figurative not only in their metaphorical substitutions but also in that the very reality they deform is actually already a linguistic model, a compound of artistic codes developed in the ongoing tradition of art in our civilization. To take an example, one of the "Ariettes oubliées" by Verlaine which Tolstoy quotes disapprovingly in his essay begins as follows:

Dans l'interminable
Ennui de la plaine
La neige incertaine
Luit comme du sable
Le ciel est de cuivre,
Sans lueur aucune

On croirait voir vivre
Et mourir la lune.

The comparison of sand to snow rests on long-known associations in art between these two uncertain textures and the impermanence of life, the passing of time. The image of the waxing and waning moon in relation to unblinking, copper-hued sky, reinforces the relationship of contrast between deadly permanence and the transitoriness of living things. Further in the poem, we find indeterminate horizons of oak trees floating in the mist, of cloud-like forests, among which crows and wolves wander, their hunger unappeased, their mortality echoed by the now living, now dying moon. These predatory animal motifs, combined with associations that may be evoked by the shieldlike copper sky, could even permit the imagination to enter among forgotten lives of heroic quest and myth. A French critic has also noted a similar balance between the strict symmetry of the poem's structure and its indeterminate imagery which, paradoxically, even calls into question the reality of the landscape.[25]

Tolstoy, however, refuses to consider the text as written in the special language of artistic tradition within its own semantic field, where it constitutes a universe not only of meanings, but also of signs of other meanings. Instead, he simply looks at Verlaine's poem as if it were a direct attempt to convey an emotional response to actual landscapes seen in the world of non-literary reality:

> "How can the moon live and die in a copper sky, and how is it that snow can shine like sand? All this is no longer merely incomprehensible, but also, under the pretext of conveying a mood, presents a collection of false comparisons and terms" (Maude, 165; *PSS, 30*, 98).[26]

In Tolstoy, indeterminate and misty landscapes may also represent sign systems pointing beyond themselves to a variety of complex issues and associations. They will, however, be drawn directly from nature, without metaphorization, and their symbolic implications will emerge from their context and links with other elements in the structure of the narrative. We may take, for instance, the description of an early morning in *The Cossacks*:

> They could feel by the air that the sun had risen.
> The mist was clearing but it still enveloped the tops

of the trees, making the forest seem immensely high.
With every successive step things changed: what had
appeared to be a tree turned out to be a bush, and a
reed looked like a tree (Penguin classics, p. 244).

Here Olenin, guided by Erosha, is entering for the first time the thick forest in which, on another hunting day, he will have his great insight in the meaning of life as universal love. Reading this passage in the manner suitable to Verlaine, we might be permitted symbolic associations in our own mind with the "dark woods" of Dante's *Inferno* which also attended the beginning of a journey of moral discovery. With Tolstoy, however, what matters is that Olenin's great moral illumination — to live a life of love and sacrifice for others — turns out to be an illusion in the story, since Olenin's altruistic gestures will be totally misunderstood by the Cossacks as being devious selfish moves, as when Lukashka understood Olenin's gift of a horse to be in effect a sort of "payment" for Maryanka. In this context, the mist around the trees and bushes, creating the illusion that mere reeds are tall trees, encodes and prophecies Olenin's coming failure. We might also remember that the early morning mist just before the battle of Austerlitz had a similar artistic function of evil foreboding.

Verlaine suffers once more for his incomprehensibility in another "Ariette" containing the lines: "Cela resemble au cri doux/ que l'herbe agitée expire." The premise of such a metaphor is not common sense or verisimilitude, but the entire configuration of Symbolist thought around the notion of *correspondances*, itself an end product of a long line of images in the history of art, ranging from Ovid's *Metamorphoses*, with the human cry of anguish enchanted in trees and grass as the angry gods transform their human rivals, through medieval mystic symbolism implicit in the tapestries with *mille fleurs* which echo subtly and intricately the complex profundities of human and mythological events being portrayed, and finally, to the common romantic imagery of later time. Tolstoy will have none of all this. In his own works, the sounds made by grass are very different indeed from those in Verlaine. The readers of *Anna Karenina* might recall the faint crackling noise made by the grass pushing through last year's dry foliage, as Konstantin Levin hears it in his fields on a Springtime morning:

In the intervals of profound silence last year's leaves
were heard rustling, set in motion by the thawing of

the earth and the growth of the grass.
"Just fancy! One can hear and see the grass growing," thought Levin, as he noticed a wet slate-colored aspen leaf move close to the point of a blade of grass" (*Anna Karenina*, Norton, p. 148).

This is not an artistic image validated by tradition but an actual sound in nature. The emotion which here communicates itself to the reader comes, first, from the astonished recognition of how sensitive is Tolstoy's perception, and second, from the reader's knowledge that, at this point in the novel, Levin is painfully trying to teach himself solitude while life is opening out all around him. Then we begin to see the structural function of this little detail: the faint crackle of grass can eventually be recognized as a sign for the reader on the interpretative plane, and for Levin perhaps unconsciously, as a voice coming ultimately from the moral dimension.[27] Tolstoy understood that, in order to unite in a text both the depiction of reality and the meaning of the question "how to live?," the writer needs a context, a narrative structure that frames a single given experience. In the grand design of the novel, this faint crackle of the grass at this given moment is one of hundreds of little impressions which Tolstoy allows to accumulate in our minds, all of them growing into some sort of subliminal knowledge that Levin's solitude cannot endure, that the energy of life will overcome it and bring him and Kitty together again. When this happens, in an irresistible flood of joy, we have already been prepared by the author to comprehend the full depth of this inevitability.

In other words, Tolstoy works not through metaphorical deformations, as does Verlaine, but through the placement of delicately perceived facts exactly where they will link up with the most crucial events and with the most powerful emotional associations.[28] A similar effect is achieved with the help of another small sound, this time from *War and Peace*: the "i piti piti i titi" of the constantly rising and falling edifice of tiny glass needles which Prince Andrey sees in his delirium after being wounded at Borodino (Norton, *War and Peace*, 1022). A meaningless visual and auditory hallucination, it yet symbolizes the insubstantiality of intellectual constructs by which Andrey had tried to live, and in this sense serves as structural counterpart to the watery globe which Pierre sees in his crucial illuminating dream. The symbolic dimension of both arises from this juxtaposition and not from any metaphorical quality in the images themselves. In the literal context, Prince Andrey's cobwebs of brittle light may quite simply represent what his feverish eye can see in the reflection of dust particles in the air in the ebb and flow of flickering light in the hut, and the sound — just a delirious ringing in his ears, or perhaps a buzzing fly. Thus one might say, perhaps, that in Tolstoy it is not the metaphor which encodes reality, but reality which comprehends the potentiality of metaphorical meaning that may be realized as a structural function of given context. Pierre's dream is rather different in that the explained meaning of the watery globe is but a part of the dream itself, and the very word "understand" is a composite of two voices other than Pierre's: one is a memory in which the kindly old Swiss teacher speaks to him, and the other is the shout of a French soldier breaking through the thin partition from outside reality. Other components are the memory of Karataev, of whose death he becomes aware just as he sinks again into sleep and there into a totally fortuitous recollection of a summer evening with some Polish lady. There is also water, swimming, and sinking into deep sleep. Nevertheless, just as with Andrey's feverish visions, each of the parts in this complex is by itself not a symbol or a metaphor of anything, even the experience, in half-sleep, of perceiving the globe as a symbolic construct, but all of them are reality capable of encoding symbolic meaning, of configuring itself into a metaphor of Pierre's entire spiritual quest, thus also, implicitly, of the principle according to which the novel is structured (see Norton, *War and Peace*, pp. 1183-4).

Due to the very nature of artistic language, Tolstoy also could not avoid using various objects as figurative equivalents to human beings or to their states of mind. There is, however, a difference of principle which may be seen, for instance, in Baudelaire's use of the metaphor of roses as a signifier of a complex cultural and artistic tradition in the poem "Duellum" which Tolstoy quotes and utterly refuses to understand, as distinguished from Tolstoy's own treatment of people and flowers as mutually equivalent entities without bringing in an additional cultural dimension through metaphorization. Baudelaire writes like this:

> Dans le ravin hanté des chat-pards et des onces
> Nos héros, s'entreignant méchamment, ont roulé,
> Et leur peau fleurira l'aridité de ronces
> (*PSS*, *30*, 94; Maude, 161).

Torn, bloody skin, thorny brambles, roses. The full effect of this text requires our awareness of the symbolic function of thorns in the tradition of Christian imagery of faith which begins with the wreath of agony crowning the head of Christ. Suffering and holiness, linked with suffering, love and beauty, helped create the entire medieval system of symbolic references in which the status and ideals of knighthood, of knightly love, were frequently tied in with the images of hunt, and with animal representations of persons human and divine, as well as roses, thorns and various flowers. Indeed, the leopard, or panther, has been interpreted in medieval bestiaries as a symbol of Christ.[29] As Baudelaire enters this chain of images, his poetic language becomes completely metaphorical inside the framework of personal references and the artifices and artifacts of culture which constitute multiple subtexts both for the image and for the entire poem. Evidently, this requires a sufficient degree of knowledge and sophistication on the part of the reader, so that he could use his imagination to relate all such associations together in a meaningful whole.[30] Such a reader will be able to accept what Baudelaire offers, which is neither directly a description of reality nor exclusively the experience of any given individual, but beyond that an utterance that becomes an event, a new link in the ongoing history of culture in art. The poem "Duellum" has also been shown to have semantic links not only with the history and symbolism of art, but also with the pictorial dimension and also to refer to Baudelaire's own particular relationship with Jeanne Duval, the object of a number a of poems in *The Flowers of Evil*.[31]

In Tolstoy, on the other hand, when we do find imagery of blood and flowers together, it is placed in the context not of literary but moral issues, and therefore it pertains to the moral rather than literary history of mankind. For example, in the *Sevastopol' Tales* there is this landscape:

> Let us watch that ten-year-old boy, with an old worn cap on his head which doubtless belonged to his father, and with naked legs and large shoes on his feet, dressed in a pair of cotton trousers, held up by a single brace. He came out of the fortifications at the beginning of the truce. He has been walking about ever since on the low ground, examining with stupid curiosity the French soldiers and the dead bodies ly-

ing on the ground. He is gathering the little blue field-flowers with which the valley is strewn. He retracts his steps with a great bouquet, holding his nose so as not to smell the fetid odor that comes on the wind. Stopping near a heap of corpses, he looks a long time at a headless, hideous, dead man. After an examination, he goes near and touches he presses harder on it the arm moves and falls into place. The boy gives a cry, hides his face in the flowers, and enters the fortifications, running at full speed (Tolstoy, *Sebastopol*, Ann Arbor, 1961, pp. 107-8).

Everything in this passage refers directly to a depicted, and also historical, reality, and all relationships, associations, are adequately meaningful without reference to any outside set of signifiers from literary tradition. The aesthetic response expected of the reader is then such that it will lead to a moral understanding. The juxtaposition of corpses and flowers in the meadow is meant to arouse indignation at the horrible stupidity of mankind bent on self-destruction. That stupidity itself becomes, as it were, impersonated in the boy's face, even as it remains also a straight descriptive element. The boy, holding the flowers and touching the corpses, acts upon our minds as a literary metaphor would, that is in terms of the opening flower of life, its tender growth in youth, and its end in death, only after the sight depicted has evoked in us a feeling of moral shock that can turn our minds to generalizations about human nature and fate. From the very beginning of his concern with art Tolstoy did not perceive that the associations issuing from literary and cultural tradition constitute a particular reality which is to be imitated by the artist; he felt, rather, that the material reality and the reality of human feelings outside the realm of literary conventions is the true concern of the artist. As early as 1853 Tolstoy noted in his diary that the true basis for a literary work is an accumulation of observations from actual life, and not from other books:

The idea of writing down, on the basis of various books, one's own thoughts, observations and rules is altogether strange. It is much better to put everything down in a diary which one must attempt to keep regularly and accurately, than to write in such a way that the thing becomes a literary exercise for me and no more than entertainment for others. At the end of each month, looking over this diary, I can select and extract from it everything that may be remarkable (Tolstoy's diary, October 23, 1953. *PSS*, *46*, 179).

If the semiotic density of the French Decadents and Symbolists depends on signs that stand at the crossroads of many intersecting literary and artistic traditions, with Tolstoy, we have a very different process. The initial figure of speech may be quite direct and simple, clear without any subtexts, but then it will go on producing widening circles of associations surrounding a crucial experience in the life of a particular person.

Remembering again Baudelaire's flowers of blood, we may look at a detail from *Anna Karenina*. Describing how Kitty arrives at a ball, Tolstoy says that a staircase leading to the ballroom "was decorated with lackeys and flowers" (*Anna Karenina*, Norton, 70). Young Kitty, who is climbing this staircase, past all these lackeys looking like potted plants, is herself all dressed in fluffy white and looks just like a flower. This, however, will be the very evening when Vronsky, totally enchanted by Anna, will callously abandon Kitty, paying no heed to the expectations he had created that he will propose to her. Thus an image initially employed to convey the atmosphere of exciting promise for Kitty as she enters the festive hall develops in the end into a picture of lonely dejection. Much of the impact of Tolstoy's image resides in the perception that Kitty, as well as the footmen, human beings, are given not human, but object-functions — they become decorative details in the description of the place. Like with the dead soldiers of Sevastopol', the point is ultimately moral and deals with either physical or spiritual depersonalization of a human being, thus with an issue of moral purpose in art. This is fully consistent with the development of the plot, since the ballroom scene marks the beginning of Anna's tragic love affair and Kitty's painful liberation from her enchantment with Vronsky.[32] All such frames of reference, however, remain strictly within the novel itself and do not enter into any of the Baudelairean semantic fields, overgrown as these are with their bloody brambles. Similarly, the well-known passage in *War and Peace* about Prince Andrey and the oak tree in Spring does not expand toward any contexts of death and resurrection as these may have been established in literary tradition, but stays within the bounds of one individual's personal experience. The point is that the parallel between Andrey and the oak is not an instance of pathetic fallacy, or a metaphor, or even a simile developed by Tolstoy in his role as a narrator, but rather a direct insight into the thoughts and feelings of Andrey himself, for it is he, and not the author making poetic figures, who responds in this manner to nature, saying in his mind to the tree: "you are right a thousand times."

Considering the extensive quotations from French Symbolist poets, even if Tolstoy did sardonically choose their poems arbitrarily, "from page 28 each," some readers were curious why did Tolstoy not discuss any Russian poets in his essay; poets about whom he may safely be presumed to know more than about the French. Tolstoy did carry on extensive correspondence with one outstanding Russian poet, Afanasy Fet, and his letters do testify to his thorough knowledge and great sensitivity to Russian poetry, even if he did at times object to the genre as such. In Tolstoy's "Preface to the Novel by Polentz *Der Bütnerbauer*," written in 1898, the same year as the essay, there is a summary comment on Russian poets, which in spirit quite resembles his discussions of the French, being equally conservative and condemnatory of all latest developments:

> In Russian poetry, for instance, after Pushkin and Lermontov (one usually forgets about Tyutchev), the poets' glory was at first transferred to quite doubtful poets: Maikov, Polonsky and Fet, then to Nekrasov, who altogether lacked the poetic gift, then to the artificial, prosaic versifier Aleksey Tolstoy, then to the monotonous and weak Nadson, then to the altogether talentless Apukhtin, and then, after that, everything becomes mixed up together, and versifiers appear whose name is legion and who do not even know what poetry is, or what is the meaning of their verse and why they write it.[33]

It seems rather strange to have Fet included among dubious poets, for that is not the tenor of Tolstoy's correspondence with him. The denial of poetic talent to Nekrasov is also less than just. Nadson and Apukhtin, however, would very likely find fewer defenders than the other poets mentioned by Tolstoy. For him, their eroticism and superficial romanticism may also have looked like true signs of the decadence into which society of his time was sinking.[34]

From Tolstoy's comments about the French poets, one may perceive that he refuses, both in his essay and in his art, to follow the literary convention that substitutes metaphorical associations for an unmediated link between perception and reality. Tolstoy's argument is that only such "unadorned" writing can sustain the simplicity and truth of spontaneous human feeling, in his view, the only kind that can infect others. Consequently, he also avoids the intellectual mode of writing, because it is there that word games begin and the skills of artifice become more important than the telling of truth. What meaning there is in art must reside, for Tolstoy, in the quality of feeling being communicated and not in what Roman Jakobson once called the poetic function, that is, in the construction of poetic language as a message about itself. Tolstoy understood "message about itself" in art to mean "art for art's sake," a meaningless thing. Nevertheless, Jakobson's notion of poetic function continues to apply even to an artist like Tolstoy, who insists that a message is valid only if it says something important and sincerely felt, because even then it will move us only through the way it is formulated in artistic language. Understanding "poetic" to mean "borrowed" (see *PSS*, *30*, 116; Maude, p. 186), that is, to be merely a collection and rearrangement of other peoples' artistic devices, Tolstoy in his later writings increasingly sought the greatest possible simplicity of statement, without any aura of literariness around it, relying for communication on the content of his message, that is, on its moral significance. Such dramatic simplicity characterizes a number of scenes in his story *God Sees the Truth, but Waits* — one of the only two works of his acknowledged in *What Is Art?* to be good art. We may look at the following excerpt from that story to understand what Tolstoy meant. The story tells of a merchant, Aksenov, who is flogged and sent to Siberia for life because of a murder actually committed by another man. An honest and simple person, he is extremely hurt when he sees that all his acquaintances believe him to be guilty. Here is the moment when Aksenov understands that his wife also suspects him of murder:

> And she began to stroke his hair and said:
> — Vanya, my dearest, tell the truth to your own wife: did you do it?

> Aksenov said: "So, you too think I am guilty," covered his face with his hands and broke out in sobs. Then a soldier came and said that his wife and children have to go now. And Aksenov said goodbye to his family for the last time (*PSS, 21*, 248-249).

The emotional charge in the plain statement "a soldier came" has all the power of the most exalted rhetoric precisely because it contains no "art," no stylistic intensifiers that would point only to their own presence in the text. That soldier, seen from Aksenov's own perspective becomes, at that moment, the only and total reality, just like death was for Ivan Ilyich in his last few days. For Aksenov, and the reader, he is the single sign of the totality of his fate. Anything else added to this plain statement would be not only superfluous but even inherently absurd.

Nevertheless, this simplicity of statement remains, after all, an artistic device, thus also a kind of convention, because its effect depends upon great many thoughts and feelings arising from the context as structured by the author. This ability to make a single minute detail suggest a universe of meaning must be what Tolstoy had in mind when he spoke in his essay of the "wee bit" on which the distinction between art and non-art must rest. His earlier works, those he denounced as poor art, for instance, *Anna Karenina*, are also full of such single, yet universal atoms of experience, but the difference often is that there Tolstoy enters his text in his role as narrator to explain exactly how this instantaneous communication of feeling takes place. Let us look at the first time Kitty and Varenka meet in Germany:

> Every time they met, Kitty's eyes said: "Who are you? What are you? Surely you are the delightful creature I imagine you to be? But for heaven's sake — her look added — do not think that I shall force myself on you. (Norton, *Anna Karenina*, pp. 196 - 7)

Tolstoy does not say what Kitty *felt* — he stands outside of Kitty and verbalizes, decodes for us the meaning of her glance, thus turning from narrator to interpreter. If we overlook that slightly comic awkwardness of such a construction as "her look added," the effect of this passage can be unexpectedly powerful: we may get an impression how unfathomably rich must be this our human life in its totality if it takes so much telling about at any of its fleeting moments. Reflecting back upon Tolstoy's claim in the essay that true art communicates instantly and completely, we may now realize that this "instantaneous" event in essence resembles precisely the long narrative structure of the momentary encounter between Kitty's and Varenka's eyes.

In Tolstoy's works, we come upon such "universal moments" over and over again — moments like the first encounter between Anna Karenina and Vronsky, when just one touch of something special, as Vronsky felt it, in Anna's eyes,[35] implicitly contains the entire structure of the novel, that is, the fulfilled, predetermined destiny of both Vronsky and Anna. It is on that basis, one might think, that Tolstoy denied in his essay that art can be analyzed, explained, taught, as if its essence, and not its paraphernalia, were a thing made of many parts to be measured, counted and weighed against one another.

The difference between Tolstoy and what he called "modern" art, may actually be an issue of modeling. An artist who consciously works with the norms of literary convention, whether he follows or breaks them, is in effect building a model of his perception that art is something else than reality against the framework of other such models. Tolstoy, on the other hand, is interested in communicating the joy of his discovery that he and the world are really the same, and he builds a model not of art but of that emotion. The images of the world in Tolstoy are not encoded in the devices of artistic convention, nor do they reflect models of inner worlds themselves already deformed to represent some particular set of artistic conventions or devices of civilization. When the world does become deformed in Tolstoy, "made strange," it is in reference to some character's spiritual condition, feelings, and not in reference to other "literature." Natasha's reaction to the opera in *War and Peace* is a famous examples of such Tolstoyan deformation. Another good example is the description of Levin's and Kitty's euphoria at their second meeting that eventually led to betrothal:

> Everybody took part in the general conversation except Kitty and Levin. At first when the influence of one nation on another was talked about, thoughts of what he had to say on the subject involuntarily came into Levin's mind; but these thoughts formerly so important to him, now only flickered through his mind as in a dream and were not of the slightest interest. It even struck him as strange that they should

care to talk about things that could make no difference to anyone. In the same way what was being said about the rights of the education of women should have interested Kitty. How often she had thought about that question when she remembered her friend abroad and the irksome state of dependence in which Varenka lived, how often she had wondered what would be her own fate if she did not get married, and how many times she had argued about it with her sister. But now it did not interest her at all. She and Levin were carrying on their own separate conversation, and it was not even a conversation but a kind of mystic intercourse, which every moment bound them closer and closer and created in both a feeling of joyful fear before the unknown upon which they were entering (Norton, *Anna Karenina,*, 355).

A little later that very evening, Levin and Kitty, in their "mystical union," can communicate deep and complicated feelings to each other by simply writing down the first letters of each word they want to say.

This passage conveys precisely the kind of communication, infection with emotion that Tolstoy speaks of in his essay as the activity of art. Here we see something like a bridge arching between Levin and Kitty across the many long years of their separation to link them together again, and in such a way as to establish the unity of all human experience: art is really like love, love is the fullness of life itself, and the joyful perception of that fullness in mutual love is what Tolstoy actually means by "religious consciousness."

CHAPTER SIX

THE LEGACY AT HOME

The response of pre-Revolutionary Russian critics to Tolstoy's treatise was, on the whole, limited in its intellectual scope. Very few readers placed the treatise in the larger context of Tolstoy's total personality, his moral-philosophical quest, and his artistic works. Instead, the tendency was to consider the essay in the limited context of aesthetic theory and to respond to it on that level alone.[1] Having thus diminished the relevance of Tolstoy's essay to his art, the critics made it seem even smaller by chipping away at it each with his own set of professional tools brought over from any given area of competence or interest. Practicing artists felt that Tolstoy was speaking of the arts as if he were an amateur and not the great writer that he was;[2] philosophers and literary critics found his reasoning cloudy, his research superficial and unsystematic, and men of the cloth objected to his notion of religious consciousness which did not postulate a personal God in the traditional orthodox sense.[3]

Indeed, tradition understood as civilization — the accumulated thought and experience in philosophy, religion and the arts — was then (and still is) the shield separating in readers' eyes Tolstoy the artist from Tolstoy the theoretician of aesthetics. As an artist, he belonged within that tradition; he had met the generally established criteria of excellence in literature and was greatly admired by all. His thoughts on art, however, did not answer to the ideas and conventions developed in the discipline of aesthetics and seemed therefore to be unprofessional and even incomprehensible. This artificial distinction made by most of Tolstoy's friends, readers and critics effectively demonstrates the depth of his intellectual solitude. Tolstoy spoke as an individual alone, thinking matters through from the beginning, out of his great need to understand the truth in art as it must exist for him personally. His commentators, on the other hand, represented, gave expression to, conceptual systems and conventions that had accumulated around the topic of aesthetics in the history of civilization. The end result was that the Russian critics of the 1890s, as the Soviet scholar V. Zubov pointed out in 1929, failed to understand the essay as a document testifying to the inner drama of Tolstoy's life and "argued with Tolstoy's thoughts and propositions but not with Tolstoy."[4]

The response to Tolstoy's essay was for the most part focused upon the central issue of feeling as a decisive concept in the definition of art. Many critics were anxious to establish a distinction between feelings as they are ordinarily understood in life and the special aesthetic experience that can be called feeling in art. From this distinction it was possible to conclude that Tolstoy, by confusing the two kinds of emotion, assigned unwarranted breadth and depth of function to art in society. Instead of regarding art essentially as an ornament to civilization, requiring the development of a special sensibility and knowledge for its appreciation, he turned art into the central and universal human value, not in essence clearly distinguishable from religion. In the minds of some of the critics, this was a matter of distinction not only of aesthetic and "natural" feelings (almost, as it were, a matter of a "langue" and "parole" of emotions in art) but also of moral and aesthetic values in art, that is, basically, an issue of what Tolstoy meant, or should have meant, by "religious consciousness" as the highest aim of art. In this context, some critics defended the traditional notion that Beauty, the specific aesthetic encoding of all ultimate values, was the essence of art and the aesthetic counterpart of Religion, and that Tolstoy was again wrong in his moralistic stance of regarding Goodness alone as the criterion of ultimate value in both art and life. At least one critic, Lev Shestov, went so far as to imply that Tolstoy's essay on art, like, indeed, all his other works, amounted to a claim of sole possession of this Goodness — everything: goodness, religion, aesthetics and perhaps also beauty, were nothing else but just Tolstoy himself.

Tolstoy's proposition that art communicates and infects with feeling was understood too narrowly by many critics as pertaining to feeling in the special sphere of traditionally understood aesthetics alone. Taking this as a mere theoretical point made with insufficient precision, many critics soon became entangled in the complexities of establishing valid distinctions between feeling in life and feeling in art. Even while agreeing with Tolstoy that in human relationships art serves the need for sharing feelings — a task no less important than the cognitive function of language — it seemed difficult for the critics to accept the idea that there is only one kind of emotion for both art and life, as Tolstoy seemed to maintain, judging by such statements in *What Is Art?* as the following:

> The activity of art is based on the fact that a man receiving through his sense of hearing or sight another man's expression of feeling, is capable of experiencing the emotion which moved the man who expressed it. To take the simplest example: one man laughs and another who hears becomes merry, or a man weeps, and another who hears feels sorrow. A man is excited or irritated, and another man seeing him is brought to a similar state of mind.[5]

According to this "simplest example," infectious laughter would also be a work of art, or could at least be regarded as a product of artistic activity, a "text," as the Structuralists might call it. In opposition to that, Tolstoy's critics, maintained, as the musician V.T. Val'ter did in his book called *In Defense of Art* that:

> The creator of art experiences not real feelings, but reproduced, imagined ones ... and those who become affected by art experience not real feelings but aesthetic ones.[6]

The difference between "real" and "aesthetic" feelings Val'ter describes in terms not very different from Immanuel Kant's notion of art as "Vergnügen ohne Begehren":

> Feelings evoked by art are aesthetic feelings, which differ from the real ones in that they are not accompanied by longing (desire to acquire an object) nor by fear (however terrible the thing depicted) nor by suffering. Esthetic feelings are only feelings in the sense of a game, and this is why they are always accompanied by an element of pleasure.[7]

As Mr. Val'ter was a musician, it might be a propos to accompany his remarks with those of Pozdnyshev, Tolstoy's main hero in *Kreutzer Sonata*, who stated very insistently that in music, precisely, the aesthetic feelings indeed *are* accompanied by longings, and that the impossibility of fulfilling these longings in society is the whole problem with music:

> Take that *Kreutzer Sonata*, for instance, how can that first presto be played in a drawing-room among ladies in low-necked dresses? To hear that played, to clap a little, and then to eat ices and talk of the latest scandal? Such things should only be played on certain important significant occasions, and then only when certain actions answering to such music are wanted; play it then and do what the music has moved you to. Otherwise an awakening of energy and feeling unsuited both to the time and the place, to which no outlet is given, cannot but act harmfully (Maude, "Kreutzer Sonata," *The Death of Ivan Ilyich and Other Stories*, p. 220).

Herein lies the distinction: what for Val'ter is a game, for Pozdnyshev is very serious business indeed, and for Tolstoy, his creator, there is no justification for art that does not take itself thus seriously.

The idea that art resembles a game, and that the pleasure, the emotion inherent in creating an artistic structure emerges from the way in which this "game" is played, implies a reversal of the Tolstoyan sequence in which the point of origin is a genuine human emotion rooted in life itself which then stimulates artistic creation. Now we first have the game of art, and only then comes the aesthetic feeling which is itself the child of pretense in its inception and of artifice in its accomplishment. In this context, D.N. Tsertelev, a well-known conservative critic and editor of the journal *Russkoe obozrenie* (The Russian Review), answered Tolstoy's idea that no feelings can be transmitted unless they are experienced by the artist himself with the observation that, for an artist, a reduced clue, implicit in a given fictional situation, is enough to reproduce, actually to create, the complete emotional experience. A propos of Tolstoy's story "Master and Man" Tsertelev wrote:

> Did the author ever actually experience the perceptions and feelings experienced by the freezing master? Of course not, but this is not necessary, either: one hint was enough for him to have these two people and the surrounding setting present themselves clearly to his imagination, even if their inner world was so dissimilar from his own.[8]

If we consider that "Master and Man" may well convey Tolstoy's own great moral anguish, his remorse over the fact that he, as a member of the ruling class, has failed to perceive humanity in the "slaves" who often were ready to give up their lives for him, we may understand that the realities of Tolstoy's troubled conscience may well be directly commensurate with the imagined sensations of the "freezing master." It is not really a question, as Tsertelev put it, of having a small clue from which to create a complete physical illusion; what we have is the described sensation of the body functioning as a metaphor for the anguish of the spirit that was a moral reality, and not a "game" of artifice.

The point remains, however, that Tolstoy's critics wished to separate clearly the communication of real emotions from the creation of an artistic experience. N.K. Mikhailovsky, an important populist critic and editor of the journals *Obshchestvennye zapiski* (Notes on Society) and *Russkoe bogatstvo* (The Russian treasure), stated the issue as follows:

> Art expresses not direct feelings, but reflected ones, and all good works of art give an illusion, as complete as possible according to the ability of a given branch of art, but still an illusion. And we know this.[9]

Ultimately, this entire issue comes back to the distinction between true and counterfeit art in Tolstoy's essay. The illusion of a feeling must be created by manipulating aesthetic signs according to the rules immanent in the game of art. In doing so, the artist enters aesthetic tradition, the history of artistic devices, and works from within it. In his essay, Tolstoy described such a process as one of producing counterfeit art. The counterfeit is the imitation, illusion of feeling, and the false art which is built on that has no significance at all in view of anything important, like, for instance, the question asked by the itinerant mendicant Grisha in Tolstoy's *Youth*: "how shall I live?"

The placing of art in a dimension autonomous to itself will tend to reduce the function of art in life. Some of Tolstoy's critics understood this and indeed asserted that it should be so. To them it seemed that Tolstoy had deprived art of its proper place, which is to be essentially a marginal activity, a relatively secondary component in the structure of civilization. The critics felt that Tolstoy had thrust art to the very center of human affairs instead of accepting it in its minor, "Aristotelian" function — to amuse and to instruct. "Art is only a small branch of life," said one critic, D.S. Trizna, "but to Count Tolstoy it is the kernel of life"[10] and therefore Tolstoy is prey to exaggerated hopes of "establishing a paradise on earth with the help of art." Trizna also argues, rather like Tolstoy himself has done in his works, that organic living necessities, and the logic of facts and phenomena, rather than the artifices of aesthetics, are what determines the course of life. He fails, however, to complete the connection between Tolstoy's art and his thought on art, to perceive it as a continuum of one and the same flow of reality in the mind.

If art is not to be something inherent in the very processes of living, but rather a superstructure, or an ornament upon the edifice of civilization, then the question of what it has to communicate, and indeed, the importance of communication in itself, acquires a different aspect from that understood by Tolstoy. The process of creation becomes more of an artist's dialogue with himself than an exchange of messages with others. On such grounds, V.A. Posse, the editor of the journal *Zhizn' dlya vsekh*, (Life for All) who, perhaps ironically, had published a number of Tolstoy's late works, including *What is Art?*, objected to Tolstoy's definition of art in principle, because it stresses the communicative rather than the creative function:

> ...in a definition of art, the center of gravity must be transferred to the aspect of creation and not to the aspect of reception by a listener, viewer or reader of the artist's work.[11]

Naturally, such a transfer reduces the circle of an artist's audience and changes its composition: now it must consist of those who have the training and education to decode an artist's dialogue with himself; creating and sharing art becomes the activity of a select intellectual elite. Tolstoy's own views were radically opposed to this. In his opinion, the universal accessibility of art is related to its moral purpose because art, in essence, serves not only as a vehicle for the communication of feelings, but also as an embodiment of man's relationship to God:

> People talk about incomprehensibility; but if art is the transmission of feeling flowing from man's religious perception, how can a feeling be incomprehensible which is founded on religion, that is, on man's relationship to God? Such art should be, and

has actually been, comprehensible to everybody, because every man's relation to God is one and the same (Maude, p. 178)

These ideas encountered critical comments from several directions. Ya. Borisov, writing in the periodical *Russkaya mysl'*, (Russian thought) perceived an inconsistency in Tolstoy's thought concerning the stewardship of moral values by the broad masses of people on the one hand, and the achievement of religious consciousness — the highest aim of art — on the other:

> Count Tolstoy himself says that the feelings of brotherhood and love are accessible at the present time only to the few best people. In that case, a work of art which expresses such feelings is not universally accessible at the present time.[12]

The inconsistency is only here, however, if by "the best people" Borisov means those distinguished by talent and education, thus also by their social standing. Tolstoy, on the other hand, found his "best people" from among the peasants, pilgrims and homeless wanderers whose wisdom was not a personal quality, but a state which they had reached by listening to the voice of God inside them. Yet, the problem of communication — how is one individual who has lived through the intense experience of a new insight to convey that insight to all others — was one of the most troublesome and complex problems Tolstoy had to face both as a moralist and as an artist.

Another critic, F.D. Batyushkov, understood better Tolstoy's intent to point up the difference between the corrupt values, of the privileged classes, and the sane moral sense of the working people, but he then extended the concept of "work" beyond Tolstoy's limitations to manual labor, especially by the peasants.[13] Batyushkov's own criticism is directed against the identification of moral with aesthetic values by Tolstoy. He points out that:

> Esthetic emotion, of course, is not the same thing as moral feeling, and it happens quite often that the pursuit of beauty may turn into a retreat from goodness. But from this one cannot deduce the concept, referred to repeatedly by L.N. Tolstoy, of an incompatibility of the one with the other (*ibid.*, p. 22).

This confuses the issue: Tolstoy held the concept of "beauty" inapplicable toward the definition of art but not necessarily incompatible with goodness. It is the false, counterfeit art, which has embraced the notion of beauty and, for Tolstoy, thus also of pleasure, that is incompatible with goodness. N. Mikhailovsky went even further and suggested that the art of the masses, like that of the privileged minority, has also preferred the pursuit of pleasure to a moral ideal. In fact, it may well have been the educated classes which tried to enforce moral values in art, while the people themselves regarded it as mere entertainment:

> It is clear that the people, before the time of Peter I as well as afterwards, not only did not reject pleasure in art, but, on the contrary, sought it, and it was the persons with book learning in positions of power who struggled diligently but in vain against it in the name of an ascetic ideal.[14]

Mikhailovsky added that there are many erotic elements in the folklore of simple people, so that even "lust" is not the exclusive province of the art of the spoiled rich. As for the depth and profundity of the art of the common people, (in Tolstoyan terms, ultimately its moral value), as against the art of educated classes, Batyushkov observed the following:

> If Tolstoy is referring to certain tales and legends which have now become the property of the people, then the question of their origin is quite complex. Precisely those legends which strike us by the depth of their content and the elevation of their moral image in most cases have penetrated down among the people instead of being created by them.[15]

It is hard to say which tales or legends Batyushkov had in mind, but whatever the case may be, both he and Mikhailovsky have raised some valid points. Many of the popular tales in old Russian literature, in particular the picaresque adventure stories, and also the lives of saints, can ultimately be traced to West European written sources. The Russian folk tales, on the other hand, contain as many elements of universal human greed, cruelty and hedonism as they do of universal wisdom. Even the most important Russian folk creations, the ancient heroic epics, the *byliny*, singing the deeds of real and imaginary heroes of the past, are as full of human foibles as of moral awareness of the highest sort.

The idea that the art which is understood and enjoyed by the working masses is not necessarily distinguished by any great striving for virtue is consistent with the denial in principle of moral purpose as an essential quality of art. The critics of Tolstoy's treatise understood this and followed through the implications of their position explicitly, just as they had argued that aesthetic feelings are not the same as feelings in real life, for which a person may be morally responsible. The musician Val'ter said that "the moral influence of art is doubtful because feelings aroused by art do not lead to actions which real feelings of the same kind would provoke."[16] D.N. Tsertelev also separated the notion of quality in art from that of moral value:

> There may be in art works whose aesthetic excellence cannot be disputed, even if their enjoyment is connected with unhealthy or immoral impressions.[17]

Some of Tolstoy's critics tried to show that beauty can indeed be regarded as a moral and philosophical norm and thus a suitable cornerstone for a system of aesthetics. This was the opinion of N.K. Mikhailovsky, who wrote that there have been formulations of aesthetic theory where "the idea of a so-called objective beauty is replaced by the idea that there are things which *must* please."[18] He also gave ground to Tolstoy on the question of pleasure, agreeing that mere pleasure does not exhaust the purposes of art. However, he insisted that pleasure does belong to the sphere of art: "Art is not pleasure — these two concepts do not cover each other; however, pleasure is the necessary condition of art" (*ibid.*, p. 142). Moreover, pleasure, for Mikhailovsky was a much nobler concept than the hedonistic drive for satisfaction which Tolstoy understood it to be, because in the works of art it included a special kind of suffering: "The point is," said Mikhailovsky:

> that infectiousness does, after all, follow pleasure in art, and it is pleasure of two kinds: first of all, it is aesthetic, and secondly, it is a special, very complex, often frightening pleasure which borders on suffering and which we experience in empathy with someone's life or with certain moments in it (*ibid.*, p. 138).

D.N. Tsertelev did not challenge Tolstoy on the point that in art aesthetics must be subordinate to ethics. But, whereas for Tolstoy the moral purpose of art — to bring people together in love — was a quite different thing from beauty, Tsertelev, following the aesthetics of German idealism, elevated beauty itself to the status of moral value. The unification of people, said Tsertelev, "is by far not the final purpose, not the ultimate ideal, but only a transitional stage, a brief moment in the striving for the eternal," and therefore "the concept of art as an expression of eternal beauty is incomparably higher than the notion that art is a means for bringing people together."[19] The metaphysical view of the moral dimension in beauty was shared by F.Ya. Batyushkov. He first of all rejected Tolstoy's statement that beauty is, after all, a subjective matter. "One can only compare that which pleases," said Batyushkov "with that which is useful but not with the highest definition of good as a metaphysical concept." In his essay Tolstoy had denounced the "Baumgartenian Trinity" of Goodness, Beauty, and Truth, according to which it appears that the very best that can be done by the art of nations after 1900 years of Christian teaching is to choose as the ideal of their life the ideal that was held by a small semi-savage, slave-holding people who lived 2000 years ago, imitated the nude human body extremely well, and erected buildings pleasant to look at (*PSS*, *30*, 78; Maude, p. 140). Batyushkov, quite to the contrary, proceeds to expound the proposition that love, truth and beauty are in essence the same thing in their highest, ideal conception:

> Why shouldn't we acknowledge that there is beauty which cannot be defined by reason, in the highest meaning of the word, as there is goodness in its highest sense? The good is elevated over the concept of usefulness, or advantage, by that element of love which we contribute to it, love which serves as a counterpoint to egoistical advantage and to the self-preserving instinct of searching for usefulness only for oneself. And in beauty, in the highest meaning of the word, such an element is truth, which inspires us see that not everything is beautiful which pleases but only that which is truthful, that which does not always exist but must come, and this striving for the highest artistic truth is the only level of art, not of all art, of course, but of the best and true art.[20]

In constructing his equation: goodness-love, beauty-truth, Batyushkov apparently aimed to reestablish the validity of the ancient Greek ideals by adding to them the specifically Christian element of love. Tolstoy, however, proceeded from entirely different premises. Unlike Batyushkov, in whose view goodness and truth in art existed most ideally in their aspect as beauty, Tolstoy took goodness to be the striving toward God, the highest aim of life and thus something quite separate from beauty and truth which are concepts of a much lower order and cannot be put on the same level with goodness without confusing the issue altogether. Beauty is that which happens to please, and it has no moral quality at all:

> I know that to this people always reply that there is a moral and spiritual beauty, but this is merely playing with words, for by spiritual and moral beauty nothing else is understood but goodness (*PSS 30*, 79; Maude, 141).

Truth, in turn, is nothing but the correspondence of "an expression or of the definition of an object, with reality, or with an understanding of the object common to everyone, and therefore it is a means of arriving at the good" (Maude, p. 142). Furthermore, for Tolstoy goodness was a concept "which cannot be defined by anything else but which defines everything else." Goodness so understood acquires the character of an absolute, because usually one refers to God Himself as that which is indefinable but defines everything else. What Tolstoy says, in effect, is that in itself the striving toward God is goodness, is God — a dynamic conception of deity not as a static entity but as man's progress toward his own perfection. In Tolstoy's equation, as opposed to that of Batyushkov and the Romantics, goodness, love and God (not goodness, truth and beauty) become in essence one and the same thing, and they all amount to a striving, a movement, a historical process.[21]

A similar discrepancy of thought emerges from the critical comments concerning that which Tolstoy considered the highest purpose of art — the achievement and communication of religious consciousness. In the essay, religious consciousness is described as follows:

> Humanity unceasingly moves forward from a lower, more partial and obscure, understanding of life to one more general and more lucid. And in this as in every movement there are leaders — those who have understood the meaning of life more clearly than others — and of these advanced men there is always one who has in his words and by his life expressed this meaning more clearly, lucidly, and strongly, than others. This man's expression of the

meaning of life, together with those superstitions, traditions, and ceremonies, which usually form around such a man, is what is called a religion (*PSS*, *30*, 68; Maude, p. 127).

Again, the critics did not really speak to this point at all, but instead discussed the established notions of religion and its relationship to man as if that were what Tolstoy was talking about. There exists, for instance, a set of ideas sanctified by religious convention having to do with man's imperfection, his fall from grace, his consequent failure to embody religious values as an absolute ideal. From this framework, the critic V.N. Mochul'sky dismissed as utopian in principle Tolstoy's demand that art should contain the expression of Christianity:

The Christian ideal is so high, and the value of life is so low and sad that the implementation of Christian ideals on earth is, for the time being, a utopia. In the same way, many scientific and social theories are utopian as well. And to demand after this that art should be an expression of religious consciousness amounts, in my opinion, to playing games in Utopia.[22]

The critic Ya. Borisov spoke from another set of intellectual conventions, according to which religious teaching, and consequently also religious consciousness, is understood to emanate from the various churches and systems of faith. Failing to perceive that for Tolstoy religious consciousness is something outside such systems, Borisov reproached Tolstoy for not understanding that religious consciousness is not a matter of any set of religious beliefs:

Count Tolstoy acknowledges that a religious teaching may be false, but the art which arises from such false or distorted teaching will be true nevertheless, because it corresponds to the religious consciousness of the people.[23]

Actually, Tolstoy understood that very well. What Borisov failed to grasp, on the other hand, was that by "religious consciousness" Tolstoy did not at all mean religiosity in the generally accepted sense, as an emotion or faith issuing from the ambience of a particular church or ritual. The Russian people had God in their hearts, and that sort of consciousness has nothing to do with the piety of the faithful. In the opinion of another critic, P.K. Engelmeier, however, Tolstoy's very idea that such a religious awareness develops independently of church doctrine is wrong. When Tolstoy spoke of understanding the meaning, i.e., the purpose of life, he was not dealing with any "conceptions" that can be "constructed," but Engelmeier thinks that he was:

> Another weak point in Tolstoy's teaching is that he considers "the understanding of the purpose of life" to be something unique, clear and indisputable and therefore obligatory for a given time and society. Of course, if we postulate Revelation, then this could be asserted, but Tolstoy thinks that this conception of the purpose of life is constructed by us in the same way as any other conception.[24]

For Tolstoy, that purpose is clear enough in every true peasant's heart, but it cannot be encoded either in some Revelation, or some theological doctrine, or in any rational construct. He wrote of God, art and man not as a prophet to whom God's truth has been revealed but as a seeker, from his own compelling vision. Failing to understand that Tolstoy was only trying to explain clearly what he saw as truth, his readers decided that he was himself usurping that throne of authority from which he had removed the image of God and the wisdom of men. To Mikhailovsky, Tolstoy became a ruthless tyrant:

> One would hardly find any anyone to equal Count Tolstoy in arrogant self-assurance and intolerance. The most despotic arbitrariness, cruel and merciless, holds sway in all his later works. It does not bother him in the least to cripple, distort or dismiss altogether any manifestation of life if it so pleases his own capricious thought.[25]

What Mikhailovsky terms "capricious" is really the fact that, whatever the profundity of Tolstoy's thought, he could never join the ranks of objective scholars as his critics understood, and we still understand, scholarship. He did not contribute to the pyramid of accumulated thought — he burrowed under it to question the validity of its foundations. Moreover, according to some, as an acknowledged creative artist, Tolstoy should not have tried to enter the precincts of scholarship at all. Engelmeier puts Tolstoy back in his place with a touch of pathos and sarcasm:

> But the great change in Tolstoy came about because he himself suddenly began to despise his highest, rarest and most useful gift from heaven and conceived a thirst, at any price, for another kind of glory, the glory of a thinker, a scholar, a learned man of letters.[26]

Actually one may say that in his thoughts on art Tolstoy drew his confidence not from any authoritative self-image as a scholar, but from what he saw as the spontaneous understanding of a simple working man. It is, of course, another question whether or not such a truth-bearing common man was, after all, just a figment of Tolstoy's imagination. Some of Tolstoy's critics, for instance, Mikhailovsky, did suspect this to be the case and challenged his intellectual honesty:

> It appears as if he were extremely democratic in inviting us to listen to the voice of nine-tenths or 99/100 of all mankind and to be ashamed before this multimillion voice. But actually it is his personal voice, and he, like Louis XIV, who asserted that "l'état c'est moi," could have said: 99/100 of all mankind is me."[27]

The point that Tolstoy presumed to speak for the masses without by some method finding out what they really thought is well taken but in essence not very relevant to the issue at hand. Tolstoy had a sense that some things, perhaps the most important, are naturally and instinctively true before the process of ratiocination can becloud matters, and he perceived of it not as his own infallibility, but as the infallibility of nature, where an animal, say, knows exactly where to look for food, and so does a simple human being know exactly what is true art.[28]

The famous Russian philosopher-critic Lev Shestov went even further and, in his book *The Good in the Teaching of Count Tolstoy and F. Nietzsche* in essence accused Tolstoy of moral hypocrisy as well. It was a very special kind of hypocrisy: not that Tolstoy was evil and pretended to be good, but that he pretended to give voice to the moral values of mankind in its entirety while actually usurping them all to himself. "Tolstoy," said Shestov, "does not describe life; he interrogates it," like a prosecutor, in the name of moral goodness, of which he feels entitled to be the arbiter. This according to Shestov, was already evident event in Tolstoy's manner of living. When he took up the plow in allegiance to the exploited peasants, this did not help the peasants any but it did enable Tolstoy himself to feel that he is now engaged in a meaningful and morally good activity. Similarly, all of Tolstoy's philosophy, including his theories on art, seemed to Shestov a defense of his right to goodness:

> There is one thing that he [Tolstoy] will not give up, and that is his right to moral good. If there be any encroachment upon this right, Count Tolstoy will show the same greed for it as Shakespeare's Henry V did when it was a matter of glory. They both — Count Tolstoy and Henry V — think that in their given case greed is not a failing, and that not only can they not be reproached for it, but it must be considered a virtue of theirs.[29]

And so, in Shestov's opinion, the whole purpose of Tolstoy's essay on art is "to proclaim to people: you are immoral, but I am moral, that is, the highest good is with me and not with you (*ibid.*, p. 59). That may be an interesting idea, but Shestov conceives it too narrowly, too much for the forensic effect of his bold attack on Tolstoy. Having gotten this much satisfaction, he also misses the point that could have made his thought much more significant, namely, that it is not an issue of Tolstoy's moral arrogance, but rather of the form and substance of his entire personality, of the total unity of his art, conscience and thought. Tolstoy did not claim any exclusive moral excellence; rather he made a tremendous effort to be totally and completely himself in all he was and did, and thus he became a universe. The English critic Vernon Lee understood this better than Shestov when he looked at Tolstoy in terms of the overpowering single-mindedness of certain great men:

> For it would seem — we notice it in two other great lay prophets, Carlyle and Ruskin — that the gift of seeing through the accepted falsehoods of the present, and foretelling the improbable realities of the future, can arise only in creatures too far overpowered by their own magnificent nature to understand other men's ways of being and thinking; in minds so bent upon how things should be as to lose sight of how things are and how things came to be.[30]

Shestov must be credited at least with some understanding

that this is so. His spirited essay is different from most other prerevolutionary Russian responses to Tolstoy's treatise on aesthetics in that he places Tolstoy's thoughts on art in the larger context of his personal development and his fictional works. Shestov noted, for instance, that Tolstoy's relentless moral imperative, permeating his aesthetics, is also characteristic of everything else he wrote late in his life. But Shestov could only understand Tolstoy's thrust as an effort to impose himself upon his readers: "All of Count Tolstoy's works in recent years, even the artistic ones, have an exclusive purpose: to make the world-view he had worked out obligatory to all people" (*Shestov*, p. 20). This, in turn, led Shestov to the naive notion that Tolstoy's passion for goodness as an exclusive personal possession has made him cold and cruel to those of his fictional characters who embody an appetite for life which he had come to reject, as for instance, does Anna Karenina:

> This may appear strange to Count Tolstoy, but many readers reproach him for coldness, insensitivity, callousness. To lead Anna Karenina under the train without a sigh! To follow the agony of Ivan Ilyich without a tear! This seems to many readers incomprehensible and outrageous to such a degree that they are even ready to withdraw recognition of artistic genius from Count Tolstoy (*ibid.*, p. 31).

On this point of righteous cruelty, Shestov compares Tolstoy to both Dostoevsky and Nietzsche. Tolstoy and Nietzsche, according to Shestov, liked Dostoevsky for opposite reasons, but still also for his "cruel talent":

> The underground thoughts of the first part of *Crime and Punishment* were close to Nietzsche. He himself, ever since he became hopelessly ill, could only see the world and its people from his own underground, and to substitute thoughts of power for real power. He readily forgave Dostoevsky for the second part — punishment, because of the first, the crime. Count Tolstoy, on the other hand, forgave the first part because of the second (*ibid.*, pp. 68-69).

It almost seems that, according to Shestov, if Dostoevsky was the great "criminal" in Russian literature, Tolstoy was the great punisher, merciless for moral reasons. In that sense, *What Is Art?*, would also amount to such a punishment of society as a whole, or at least a vehement attack on it from moral positions incomprehensible to the social establishment:

> In his book *What Is Art?* Count Tolstoy, not for the first time, but with all the passion of a man fighting his first battle, attacks the contemporary society. The book is called *What Is Art?*, but no special argument is needed to understand that the real question is not one of art, that it isn't art which occupies the author's mind. Count Tolstoy says that this work was conceived 15 years ago but could not be completed because his thoughts on the subject were not completely clear to him then. In essence, this is not quite so. Fifteen years ago there appeared an article by Count Tolstoy called "Thoughts evoked by a Correspondence in Moscow," and the basic propositions of *What Is Art?* were already fully expressed in it. That spiritual storm which tore Count Tolstoy away from Russian intelligentsia and took him to alien shores, where he learned to speak words strange and alien to us is a matter of times now long past. *What Is Art* is only a concluding word in a long sermon that was begun many years ago (*ibid.*, pp. 19-20).

Shestov thought that the basic driving force of Tolstoy's work was not really Christian love, as so many people had assumed, but a kind of rage against the incomprehensibility of life:

> For this reason, he does not see anything good in the contemporary society, in the people of his circle. He does not need the good, he needs the bad so he would have someone upon whom to vent the fury which has accumulated in his heart against the mysterious and stubborn insolubility of torturous questions of life. In spite of the fact that he always refers to the Gospel, there is very little of the Christian spirit in his teaching (*Ibid.*, p. 94).

There is an inner void, a lack of faith in Tolstoy, thinks Shestov, and Tolstoy's work is built over this void:

> Count Tolstoy thinks it possible not to tell his pupils of that emptiness in his heart over which he erected the structure of his teaching, so brilliant in its literary aspect (*ibid.*, p. 118).

We may say at least this for Shestov: he understood something that certain other critics of Tolstoy did not clearly see. Tolstoy's essay on art is not in essence just a treatise on aesthetics containing all its basic premises within itself alone. The reasons for any given opinions of good and bad art stated in the essay will often originate in Tolstoy's thoughts and feelings of long time past which were then not necessarily in any way connected with aesthetics as a specific intellectual discipline. Thus, Tolstoy's ideas expressed in the essay cannot be properly discussed without thinking of his art in general and of his inner struggles, his challenge to society.

Whether or not Tolstoy spoke from an inner void in all his works, including his essay on art, may be difficult to decide. It would seem simpler to look at the question in a somewhat different way. If Tolstoy's critics, the representatives of modern civilization which Tolstoy considered perverted, were to accept his ideas as to the meaninglessness of their lives, then indeed they would have nothing left to believe in, and it might seem to them that they are looking at a void. Not being able to conceive of other sets of moral values than the ones nurtured by the conventions of civilization and established religion over the centuries, they could not understand what Tolstoy really stood for, and thought, with Shestov, that he also had no faith.

This entire mode of talking about Tolstoy in terms of the rightness or wrongness of his views on art, religion, and morality without the restraint of a rigid intellectual horizon imposed on the critics from outside, came to an end with the Bolshevik revolution. The Soviet regime changed the context in which literature was to be read in general and the nineteenth-century Russian masters in particular. It provided a comprehensive ideology reaching into all aspects of life with its own standards and avenues of approach toward the work of all past writers including, of course, Tolstoy. Tolstoy's ideas on art could be of very special interest to Soviet scholarship, because on at least one basic matter and a number of subsidiary issues they could be seen to run a tantalizing parallel with the governing assumptions of Marxist aesthetics. The basic similarity between the Marxist and the Tolstoyan approach is that the definition of art must satisfy the demands of some philosophical or political principle extraneous to art itself. Art could not be assumed, or permitted, to have a capacity for self-definition on its own terms that would continuously evolve from the accumulating substance of meaning achieved in artistic practice. The real question for both Tolstoy and a Soviet ideologist was how to establish some general rules for judging both overall trends and individual artists. As R.F. Christian points out:

> Aesthetics is less helpful than art criticism when it comes to understanding art. But if Art with a capital A is meaningless, how can individual works of art be meaningful? This is the question which tormented Tolstoy and he would not have been satisfied to have been told that it was not the right question to ask. That it is still being asked and that a solution to it is still being sought in terms as comprehensive, dogmatic and socially oriented as Tolstoy's is evident from the writings of the exponents of Socialist Realism. For, like Tolstoy, they acknowledge that the power of art for good or evil is so great that it must be forced to serve society, not the pleasures of the ruling few. Where Tolstoy saw art as a quasi-religious activity whose object was to promote the brotherhood of man, socialist Realism assigns to it the secular goal of the brotherhood of socialist man.[31]

With Tolstoy, the answer to the question "what is art?" came from a lifelong search for the meaning of life reflected in both his artistic works and in his moral philosophy. The Soviets elaborated their ideas on what art should be during the years of revolution, "dictatorship of the proletariat" and systematic regimentation of all aspects of life in support of the regime. Both have therefore acquired from their respective experiences a sense of conviction, of inevitable rightness of their stand on all issues of life, including judgments on art, however strange these might appear to the uninitiated. Thus, for the Soviets good art is defined by the political realities of class struggle and it is but an aspect of the revolution. For Tolstoy, good art is, ultimately, an aspect of religious consciousness.[32]

Another point of at least seemingly close resemblance is the insistence by both Tolstoy and the Marxists upon the accessibility and relevance of art to the great majority of mankind, namely, the working masses, understood by Tolstoy mostly as the peasants and by the Soviets as the proletariat. In his essay, Tolstoy was ready to discard all the artistic works which failed to meet this demand. Like the Marxists, he maintained that art must not be decadent and exclusive in its aristocratic and individualistic incomprehensibility. It must be a factor contributing to change in the quality of people's lives rather than an inconsequential toy in the hands of a parasitical few. It must, in other words, be art for the sake of life and not for the sake of art. On the Soviet side, during the first years of Bolshevik rule, there was much discussion about the creation of a specific proletarian culture, stemming from and intended for the working class, which would renounce all the past artistic achievements of "bourgeois" and "feudal" societies as meaningless to them, and therefore also meaningless in principle. Even Western commentators have understood that the radicalism implicit in Tolstoy's views on art has its points of similarity with the radicalism of the bolshevik revolution, particularly insofar as the standard notion of Western civilization, called by the Soviets "bourgeois" culture, is concerned. Hugh I'Anson Fausset even compared Tolstoy with Trotsky:

> Tolstoy's theory of post-Renaissance development may be usefully compared with that of another Russian, with whom he would have had little sympathy. Trotsky in his *Literature and Revolution* argues, like Tolstoy, that post-Renaissance art has always been class-conscious. He too claims that it has increasingly reflected a vicious egotism and that man has grown farther and farther away from his roots in social life.[33]

Observing such basic similarities in outlook, particularly if one could interpret the Tolstoyan "religious consciousness" as an equivalent, however obsolete, of the vision of Communist millennium,[34] the Soviet critics might have sought ways from the very beginning to assimilate Tolstoy's view of art to their own ideology. This, however, was not the approach they took at the beginning. Rather, their attitude toward Tolstoy was determined by two main factors, one relatively temporary and the other long-lasting, still in force even today, with some possible softening in the era of "glasnost'." The permanent factor was Lenin's early articles on Tolstoy, particularly his "Tolstoy as a Mirror of the Russian Revolution," which forever branded Tolstoy as being the voice of what Lenin called "patriarchal peasantry," meaning presumably the richer and more conservative peasants, but perhaps also the entire peasant class. The temporary factor, prevalent until the early thirties was the revolutionary ardor and dogmatism of the first years of Bolshevik rule which called for a clean break with the past and led many critics to regard Tolstoy as an alien presence in Soviet society.

Lenin's article on Tolstoy as the mirror of the Russian revolution, though written in 1908, is still, after these many years of laborious Tolstoyan research, the ultimate standard and inspiration for the true understanding of Tolstoy available to the Soviet scholar. The initial premise of the article, namely that if Tolstoy is really a great artist then he must reflect at least some of the essential aspects of the revolution in his works, squarely places the measure of Tolstoy's value in his relevance, or lack of it, to the political issues which alone interested Lenin.[35] From these positions, after describing "crying contradictions" in Tolstoy's thought, Lenin proceeds to define Tolstoy's greatness and weakness:

> The contradictions in Tolstoy's views must be assessed not from the point of view of the workers' movement and contemporary socialism (such an assessment, of course, is necessary, but insufficient), but from the point of view of that protest against encroaching capitalism, impoverishment and deprivation of land which had to arise among the patriarchal Russian peasantry. Tolstoy is ridiculous as a prophet who discovered new recipes for saving mankind — and for this reason quite miserable are the foreign and Russian "Tolstoyans," who desire to turn into dogma exactly the very weakest aspect of his teaching. Tolstoy is great as a voice expressing those ideas and sentiments which had accumulated among millions of Russian peasants by the beginning of the bourgeois revolution in Russia.[36]

Since all this has little or nothing to do with Tolstoy's aesthetics, one does eventually come to admire the ingenuity of Soviet scholars in finding various ways to make Lenin's political pamphlet the guiding beacon of their literary-humanistic quest. In the early years, they directly followed Lenin's footprints toward the conclusion that Tolstoy's ideas on art were of no help at all to "the people" understood as a militant political class. In 1926, L.I. Aksel'-

rod-Ortodoks explained in the magazine *Krasnaya nov'* (Red News)[37] that in calling for an art which would unify all people in love Tolstoy was actually going against the demands of class art, since the art of the people, in the name of class struggle, would certainly strive for conflict rather than unification. As for Tolstoy's attacks on the sophisticated art popular among the "ruling classes," Aksel'rod comments that the great writer did not have specific Marxist aims in mind, or indeed any aims consistent with social progress, but was instead concerned, as, for instance, in his critique of Wagner, with "presenting art as such in a caricaturized, ridiculous manner, attacking it for the sole reason that it was not actually reality" (*ibid.*, p. 157). Apparently, Aksel'rod had in mind the art that Tolstoy called "counterfeit," a brain-spun invention and imitation of other such inventions having nothing to do with any significant reality. Finally, Aksel'rod rejected the very core of Tolstoy's essay — his demand that art should unify all people in love:

> This formulation becomes erroneous even with respect to religious consciousness as soon as we leave the abstract level and remember the concrete forms in which religious consciousness manifests itself. The point is that even religious art can only unite people who confess one and the same religious doctrine (*ibid.*, p. 155).

An even more negative attitude was taken somewhat later by L.Ya. Zivel'chinskaya in a book entitled *An Essay at Marxist Analysis of the History of Esthetics*, published by the Communist Academy in 1928.[38] In this Marxist textbook Zivel'chinskaya seems determined to throw Tolstoy out altogether to what the Soviet rhetoric likes to call "the trash heap of history," saying that he was merely a "helpless medic" (bespomoshchnyj lekar') writing prescriptions in the vain hope of saving the doomed ruling class. After quoting Tolstoy to the effect that if you free the slaves of capital, it will become impossible to produce refined and decadent art, the author adds her own ingenious explanation of Tolstoy's reasons for saying this: "Precisely because it is not possible to free the slaves of capital — so thought Tolstoy — it is better to give up the sophisticated art and to work with the art of the people in order to afford some consolation to the slaves of capital, so as to escape their inevitable and furious revolt." (*ibid.*, p. 328). In the context of the passage in *What Is Art?* to which Zivel'chinskaya was referring, her comment makes no sense at all. Tolstoy was saying that the meaningless, exclusive art rests on the backbreaking labor of the masses and would itself disappear if these masses were free.[39] Whether or not it was possible to free them, and how this would occur, had no bearing on Tolstoy's argument at this point. But Zivel'chinskaya's apparent intention was to imply that Tolstoy regarded art — even the meaningful art accessible to the working masses — as an opiate for the people. Her logic would then lead us to understand Tolstoy's idea of religious consciousness as a description of precisely that opiate, a mind-bending drug that produces hallucinations of universal love and sends the working people on some sort of a soma holiday.

This basically negative attitude toward Tolstoy's aesthetics continued through the 1930s and even beyond. In 1935, B. Bursov, in the periodical *Zvezda* (The Star) asserted once more that "the Tolstoyan system of aesthetics on the whole is extremely reactionary and unacceptable."[40] In Bursov's opinion, the early Tolstoy did what he could to make his aristocratic heroes beloved by everybody, including the working masses. This, in his interpretation, amounted to an attempt to stifle the revolutionary consciousness of the people, a sin of which Zivel'chinskaya had already accused Tolstoy in 1928. As for the late Tolstoy, who himself denounced upper-class art, Bursov explains that the only reason for this was the ineffectiveness of such art among the working people whom Tolstoy was anxious to influence in favor of the prevailing social structure. The radical break in Tolstoy's views in the 1880's signifies, for Bursov, the transition from the positions of the landowning class to those of the patriarchal peasantry. This peasantry, in essence politically passive, conservative and opposed to revolutionary changes in society, prefers a vacuous moral "self-perfection" to any militant mass movement. Lenin's attitude, translated into the specific terms of aesthetics, receives its expression in Bursov's conclusions about Tolstoy:

> The strength of Tolstoy's aesthetics is that, from its point of view, Tolstoy first of all dealt a crushing blow to the perverted bourgeois and landowner art and, secondly, proved that the true creator of culture and art is the people. The weakness of Tolstoy's aesthetics is that, from its point of view, Tolstoy first of all rejected all the world culture and literature,

and secondly, turned the future art of the people essentially into an accessory to religion." (*ibid.*, p. 208)

Since it is very doubtful that the "patriarchal peasantry" had any particular educated views on art at all, the Soviet accusations that Tolstoy expressed the position of this class seem to be based on nothing more than Lenin's article and, in support of it, on the opinion that Tolstoy was a "patriarchal" person in his own household and that he expressed loyalty to the peasants' way of life. The same Leninist view of Tolstoy as a faithful mirror of both the strengths and weaknesses of the peasant class during the time of far-reaching changes in the fabric of Russian life is maintained also by M. Rozental' in an article entitled "The 'Temporal' and 'Immortal'," printed in the magazine *Literaturnyj kritik* (Literary Critic) in 1935. Rozental's conclusion is that "while struggling against the 'temporal' and striving to pass beyond the limits of the 'finite' into the 'eternal' he expressed in essence an extremely temporal, historical situation in a specific temporal-organic slice of life taken from the development of human society,"[41] namely, the attitude of patriarchal peasantry toward the coming revolution.

Anti-Tolstoyan voices, however, were not the only ones heard during the early decades of the Soviet regime. Before Stalin took control of the entire Soviet literary establishment, there was room for a variety of opinions, among other matters, also with regard to the aesthetics of Tolstoy. Authors like Aksel'rod and Zivel'chinskaya represented more the left ideological wing of literary critics, but there were also other positions, more oriented toward serious analysis of the issues at hand than toward political pamphleteering. A fairly representative body of good professional Tolstoy scholarship appeared as a collection of articles in a book called the *Aesthetics of Leo Tolstoy*, published in 1929 by the State Academy of Belles Lettres, then a relatively independent group.[42] The general editor, P. Sakulin, in an article entitled "The Working Man's Aesthetic" does recognize the possibility of building a bridge from Soviet aesthetics to Tolstoy, because the latter was, after all, concerned with the social significance of art and therefore could be counted among the "revolutionaries of aesthetics." T. Rainov contributed an extensive and interesting article "Tolstoy's Aesthetics and His Art" in which he related Tolstoy's ideas on art throughout his life to his novels and short stories and found a steady and consistent development of views along both channels. Indeed (p. 27)

Rainov even thinks that Tolstoy's essay on art represents, in a sense, an extension of the multiple revisions Tolstoy made when composing his fiction — revisions not in the margins of his manuscripts, but in his own mind, about the very basic approaches to his art. In support of this notion, Rainov develops a consistent argument to the effect that the various radical breaks in Tolstoy's views on life and art were more like stages in a steady development. Rainov notes the first stage in Tolstoy's 1860 letter to Fet, stating that there is a need in the soul to speak the truth, but that art is a beautiful lie. This does indeed set the basic dichotomy of *What Is Art?* many years later. The next stage, as Rainov sees it, appears in 1882, in Tolstoy's letter to A. Aleksandrov to the effect that he, Tolstoy, now a famous writer, in actuality did nothing but titillate sexual lust in his works (Sakulin, *Èstetika*, p. 29). From there one needs to go only a very short distance to *The Confession* and the essay itself. In spite of all this, Tolstoy's fiction, as Rainov notes correctly, was after all, always in essence an educational experience, a quest for the meaning of life, just as there was also a good deal of art in his treaties on moral and social issues.

Tolstoy's basic definition that art is an activity which communicates feelings was understood by Rainov better than by some later Soviet critics. Rainov recognized that there was an element of thought, of intellectual experience, in what Tolstoy called "feeling" in art,[43] but other commentators preferred to say that he spoke of feeling alone,[44] thus excluding art from participation in a rational social philosophy, such as, say, Marxism, and supposedly plunging it into meaningless Christian mysticism instead. Misled by their literal understanding of Tolstoy's terms, these later critics even found it difficult to accept Tolstoy as a realist in his fiction, because it seemed to them that in his intense concern for the transmission of feeling Tolstoy lost the true sense of reality which is provided by an overall rational perspective, and therefore did not understand the meaning of the life he was depicting.

Among the other contributors to the book one ought to mention N.K. Gudzy, whose objective and scholarly report on Tolstoy's opinions about other writers[45] is typical of what might be called a "second line" of Soviet critics. These were people who did not claim a decisive voice in the formulation of an orthodox Communist interpretation of Tolstoy, but whose work, remaining in the background throughout the decades of changing official attitudes, continued to advance the cause of objective scholarship. Some of these writers, for instance, N.N. Gusev, were older persons, former friends and disciples of Tolstoy, and others, such as Boris Eikhenbaum, belonged to the so-called Formalist movement. As time went on, there came other critics who joined this group, such as S. Breytburg, V. Asmus, A. Anikst, P. Babaev, Lakshin and others. In spite of occasional declaratory, politically inspired "policy-making" pronouncements on Tolstoy's aesthetics, their work is recognizable for its independent, at times profound, insights into the very nature of Tolstoy's mentality and his art, and for factual studies related to Tolstoy's ideas on art contained in his diaries, correspondence, in various little-known manuscripts and also implied or expressed in his fiction.

The Russian Formalists, whose ideas on literature started taking shape around 1916,[46] were interested in literary texts on a theoretical plane of quite a different order than any criticism based on ideas applied to artistic texts from outside the realm of art, or any descriptive - historical scholarship. Their focus was upon the specific qualities of the literary language itself, the "literariness" of fiction, as Roman Jakobson described it. This meant that artistic structures were to be analyzed as a sum total of specific artistic devices and not in terms of a "religious consciousness," nor in those of some political - economic order of society. Consequently, Tolstoy's essay on art was largely ignored for its lack of direct relevance to the Formalists' concerns. Furthermore, their intense concentration on the intimate complexities of interrelationships among various devices in the language of art often led them to chose their materials in the genre of verse rather than prose.

Nevertheless, some of the Formalists were quite interested in the problems of artistic prose, and among them particularly Boris Eikhenbaum[47] and Viktor Shklovsky, did make pivotal contributions to the study of Tolstoy. Eikhenbaum's general observations on Tolstoy's fiction can often be made applicable also to his views on art. Perhaps the most valuable insight offered by Eikhenbaum was that the various crises and radical breaks with the past in Tolstoy's life could be more usefully studied not in the personal dimension but as "deliberate creative acts," in the evolution of his work. In this spirit, Eikhenbaum said in 1919:

> Tolstoy was always an artist and never ceased to be that, least of all when he renounced his art and

wrote religious-moral articles. The crisis [in the 1880s], like all other "pauses" of Tolstoy is not merely a spiritual manifestation determined by character or life's circumstances, but a definite creative act, a moment of liberation, of evolution. The "duality" of Tolstoy, of which there is so much talk as a spiritual peculiarity, is for us not a passive manifestation of his *nature*, but an act of *consciousness*, developed in the search of a new artistic base.[48]

This approach obviates the long-standing arguments as to whether or not Tolstoy became hostile to himself as an artist in his yearning to make some other, more significant contributions to society, and places the entire issue on the proper track, in pursuit of a description of Tolstoy in terms of interrelationships among the many discrete genres, including that of expository prose (thus also his statements on aesthetics) in which he worked. Eikhenbaum is also right when he continues to say that the entire Russian literature, after romanticism, was looking for new approaches and new traditions during the 1850s to 1870s, and that this gave rise to that special type of Russian art in which elements of consciousness are not drowned in "unconscious" inspiration but rather appear on the surface:

> The events of personal spiritual life do not drown in the swelling creative imagination and are not raised to the plane of exceptional experiences, but are introduced into the creative work itself, lending to it a quality of autobiographical confession. Life becomes as if the measure of art — this is why we know so much about the personal life of Tolstoy. The creative act is complicated by self-perception as a central point morally responsible for an entire generation, for the entire culture("Lev Tolstoy", pp. 19-20).

It is clear, therefore, how Tolstoy the philosophical moralist in the discipline of aesthetics, and Tolstoy the penitent, scourging himself in the essay for his own bad art is also, and above it all, still an artist shaping the totality of his being into a text that must open innumerable channels of communication with all the wonders of his inner world.

The most productive contribution made by Victor Shklovsky to the study of Tolstoy's stylistics evolved from his concept of "making strange" as a literary device, particularly with respect to Tolstoy. Shklovsky's premises are as follows:

> Art exists that one may recover the sensation of life; it exists to make one feel things, to make the stone *stony*. The technique of art is to make objects "unfamiliar," to make forms difficult, to increase the difficulty and length of perception because the process of perception is an aesthetic end in itself and must be prolonged.[49]

From this, his comment on Tolstoy:

> Tolstoy makes the familiar seem strange by not naming the familiar object. He describes an object as if he were seeing it for the first time, and an event as if it were happening for the first time. In describing something he avoids the accepted names of its parts and instead names corresponding parts of other objects (*ibid.*, p. 13).

We may apply these ideas of Shklovsky to Tolstoy's aesthetics and consider, for instance, that his entire argument on art was in essence a device to "make aesthetics strange" so as to enable us all to experience it anew. This does not require that Tolstoy should consciously strive to shape his essay as art, although Eikhenbaum's insight would certainly permit such an inference, but it is quite easy to see how an ordinary reader, if only in self-defense, could be stimulated to think through the automatic notions of "Beauty, Goodness and Truth," existing somewhere in a realm of no concern to him, after they have been made strange, as if naked, without their usual contexts, in front of one's eyes, after they have been "named" anew by Tolstoy. Unfortunately, what actually happened in so many cases was that Tolstoy's statements were simply shrugged off as not relevant to the discipline of aesthetics.

Sakulin's *The Aesthetics of Leo Tolstoy* is not based on Formalist premises, but rather reflects a historical-analytical point of view based for the most part on Marxist aesthetics. Nevertheless, it came under attack early in the 1930s, during the time of the so-called "vulgar sociologism."[50] The first to strike were the critics connected with the Russian Association of Proletarian Writers (RAPP), a militant leftist group which, under the energetic leadership of Leopold Averbakh, became a virtual dictator of all Soviet letters until it was dissolved in 1932. In 1931, A. Mikhailov wrote an article for a journal with the inspiring Soviet title *Na literaturnom postu* (On Literary Guard)[51] in which he called the State Academy of Sciences in the Arts — the publishers of *Aesthetics*, "a stronghold of bourgeois idealistic theories in the science of aesthetics" (*Ibid.*, p. 28). Mikhailov rejected Sakulin's idea that Tolstoy might be considered a potential Marxist because such an interpretation would require glossing over the religious basis of Tolstoy's aesthetics. Rainov's argument that there was no crucial break in Tolstoy's outlook on art in the 1880s was also repudiated, not on any factual basis, but simply for the reason that "rejection of this break in essence means affirmation that an evolutionary approach is sufficient to explain the aesthetics of Tolstoy." In actuality, however, says Mikhailov, such evolutionism simply throws out "the *dialectics* of Tolstoy's aesthetic views" (*ibid.*, p. 30). This amounts to saying that there had to be a radical break because the Marxist dialectics needed one.

Mikhailov's own view is that before his radical change of outlook Tolstoy was a supporter of socially irresponsible "pure art," and afterwards — from the 1880s — he became an apologist for "religious-utilitarian, popular art." "There is no need to point out," says Mikhailov, "that this preaching of religious art makes Tolstoy's aesthetic views harmful and unacceptable as a whole, in spite of the fact that they do contain certain revolutionary-critical elements" (*ibid.*, p. 28). The question of religious, Christian elements in Tolstoy's essay was discussed in later years in more sophisticated terms, as an interplay of paradoxical positions not quite grasped even by Tolstoy himself. Here, for instance is the opinion of V.P. Malinovsky:

> Art must serve the people, and art must be Christian — here are two propositions which Tolstoy attempts to unite, which is in itself paradoxical and functions as a basis for many other paradoxes. More exactly: this is paradoxical from the positions of the scientific world view of the present epoch, but not from the point of view of Tolstoy himself. Moreover, the paradoxical nature of one of the aspects of the problem of popular art in Tolstoy consists in that the writer tried to find means of expressing people's interests in the form of seeking the true faith.[52]

It appears that Sakulin's book remained a thorn in the ideological side of Soviet critics. As late as 1979, E. Nuralov in his book *The Aethetics of Lev Tolstoy in the Judgment of Literary Criticism* made the claim that the authors "ignore Lenin's articles about Tolstoy."[53] Rainov is accused of trying to show that "Tolstoy's aesthetics is abstract, that one cannot discern in it the class-conscious positions of the writer, that it does not reflect the writer's transition to the positions of the patriarchal peasantry" (*ibid.*, p. 30). To ignore Lenin's articles means, of course, to forfeit any claims to at least the Soviet version of literary scholarship. B. Gornung's article in the collection, "Tolstoy and the Traditions of the 'New Art'" is found to be erroneous in that Tolstoy is alleged to have "rejected the basic properties of poetry." All in all, however, Nuralov takes a forgiving attitude:

> While criticizing the articles by Rainov, Gornung and others, as well as some propositions in D. Sakulin's contribution, one must also admit that this collection was a reflection of the time in which it was published (*ibid.*, p. 34).

The time was 1929, a few years before Stalin imposed his total control over literary scholarship as well as all other aspects of cultural life.

It was evident, however, that discarding Tolstoy would be too great a loss, particularly since the regime began to advance its claims to be the legitimate heir of the very best traditions of Russian culture. From any possible point of view, it had to be admitted that Tolstoy's legacy did constitute a large share of these traditions. Since Tolstoy, as well as the other great writers of the nineteenth century, did not readily fit the Bolshevik frame, the solution was to remake them, to provide such a reading of their works that they would appear to be the followers and co-militants of the "progressive" movements in past Russian literature and criticism. This direction of thought became particularly clear after the writers' congress of 1932, during which the Soviet Writers' Union was established under central Party control. In distinction from the boundless revolutionary enthusiasms of the previous semi-independent groupings, such as The Russian Association of Proletarian Writers, the new Union was much more conservative in its outlook and much more eager to reestablish ties of continuity with the Russian past. To accomplish this, literary commentators turned first of all to the socially-minded critics of the nineteenth-century, particularly Vissarion Belinsky, Nikolay Chernyshevsky and Nikolay Dobrolyubov, claimed by the Soviets to be their precursors in cultural and political thought, who clearly dominated all discourse on literature at that time. It was quite natural that the Soviets should seek to develop arguments suggesting an affinity between these critics and the nineteenth-century classics. The functional concept applied to the critics and writers was "critical realism," a counterpart of "progressive aesthetics," and Tolstoy, together with others, was to be fitted between these two terms. The validity of the Soviet position rests on but does not extend beyond the fact that the complex interrelationships among art, politics, philosophy, attitudes toward public affairs and intellectual life in general did occasionally bring similar and dissimilar people to express comparable views. In Tolstoy's case, one may indeed compare with some profit his thoughts on art with those of Chernyshevsky, who articulated his views on the theoretical plane to a greater extent than either Belinsky or Dobrolyubov.[54] First of all, as Victor Terras points out:

> The key notion of Chernyshevsky's aaesthetics proper is a total rejection of the Kantian doctrine of the autonomous and specific nature of the aesthetic fact. Chernyshevsky did everything to destroy all the barriers separating art from science, from politics, from publicism, and from ordinary practical activity.[55]

This makes it feasible for anyone so inclined to relate Tolstoy's principle that art is a normal and necessary function of living to Chernyshevsky's view that art is an "ordinary practical activity." Furthermore, Chernyshevsky, like Tolstoy, rejected the traditional aesthetic category of the Beautiful, translating it from philosophical concept in aesthetics to simply the experience of the joy of being alive:

> The nearest and dearest thing to a human being is — the human being, the human life. If we then look at what is called "beautiful" and "beauty" in a human being, we shall find that we find that beautiful in a human being in which a joyful, full and prosperous life finds its expression.[56]

This may sound a bit hedonistic and is considerably different from Tolstoy's "religious consciousness,"[57] but nevertheless, the thrust of the concept of beauty in both instances is directed toward actual life, a manner of living, instead of being an abstract category of aesthetics.

One might add another point of relationship between Tolstoy and Chernyshevsky, noted by James P. Scanlan, namely, their mutual interest in Rousseau. Chernyshevsky, as Scanlan convincingly argues, was much more influenced by Rousseau than is generally supposed, and on at least one point, the issue of what is or is not a true human need, all three: Chernyshevsky, Rousseau and Tolstoy seemed to be in fair agreement. According to Scanlan:

> the strongest and the clearest echo of Rousseau in Chernyshevsky's aesthetic thinking is once again the distinction between true and false needs. The point is made clearly enough in the main text of *The Aesthetic Relations*, where Chernyshevsky insists that "a distinction must be drawn between real desires and imaginary, fictitious desires" and where he uses the distinction to attack the fine arts, in passages redolent of Rousseau's *Discourses*.[58]

One more instance of real or seeming similarity with Chernyshevsky, as Terras points out, is in their views of Shakespeare:

> Chernyshevsky anticipated Tolstoy's rejection of Shakespeare, and on much the same grounds. He even anticipated Tolstoy's observation that romantic aesthetics was created *ad hoc* to fit Shakespeare's art (Terras, *Belinsky and Russian literary Criticism*, p. 239).

Curiously enough, not a great deal has been written by the Soviets directly about Tolstoy and Chernyshevsky, or indeed about Tolstoy's relationship with the other "revolutionary democrats," as the Soviet term has it, of nineteenth-century Russian literary criticism. The preference over the years has been for scattered remarks to the effect that there were significant affinities between Tolstoy and those critics, but a systematic analysis, or a theory, of these relationships has not been elaborated.[59]

In the course of time, as the construction of a "Soviet Tolstoy" went on, his aesthetics, under the scrutiny of Soviet critics, became, so to speak, irrelevant to itself and turned into a socio-political issue. Tolstoy was condemned, or else given credit, for reasons having little to do with the intrinsic merit of his theories on art. His works were scanned for individual statements that could be quoted to support the notion of continuing tradition leading ultimately to revolution. Any statements that did not fit this mold were seen as examples of Tolstoy's inner contradictions. This shift of focus toward politics, also created the conditions for the eventual "rehabilitation" of Tolstoy on the Soviet critics' own terms. It became possible to pass over the complexities of Tolstoy's artistic and spiritual concerns and to discuss in isolation his specific opinions of various aspects of socio-political life in Russia in such a way as to make him appear to be the champion of progress and of the working man, as these terms are understood in the political vocabulary of the Soviets themselves.

During the 1940s and 50s the Soviet critics gradually developed a more favorable approach to Tolstoy's aesthetics, mostly by cultivating the image of Tolstoy as a Russian patriot and a "critical realist" in his art. This was especially important in view of the strong emphasis on Russian nationalism during and after the war, which required a positive revaluation of all the great Russian cultural figures of the past. Important service on this "front" was performed by the critic N.K. Lomunov, who wrote a series of articles in the early 50s, aimed at creating a new image of Tolstoy as a great champion of the Russian people. In 1951 Lomunov published an article entitled "Tolstoy in the Struggle Against Decadent Art," for the book *Lev Nikolaevich Tolstoy, a Collection of Articles and Materials*, edited by D. Blagoy I. Uspensky and Lomunov himself.[60] At the very beginning he declared that, for Tolstoy, the main question was whether or not art served the interests of the common people. Decadent art, of course, goes against those interests, serving as it does the whims of the exploiting classes. This, according to Lomunov, was the reason why Tolstoy opposed the decadents. Tolstoy was also against Nietzsche and Wagner and the whole ideology of the "superman" — the same ideology, the article implies, which was espoused by the Nazis, and which also dominates the thinking of the capitalists. "The great writer-realist," says Lomunov, "convincingly demonstrated that, in defending the theory of 'pure art', of 'art for art's sake' the Decadents were creating works for the select (for 'superman') and that they were completely dependent upon the 'rulers of life', upon the 'money bag'" (*ibid.*, p. 84).

This interpretation, in spite of its political partisanship, might still seem fair enough on the face of it, because Tolstoy did in fact oppose both Nietzsche and Wagner as well as the Decadents, although for reasons having to do with his philosophy of art rather than with politics. Lomunov, however, draws his own nationalistic, anti-Western political line from Tolstoy's cosmopolitan ideological premises to his views on Nietzsche, Wagner, Baudelaire and Verlaine, and then to Hitler and the American capitalist system, lumping all these complex and multifaceted personalities, ideas and issues into a single world-view supposedly representing the ideology of the "exploiting classes." The resulting implication was that Tolstoy also opposed Western civilization, as defined by Lomunov, and that therefore he could be exploited as a Soviet ally in the cold war. The only shortcoming of this Soviet Tolstoy was that, according to Lomunov, he "rejected the revolutionary path of liberation of the oppressed masses," that is, the path of politically inspired violence.

Another article by Lomunov, entitled "Leo Tolstoy in the Struggle for Realism in Art," in *Problems of Philosophy*, 1953[61] begins with an attack on the American critics, in particular Ernest J. Simmons, for being interested in Tolstoy's moral and religious search and for saying that Tolstoy's central problem was the problem of man's relationship to infinity. This, for Lomunov, is mystical bourgeois nonsense — what interests the Soviet critic is Tolstoy's "stormy protest against any and all class inequality, permeating his stern criticism of the 'lordly' bourgeois-aristocratic art" (*ibid.*, p. 182). The expressions used by Lomunov; "struggle for realism," "stormy protest" and the like, come straight from Pravda editorials, replacing the language of Tolstoy in the same way as the Soviet criticism itself had replaced his image with a product of their own making. This new Tolstoy, according to Lomunov, even believed in some of the basic tenets of what later became Socialist realism, such as the notion that the typical in art expresses the ideals of the future at least as much as the prevalent reality of the present. "It is important to emphasize," writes Lomunov, "that Tolstoy considered the typical to be not only the prevailing, dominating traits, but also traits expressing new facets of phenomena, depicting that which still 'must be'" (*ibid.*, p. 186).

Another step toward this politically oriented rehabilitation of Tolstoy as a literary critic and theoretician of aesthetics came when the Soviet critics looked again at his attacks on Shakespeare in 1903 article entitled "On Shakespeare and on Drama" in which he vigorously attacked the English playwright for lack of historical sense and verisimilitude in his plots, for amorality — absence of the Tolstoyan "religious consciousness" — for bad taste, inability to create individual characters, bombastic rhetoric and, finally, for crude and repugnant violence on the stage. The Soviet critics of the 1930s preferred to avoid the intellectual challenge posed by Tolstoy's highly unorthodox opinions and instead looked for an explanation in Tolstoy's passive "patriarchal-peasant" attitudes to life. B. Bursov had the following to say on the matter:

> The struggle of passions — this is what made Shakespeare's plays unacceptable to Tolstoy, this is what seems to him unnatural, thought-up to create effect, false. Instead of the struggle of passions Tolstoy proposes a feeling of submission, of acceptance. But Shakespeare's characters lack this quality. This is why Tolstoy accuses Shakespeare of a lack of sense of proportion and of other similar sins."[62]

It is perhaps ironic to remember that precisely the movement of passion in Shakespeare's plays was considered by Tolstoy to be their only redeeming feature.[63]

By 1953, however, Tolstoy's passive religious mysticism was withdrawn from the center of attention and his dislike for Shakespeare was explained in standard anti-Western, class-conscious terms. P. Solntsev noted in his master's dissertation on Tolstoy's aesthetics in the 1890s that:

> Tolstoy's negative attitude toward the works of Shakespeare was provoked by the fact that in Shakespeare's person he saw a clear representative of the bourgeois culture. Shakespeare was a great representative of the Renaissance. According to Tolstoy, however, the Renaissance was the greatest mistake in the history of world culture.[64]

Solntsev's idea is in a sense closer to the mark than the comments of previous critics, for even if Tolstoy did not use any such Soviet terminology as "bourgeois culture," he did, in his essay *"What Is Art?"* regard the Renaissance as a catastrophic period of betrayal of religious consciousness in art, because the upper classes ceased to believe in God, and yet used religion to keep themselves in power. On the other hand, in the article "On Shakespeare and on Drama" Tolstoy did not at all accuse Shakespeare of having lost faith in either Christianity or its perversion — the Church, but confined himself largely to matters of the playwright's artistic skill and integrity.

There still remained certain facets of Tolstoy's aesthetics which barred the way to his complete acceptance on Soviet terms. The discussion of these had to wait until the mid 1950s, when the more permissive post-Stalin atmosphere allowed experiments in writing which seemed most directly opposed to a Communist world-view. One such idea of Tolstoy was the crucial matter of religious consciousness. It did not help to dismiss this concept as "reactionary mysticism," because without it Tolstoy's aesthetics would lose the principal cohesive force holding it together as a system of thought. Another difficulty was caused by Tolstoy's denial that it was possible to teach art in schools and by his rejection of the traditional artistic devices which could be analyzed and explained by people engaged in what, to him, was the meaningless busywork called literary scholarship. A brave attempt to confront these issues was made by G. Kulikov in his master's thesis in 1955.[65] Kulikov explained that Tolstoy did not really reject art schools as such (which is precisely what he did), but only the bourgeois schools which did not truly teach art, since bourgeois art is, of course, counterfeit. The Soviet schools, on the other hand, of which, the implication is, Tolstoy would approve, teach man how to "free himself from individualism, from the habits and opinions issuing from the instinct for private property" and "promulgate the spirit of collectivism" (*ibid.*, p. 8). Collectivism, then, is the word applied to one of the most individualistic of all writers to explain his demand for unity of mankind in love. As for religious consciousness, Kulikov finally devised a formula to get around the difficulties of the earlier Soviet critics who took the word "religious" literally. His interpretation was that "true art is connected with the advanced social consciousness of the people, called by Tolstoy religious consciousness" (*ibid.*, p. 7). Such an interpretation would be quite close to the mark if it were not for the fact that Kulikov uses the term "social consciousness" in the specific Soviet sense, implying the divisive and even hate-filled emotions attendant to class struggle, whereas Tolstoy felt that no meaning in life can be possibly discerned by those who feel that they must direct their hatred against anyone at all.

In general, Kulikov finds Tolstoy acceptable in the Soviet context because his aesthetics reflects "the advanced democratic tendencies of the peasant movement toward the revolution of 1905," and also because it "continues and completes the achievements of critical realism" (*ibid.*, p. 3), meaning, apparently the critical theories of Belinsky, Chernyshevsky and Dobrolyubov.

Kulikov turns to the questions of artistic devices in an article entitled "L.N. Tolstoy's Struggle Against Decadent Art," published in a scholarly series of the Urals Pedagogical Institute in 1956.[66] The basic argument is again that Tolstoy really attacked only the devices of bourgeois-decadent art. For instance, his denunciation of artistic devices designed to make a novel or a story interesting, such as an abundance of historical detail and the like, is understood by Kulikov as a protest against the efforts of the decadents to "paralyze the rational will of the reader" (*ibid.*, p. 213). The reason why the Decadents wish to do this is explained by Kulikov as follows: "The aim of the decadent art is to dull the active and creative initiative of the reader, to lead his attention away from the questions of class struggle, of social contradictions, toward unnecessary and empty pastimes" (*ibid.*, p. 214). In other words, Tolstoy was really opposed to art if it were to become a form of opiate for the people, rather than for it on those grounds, as the earlier critics would have it.

The acceptable view of Tolstoy's aesthetics worked out by Soviet critics in the 1950s remained valid for them into the 60s as well. For instance, in 1965, E. Nuralov confirmed in his book *On the Aesthetic Views of L.N. Tolstoy* that the great writer does indeed belong to the line of succession leading from the "progressive critics" of the nineteenth century to the Soviet period.[67] Nuralov's book pays a great deal of attention to Tolstoy's critique of "decadent art," the German idealist philosophers, and of Wagner.[68] These were also the topics of particular interest during the last years of Stalin's rule and up to 1956 to such critics as N.K. Lomunov, who wrote then in the spirit of the "cold war." In Tolstoy's essay, these topics really perform an auxiliary function, supporting his main body of thought. Chapters II through IV, where Tolstoy discusses various theories of art, Chapter X, an attack on the "Decadents," and Chapter XIII, which launches a heavy attack on Wagner, could be regarded in structural terms as separate bodies, supporting evidence which could have easily been placed in an appendix without doing harm to the central line of argument.[69] On the other hand, precisely these matters seem most comfortable for some Soviet critics to deal with, because there Tolstoy's views come very close to the official anti-modernistic Soviet line in the arts, and thus his great authority can be enlisted in the ideological struggle against the West. Nuralov also echoes some earlier militant Soviet statements directed against Western scholarship. He repeats, for instance, Lomunov's scheme linking Nietzsche, Wagner and the Symbolists with the decadent, imperialistic West, and then fires a salvo at E.J. Simmons, Gleb Struve and others, just as Lomunov had done in 1953.[70]

On the troublesome matters raised by Tolstoy in Chapter XII of his essay, namely that there should be no schools of art, since they can only teach the techniques of counterfeiting art, that there really isn't any such thing as literary criticism, etc., Nuralov holds to the positions A. Kulikov proclaimed back in 1935, where he said that Tolstoy must, of course, have meant the bourgeois schools and critics. Here Nuralov sounds an ominous note against unspecified "revisionists" who might possibly be some Soviet scholars of the more liberal persuasion. In spite of some mistakes, says Nuralov, Chapter XII does make important statements on the class nature of art. Then he adds:

> These statements acquire a special significance in our time, when revisionist scholars in the arts are again dragging from the trash heap of history all sorts of theories about an artist's intuition, about the elevation of art above class conflicts, etc.[71]

Expressions like "the trash heap of history" bring back echoes of an even earlier, extremely negative Soviet rhetoric against Tolstoy, such as Zivel'chinskaya's statements of 1928.

In 1979, the same Nuralov devoted a long chapter to what he called Tolstoy's "Critique of Bourgeois Theories and Trends in West-European and Russian Literature and Art at the End of the Nineteenth and the Beginning of the Twentieth Century."[72] Most of the chapter summarizes Tolstoy's review of West European writings on aesthetics in his essay, but Nuralov does keep using the term "bourgeois" to build up an impression in the mind that what Tolstoy sought first of all was not a proper definition of art, but an exposure of the evils perpetrated by the ruling clique of a doomed class that must be replaced by the revolution. In this way, Nuralov comes as close as anyone in creating a Soviet Tolstoy — a writer indignant at class exploitation who in the name of the working people fiercely consigns to the "trash heap of history" all the ideas of that oppressor class. Thus making Tolstoy's human indignation appear as an equivalent to political doctrine, Nuralov chooses to ignore Tolstoy's oft-repeated opposition to the division of humanity into hostile social classes, or even nations.

Nuralov ends his discourse with sentiments exactly resembling the Stalinist notions of the fifties concerning Western attitudes toward Tolstoy's aesthetics:

> Certain contemporary bourgeois scholars in literature are trying to disparage the meaning of Tolstoy's critique of decadent art, often resorting to coarse and dishonest means. Now, when the bourgeois countries are widely propagating and supporting materialistic-decadent-mystical art, Tolstoy's thoughts about the mutual relationship between art and social classes, about the place of the artist in the public life of a country, acquire a new meaning (Nuralov, Èstetika, p. 186).

Reading these official pundits, lackeys of their regime, one is tempted to become discouraged by their repetitious, unchanging political cant throughout the long decades of Soviet rule. Fortunately, one can also find different critical approaches, like that in E.P. Babaev's monograph, *Tolstoy on Art*, 1960. Writing in an easy, informal style, Babaev presents a number of refreshing insights, particularly on matters related to the continuity of Tolstoy's thoughts on art throughout his life. There is, for instance, an interesting discussion of Tolstoy's early relations with Turgenev, Fet and Druzhinin, who were then friends of art, beauty, and civilized ease. As Tolstoy's restless struggles with moral imperatives intensified, his attachment to his "aesthetic friends" gradually lost meaning, and Tolstoy became more distant from them. However, Babaev points out, traces of their views on art and life can be found in *Anna Karenina*, particularly in the character of the "modern epicurean" Stiva Oblonsky. The counterpoint between Levin and Oblonsky, says Babaev, prefigures the opposition, on an ideological plane, between the traditional concepts of art, based on beauty, and Tolstoy's own morally oriented values in his essay. In general, Babaev says:

> During the years when *Anna Karenina* was being written, Tolstoy was at a crossroads, and the question of new demands in life and art was posed there, only posed but not solved. But it was so formulated that one can move directly from the novel to the treatise *What Is Art?* with full confidence that at the core of it we will find issues we knew about already.[73]

This is certainly true, and not only of *Anna Karenina* but of all of Tolstoy's fiction. The issues are the same, and only the articulation is different: in fiction it is accomplished according to the demands of art, and in the essay — according to the demands of conscience as Tolstoy perceived them, rightly or wrongly.

In 1961, V.A. Asmus contributed a significant article to the *Literaturnoe nasledstvo* (Literary Heritage) series in which he discusses Tolstoy's world-view, particularly in terms of moral implications inherent in the demands for comprehensibility of art made in the essay. "Comprehensible art," says Asmus "is truthful art, and truthfulness is the most indispensable condition of both life and art."[74] In this spirit, Asmus describes Tolstoy's realism as a realism of the author's own feelings:

> The special quality of Tolstoy's realism is that it does not so much depict an object or a phenomenon as it depicts them by means of the transmission of feeling which that object has evoked in the author ("Mirovozzrenie Tolstogo," p. 93).

Nevertheless, Asmus has objections to Tolstoy's definition of art in terms of feeling:

> The meaning of art is *not only*, as Tolstoy thought erroneously, in that art "infects" people with the feelings which the artist has experienced and then consciously reproduced in his work. In addition to the effect of art on feelings, a point especially stressed by Tolstoy, art also affects, by means of its images, the entire sphere of our *conceptions* and *ideas*. Art is capable not only of changing the structure of our feelings, but also the structure of *our thoughts* (ibid., p. 93).

This is not a new idea, since the pre-revolutionary Russian critics had also explained Tolstoy's notion of feeling as a blend of emotion and thought, some adding that it is a blend peculiar to aesthetics. Nevertheless, the discussion around the concept of feeling in Tolstoy's definition keeps recurring in Soviet commentaries on his treatise. In the Soviet context, the idea that art can also affect our thoughts, i.e., also convictions, is very important indeed. The regime would probably never trouble itself to exercise control over the arts if it did not believe in their importance precisely in the development of a person's world-view, indeed, of the world-view of an entire society. On these terms, Tolstoy was being called to service along with all other writers, "engineers of the human souls," according to Stalin's famous definition.

In his study Babaev does not deal primarily with Tolstoy's treatise itself. He limits himself to pointing out occasional moments, landmarks in Tolstoy's progress toward the final systematic formulation of his views on art. In contrast to this, E. Kupreyanova, in a major work, *The Esthetics of L.N. Tolstoy*, 1966[75], thoroughly investigates various aspects of Tolstoy's artistic and ideological experience leading to the development of his aesthetic thought. Like so many Soviet scholars, she also uses Lenin as a starting point, but with one crucial difference: her focus is shifted from Lenin himself to those critics who have misinterpreted his remarks about profound contradictions in Tolstoy's world-view to mean that there was a dichotomy between Tolstoy the great artist, and Tolstoy the weak, reactionary thinker. Kupreyanova maintains that, on the contrary:

> The world-view and the ideas of a true artist are such that they cannot be formulated and in the process of their formulation expressed in any other way except the language of art, the language of artistic images. And for this reason, the creative work of an artist depends on his world-view to the extent that the latter possesses a specific aesthetic quality. It is another matter that, after the ideas of an artist have already been formed and embodied in artistic images, the artist may formulate them directly in words, that is, in the language of concepts (Kupreyanova, p. 21).

This excellent approach leads Kupreyanova to her basic point concerning Tolstoy's aesthetics and his art:

> Tolstoy's teaching did not develop from theoretical considerations but was only a generalization of a

grandiose artistic experience of the great writer, a generalization performed by himself in a noble but unsubstantiated effort to elevate the results of that experience to the height of all-encompassing, universal truth (*ibid.*, p. 87).[76]

In this spirit, Kupreyanova investigates various factors acting on the formulation of Tolstoy's world-view. According to her, Tolstoy was first influenced by the Swiss moralist F.R. Weiss, who expounded his utilitarian and rationalistic ideas on self-perfection of man, best achieved by means of art. These blended with the philosophy of Rousseau and reached the stage of "moral imperative" found in the philosophy of Kant. Of special importance, in Kupreyanova's opinion, was the so-called "Stankevich circle" of Russian intellectuals in the 1830s, because of their concerns with "man, his purpose, the meaning and moral value of man's life" (p. 66), precisely the main questions of Tolstoy's own search for a philosophy of living. According to Kupreyanova, the point is not that Tolstoy was directly influenced by the Stankevich circle, but that its ideas dominated the thinking of the time and left their mark on Tolstoy's own mind. Tolstoy carried out in practice, in his creative work and aesthetic thought, "the application in life of the ideal of moral perfection, worked out theoretically by Stankevich" (p. 74).

Against this background, the author turns to Tolstoy's early diaries and drafts in search of preliminary formulations relevant to his aesthetics. Starting with the need to seek for elemental principles of truth from direct experience of reality and not from some other thought, Tolstoy arrived at the notion that what a person truly experiences must be evidently true in the objective sense as well, because our feelings, unlike our thoughts, are grounded in reality and not in abstract mind-made patterns. Thus, says Kupreyanova, "Tolstoy's world-perception and his aesthetics reflect the world as governed by the laws determining the perceptions of his own psyche" (*ibid.*, p. 113). Here, in her opinion are the roots of Tolstoy's "mysticism," as reflected in his aesthetics. If something is true in terms of experience (say, a meaningful connection in the mind between bloody bodies on the battlefield and a blood-red evening sun), it may not be true in the scientific-objective sense at all. Yet, Tolstoy tended to assume his own perception to be objectively valid, in part because he felt his own psyche to be only an aspect, a manifestation of a truly existing "universal mind." This is

not so in Tolstoy's art, but it does affect the non-artistic formulations of his thought:
> The point is that being an elemental-materialistic category of aesthetic consciousness, the psychological reality acquires an entirely different, idealistic meaning as soon as it changes from the aesthetic to the philosophical category (*ibid*, p. 175).

The implication of Kupreyanova's argument is that this tendency of Tolstoy might provide a conceptual bridge between Tolstoy's definition of art as transmission of feeling and his postulate that the best and noblest art expresses religious consciousness — the understanding of the meaning of life in general. The truth of a personal experience becomes elevated to a universal verity. Moreover, in Kupreyanova's opinion, Tolstoy, from his studies of folklore, came to feel that:
> only the spiritual culture of "working people" has an absolute, i.e., universally human value, while the culture of the civilized society only possesses value which is relative, existing only for a narrow circle of people, and therefore artificial (*ibid.*, p. 238).

The radical break in Tolstoy's outlook, according to Kupreyanova, really began in the 1870s, when "the testing of civilization against the idea of the people" became a declaratory principle of his art. From this point on, Tolstoy developed the notion of God as "an artistic personification of the highest spiritual and moral essence of man" (p. 257) and transferred "the meaning attributed earlier to art to what he called religion" (p.260). This, Kupreyanova thinks, constitutes the essence of Tolstoy's fundamental change in the 1880s.

From these premises Kupreyanova proceeds to a brief commentary on Tolstoy's treatise itself. Disappointingly, the rich and often very penetrating analysis of Tolstoy's preceding thought leads the author to conclusions in essence no different from those of other less thorough and perhaps less perceptive Soviet critics. She says, as others have, that Tolstoy's religious consciousness could be understood in the Soviet context as the idea of social and economic progress leading to the Communist millennium, that his reliance on the common people agrees with the basic tenets of Chernyshevsky, that Tolstoy saw in the Renaissance a manifestation of "bourgeois individualism" and, finally, that in his opposition to Nietzsche and Wagner, Tolstoy, "and, as far as we know, only Tolstoy, foresaw the direct connection between the degradation of bourgeois art and the imperialistic philosophy of power" (p. 316). Such a critique is clearly inadequate, but Kupreyanova's excellent preliminary survey will enable future students of Tolstoy's aesthetics to do more substantial work on the treatise itself.

Another serious study *The Problem of Esthetics of L.N. Tolstoy in His Late Period*, by G.N. Ishchuk, came out soon after Kupreyanova's book, in 1967. It focuses more closely on a series of unfinished drafts and smaller article written by Tolstoy in the interval between 1879, when he published his *Confession*, and 1897, when *What Is Art?* was finished. Ishchuk divides Tolstoy's preliminary search into several stages, beginning with *The Confession*, where some thought is given to the exploitative nature of art and a strong revulsion on Tolstoy's part toward his own activities as a writer becomes manifest. During the second stage, in 1882, Tolstoy began groping toward reliable criteria of art, and also underwent a strong moral shock upon witnessing the condition of the poor in Moscow — a shock which produced his famous essay *What, Then, Are We to Do?*

Between 1881 and 1891, when Tolstoy worked on such pieces as *Kreutzer Sonata* and the play *The Fruits of Learning*, he also produced numerous short, probing investigations into the nature of art, most of which show considerable confusion and great emotional tension. At that time, Ishchuk says, Tolstoy began to turn against "bourgeois social values" and against the idea of art for art's sake. Around 1889, the notion of the people, bystanders and judges of what the bourgeois society calls art, begins to develop. A crucial moment in Tolstoy's preliminary investigations of art was the preface to a Russian translation of the works of Maupassant, written in 1893-4. There Tolstoy understood that talented works of art can be produced from amoral and even immoral positions, that "there is something in creative arts that lies on different planes" than morality.[77] At that time, according to Ishchuk, Tolstoy also understood that talent, or sincerity in an artist "is a natural, elemental force through which an artist experiences the pressure of the very material of life."

Finally, in the last two years before the appearance of *What Is Art?* a great number of "decadent" works appeared both in Western Europe and in Russia. This especially strengthened Tolstoy's resolve to oppose the modernistic tendencies in his own essay.

In this section of his book Ishchuk gives a systematic and clear picture of Tolstoy's progress from a crucial religious-moral experience (*The Confession*) through social indignation and reaction against modern art, which culminated in a unified idea that, with the loss of religious values, society also instituted injustice and degraded art. On the other hand, Ishchuk does not draw a line backwards in time to earlier works and thoughts of Tolstoy where the same basic issues were already germinating and developing in the writer's mind. Ishchuk becomes a little disappointing when he turns his attention to the essay itself. Here the reader is again treated to the conventional Soviet listing of Tolstoy's "strong and weak sides" from the Marxist point of view, such as that Tolstoy's "class consciousness" shows him at his best, while his "religious consciousness" — at his worst, and so on. Ishchuk does, however, note that there is a "certain one-sidedness" (p.34) in Soviet criticism discussing Tolstoy's struggle against the decadent art, in particular, a failure to point out that, whatever Tolstoy thought of them, not all "decadents" were bourgeois-minded and against social change. On the other hand, he attributes Tolstoy's failure to understand this to his "patriarchal peasant" mentality — a phrase first used by Lenin, which has kept meandering through the Soviet criticism of Tolstoy through the years until it lost most of its meaning, whatever that was in the first place.

Further in the book Ishchuk continues to advance the Soviet claim that Tolstoy was really like-minded with Chernyshevsky and the other "progressive critics." One small, refreshing difference is that Ishchuk takes the trouble to point out that it is not a question of direct influence but rather of analogous development at a given time in Russian social history. Ishchuk also complements Kupreyanova's list of Western European influences on Tolstoy's aesthetic thought by pointing out that he was familiar with John Ruskin's[78] directed against the modern technocratic society.

Another fairly recent major study of Tolstoy's aesthetics, *Èstetika L'va Tolstogo*, comes from the prolific pen of N.K. Lomunov. Lomunov undertakes to trace Tolstoy's ideas on art from early notes in his diaries through the Yasnaja Polyana period, the turning point in the 1880s reflected in *The Confession* and in *What, Then, Must we Do?*, the preliminaries to the essay on art, such as Tolstoy's article on Maupassant, to the essay on art itself, and finally to Tolstoy's late thoughts. For the most part it is a descriptive work, richly embroidered with references to Tolstoy's own statements and to pre-revolutionary Russian, Soviet and Western criticism of Tolstoy's aesthetics. Lomunov does understand that Tolstoy's aesthetics must form an inseparable, organic unity with his art, but does not develop this point sufficiently to make his book a significant contribution in terms of new critical thought. In this volume, Lomunov continues to hold his earlier opinions, tying Tolstoy in with the "revolutionary democratic" critics of the nineteenth century, making him an enemy of Western culture and art in principle, even implying that Tolstoy foresaw the "kernel of fascism" in the work of Wagner and the French Decadents.

CHAPTER SEVEN

THE LEGACY ABROAD

The range of contemporary responses to Tolstoy's essay among the English-speaking critics in the West extended all the way from full approval to sarcastic rejection. Not surprisingly, one of the most enthusiastic echoes came from Tolstoy's long-time friend, translator and disciple Aylmer Maude. For him the essay was a brilliant achievement bringing succinctness and clarity to the whole issue of aesthetics:

> In its construction, in coordination in concise form of many converging thoughts, this is, probably, the most masterly of all Tolstoy's works. Of the effect the book had on me personally, I can only say that, though sensitive to some forms of art, I was, when I took it up, much in the dark on questions of esthetic philosophy; when I had done with it, I had grasped the main solution of the problem so clearly that, though I subsequently read a number of conflicting opinions on the subject, I never again became perplexed upon the central issues.[1]

In contrast to this, an editorial in the journal *Literature* called Tolstoy's views a "fantastic doctrine," opposed the notion that an established, even famous writer has any business commenting on the question of what is art and refused outright even to discuss the essay:

> Of Count Tolstoi no one who can appreciate the commanding qualities displayed alike in the conception and the execution of "Anna Karenina" — to name but one of the author's masterpieces — could wish to speak without respect. But there never was any reason for inferring from the powers revealed in this and other works of fiction that Count Tolstoi's opinions on the philosophy of art would be worth the

paper on which they are written; and the history of his opinions on other subjects, political and religious affords the strongest ground for expecting that they would be unreasonable and unsound.²

The editorial goes on to speak in even stronger terms:
Nobody, however eminent as a novelist, or in whatever other walk of art, has any business to invite his fellow-men to step with him outside the region of sanity (within the boundaries of which there is abundance of interesting and rational matter of discussion) and sit down beside him like Alice beside the Hatter or the March Hare for the solemn examination of so lunatic a thesis as this (*Literature*, p. 74).

Having thus introduced Tolstoy to this illustrious company of literary madmen, the article proceeds with a medical diagnosis:
The utmost vigor of logic is a phenomenon frequently displayed by a class of persons whose theories are never seriously discussed, except with the object of humoring the theorist: and it seems to us much more to the purpose in this case to attempt a preliminary diagnosis of the theorist's own case. It is not a reassuring history. Count Tolstoi, after establishing a brilliant record as a writer of fiction in early life, took up at about the age of fifty with Socialism of the crudest sort, started what was practically a new religion based upon a highly eclectic form of Christianity, and developed sundry views as to the relation of music — and cigarette smoking — to sexual morality which would have earned for any less distinguished and respected person the slang American epithet of a "crank" (*ibid.*).

It seems that what really offended the sensibilities of the Victorian establishment in America was the whole Tolstoy, in the entirety of what he represented — a disturbing force of conscience and of prophetic vision destructive to the entire fabric of conventions and illusions made to cover the nakedness of the Victorian fear of life. It fell to another iconoclast, a "mad Irishman," George Bernard Shaw, to present a saner and more balanced view of Tolstoy's aesthetics. While no one would consider Maude and Shaw to be true ideological bedfellows, the two did agree on some positive aspects of Tolstoy's treatise. In his own puckish way, Shaw first of all enjoyed the good fracas which, he thought, Tolstoy, the great prophet of non-violence, provoked on the literary battlefields:

> There is always something specially exhilarating in the spectacle of a Quaker fighting; and Tolstoy's performance in this kind will not soon be forgotten. Our generation has not seen a hartier bout of literary fisticuffs, or one in which the challenger has been more brilliantly victorious.[3]

Tolstoy's "brilliant victory" really consists, in Shaw's view, of the essential truth of his central definition of art, namely, that art concerns the transmission of feelings. "This is the simple truth," says Shaw. "The moment it is uttered, whoever is really conversant with art recognizes in it the voice of the master" (*Pen Portraits*, p. 257).

Shaw was not altogether willing to accept all of Tolstoy's propositions. "Clearly," says Shaw, "this book of his will not be valued for its specific criticisms, some of which, if the truth must be told, represent nothing but the inevitable obsolescence of an old man's taste in art" (*ibid.*, p. 255). Shaw was least of all impressed with Tolstoy's idea that the ordinary peasants are the ones capable of appreciating art. To this, he was amused to observe that Tolstoy acted like the true Russian aristocrat, as proud of the peasants' ignorance as of his own. According to Shaw: "there is nothing whatever to choose between the average country gentleman and his gamekeeper in respect of distaste for the Ninth Symphony" (*ibid.*, p. 257).[4]

Shaw's remarks seem relatively gentle, compared to those of another critic, John Albert Macy:

> Though he [Tolstoy] has a great height from which to view the world, his eyes are bad; and for all the contagion of good will and brotherly love which he preaches, his own heart is not warm enough to make us forget in the fervor of his belief the fallacies contained in it. Neither the truth nor the error of his teaching stirs us very deeply. The reaction on his doctrines is cold, and the very incitement to better things which he preaches as the great glory of true art fails to beat in the blood.[5]

Macy's well-aimed blow is made even more vicious by his *ad hominem* reference to Tolstoy's old age: "he shows rather the irascibility of old age than its tempered wisdom." We get the portrait of an unwise ancient with withered feelings propounding angrily and impotently that true feeling is the crux of art. Macy furthermore permits himself a perspective of cultural superiority to Tolstoy in what he calls "the crotchety side of his doctrine":

> One bias is evident: Tolstoi is a Russian. In Russia class distinctions are cruelly manifest, and Tolstoi's socialism and hatred of aristocracy are too sectional to form the basis of a universal theory of art. Russian art, moreover, with notable exceptions in fiction and music, does not rank with the best art of modern Europe and the narrow range, marked by the special works of art which Tolstoi selects to praise or to blame, makes one question whether he is well enough acquainted with the art of other countries (*ibid.*).

This accusation of ignorance has been repeated by both Russian and French critics of Tolstoy. There may be a point to it, but even if Tolstoy had known a great many more Western writers and artists than he mentions in the essay, chances are his opinions would not have changed perceptibly. It is not a matter of statistics, but of a particular *stance* toward the arts — a declaration of what art should be rather than a noncommittal description of the kind one might expect in the "hard" sciences. As Aylmer Maude pointed out (*Tolstoy and His Problems*, p. 45.), "the basis on which the work rests is a perception of the meaning of human life," a unified view:

> His [Tolstoy's — R.Š.] whole philosophy of life — the "religious perception" to which, with such tremendous labour and effort, he had attained — forbade him to detach art from life, and place it in a water-tight compartment where it should not act on life or be re-acted upon by life (*ibid.*, p. 44).

This point was much more clearly understood by Arthur Symons, another critic. Even though he remains rather skeptical about many issues in the essay, he does recognize the vitality in it of Tolstoy's own genius. As a first thing, Symons recognizes the sincerity of Tolstoy's commitment and can see that it is a value in

itself, regardless of the particular opinions on art:
> He is unique in our time in having made every practical sacrifice to his own ideal. Everything he writes, therefore, we are bound to receive with that respect which is due alike to every man of genius and to every man of unflinching sincerity. It is impossible that he should write anything which is without a value of its own, not necessarily the value which he himself attaches to it.[6]

Symons also understands precisely the moral intensity which underlies both Tolstoy's fiction and his statements on art. Speaking a propos of *Anna Karenina*, he says:
> There are none of the disguises of the novelist with a style, or of the novelist with a purpose. It is so real that it seems to be speaking to us out of our own hearts and out of our own experience. It is so real because it is the work of one to whom life is more significant than it is to any other novelist. Thus the final step, the step which every novelist, if he goes far enough, may be impelled, by the mere logic of things, to take, is easier, more inevitable for him than for any other. The novelist, more than any other artist, is concerned directly with life. He has to watch the passions at work in the world, the shipwreck of ideals, the action of society upon man, of man upon society. When he is tired of considering these things with the unimpassioned eyes of the artist, he begins to concern himself about them very painfully: he becomes a moralist. Perhaps he has been one: he becomes a reformer (*ibid*, pp. 83-4).

L. William Flaccus, also speaking of *Anna Karenina*, shows a similar understanding that the integrity of an artistic text comes from an author's integrity in perceiving that life must have an underlying moral quality:
> What Tolstoy means is that art must be rooted in a *Weltanschauung*, a life attitude, and that this, and not character or plot, is the true principle of unity in a novel or play. Life is thought to have an inherent moral quality; this the true artist is to give intensely and objectively (Duffield, p. 89).

One of Tolstoy's most contentious statements in the essay, that Beauty cannot function as a criterion defining art, not surprisingly has given rise to some of the most vigorous responses. The Russian critics, as we saw, tended to defend Beauty in terms of an Ideal superior even to love of humanity and coming very close, within the sphere of aesthetics, to the notion of Goodness — precisely what Tolstoy most vigorously denied. Macy, however, puts it in a much simpler and more determined way. He says (Duffield, p. 71) that "the chief noun in esthetics is beauty. Since Tolstoi rules beauty out of art entirely, his work is not so much a treatise on aesthetics as an attack on the very existence of this branch of philosophy" It is, of course, an overstatement to say that Tolstoy rules out beauty "entirely"; what he does is to place it in its proper context as one of the elements that may contribute to the value of a work of art. As for Tolstoy's point that beauty cannot be defined objectively enough to be a criterion Macy dismisses it as follows:

> These fallacies are due to Tolstoi's lack of training in philosophy. He does not see that the same subjectivity that destroys for him the value of judgments about beauty holds in all the judgments we make. Like beauty, all things that men think about and believe in — God, goodness, truth, all the conclusions of science, religion, ethics — depend on the biased individual. (Duffield, p. 71).

It may be reassuring to believe that Macy would not exclude himself from the number of "biased individuals" discussing Tolstoy's work. There is, however, a more interesting point. Tolstoy, as is common knowledge, was a truly great master in presenting in his fiction subjective experiences and beliefs by individuals who thought that what they perceive does not even come from them, but is, so to speak, Nature, the objective reality of the world itself, and not a matter of opinion. We need only to remember how Olenin felt that "the whole of God's universe, the whole of Nature" required that he love Maryanka, and how wrong he was about her love for him, or how Karenin deceived himself into believing that, being in the right, he "cannot be unhappy," or how long and hard Death had to torture Ivan Ilyich until he finally began to grasp that his own life had been lived wrong. After all this, Tolstoy may have become tired of his own skill in depicting human illusions; as he brought them into being one after another in his work, a conviction could begin to develop that something else altogether is necessary for life to have meaning — a statement on art generated not by the study of artistic devices, but by a moral principle.

Vernon Lee also defends the notion of Beauty as a fit criterion and essence of art, but, lacking Macy's philosophical candor about us all being biased, he does attempt to define beauty and comes up with a complicated statement that is not very helpful at all. He speaks of:

> that particular relation between certain visible and audible forms and the human being which is brought about by what we call *beauty*, as a relation involving, whatever its particular kind, a general momentary advantage to the vital, nervous, mental and bodily conditions, and accompanied, as all beneficent conscious phenomena are, by the condition called *pleasure* (Duffield, p. 660).

Then Lee gives up and calls beauty "a specific sort of pleasure at present neither analyzable nor explicable which, like all the other varieties of pleasure, can be instantly identified, though not described, by any one who has experienced it" (*ibid.*). At this point, it does seem simpler, as Tolstoy suggested, just to dispense altogether with the notion of Beauty as a factor in the definition of art. Yet, Lee proceeds to hold on to his position and even uses it to intimate that Tolstoy, at least in his essay, did not show much understanding of the organic and beautiful complexity of life:

> ...the constant return to the belief that art's eventual aim is to produce beauty, and even the very mystery which at present surrounds this indefinable and as yet inexplicable quality, go to prove that, in a world different from the monotonous ascetic, inorganic world conceived by Tolstoi, in a world of life the most complex, overflowing and organic — not merely the negative moral virtue, but physical beauty, as much as intellectual lucidity, is required, and, by the nature of things, will eternally be required and produced (Duffield, p. 61).

Anyone who has ever read Tolstoy's works with some attention knows just how rich and organic they are in their recreation of the fullness of life. If the essay is not an inexplicable aberration, which it is not, perhaps it may be perceived to speak in its own language of just the same richness and complexity as an infinitude of possible forms of religious consciousness, that is, of love for life as it blossoms out all around us. [7]

To Macy, the rejection of beauty as a criterion means also the rejection of pleasure and, since pleasure is a feeling, Tolstoy in effect has rejected his own definition of art as a transfer of feeling, and so:

> ...not only is Tolstoi wrong in saying that judgments about art must not depend on our pleasures, but if he understood psychology, he would see that his own theory, his book, all that he writes, is an expression of his pleasure, his personal sense of value, the very sort of ground which he would draw from under the structure of aesthetics (Duffield, p. 72).

Macy seems to place the word "pleasure" on the plane of abstract psychological principle and of philosophical relativism. From this height, the word simply does not describe what Tolstoy had in mind, namely that the rich and powerful of this world have indulged in personal and class hedonism and have given the pleasure they derive from it the name of Beauty, the aim of all art. What Tolstoy's critique of beauty and pleasure really means is that there is no abstract, theoretical reality where they exist as indigenous phenomena, just as there is no reality to the mental construct called "art" and the "aesthetic feeling" which art conveys, as distinguished from "ordinary feeling" If so, then Tolstoy's question "what is art?," which for him is concrete and real and fraught with factual consequences pertaining to how one should live, simply is not addressed to philosophy, psychology or the discipline of aesthetics. Or, to put it differently, the terms of discourse used by Tolstoy and by his critics are so different that there is no true meeting point where one could be articulated to the other.

This lack of communication, ironically, becomes especially evident when we compare what Tolstoy and what his critics say about the communicability of feeling. Tolstoy maintains that all true feeling is instantly and universally communicable because every person's relationship to God is the same. His critics say that feelings are communicable only when the artist and his audience learn to work with the same code, because every person's relationship to the history of culture is different. This, at least, seems to be

the gist of Macy's statement:
> Defining art as the transfer of feeling, Tolstoi makes the supreme assumption that any sane human being can feel again the expressed feelings of another. "Good art," he says, "is always intelligible to every one" Here is a great error. Art cannot suggest to a man a feeling which he has not had before. The previous experience of a reader, his capacity in general, determines how much he shall receive of emotional pleasure or of moral stimulus from the work of a great artist (Duffield, p. 76).

Vernon Lee also makes a similar point:
> What Tolstoy mistakes for a naturally, inevitably intelligible and enjoyable character in art is in reality an affinity, a resemblance, with forms of art already familiar (Duffield, p. 63).

Macy's statement that "art cannot suggest to a man a feeling which he has not had before" and Lee's point about Tolstoy's "mistake" suddenly reveal a deep affinity between Tolstoy's fiction and his statements on art. The term "making strange," made famous by Viktor Shklovsky precisely with reference to Tolstoy[8], indicates that the artist displaces the frame of reference, "forgets the rules of the game" (or "the forms of art already familiar") in talking about otherwise well-known things, with the result that they appear to us entirely new and strange, as if seen for the first time. The reader, then, in his astonishment at suddenly understanding this strangeness, is indeed infected with a feeling he has not had before. It seems clear that this "refusal to know the rules," this method of opening new insight by means of a context displacement that changes all relationships is, though on different levels, in different categories of discourse, precisely the same in Tolstoy's fiction and in his essay on art.

Another way found by the critics to dispute Tolstoy's idea of the universal accessibility of art was to assert, in exact opposition to Tolstoy, that the "common people" are far less capable of appreciating great art because they have not been informed and educated to its complexities, its levels of associations in the history of culture. Symons, for instance, says that Tolstoy's claim is:
> ...absolutely unjustifiable: it has no foundation in fact. The "Iliad," to an English labourer, would be

completely unintelligible. Imagine him sitting down to the simplest translation which exists in English, the prose translation of Lang, Butcher and Leaf: "Upon the flaming chariot set she her foot, and grasped her heavy spear, great and stout, wherewith she vanquisheth the ranks of men, even of heroes with whom she of the awful sire is wroth!" (Duffield, p. 86)

Symons's point really pertains to style (actually, a constipated Victorian English style) and indicates nothing at all about how well the common people might understand the substance of the *Iliad* if it were not obfuscated by such "simple" prose. Indeed, Tolstoy rose up in arms precisely against this sort of stylistic clutter and pomposity and, particularly in his old age, wrote a great many stories for the peasants in which severe simplicity of style went hand in had with full complexity of ideas. T.S. Knowlston, on the other hand, turns to A.E. Fletcher for support of his view that, style notwithstanding, the broad masses cannot understand art because:

...the majority of men are the victims of ignorance and prejudice and selfishness; and it is impossible, therefore, that they can appreciate that which is great by reason of its freedom from these characteristics, until at least their nobler instincts have been awakened by the contemplation of perfection.[9]

Tolstoy's position is, of course, just the opposite: only the few are corrupt, and what Victorian Englishmen might call "contemplation of perfection" is nothing but hypocrisy. In general, the English-speaking critics tend to approach the essay less from theoretical positions as such than through Tolstoy's examples of good and bad art, and to draw from these their critique of Tolstoy's propositions. Flaccus puts this point forward quite succinctly:

...if a theory is no stronger than its weakest dictum or application, little can be said in favor of his views on art. What can be held of a man who regards King Lear as a mere clutter of improbabilities and denies Shakespeare grasp, sense of measure, and true characterization; of one who rejects Dante and Michael Angelo nonchalantly, and shows as little understanding of the trenchant intellectualism of Ibsen as he does of the elusive art of Maeterlinck or

Baudelaire and the rich art of Boecklin, Beethoven, and Wagner? (Duffield, p. 87)

Macy refers to such and similar judgments by Tolstoy simply as "rubbish which must be cleared away before one can get to the good of Tolstoy's work" (Duffield, p. 68). It is probably true that the particular pronouncements of Tolstoy as to the worth of various works of art, such as his dismissal of classical Greek civilization as one produced by a little "semi-savage, slave-holding tribe," or his praise for "Uncle Tom's Cabin," or his reference to Michelangelo's Last Judgment as "absurd," are one of the main reasons why the essay is not often taken seriously today by very many people. Yet, it is good to remember Macy's statement that after all this there is the "good" of Tolstoy's thought; it is also more than a little tempting sometimes to hear someone's authoritative last judgment as to why the Last Judgment is not indeed absurd, or if the savagery of the ancient Greeks was not, after all, a fact. Tolstoy did not know how to express "safe" opinions; he spoke as his inner need led him to speak, and in some ways his very sincerity and courage of his convictions may well become the measure of both his genius and his solitude.

Since Tolstoy in his essay delivered some harsh judgments on the art of contemporary France, it is of some interest to see what the French had to say about it. Their responses, many of which were collected by E. Halperine-Kaminsky in *La Grande Revue* in 1899, after he had sent his translation of *What Is Art* to various French critics, writers and artists, in large part may be well explained by what Romain Rolland said in his biography of Tolstoy:

> The negative part — sarcasms and insults — is so vigorous that it alone has struck the artists. This hurt too much their superstitions and their susceptibilities, so that they failed to see that the enemy of their art is not the enemy of all art.[10]

E. Halperine-Kaminsky provided a thoughtful introduction to his questionnaire, in which he, first of all, succinctly stated the basic ideological position in Tolstoy's essay:

> Tolstoy presents the following principle: art, in all its manifestations, must pursue a moral goal and contribute to the realization of the highest ideals of each epoch. Modern art should also become inspired by that supreme ideal which should guide our ac-

tions. That ideal is still the same as was shown by
Christ nineteen centuries ago, but it has been so
much obscured by the dogmatic interpretations of
the Church that only now, after a long night, do we
see it return in our day with all its clarity: love for
thy neighbor and brotherly union of all humanity.[11]

Some of the responses do, however, demonstrate, that there was a good measure of cold Gaelic fury on the part of the slighted French artists, even if they were not referred to by name in Tolstoy's essay. Monsieur G. Rochegrosse says simply that he cannot even comment on:

This book, which may be admirable from the human
point of view, but which wounds all that I love and
venerate and which I therefore hate profoundly.[12]

Rochegrosse then adds a damning offhand comment: "question de race et de temperament sans doute" which presumably explains fully how only a Russian like Tolstoy could have written his impossible essay. Charles Garnier wastes even less time; for him the essay is "un nuage": "je trouve bien de la fumée dans les explications de Tolstoï" (*La Grande Revue*, p. 629). C. Saint-Saens simply cannot understand what would a barbarian like Tolstoy have to say about art to a cultivated Frenchman:

Tolstoy said that it was wrong to change one's shirt
and to take a bath, that it was criminal to perpetuate
the human race; Tolstoy said that property was one
of the shapes of pride; hence, whatever Tolstoy may
or may not say about art is of profound indifference
to me...(*ibid*, p. 638).

Some critics, like Daniel Lesueur, thought that Tolstoy's attack on the French modernists distorts his entire argument because of lost perspective:

In so vast a subject, he remains beset with his narrow
preoccupation, blinded by his singular bias. The entire history of art is barely touched upon with a
stroke of the pen, and the most universal issues seem
to run up against an anathema, and against what?
Against a small artistic movement that is limited in
duration and in its productions, and in its effect, concerning which it is not yet possible to predict if it will
even have some final influence, and which will prob-

ably disappear in the victorious progress of the Ideal of tomorrow, will not count for anything in the future (*ibid*, p. 650).

If Lesueur is belittling the achievement of the French Symbolists, he is playing into Tolstoy's hands. More importantly, however, his claim that Tolstoy shrugged off the entire vast field of art in order to base all his judgments upon "an anathema" against a little and probably inconsequential movement in literature shows that he had not followed the full outline of Tolstoy's thought. For Tolstoy, modern art was not a small aberration, but rather the logical consequence of the betrayal of faith by the Renaissance.

Henri de Regnier refuses to disparage the French modernists, preferring instead (like a number of others) to accuse Tolstoy of ignorance. He also repeats the reactions of a number of French and English-speaking critics to the effect that Tolstoy, the great artist, is no longer himself in the treatise — he must have deteriorated, lost his touch:

> If the ideas expressed in his book [*What Is Art?* — R.Š.] were those of the great novelist, author of *Anna Karenina* or *War and Peace*, it would be appropriate to discuss them with respect. No. These ideas are those of an old man who, to be sure, is famous, but who has fallen into the mania of a humanitarian and religious apostle, who has taken pains to deny to himself his own glorious past and to renounce his own admirable literary accomplishments. This fact removes, in a true sense, all meaning from his latest work, and I see no sense in discussing its principles.
> And as for details, he demonstrates such an ignorance of the French literature that it is impossible to listen to someone who has read so little and so poorly, who confuses everything for he has understood nothing, at least with respect to the actual works (*ibid*, pp. 461-2).

Many readers have remarked upon Tolstoy's narrow range of references to various works of art. It is quite possible that his acquaintance with modern European literature, perhaps also most particularly painting, was not very thorough, but then we must also remember Tolstoy's own caveat in the essay to the effect that the particular examples cited are of no special value and that some may indeed represent the consequences of his own conventional, possibly limited education, or "corruption," as he called it. The point is not there — what counts is Tolstoy's spiritual evolution as an artist and thinker about art, an evolution which made his ultimate opinions, right or wrong, truly consistent with his own mindset and therefore inevitable.

Some readers, unable to imagine how Tolstoy could say all those strange things about art, unable to consider him in the perspective of his total work, but still wishing to understand him somehow, went back, as some English critics did, to his "race," his Russian heritage and its limitations. Thus Flameng, a portrait painter who had spent some time in Russia, waxes positively poetic about Tolstoy's unfortunate land of birth:

> The immense distances under a leaden sky of nothing but the almost perpetual snow and night, a cold that penetrates straight into the heart, a social organization that is of necessity authoritarian and hierarchical, bear upon the Slavic soul with all their weight, making it but little disposed toward platonic contemplations, to exhilarating responsiveness before the spectacle of pure Beauty (*ibid*, p. 613).

As far as the ability of "âme slave" to be intoxicated before the spectacle of pure beauty, Flameng should have read his Dostoevsky, where he would have found out that Dmitriy Karamazov, for instance was not only prone to be so intoxicated, but could also add a special twist to his ecstasy: to worship simultaneously the purest ideal Beauty of both of Sodom and Madonna.

Among the critics who sought a more balanced view, some were prepared to admit that there was some value in Tolstoy's judgments, but they also felt either that he had been too sweeping and too dogmatic, or else that his criticism of modern society had only limited validity. Among the latter, Alfred Fouillée, in contrasting Tolstoy with the French philosopher Guyau to whom Tolstoy had referred in his essay, thinks that Tolstoy's ideas, while they have their value, suffer from his amateurish, personal impressionism:

> Tolstoy mixes into his great truths various paradoxical exaggerations and impermissible whims; his doctrines seem too amateurish and reveal the insuffi-

ciencies of his philosophical education. It is no less true that if one wishes to separate truths and errors in his work... the simplest and shortest means would be to compare *Art from the sociological point of view*, which contains all the essential ideas for a theses on social aspects of art, with Tolstoy's book, where accessory ideas are brilliantly expressed. The great Russian writer has mixed in a multitude of *personal impressions*, often inexact, which take up too much of his beautiful book that is nevertheless dedicated to art outside of the personal; a book individualistic nonetheless and, for this reason, enveloped in isolation. In philosophy and in sociology, Tolstoy remains an impressionist at the very same time as he would like to be an apostle to humanity.[13]

Others, for instance C. Renouvier, objected in principle to Tolstoy's definition of art:

Does Tolstoy's definition of art have the true characteristics of a proper definition? —No, because the *moral organ* is confused there with the esthetic organ, and moreover, a particular morality and a particular religion are prescribed by the creator of this organ.

Remy de Gourmont states the point of opposition between art and morality much more firmly than Renouvier:

In the *transmission of feeling*, regarded as the proper activity of art, one should distinguish between a natural and an artistic transmission (*La Grande Revue*, I, 285).

If art is given the purposes of morality, it ceases to be, because it ceases to be non-utilitarian. It is not possible that a work should comprise morality and art at the same time; the antinomy between them is absolute (*La Grande Revue*, I, 307).

When we remember that for Tolstoy art had a moral "utility" of the same order as food has "utility" of survival, and that this was precisely what gave art a meaning and a place in the total organic unity of life, we can indeed perceive clearly how radically different Tolstoy's position was from anything at all that can be subsumed under the commonly understood category of aesthetics. The antinomy, as Gourmont says, is absolute. No wonder that Tolstoy has by now become essentially irrelevant to aesthetics, and aesthetics, according to Tolstoy, was always irrelevant to life.

Among the French critics who assert against Tolstoy the "elitist" principle in art, we may quote F. Cormon:

> The purpose of art is to procure the most intimate joys that would not, of course, be lacking in nobility, in elevation of spirit, but accessible only to an elite capable of experiencing this (*ibid.*, p. 605).

He is, however, also willing to agree that the social elite is not the same as the intellectual one, and that the simple workers may not be any worse than some "*sots*" in the aristocracy, but that in either case, this says nothing about the relevance of judgments by either class to the values of art:

> I recognize... that Tolstoy is right when he states that artistic feeling of our epoch is that of the worldly classes, and that this feeling is false, pretentious, insipid and neurotic. He prefers the naive judgment of a worker to that of the worldly person, corrupted by faulty education. I believe this to be an exaggerated notion. The "Monsieur" is too often nothing but a fool, but the worker is ignorant. In reality, neither the one nor the other understands anything (*ibid.*, p. 607).

Some of the authors mentioned by name in Tolstoy's essay also responded to it. René Doumic, whom Tolstoy quotes approvingly in his essay a propos of his negative judgment against the new French writers (cf. Maude, p. 153) and the cult of obscurity which they embrace (Maude, p. 159) does point out, on the other hand, that Tolstoy failed to understand the function of artistic form:

> Tolstoy totally fails to recognize the value of form, by means of which the language of art is distinguished from any other language. The artist is one who can express better than other people the feelings experienced by them, even if often more vividly and more profoundly than he does. From this initial error [Tolstoy] has condemned art as a profession, as a discipline.[14]

Aside from some, who thought works like *War and Peace* were "loose baggy monsters," most readers of Tolstoy do recognize in him a true master of artistic form, and many of them are also enthusiastic about Tolstoy's ability to make people recognize in his works their own feelings brought to a much greater degree of intensity and perfection. Tolstoy did condemn the profession of art and of literary criticism, but he never said that mastery of artistic form is acquired in schools of art. From a Tolstoyan perspective, Doumic is merely operating in the same superstructure of abstractions called civilization which has nothing to do with either art or feeling. Doumic's own comment in another article seems to confirm the Tolstoyan view:

> He [Tolstoy] has fashioned for himself a soul resembling those of the simple-minded, whose condition he dreams of improving. Or, if you wish, once the veneer of civilization cracks, one sees the essence of barbarity coming to flourish in the Slavic soul.[15]

Here Doumic refers to the passage in *What Is Art?* where Tolstoy describes the opera rehearsal as a strange, grotesque ritual devoid of meaning. Apparently, in Doumic's view, Tolstoy's rhetorical gesture on behalf of those oppressed by a meaningless activity that passes by the name of art is proof of his own, Tolstoy's, barbarity. This is indeed where the issue is joined: to Tolstoy, in his essay as well as in his novels, for instance, in the descriptions of Anna Sherer's *salon* in *War and Peace*, Doumic's concept of civilization describes no reality and is a mere screen to hide the awful truth about our lives, while to Doumic this same concept implies our only hope for decent human existence.

On other points, however, Doumic tends to agree with Tolstoy. One of the most important issues on which both seem of the same mind is that of the communicative function of language in art. Doumic says:

> If art is a language spoken to be heard, then art cannot address itself only to the initiated and become the privilege of an elite; this is the great danger threatening modern art (*Études*, p. 205).

This, of course, is exactly Tolstoy's point: if art is any sort of a special language, its discrete characteristics should not include incomprehensibility. Doumic also gives a fair overall summary of Tolstoy's ideas in the essay:

> To keep in mind what is being said, and not merely the manner of saying, to appreciate a work of art ac-

cording to the degree of its universality, to respect simplicity above all the other qualities of expression, to restore the notion of morality to its rights, to demand of an artist that he should be, in the narrow as well as in the broad sense of the word, an honest human being — these are the essentials of Tolstoy's doctrine, once you separate them from the appearance of paradox and excesses of expression. These same demands constitute the classic and, I think, any sane doctrine of art (*ibid.*, p. 217).

On the other side of the coin, Doumic also understands the distortions of the concept of art which may result from an all-too-logical manner of arguing a valid point that leads to confining definitions:

We too are ready to pay homage to truth. Yet, we shall not push the superstitions of formulaic statements to the point of sacrificing works of art to them. And it is enough for us to see that a criterion allows one to reject Beethoven and to accept Dumas the father to realize that it is incomplete (*ibid.*)

Doumic seems to have perceived better than Tolstoy that aesthetics tries to understand why great art is great and not to define a priori what great art must be; that it is a search and not a prescriptive doctrine.

Stephane Mallarmé, whose poem "De la musique avant toute chose" was quoted in the essay with the subsequent comment that he, Mallarmé, who has also contributed to making dogma out of the cult of obscurity (Maude, p. 159) responded cautiously and not unfairly:

I would fear an erroneous interpretation, such as I see, for instance, in the tenor of the comments upon one of my poems. Leaving aside the specialized aspects of this treatise and considering only the generalized and disinterested ones, it seems to me that the illustrious apostle assigns to art, as a matter of principle, a quality which in actuality is rather a consequence. In effect, art is essentially *communicative* while in fact it is also exclusive (Halperin-Kaminsky, p. 637).

An angry response came from Sar Peladan, whose book *L'art*

idéaliste et mystique (1894) Tolstoy described as "very fantastic and very illiterate" (Maude, p. 106), because it refers to beauty as one of the manifestations of God. Peladan wrote an entire monograph as a response to Tolstoy[16] in which he, like some of the other French intellectuals, often substituted mere abuse and name-calling for argument. As long as Peladan observes at least the appearances of being rational, he does offer a reasoned critique of Tolstoy's manner of thinking, adding to it, unfortunately, a bitter dash of bigotry:

> What Tolstoy's conceptions lack is the ability to respect the inherent meaning of each verbal construct, not to subordinate one topic to another in an abusive manner and to sustain the logic of each matter at hand: this is what Russian thought will never have (Peladan, p. 103).

Peladan's arrogance quickly reduces him to name-calling even as he pretends to be speaking seriously of essential matters pertaining to his own and Tolstoy's notions on art. The issue Peladan takes with Tolstoy on the question of Beauty, Truth and Goodness, for instance, soon degenerates to a matter of Russian stupidity and Russian vodka:

> For Tolstoy, the Beautiful, the True and the Good are words without any meaning, and he sees a triple antinomy where there is a triple harmony. The Beautiful is the True that can be perceived, the True is the Beautiful that can be contemplated; the Good is the Beautiful and the True as realized.
>
> But this apostle envisages a populace that can only understand what is said by priests and vodka, and he wishes to reduce the intellectual domain to what a vodka drinker is capable of assimilating (Peladan, p. 60).

Without exactly accusing Tolstoy himself of drunkenness, Peladan does paint a picture of the great and complex artist as a sort of primitive without much of any thought in his head:

> The Russian reformer is what one would call in literary jargon a "simplist": he is short of ideas. To make up for this lack, he pushes the ideas he has to the extreme and makes them become brutal, absurd and even dangerous (*ibid.*, 109).

In the end, Peladan throws all pretense at civilized argument to the winds and stands naked before Tolstoy in all his injured and arrogant pride:
> It is intolerable that a Slav should instruct the Latins and that a preacher to the peasants should arrogate to himself the right to abuse our dogmas and our gods (*ibid.*, pp. 226-7).

Such lack of professionalism is particularly noticeable in contemporary Western, and indeed, Russian, responses to Tolstoy's essay; his readers and critics seem caught up in the prejudices and rhetoric of another age. Aside from theoretical issues pertaining "purely" to literature, as these may be understood, for instance, in Russian Formalism or European Structuralism, Tolstoy's contemporary critics also lacked, or were unwilling to accept, a perspective outside of art proper from which Tolstoy's ideas would appear to have acquired altogether new meaning and purpose. Unfortunately, only the conventional Stalinist Soviet approach to Tolstoy provides such a perspective as it also distorts him completely.

The English-speaking critics tended to focus first of all on Tolstoy's basic premises from which he arrived at his definition of art. Some, like George Orwell, began by simply dismissing Tolstoy's theories on the grounds that they are built on unwarranted and arbitrary assumptions.[17] The scholarly community, however, responded with greater care, and some attempts were made to subject Tolstoy's premises to an analytical description. Israel Knox, for instance, wrote in 1930 that:
> Tolstoy's philosophy of art consists of two distinct elements: the first is aesthetic in purpose and meaning and defines art as the infectious communication of emotions; the second is socio-religious, and is concerned with the moral value of the emotions or experience transmitted by means of art.[18]

This simple division provides two planes on which to discuss the essay and may help to introduce some clarity in Tolstoy's line of thought, from his definition of art as infection with feeling to the description of it as a mode of expression for religious consciousness. Tolstoy's classifications of art into true and counterfeit, combined with the discussion of true art as "bad" or "good," depending on the quality of feelings transmitted, tend in the essay to lose their outline, because of the impression one soon gets that the real division Tolstoy makes is between art that is "true and good" and one that is "counterfeit and bad," and also that the counterfeit art, although it is not supposed to convey any real feelings, does affect its audience in a morally destructive way. Knox, then, does straighten out the terms of the argument, but there is also the danger that his two planes of discussion may in the end lose some of their relevance to each other and leave us with a fragmented image of what the essay is all about. As for the definition of art itself, Knox' approach is similarly analytical:

> Three concepts are involved in this definition: that art is communication; that it is infectious communication; that it is the infectious communication of emotions. The three words, "communication," "infectious" and "emotions" are focal in Tolstoy's esthetic approach to art and their meanings and implications must be closely considered (*ibid.*).

Among such implications, there is the question whether or not art is really communication at all, rather than expression, and also the issue of what "feeling" means in the essay. Tolstoy's contemporaries both in Russia and the West, as well as Soviet critics, were much concerned with these matters. Knox, however, is able to dispose of them with ease. As to expression versus communication, the problem does not really exist:

> The controversy as to whether art is essentially expression or communication seems to me entirely fortuitous. The solution is simple and lucid: art is expression for the sake of communication (*ibid.*).

Such a solution clears the ground neatly, but it does not meet Tolstoy's requirement that infection with emotion must actually happen before we can say of any given text that it is art.[19] "Expression for the sake of communication describes no more than a preliminary stage of the event of art.

On the issue of feeling: ordinary versus aesthetic feeling, and mere feeling versus feeling which also includes aspects of thought, Knox is again quite confident:

> The reality of great art consists in the perfect blending of inspired thought and inspired emotion, in the luminous intuition which the imaginative reason fashions into a concrete, vivid, communicable image. It is fallacious to attempt to dissociate feeling from

reflection. What is true is that in the realm of art, an idea may not be analyzed as an abstract, detached speculative problem, but must be planted in a living heart and chronicled as an emotional experience. It would be better therefore to substitute for the word "emotions" in Tolstoy's definition the word "experience," and to interpret experience as that spiritual synthesis of thought and feeling which constitutes the stuff of life (*ibid.*, p. 70).

Perhaps the greatest profit from Knox' statement can be gained by regarding it as an effective description of what actually goes on in Tolstoy's fiction, whatever the theory. The characters there do indeed come before us as vivid, communicable and communicating images, as the stuff of life, essentially for the reason that they perceive their own thoughts as emotional experiences. Indeed, "perception" may be a more suitable term than "experience" to describe how Tolstoy's characters come to be created to the full illusion of life.

At a later date, 1975, another careful attempt to provide clear analytical categories for Tolstoyan premises on art was made by Gary R. Jahn in order, as he claims, "to follow the path indicated by Knox and divorce the aesthetic from the moral component"[20] Jahn postulates that there are three assumptions made in *What Is Art?*: 1) that art is a form of communication; 2) that what happens in the process of communication is properly described as "feeling," and 3) that art consists of two categories, one large, a general category that contains all communications of feeling and subsumes the other, small, "art in the full meaning of the word," which contains only those works which communicate feelings proceeding from religious perception.

Such an analysis may seem dangerously near to tautology: Tolstoy said art was the communication of feelings because he assumed that art is communication and that what it transmits are feelings. Nevertheless, describing these things as "assumptions" does help to transfer the discussion to a theoretical plane, approachable to the scholarly methodology of analysis. Gary Jahn proceeds to do so, particularly with regard to Tolstoy's understanding of "thought," and "feeling." As to thought, Jahn finds a solution with an assumption of his own, hard to argue with, namely that:

...by "a thought" Tolstoy meant anything which may be objectively the same for all persons: mathematical calculations, geometric theorems, matters of accepted historical fact, observable natural occurrences, and the like (*ibid.*, p. 62).

"Feeling," on the other hand is described as follows:
In short, "feeling," as it is used in *What Is Art?* may include all human experience, for it is not an entity or a list, however long, of entities, but rather the subjective mode of regarding any entity (*ibid.*).

All this is reasonable and clear, but there may be some in whom these conclusions will seem devoid of any real substance as pertains to demonstrating any specific contribution made by Tolstoy, because of their obvious applicability anywhere, inside and outside Yasnaya Polyana. But Jahn only enters into these considerations, first, for the modest purpose of separating the aesthetic from the religious plane in Tolstoy's essay — something already done by Knox — and, second, in order to substantiate his conclusion that Tolstoy, having made perfectly defensible assumptions about art, should be given more credit for his essay than he has been. Tolstoy's main fault, according to Jahn, is that he applied a moral scale to determine which works merit censure. As a result, Jahn says, "unfortunately, the aesthetic underpinning of *What Is Art?* has suffered as well, an apparent victim of guilt by association (*ibid.*, p. 64).

If Tolstoy could be asked today to respond to this, he might very well say that without the application of his "assumptions" on a moral scale there cannot be any defense of art, however defined. He quite justly remembered Plato's suggestion that artists should be simply driven out of the republic for the harm they may do.[21]

There is, of course, an essential difference between Plato's and Tolstoy's approach to art, as many critics have clearly perceived. Hugh I'Anson Fausset, for instance, says quite rightly that Tolstoy rejected Plato's metaphysical and symbolic conception of art in principle:

Tolstoy... began by rejecting a metaphysical conception of art. He did not merely reject the Platonic conception, because it was not grounded in human life and so, like the other-worldliness of the Church's Christianity, could be debased by the self-indulgent.

> He did not admit that the Idea of Beauty might be distinguished from a mere sensation of pleasure through being related to Truth, as Keats conceived it, the truth of human life disinterestedly experienced.[22]

Rejection of the platonic ideal, as Fausset well understood, also meant rejection of the ideal and myth of ancient Greece — the wellsprings which nourished the Renaissance. In direct contradiction to Tolstoy, he asserted that indeed, religious consciousness as defined by Tolstoy is precisely what characterizes the Renaissance in the flow of the tradition of culture:

> And this view we would oppose as being altogether too summary and as failing to express the true religious significance of the Renaissance as a new movement in the evolution of the human consciousness having its roots indeed in the continuous tradition of culture inherited from the ancient world but seeking to adapt that culture and the impulses which it expressed to the needs of a finer and more informed humanity.
>
> The finest minds since the Renaissance have rejected Church-Christianity, like Tolstoy himself, but they have not, in any true sense of the word, rejected religion (*ibid.*, p. 274).

The general impression is that English-speaking Western critics did not really know how to confront Tolstoy's views, so strange to them, so out of the mainstream of critical tradition. Concepts and categories with which conventional aesthetics generally operate in the West simply do not articulate at any meaningful point with Tolstoy's positions. It may be true, after all, that the framework of aesthetics, or of the theory of art, is not appropriate for measuring the worth of Tolstoy's ideas and the manner in which they were expressed. It is really an existential question, the same question as Tolstoy confronted so intensely in his fiction, the question which translates "what is art?" into "how shall I live?" William B. Edgerton, for one, seems to have understood this clearly when he said:

> Tolstoy's extreme statements may make it hard at times to resist the temptation to dismiss him out of hand — particularly when his dogmatism leads him

to disparage the art of such masters as Beethoven, Dante, Goethe, Raphael, and Shakespeare. The temptation must be resisted, however, because when we look below the surface of his extremism, we can see that Tolstoy here is grappling with a genuinely serious problem. This problem is the relation of art, and science, to humanity.[23]

The relation of everything Tolstoy was as an artist and a thinker to humanity is fully embodied in his fiction. Yet, this fiction itself has so many close ties with the convictions expounded in the essay on art that one must needs entertain the possibility that this essay, too, was in an important sense part of Tolstoy's general creative act, a particular mode of continuing, developing and enriching the insights into the human condition that his art itself provided him with. It is well to remember Fausset's significant insight:

But surely the reality of great art consists in this, that it *cannot* be translated into "the form of an argument," that it is neither understood as logic is, nor felt as sensations are, but that it is inextricably blends feeling and thought, being and knowing, that the two cannot be dissociated. And to experience it we too have to renew in ourselves the intuition which the artist expressed (Fausset, p. 278).

CHAPTER EIGHT

CONCLUSIONS

We have seen that Tolstoy's fiction as a whole exists within the framework of his continuing thought on art. We can read and ponder these two modes separately, of course, but the intimate relationship between them in itself can be regarded as an entity, an unrealized "zero-text" which, like some force-field, shaped all that Tolstoy actually wrote. In a similar way, Dostoevsky's non-existent *Life of a Great Sinner* may nevertheless be thought of as a sort of "supertext" of which all else he wrote were but partial variants. Indications that Tolstoy himself was to some degree even aware of such a "supertext" over his own work can be seen as early as 1856, when he jotted down a "Preface not for the reader but for the author" for a contemplated *Novel of a Russian Landowner*,[1] a sort of *Bildungsroman* meant to extol the virtues of country life, which he never wrote, and yet, in a sense did write all his life in and through his other works. To the degree that Tolstoy's art was also in effect a theory on art, one may say he wrote, all his life, a grand essay on art, of which *What Is Art?* itself is but an imperfect and partial realization. In that sense, what Tolstoy demanded of art and strove for in his work is not just the communication of this or that particular experience, but the transmission of his own entire selfhood to us so that, in response, we would permit ourselves to be absorbed into the enormity of that selfhood and become his world. It may seem strange to think of some godlike entity as a simile of Tolstoy, but such comparisons have indeed occurred to some,[2] even though Tolstoy himself repeatedly denied that there is any such category as "genius," maintaining instead that the same spark of divinity dwells in us all. Somewhat more modestly, one could think that Tolstoy, possibly even unbeknownst to himself, was offering his genius as a force to replace the perceived mythology of his time consisting, as he saw it, of fake Christianity, false notions of art and perverted moral values.[3]

We have seen that the idea of art as infection with feeling informs his fiction with particular intensity. It is the deepest source of the Tolstoyan "supertext," the driving force that planted the pillars of Tolstoy's moral edifice and shaped its aesthetic design. In his mind, this idea is not a static formula to be consciously applied in a sequence where feeling precedes the creative act, but a dynamic, instinctive process that directs the flow of narrative as it emerges from the imagination. In other words, the quality of the artist's feeling: its intensity, scope and communicability become realized as an artistic text — an illusion of some actual world in which we ourselves might live and be called upon to decide what is right and what is wrong. In the grip of this feeling, the Tolstoyan imagination generally works by transforming the characters, objects or actions into multivalent signs that, without becoming metaphors, do in effect function as such and produce an impression akin to poetry. As the reader discovers this poetic complexity of a Tolstoyan text, many things in it become "strange," suddenly seen in a new light that changes the logic of all relationships. In Tolstoy, this is the crucial moment of new existential insight, when ordinary things lose their inert familiarity and become discoveries of some important truth about one's own inner nature or condition.[4] In this sense, the Soviet critic E. Kupreyanova is right when she says that in Tolstoy's landscapes a barrier is removed between the depiction of the outer world and the expression of the inner one.[5] So in *The Cossacks*, the breathtaking, constantly expanding presence of the mountains before Olenin's astonished eyes is in fact the materialization of an unconscious inner process by which he discovers the implicit boundlessness of his own soul. Conversely, when under the serene Austerlitz sky Prince Andrey understands the irrelevance of puny human ambitions, that moment serves as a marker of his beginning inward journey toward concordance with death.[6] It is a sign pointing toward his ultimate discovery, as he lay dying after Borodino, that the irrelevance of wars and passions to the endless spaces of the sky is actually the irrelevance of his own life itself to the infinity unfolding within him.[7] As we see how for Tolstoy there is ultimately no meaning in anything that is separated out, be it the events of history or those of an individual soul, or just the presence of the earth and the sky, it becomes clearer how art for him is an emotion that unifies everything. On a very deep level of experience, the sense of this unity becomes what Tolstoy calls "religious consciousness".

This underlying existential perception of the unity of all things is also an equivalent of the force of feeling that shapes the structural integrity of Tolstoy's artistic texts. It controls the tension that often exists in Tolstoy between the mode of fictional narration on the one hand, and of expository discourse on the other. So in *War and Peace*, moral feeling emerging from the immediacy of an individual experience moves by a sort of osmosis across the barriers that separate fiction, history and essay, establishing a relationship of influence and transformation that unites all three and makes it possible to read the novel as a single integral aesthetic structure, in effect, a new literary genre. As we leaf backwards through the novel, we can observe how the structural logic of Tolstoy's final arguments gradually recedes into the associative logic of an artistic text in the depicted events and experiences and against the background of history. When, having perceived this, we again reverse direction and move through the novel from the beginning, we see that, as the novel's argument extends toward asserting the impermeability of reality by the arrogance of reason, the objective causality of events increasingly assumes the aspect of multiple individual perceptions, and in these, roots and causes of things become transformed more and more into images, so that ultimately, both the history and the philosophy that judges it become a single text subsumed by art.

Such a text then also has this additional quality that any particular portion of it, when closely observed, reveals its capacity to embrace, or signify, the entire structure with all its temporal and spatial dimensions. A striking example from *Anna Karenina*, is the passage where Levin and Kitty meet again at a party after long separation during which their love for each other has somewhere on the edge of their consciousness grown into an irresistible force. Now, at their new encounter, this force suddenly erupts in them and overwhelms everything:

> She [Kitty] and Levin were carrying on their own separate conversation, and it was not even a conversation but a kind of mystic intercourse, which every moment bound them closer and closer and created in both a feeling of joyful fear before the unknown upon which they were entering (*Anna Karenina*, Norton, p. 355).

This "mystic intercourse" is in essence the same moment of poetic transformation of discourse into feeling from which, in Tolstoy, art is born. Of special interest, however, is the manner in which the moment of that union also becomes a co-presence of everything that went on before in the characters' lives. A little later that very evening, precisely for this reason, Levin and Kitty can communicate deep and complex feelings to each other by simply writing down the first letters of each word they want to say. All their separate and shared past events and feelings have now blended in their minds into a single awareness, a "text" they both read in the same way. Thus a single sign acquires the quality of what is called a "fractal" in mathematics, a particular fragment that repeats the structure of the whole and thus, in literary terms, becomes a kind of multivalent synecdoche, a part which yet embodies in itself the potential to expand and be a complete world. Therefore, the integrity of a Tolstoyan text is such that the feeling in it also functions as the underlying idea and is present in its entirety at every single point and must be so perceived by the reader. All this makes any given text in its turn a single "sign" which must, as Tolstoy demands in his essay, communicate itself instantaneously, universally and in its totality.

It follows, then, that the whole of Tolstoy's work, fiction and non-fiction, in all its modes and genres, is not an aggregate of separate categories of texts, but a single text, a complex, dynamic structure of modulations and transitions which constantly interpenetrate each other encoding and re-encoding the same ultimate message in a variety of different ways. In his own commentaries to *War and Peace*, Tolstoy defined this message not as some particular idea but as an all-encompassing love of life: "The goal of the artist is not to solve a question irrefutably, but to force people to love life in all its innumerable, inexhaustible manifestations" (letter to P.D. Boborykin, 1865, *War and Peace*, Norton, pp. 1359-60). This love of life is, of course, that same feeling of which Tolstoy speaks in his essay as the wellspring of all art.

This deep striving for unity of all things also helps explain Tolstoy's peculiar attitude to science. In denying the relevance of pure scientific quest to any true human values, he in effect relegates it to the same sphere of counterfeit, artificial activities as false art and the equally false customs and standards of city culture that comprise the social, artistic and scientific traditions. In *What*

Is Art? Tolstoy states quite vigorously that neither the subject matter nor the methodology of what are called "hard sciences" make any sense, since the only thing worth studying is the question of how one should live. Therefore, scientific inquest should in its essence be a study of the various states of moral perception and not of supposed objective realities. On various occasions in his life, Tolstoy even went so far as to deny such reality to time and space, calling the one "the human ability to perceive many things in one and the same space," possible only through sequentiality, and the other "human ability to perceive many things at the same time," possible only in the co-presence of things. Both kinds of perceptions are needed so human beings could communicate with one another. "Thus," says Tolstoy, "time and space can be described as human capabilities, but they make no sense as attributes of things" (see *U Tolstogo*, III, 451).

Again, there is a direct connection between Tolstoy's ideas on science and the beliefs and feelings expressed by various characters, or in the authorial voice, in particular works of fiction. For instance, we can see in *Anna Karenina* how the "scientific" perspective of the medical profession becomes equated with moral outrage. After rejecting Levin's first proposal of marriage, and after the mortifying experience of having to watch Anna and Vronsky, her fiancee, dancing together oblivious to the whole world, Kitty became depressed, and a doctor was called. This doctor, who thought that "nothing is more natural than for a man still in his prime to handle a young woman's naked body," proceeded to do so with Kitty, who was "stupefied with shame" (*Anna Karenina*, Norton, pp. 106-7). In *War and Peace*, Tolstoy's attitude to science, in particular, medicine, very much the same as in his essay and in other works preliminary to it, is blended smoothly into the context of the novel's ideas about the "science of war" and the logic of causes and effects in history. After the humiliating episode of aborted elopement with Kuragin, Natasha, like Kitty in *Anna Karenina*, suffers a nervous breakdown and doctors are also called in. Just like the Russian generals at the council of Drissa (in Book Nine, Maude translation), these doctors "talked much in French, German and Latin, blamed one another, and prescribed a great variety of medicines" (*War and Peace*, Norton, p. 726). Their mistake was the same as, according to Tolstoy, the historians have always been making in their "science" of history, namely that the

doctors could not comprehend the infinite multiplicity of causes for any event:
> the simple idea never occurred to them that they could not know the disease Natasha was suffering from, as no disease suffered by a live man can be known, for every living person has his own peculiarities and always has his own peculiar, personal, novel, complicated disease, unknown to medicine — not a disease of the lungs, liver, skin, heart, nerves, and so on mentioned in medical books, but a disease consisting of one of the innumerable combinations of the maladies of those organs (*War and Peace*, Norton, p. 726).

Thus also in the second epilogue to *War and Peace,* speaking of the freedom of will versus determinism, Tolstoy points out the impossibility of such knowledge as would exclude any element of unpredictability, that is, of free will:
> However we may increase our knowledge of the conditions of space in which man is situated, that knowledge can never be complete, for the number of those conditions is as infinite as the infinity of space. And therefore so long as not *all* the conditions influencing men are defined, there is no complete inevitability but a certain measure of freedom remains (*War and Peace*, Norton, 1346).

Similarly, then, there is no defining a disease according to known laws that would elucidate its causes and its course. Nevertheless, Tolstoy also makes the point that those doctors are necessary after all because they "satisfied a mental need" of the patient, made him feel reassured, just like the Russian soldiers needed the confident Bagration at Schöngraben, even though the general did not seem to be issuing any particular orders.[8]

All this corresponds precisely with the ideas expressed in *What Is Art?* to the effect that there is really no "science" of literary criticism, no schools, and that in an ordinary human being who makes his living honestly, there is an infinitude of feelings each of them conducive to the creation of a true and original work of art. In the essay and in other places, Tolstoy makes his point that science deals with causes, measurements and predictions and takes for its subject of study all sorts of useless trivia (like calculating the paths of heavenly bodies). In his fiction, this idea is also repeated frequently and emphatically in all sorts of circumstances. The only meaningful science, Tolstoy says, is one that will help us learn how to live right; and precisely the same demands are made of art.

The close and extensive connections and correspondences between Tolstoy's fiction and his essay, particularly on the crucial points that art is infection with emotion, that it must be universal and instantaneously experienced in full, and that its significance lies in the moral dimension, permit the view that Tolstoy's fiction in effect also functions as a theory of art. The many just and obvious objections that have been raised against *What Is Art?* appear valid only as long as we read the essay as a separate theoretical statement which requires a judgment on a proper rational plane of the points being made. On the other hand, when the same or similar notions are presented to us as the experiences of Tolstoyan characters in the context of their own lives and not as separate and abstract formulations, the appeal is not to our judgment but to our empathy with the people depicted and to the sensitivity of our poetic imagination. Thus when Natasha in *War and Peace* watches the opera and sees only nonsense, we immediately recall the foolish and cruel goings-on at the opera rehearsal in the beginning of *What Is Art?*. The question raised there: can these inhuman idiocies be justified in the name of art? is certainly implicit also in the novel, but what we think about, are affected by, is Natasha's emotional state as a young, lonely girl, desperately needing love and having just been cruelly repulsed by the old Bolkonsky. Similarly, when young Irtenyev in *Childhood*, after his success with the false poem to his grandmother, muses that art is a lie, our mind is engaged in a dialogue with the young boy's soul and not with the theoretical or philosophical proposition ultimately articulated in the essay.

Similar juxtapositions can be found almost everywhere in Tolstoy's fiction, and some have been discussed elsewhere in the present essay. Their cumulative effect on the reader is to create an image of Tolstoy that is astounding in its massive consistency with itself. As we move in time through Tolstoy's life and works, from his earliest writings to his last, that single image constantly rebuilds itself from all the new, diverse, often contradictory messages emanating from the succession of his texts. The act of reading Tolstoy then appears to be a process of constant rediscovery that an entity called "life," infinitely complex, yet randomly distributed in its parts, keeps reconstituting itself in the shape of this amazing Tolstoyan image as a kind of moral-artistic equivalent of God.

At the same time, each of the particulars stands in contradiction to some or all of the others as often as it is in agreement with them. We are led to perceive that this unyielding monolith is not actually a structure shaped according to some ultimately harmonious system of laws. It is rather a sort of intensity, a constant struggle of opposites that sustains itself, indeed, achieves its special Tolstoyan sort of unity from the very tension among its parts.

Looked at in terms of the relationship between Tolstoy's fiction and his essay on art, this condition could be described, in still another sense, as a form of conflict between what we might call "text" and "context." By "context" we would mean the complexity of life to itself, so thoroughly attested to in Tolstoy's works, which by its very organic nature permits no imposition of a pre-conceived explanatory scheme, be it rational, moral or aesthetic. Tolstoy understood this randomness very well; indeed, according to Gary Saul Morson,[9] he developed it in its aesthetic implications to become his basic creative method in structuring *War and Peace* as well as *Anna Karenina* and other works. By "text," on the other hand, we now understand not so much some realized structure of thought as a great urgency and desire on Tolstoy's part that there should be such a thing. He felt a great need to postulate logical sets of definitions circumscribing and explaining particular phenomena which would then act upon our conscience with the force of moral compulsion. For this reason, Tolstoy asked and answered his question "what is art?" not in terms of "context" — the historical flow of multiple interrelationships between art and life that constitutes the artistic tradition, but in those of a "text" — a set of requirements art must meet in order to deserve the name. In reality, however, this set of requirements boils down to just one: genuine and effectively communicated feeling. That is not a logical construct, for its point of origin is somewhere in the as yet largely uncharted seas of the instinctive and the subconscious. Thus the rationalist, text-maker Tolstoy, in his mighty labor, actually produced but a context in which, as he believed, our feelings can respond to the miracle of art.

From another point of view, Tolstoy's formulated aesthetics as well as his own art could be considered together as one side of still another relationship, that between "text" — all that he wrote — and "supertext" — the driving force behind it all. In the relationship between Tolstoy's particular beliefs about art and the systems of aesthetic values accruing in the progress of civilization, the Tolstoyan "text" stands in opposition not to the fullness of life but to the artificialities of our society. In this other "text" - "supertext" relationship, there is a different dichotomy, between the basic thrust of Tolstoy's vitality and its realization on the printed page.

One difficulty with such binary arrangements to describe the essentially total unity of Tolstoy's art and thought is that they can become a mere static scheme, logical and balanced but explaining hardly anything more than itself. We need to take one more step: to consider the dynamics of this complex system of relationships, asking not only what it *is*, but also where it is going — what thrust or direction can we perceive in this totality before us.

Art itself, as we recall, was defined by Tolstoy much less as an entity than a process, an activity. It led to "infection with feeling," that is, a particular state of awareness, or mode of perception, which becomes "religious consciousness" with respect to good and important art. If there is indeed an all-pervading unity, if Tolstoy himself can, so to speak, be regarded as a universal "sign," then this state of awareness can be understood as the ultimate goal, and all his life and work as a journey toward it.

We know what Tolstoy said this religious consciousness is supposed to be: the highest understanding of the meaning of life, that is, of good and evil, at any given epoch. In terms of the dynamics of this issue, however, we must ask a different question, namely, can this consciousness itself be described as a path, a parabola curving toward this highest understanding, and what it is like as an experience, how does it feel as its rising tide floods the mind and the soul.

We may approach this question at the point of Tolstoy's encounter with science. First of all, if time and space are human capacities rather than attributes of things, then what we call "reality" is a world inside the mind, is a human experience. That must mean that this deeper understanding of reality is simultaneously a retreat from its physical dimensions to those of the mind. Then such a time and space can only be depicted as something that goes on inside the mind, that is, for a writer, the proper medium of conveying it is fiction, his art. Tolstoy's argument that time and space are in essence but modes of human communication, broadly understood to include conflict as well, or of human awareness of the self in dimensions that cut across those of outer reality is confirmed many times over in the great novels themselves. To take one example, for the Russian soldiers at the start of the battle of Austerlitz, what gives reality to space is that it constitutes a transition from what we are to what we cannot know:

> There was no one now between the squadron and the enemy except a few scattered skirmishers. An empty space of some seven hundred yards was all that separated them. The enemy ceased firing, and that stern, threatening, inaccessible, and intangible line which separates two hostile armies was all the more clearly felt.
> "One step beyond that boundary line which resembles the line dividing the living from the dead lies uncertainty, suffering, and death. And what is there? Who is there? — there beyond that field, that tree, that roof lit up by the sun? No one knows, but one wants to know. You fear and yet long to cross that line, and know that sooner or later it must be crossed and you will have to find out what is there, just as you will inevitably have to learn what is on the other side of death" (Norton, *War and Peace*, 151-2).

Only this fictional space is real; any other is, so to speak, fiction. For Prince Andrey, as he sees the old oak tree in its two aspects, of death and life, time is the measure of the distance between his old self and his new love, and thus, really, a metaphor of resurrection. The stormy distance on the train between Moscow and Petersburg acquires reality when it serves as the measure of Karenina's passion. The split second, just as Anna was stepping out of the railroad car upon arriving in Moscow, is an indefinite measure of time in its transformation into an infinitely extendible discourse on the future tragic love, which, however, is already accomplished, between her and Vronsky. Similarly, we can think of *The Resurrection*, Nekhlyudov's journey to distant Siberia, as an artistic realization of space in terms of remorse and love. As Nekhlyudov follows Maslova, he gradually learns that he is withdrawing from outer to inner reality of space and time and that this is at the same time a movement from the point at which the notions of meaning and purpose of life do not apply toward the meaningful, therefore real, realm of morality. In other words, time and space in Tolstoy's fiction become aspects of that parabola curving toward religious consciousness. Whatever sense and science may think of Tolstoy's arguments on time and space, they indeed come true in Tolstoy's art in the creation of a large universal metaphor — a semiotic universe where as Pasternak said, things are symbolic because they are significant.

This overall pattern and direction of Tolstoy's creative thought seems in one basic way to correspond to the structuring of events and dynamics of character development in the main novels. The advocacy of a state of perception against conventionally understood activity, and the parabola of withdrawal from the affairs of life toward a death-like state of perfection seems to be the aesthetic *dominanta* in the novels as well. Gary Saul Morson in his fine study *Hidden in Plain View* spoke of "creation by potential," in *War and Peace*, suggesting that instead of laying out firm plans that would encompass the entire novel according to what the author believes the drama, logic and meaning of events should be, Tolstoy, as it were, remained alert for a given moment's opportunity to create events and experiences that could easily have been altogether different, and with just as much justification. In other words, as an author, Tolstoy was himself retreating from the basic supposition that there must be a settled plan for any given work before it can be written and that what matters is not a particular drive toward some conflicts and their resolution, but an open state of mind and a trust in one's instinct to let life itself unfold as it will. One could extend this argument to the condition of Tolstoy's main heroes and describe them as progressing from the strain of desire or the suffering of misfortune, or the quest for truth, to some resolution in a healing state of awareness. This was so with Pierre when he acquired his inner "judge," and with Konstantin Levin when the peasant finally told him to have God in his heart and let his life proceed of itself from there — something that Tolstoy has always ardently recommended to everyone. Certainly Ivan Ilyich heaves a great sigh of relief when he sloughs off the diseased burden of a life considered by all to have been active and rational.

Most compellingly, the slow transition of Andrey from a life of tumult and striving toward the cosmic indifference of death comes to mind again and again as we read in Makovicky's diaries how the aging Tolstoy repeatedly sighed for death as the ultimate state of goodness. The fate of Anna Karenina, on the other hand, seems a terrifying variation on this theme: her life was also a movement from passion to awareness, but that awareness itself was one of ultimate disgust and terror, and death came inexorable and unconscious of itself, like that blind cosmic Dostoevskian machine.

In the world outside of fiction, in Tolstoy's daily encounters with people and ideas and in the numerous non-fiction works relating to all areas of human experience, a similar principle of withdrawal increasingly seems to apply. To take but one example from late in his life, during and after the 1905 war Tolstoy expressed strong opposition to the voices that demanded a constitution for Russia. A constitution is a measure accomplished not inside the mind but in the outer reality. It is a political concept that defines particular aims and prescribed ways of achieving them, thereby superimposing an abstract model of what is desirable upon that inner moral imperative which is the only important thing about being human. Society has many more such models used to profess morality while doing violence to the dictates of conscience, and therefore it must be understood, as Tolstoy says, that: "the concept of morality must be defined not by actions that are presumed to be useful, but by the inner demands of one's conscience. The purpose of a religious person's actions is to satisfy everything demanded of him by the law of God" (Makovicky, IV, 39). That law, according to Tolstoy, is not to be found in some theological doctrine, but rather to become manifest as that state of consciousness Tolstoy calls "religious." In other words, moral reality resides for Tolstoy not in action, but in perception. The quest for it consists of progressive withdrawals from conventional constructs pretending to purpose, meaning and reality.

The same principle applies, for Tolstoy, to the theological notions of space as heaven and earth, and of time as earthly life versus eternity. Disliking both physics and metaphysics, he relied insistently, throughout his life, on religious consciousness as the virtuous state of self-perception and perfection to strive for. Similar views emerge with respect to history. Readers of *War and Peace* will, of course, remember that the study of history as a logically explicable movement of events in time through space is equally meaningless, and that the war was won as a consequence of the feeling, again, a state of mind, shared by Kutuzov and the Russian people. Basically, Tolstoy thought of history as an unfolding of religious consciousness over time; this was the only notion of progress that he would accept.

After demolishing the respective spatial and temporal foundations of science and theology, withdrawing from abstract schemes of human conduct and reducing history to a particular mode of self-awareness, Tolstoy proceeds to reject the concept of the self as a discrete, circumscribed entity. In 1907, for instance, Tolstoy said to one visitor: "Recently it has become so clear to me that I am not Tolstoy and you are not Kartuvin, but that both you and I are this divine essence which one feels in oneself, which exists in us all" (Makovicky, I, 498). In *War and Peace*, we can see in Platon Karataev this total surrender of the self to the whole of life as a manifestation of our inner divinity. In *The Resurrection*, the one person so completely and unshakably himself that nothing can touch him is an itinerant peasant who has totally withdrawn from his own identity and from commitment to the cares of the world. In *What Is Art?*, the ultimate true artist is certainly not a professional, nor does he seek any sort of recognition; in fact, he is so anonymous, that one might say he does not really exist, and only his art is there to spread its message.

Both in Tolstoy's art and his thought the movement of withdrawal from personal identity in the secondary, outside, world is at the same time a movement toward a primary conception of life, leading to concentration upon one's inner self that is perceived not as something enclosed and with discrete content, but as an expanding inner freedom that feels like increasing love and transforms one's perception of the world from evil to good. This expanding inner freedom has its outside corollary in increasing simplicity of life, rejecting more and more of the secondary level of existence, where civilization and art exist in a refined, exclusive state.

From the evanescence of self, Tolstoy's thought leads logically to the elimination of God as a discrete entity. God to Tolstoy is not a religious idea, but only the object of religious consciousness, that is, again, not an entity, but a process, the ultimate description of how we should live, as Christ said in the Gospel: "I am the path, the truth, and the life." For Tolstoy, however, this process is one of increasing disengagement from things that ordinarily surround us in life, thus making the ultimate ideal of self-perfection also one of evanescence, of universal awareness without God, without self and without any encumbrances of conventional social structures and of material reality.

The essay *What Is Art?* and numerous other statements on aesthetics scattered throughout Tolstoy's works can also be read as if they were maps and markers tracing the route of withdrawal from all conventional standards and concepts of art carried onwards through history by the rising tide of civilization. The early parts of the essay, Chapters I through VII, present a discourse on the definition of art that seems consistently deformed by the device of alienation, the famous Tolstoyan "making strange." At the start we have a description of opera rehearsal totally lacking in any expected judgment on the quality of the artists' performance, on the music or the libretto, but filled with images of torture, humiliation and crippling of human beings who have the right and the potential of being our brothers and sisters in freedom and mutual love. Further on, Tolstoy stubbornly and meticulously stretches the distance between himself, holder of the true definition of art, and the entire enormous structure of aesthetics that was built through long centuries as suitable housing for that definition. Whatever society thinks and does about art becomes increasingly irrelevant to what art really is in the view of Tolstoy himself.

This withdrawal from established aesthetic theory brings with it a similar retreat from aesthetic practice. The entire world of the arts seems to Tolstoy like an enormous, grotesque opera rehearsal where:

> it is terrible to reflect that lively, kindly, children capable of all that is good, are devoted from their early years to such tasks as these: that for six, eight, or ten, hours a day, and for ten or fifteen years, some of them should play scales and exercises; others should twist their limbs, walk on their toes, and lift their legs above their heads; a third set should sing solfeggios; a fourth set, showing themselves off in all manner of ways, should recite verses; a fifth set should draw from busts or from nude models, and paint studies; a sixth set should write compositions according to the rules of certain periods; and that in these occupa-

tions unworthy of a human being, which are often continued long after full maturity, they should waste their physical and mental strength, and lose all perception of the meaning of life (*PSS,30*, 186; Maude pp. 252-3).

What this means is that no one can *learn* to be an artist — one can only learn to do meaningless things in a pernicious sphere of activity which in our modern world passes for art. True art wells up from the heart like a spring in the meadow, and the whole world knows what it is. This means also, as Tolstoy himself insists, that there cannot be any schools of art, nor can there be any analysis or criticism of art. True art is universally and fully present in every soul. Such universality also obviates the notion of outstanding individual talent, for what indeed is talent against the spark of divinity that resides in us all? We may note here that a certain hidden hostility to the idea of any special individual talent is already implicit in *The Yasnaya Polyana Journal*, where Tolstoy himself, an author of note by then, holds the spontaneous creativity of some village lad called Fed'ka to be superior to his own. From this sort of perspective, we can also see that Tolstoy in his fiction never dignified the idea of talent by attaching it to the positive accomplishments of his protagonists. On the contrary, he demeans it by juxtaposing the reputation for talent to characters he portrayed as small and despicable. Such is Napoleon, supposedly a genius, bungling his military operations while Bagration, depicted by Tolstoy as on the whole rather stupid, is extremely effective at Schöngraben. Even more so, Kutuzov, a man utterly without talent, always does the right thing because he is, like every true Russian peasant, indeed, like Karataev, a simple man with God in his heart. Similarly, the notion of talent does not apply to the machinations of a Prince Vassily, or of Karenin, surrounded as both of them are by the *reputation* of special abilities.

If we do not speak of knowledge, skill or talent, what can we say of art, what works can we propose as genuine and important, such as those that can infect us with the emotion they contain? Tolstoy could only give tentative examples, some, like *Uncle Tom's Cabin*, decidedly minor. The paucity of his examples, his own cautious remarks in the essay that both the good and the bad works he cites may just be choices stemming from his own corrupt education and not truly from his now genuine understanding of art, and the inconsistency of his judgments on various artists and their works throughout his life seem to point, paradoxically, to an ultimate criterion that is radically different, indeed, precisely the opposite of any one would think of using. The criterion is — non-art. True art à la Tolstoy does not bear any of the characteristics traditionally associated in our society with an artistic text, be it verbal, sculptural, musical or whatever, because it is not an artifice, an artifact, a product of our civilization — it comes from elemental human nature. If this implication is not altogether clear in the main body of the essay, it does finally emerge at the end, where Tolstoy discusses what the art of the future shall be. "The art of the future," says Tolstoy, "will be completely distinct both in subject matter and in form from what is now called art." It will consist of fairy-tales, touching little songs, lullabies, entertaining riddles, amusing jests — in other words, of various marginalia to art. According to Tolstoy, it is "incomparably more important" to produce these items "than to compose a novel or a symphony, or paint a picture," because these will only divert members of the upper classes for a little while. It is, then, minimal art, not in the sense of a Malevich or other such minimalists of the modern Russian movement of the early nineteen twenties, but in the sense of an aesthetic stimulus reduced to the very point of non-existence. It is true, of course, that a sophisticated analysis of such incidentals could engender an enormous image of their multivalent complexity, but that, to Tolstoy, would just be another example of the nonsensical labors of modern aesthetics.

From such a perspective, the gigantic achievement of the Renaissance, the genius of Shakespeare, twist themselves into grotesque and meaningless, morally repulsive shapes as they are sicklied over by the pale and angry cast of Tolstoy's thought. To the degree that the Renaissance may be said to have established a new era in the arts, one that eventually led to the modern art of Tolstoy's time and beyond, it was only natural that he should oppose the entire tradition attacking even the very edifice of contemporary Western society.

Thus we see again and again how behind any particular arguments about aesthetics and any of the infinitely varied and profound experiences of the fictional characters there is in Tolstoy that powerful impulse for withdrawal from the business of living in our civilization, or indeed, ultimately, from the burden of living at all. The overwhelmingly assertive drive of Tolstoy's own life-force also seems to resemble a process of gradual self-destruction as it leads him further and further along the parabola toward liberation from imposed norms and meanings of things, then toward religious consciousness, then to death, which in his old age Tolstoy desired as ardently as he once wished to live. The two curves — of Tolstoy's life and his art — can be seen from this perspective to run parallel to each other as the great man drew them both toward the perfection of non-being. His aesthetics, then, together with his other great moral and religious treatises and his innumerable small texts along the same lines, acquire the function of an encoding of this convergence toward death which is at the same time also a reading, an expounding of the meaning of life.

Precisely: meaning, and not meaninglessness. Tolstoy grew increasingly impatient with things that appeared true only for a time and only in some given context. In the endless movement of life there is an infinity of changing contexts; the truths emerging from them constantly cancel each other out, like the droplets that Pierre Bezuxov saw in his dream vision, and one is left with nothing: God is an unreadable, liquid crystal ball. In death, however, there are no more contexts; we stand alone, as Théophile Gauthier once said, "avec une idée en face de Dieu seul." Only then can one get an inkling of what will *always* be true. His deathward journey in the mind was for Tolstoy not one of loss and confusion, but, on the contrary, one of discovery and enlightenment. Pierre's trek across Russia with a diminishing band of prisoners who were being shot to death right and left each day might be a good analogy to Tolstoy's journey across his life with many things once dear to him dropping off to leave his mind alone, at a single point of encounter with his God. The Epiphany of Prince Andrey and of Ivan Ilyich at the moment they died is Tolstoy's as well: when there is no more space to cross, and no more time to spend, comes the light in the act of the total surrender to love. Death, then, truly is an awakening, as Tolstoy repeatedly said. In this, Tolstoy was a Christian in the most fundamental sense, as a follower of Christ, for he understood that nothing at all can lead us to salvation, nor provide the resurrection of the spirit unless we include the inevitable fact of death in the premises of our quest. His was the wisdom of a mortal, and it endures as such.

If we now ask in conclusion what has indeed endured to our day in Tolstoy's aesthetics it will be nothing much about his definition of art, but rather a sense of what must be experienced in the heart before any definitions can begin. Thus the great opponent of conventional aesthetics has laid a lasting foundation for an aesthetic that is neither an exercise of cold intellect, nor the offspring of pretended rhetorical passion, but pertains to how we feel our being, and our evanescence, as orphans in great need of love for each other in the infinite realm of death amidst the stars.

Secondly, Tolstoy's aesthetic somewhat resembles Pierre's "judge," a voice that was engendered in him after all he went through, thanks to which he knew at any given moment exactly what he must do in his life. Similarly, from the perspective of the ideas in *What Is Art?* we can also acquire a sort of "key" to what Tolstoy stands for and against at any given moment in his fiction. We know instantly that Kutuzov is right when we see that the little girl Malasha, sitting behind the stove at the war council in Fili, prefers him, "the uncle," to the other generals, because she is a peasant girl and has been spared an education in military science. We know that the prevalent social structures in Russia are an abomination when we hear the prison inspector's daughter playing Clementi's *roulades* when Nekhlyudov comes, having just heard the horrible noises of the prison. We can tell that Konstantin Levin shall eventually find the truth, because he cannot at all understand Balakirev's "King Lear on the Heath." And, of course, we tremble for Natasha just as soon as she fails to comprehend what is happening on the stage at the opera, particularly when Tolstoy tells us that the male dancer, Duport, makes sixty thousand rubles a year for jumping up and down on his naked legs. Tolstoy's judgments on art become our own judgments on society, morality and the meaning, and the meaninglessness of life. If our vision is thus distorted concerning the values of civilization, it nevertheless gains a great penetrating power with respect to the workings of Tolstoy's art. Most of all, Tolstoy's essay opens the door to an overwhelming sense of the unity of his art and thought.

Finally, Tolstoy's ideas provide an alternative to the dichotomy between the political and the aestheticist view of art in its relationship to life. The "art for art" position holds that whatever the social value systems may be, art is defined by the specifically aesthetic criteria that also comprise its purpose. The social, especially

Marxist, view holds that whatever the specific elements may be which are unique to aesthetics, what makes art art is precisely its relevance to the social value systems, or at least to their particular Marxist conception. For Tolstoy, the specific and essential quality of art is that it is a universal mode of sustaining and enhancing the human manner of our being, a natural function of the body and the mind and a key to our relationship with God.

NOTES

Introduction

[1] See *What is Art and Essays on Art*, Aylmer Maude, tr. A Hesperides Book, Oxford University Press, 1962, (first published in *The World's Classics* in 1930) p. 197, and in Russian *Lev Tolstoj, polnoe sobranie sočinenij*, Vol. 30, Moscow, 1951, p. 125. Further references to these texts will be cited in parentheses as *Maude* and *PSS*, respectively.
[2] *Maude*, 276; *PSS, 30*, 185.

Chapter 1

[1] *PSS, 1*, 178. It is worth noting at this point that Irtenyev's accusation that Lamartin tried to enrich himself by writing a worthless, and implicitly dishonest, book very much resembles Tolstoy's own in *What Is Art?*, 47 years later, where he speaks of false art usurping the material resources of society in order to enrich its adherents.
[2] Boris Ejxenbaum in *Literatura. Teorija, kritika, polemika*, 1927, reprinted in Russian Study Series No. 66, Chicago, 1969, p. 25, adds another point: "Tolstoy ... is concerned not only about transmitting his own feelings to others with all possible immediacy, but also about giving the true perception of a thing — and this is already something new in comparison with the principles of the sentimental school." One might say, then, that this moment in Tolstoy's diary stands at the pivotal point of his realism as a writer, his moral concerns, and his eventual definition of art.
[3] In *What Is Art?* Tolstoy bases the distinction between Veron's definition of art, as the expression of emotion, and his own, as the communication of emotion, precisely on this point.
[4] E.N. Kuprejanova, *Èstetika L.N. Tolstogo*, Moscow - Leningrad, "Nauka," 1966, p. 138.

[5] The notion that Tolstoy was not sensitive to poetry, supported by his own occasional grumblings about the pointlessness of embroidering one's speech with rhythm and rhyme when it is already difficult enough just to tell the truth straight out, is quickly dispelled when we read his extraordinarily perceptive and sophisticated comments on Fet's poetry in their correspondence.

[6] For a lucid, lively account of Tolstoy's introduction to the Russian literary society, read Ernest J. Simmons, *Leo Tolstoy*, Boston: Little, Brown and Company, 1946, and Henri Troyat, *Tolstoy*, New York: Doubleday, 1967.

[7] Simmons, pp. 136-7. Tolstoy had proposed a plan to free his serfs with land over a period of time, but the serfs rejected it, according to Simmons out of their "innate hostility for the master," rooted in centuries of serfdom, which made it impossible for the serfs to believe Tolstoy and his good intentions.

[8] For Tolstoy's reaction to this event, see Simmons. p. 149.

[9] Letter to A. A. Tolstaya, quoted from *L. N. Tolstoj o literature. Stat'i, pis'ma, dnevniki*, Moscow, 1955, p. 38.

[10] L.N. Tolstoy, *Perepiska s russkimi pisateljami*, Moscow, 1962, p. 159.

[11] See *L. N. Tolstoj o literature*, Moscow, 1955 pp. 49-51.

[12] *L. N. Tolstoj o literature*, pp. 9-10.

[13] Tolstoy, Letter to N.A. Nekrasov, December 18, 1857, in K.N. Lomunov, ed., *Lev Tolstoj ob iskusstve i literature*. Moscow, 1958, Vol. I, p. 359.

[14] Nekhlyudov is a thinly disguised Tolstoy. As a character, he appears again in the fragment "A Landowner's Morning" (1854) and then in the novel *The Resurrection* (1899).

[15] The incident described in *Lucerne* actually happened to Tolstoy while he was traveling in Switzerland 1857. Angered that a crowd of tourists laughed at a street singer, Tolstoy actually invited him to the hotel to share a drink, thereby offending everyone's sense of propriety. See Simmons, *Leo Tolstoy*, p. 154.

[16] See Aylmer Maude, trans. *Confession and the Gospel in Brief by Leo Tolstoy*, Vol. XI, Tolstoy centenary edition, London: Oxford University Press, 1933, p. 9, *PSS*, 23, 5:

> I, artist and poet, wrote and taught without myself knowing what. For this I was paid money; I had excellent food, lodging, women, and society; and I had fame, which showed that what I taught was very

good.

[17] A similar reaction to the Slavophiles can be seen in Tolstoy's letter to Botkin on January, 1857, at the time when Tolstoy imagined that he had found true devotees in art, and true friends, in the group of "aesthetic liberals" among whom was Botkin, Annenkov and Druzhinin: "The Slavophiles are also NOT the real thing. When I get together with them, I feel how I unconsciously become dull-minded, limited, and terribly honest, the way one always speaks bad French with those who don't know the language well. It is quite another thing with you, with the, for me, priceless triumvirate, Botkin, Annenkov and Družinin." See *L. N. Tolstoj. Perepiska s russkimi pisateljami*, p. 135.

[18] K. Aksakov, letter to Turgenev, quoted by E. J. Simmons, *Leo Tolstoy*, p. 129: "Count Tolstoy was in Moscow...A strange person! Why does he act so immaturely? Why so unsettled?... It seems as though there is still no center to him."

[19] See *Childhood*, in *Tolstoy. Childhood, Boyhood, Youth*. Tr. Rosemary Edmonds. Penguin Classics, 1964, p. 44, *PSS, 1*, 34-5.

[20] See B. Bursov, *Lev Tolstoj: idejnye iskanija i tvorčeskij metod, 1847-1862*, Moscow, Vol. x, 1960, p. 349.

[21] *Russo i Tolstoj*. Reč' Akademika M.N. Rozanova, pročitana v toržestvennom godovom sobranii ANSSSR 2 Feb. 1928, p. 4.

[22] Boris Ejxenbaum. "Lev Tolstoj," in B. Ejxenbaum, *Literatura*, p. 23.

[23] N.A. Semenova, "Problema etičeskogo i èstetičeskogo v proizvedenijax L.N. Tolstogo," A.I. Ivanov, ed., *Voprosy èstetiki. Sbornik statej*. Izdatel'stvo Saratovskogo universiteta, 1963, p. 73.

[24] Tolstoy, *The Cossacks/ Happy Ever After/ The Death of Ivan Ilyich*. Penguin classics, 1978, p. 250.

[25] B. Bursov, *Lev Tolstoj, idejnye iskanija i tvorčeskij metod*, p. 218.

[26] Karataev's natural, instinctual way of being always right may be even better understood from what Tolstoy said about the teaching of Christ and the rightness of action in his 1888 preface to a book written by G.M. Bondarev:

> A person who believes in the teaching of Christ needs as little to ask about what are the positive things he must do as a spring can ask it as it wells up from the ground. It flows and quenches the thirst of the earth, grass, trees, birds, animals and people.

See "Predislovie k sočineniju G.M. Bondareva," *Polnoe sobranie sočinenij L'va Nikolaeviča Tolstogo*, pod redakciej i s primečanijami P.I. Birjukova, Vol. 19, Moscow, 1913, p. 197.
This feeling is very much like the feeling of Pierre, after he returned from French captivity and discovered that now he always knew what and how to do, because there now was an unfailing "judge" inside him.

[27] Characteristic in this respect are some early notes by Tolstoy, written sometime between 1847 and 1852, where he feels the presence of some inner power in him: One note begins (*PSS 1*, 226): "From the time when I can remember my life, I always found in myself a certain force of truth, some kind of striving, which found no satisfaction; everywhere I saw nothing but contradictions, nothing but pointlessness." The second variant of the same thought (*ibid*, p. 227) omits the ambitious word "truth," but describes more clearly the relation of an individual consciousness to reality at large: "From the time when I can remember my life, I always found in myself a certain striving which found no satisfaction, although I did, vaguely, understand how it should be satisfied. I was aware that I was limited in everything — and at the same time I understood limitlessness, even felt it in myself." Perhaps, then, one could say that Tolstoy's early thoughts on communication in art turned around the possibility of making the reader, too, feel the limitlessness as Tolstoy felt it in his soul.

[28] Tolstoy responded in a similar spirit to other writers he happened to be reading at the time. There is, for instance, a striking reaction to a work by Karamzin, noted in Tolstoy's diary on December 20, 1853:

> I read the philosophical introduction by Karamzin to the journal *Morning Light*, which he published in 1777 and in which he says that the purpose of the journal consists in love of wisdom, in the development of human mind, will and feelings, directing them toward virtue, and I was astonished that we could have to such a degree lost our understanding of the only goal of literature — the moral goal — that if you should say something nowadays about the need for moral teaching in literature, there will be no one to understand you (*PSS, 46*, 213-14).

²⁹ For an outstanding study of Tolstoy's religious thought, see Richard F. Gustafson, *Leo Tolstoy. Resident and Stranger. A Study in Fiction and Theology*. Princeton University Press, 1986.

Chapter 2

¹ See Simmons, *Leo Tolstoy*, p. 146.
² L. N. Tolstoj, *Perepiska s russkimi pisateljami*, p. 204.
³ Thomas Mann reports the rather fascinating impression Tolstoy made on a schoolteacher in Weimar named Julius Stötzer:
> Ein Schüler des Seminars den Kopf durch die Tür steckte und meldete, ein Fremder wünsche Herrn Stötzer zu sehen. Dieser Fremde trat denn auch ohne weiteres ein, bedeutend jünger als der Lehrer, mit nicht sehr starkem Vollbart, vortretenden Backenknochen, kleinen grauen augen und einem Paar Falten zwischen den dunklen Brauen. Er Unterliess es, sich auszuweisen oder vorzustellen, sondern fragte sofort, worin heute Nachmittags unterrichtet werde; und als er erfuhr, dass erst Geschichte, dann deutsche Sprache daran sei, fand er das ausgezeichnet und sagte, er habe die Schulen von Süddeutschland, Frankreich und England besucht und möchte nun auch die von Norddeutschland kennenlernen. Er sprach wie ein Deutscher. Man musste ihn für einen Lehrer halten, auf Grund der sachkundingen und interessierten Fragen und Ausserungen, die er tat, indem er beständig Aufzeichnungen in sein Notizbuch machte. See Thomas Mann, "Goethe und Tolstoi. Fragment zum Problem der Humanität," in Thomas Mann, *Adel des Geistes. Sechzehn Versuche zum Problem der Humanität*, Stockholm: Berman-Fischer Verlag, 1945, pp. 181-2.

Tolstoy's own reaction to German schools (quite likely precisely the school he visited in Weimar) can be gauged from an unfinished article Tolstoy wrote in the form of a letter to some unknown person, written in 1861; it is rather sarcastic, mocking the thoroughly worked-out educational techniques and methodology and the lockstep procedures of teaching, without the possibility of either feeling or imagination. The picture he paints of the students is:

> All you can see are the bored faces of children who were forced to come to the school and are now impatiently waiting for the bell while at the same time fearfully expecting a question from the teacher, a question asked in order to force the child against his will to follow the lesson. See *PSS*, 8, 401.

[4] In a curious, but evidently well-meant statement, Thomas Mann attributed Tolstoy's dislike of traditional school subjects in Western Europe to his anti-humanism, and his Russian "ethnic hatred," to his resentment of the reforms of Peter I:

> Was in dieser polemischen Ausserung gegen das Studium der antiken Sprachen fühlbar wird, ja offen zum ausbruch kommt, ist die Auflehnung des russischen Volkstums gegen die *humanistische Zivilisation* selber... Er prophezeit dem "Lateinischem und der Rhetorik" einen fortbestand von noch hundert Jahren — keinen längeren, und auch einen so langen nur deshalb, weil, "wenn die Medizin einmal gekauft sei, man sie doch trinken müsse." Mit dieser Redensart ist sein Verhältnis zum Westen, zur Zivilisation, ein Verhältniss volkhaften Hasses gegen das Unvolkstümliche, Fremde, Oktroyierte, nur Bildungsmässige, kurz, die Empörung des Urrussentums gegen Peter. "Goethe und Tolstoi," pp. 301, 302.

[5] In 1858, for instance, Tolstoy undertook reforestation of his estate, prompting Turgenev to write to their mutual friend Annenkov in astonishment:

> You have astonished me with your news of Tolstoy's reforestation projects. What a man! With perfect feet, he is determined to walk on his head. ... Now he wants to prove to himself that he's a timber expert. With these capers I fear only that he will throw the spine of his talent out of joint.

See Simmons, *Leo Tolstoy*, p. 171.

[6] Z. V. Čičerin, "Rabota L'va Tolstogo nad romanom o dekabristax," *Učenye zapiski L'vovskogo Gosudarstvennogo Universiteta imeni Ivana Franko*, Vol. xxiv, 1953, issue 2, pp. 134-34.

[7] L. N. Tolstoj, *Perepiska s russkimi pisateljami*, p. 237.

[8] L.N. Tolstoj, "O narodnom obrazovanii, *PSS* 8, 5. The English text is from Leo Wiener, trans. *Tolstoy on Education*, The Univer-

sity of Chicago Press, 1967, p. 5. Main references will be to this translation.

⁹Tolstoj, "Vospitanie i obrazovanie," *PSS, 8* 231; Wiener, entitled "Education and Culture," pp. 130-31.

[10] Wiener, p. 19; *PSS 8,* 16

[11] Aylmer Maude, trans. *Leo Tolstoy. What Is Art? and Essays on Art*, pp. 120-121.

[12] Tolstoj, "Progress i opredelenie obrazovanija, *PSS 8,* 333; Wiener, p. 162.

[13] Like the story of Joseph, spanning the development of Tolstoy's thought on art between the distant points of his youth and age, or the story "God Sees the Truth but Waits," first told by Karataev in *War and Peace*, then referred to by Tolstoy in his essay as his only work of high and good art, so now the tale of Hadzhi Murat, all seem to be parts of some very deep layer of emotion experienced existentially as meaning, that nourished the roots of all of Tolstoy's thought on art and life.

[14] Countess Tolstoy, murdered by her cook, was a distant relative of Lev Tolstoy. See Simmons, p. 203, fn.

[15] Much later, in 1890, in his "Preface to Amiel's Diary," speaking of the "inner work of the soul" which alone is of value in any articulation of thought or feeling, any text, fictional or not, Tolstoy described being in the presence of this inner work in terms that very much resemble these articulated here about Fed'ka:

> It seems as if one were present, without the host's knowledge, at the most mysterious and profound, and passionate work of the soul that is usually hidden from a stranger's glance.

See "Predislovie k dnevniku Amielja," in P.I. Birjukov, ed., *Polnoe sobranie sočinenij L'va Nikolaeviča Tolstogo*, Vol. 19, p. 210.

[16] E. Dosyčeva, "Pedagogika i poetika v statje L. N. Tolstogo 'Komu u kogo učitsja pisat': krestjanskim rebjatam u nas ili nam u krestjanskix rebjat?'" *Prosveščenie, Pedagogičeskij sbornik*. Petrograd: Gosizdat, No. 2, 1922, p. 129.

[17] A. Čičerin, "Rabota L'va Tolstogo nad romanom o dekabristax," p. 189.

[18] Wiener, p. 194. In an early draft for his essay, in 1889, Tolstoy spelled out what makes a good artist:

> In order that what the artist says were expressed completely well, it is necessary that the artist master

> his skills to the degree that, while working, he would think as little of the rules of his art as a person thinks about the mechanics of movement while he is walking.
> In order to achieve this, the artist must never look back upon his work to admire it, must not make mastery his purpose, just as a person walking should not think about his walk and admire it. See *PSS, 30,* 213.

This raises all sorts of interesting issues in relation to, say, Viktor Šklovskij's dictum that art is "work constructed to be felt," and, in view of Tolstoy's suggestion that a good artist works, as it were, "automatically," to the matter of estrangement, deautomatization, felt by Šklovskij to be one of the main techniques of Tolstoy as a writer. For the moment, however, we may just note that in 1962 Fed'ka wrote exactly as Tolstoy said in 1889 that a good writer should.

[19] B. Bursov, *Lev Tolstoj, idejnye iskanija i tvorčeskij metod.*, p. 315.

[20] See L. N. Tolstoy, *Jasnaja poljana*, knižka 9-taja (Sentjabr'), 1862, pp. 12-13.

[21] George Steiner, in his book *Tolstoy or Dostoevsky. An Essay in the Old Criticism.* (New York: Vintage Books, 1961), p. 76, notes the scene in *The Illiad* where Achilles calmly explains to Lykaon, his victim, that they both have their own death and destiny, and then kills him:

> So, friend, you die also. Why all this clamour about it?
> Patroklos also is dead, who was better by far than you are.
> Do you not see what a man I am, how huge, how splendid
> and born of a great father, and the mother who bore me immortal?
> Yet even I have also my death and my strong destiny,
> and there shall be a dawn or an afternoon or a noontime
> when some man in the fighting will take the life from me also
> either with a spear cast or an arrow flown from the

> bowstring.
> So he spoke, and in the other the knees and the inward
> heart went slack. He let go the spear and sat back, spreading
> wide both hands; but Achilleus drawing his sharp sword struck him
> beside the neck at the collar-bone, and the double-edged
> sword
> plunged full length inside. He dropped to the ground, face downward,
> and lay at length, and the black blood flowed, and the ground was soaked with it.

"The calm of the narrative," says Steiner, "is nearly inhuman; but in consequence the horror speaks naked and moves us unutterably." In his opinion, no one in Western literature is more like Homer in this respect than Tolstoy.

[22] Tolstoy, *War and Peace*. The Maude translation. Backgrounds and sources. Essays in criticism. George Gibian, ed., New York: W.W. Norton & Company, 1966, p. 578.

[23] Wiener, P. 345, *PSS 8*, 112. Compare Aylmer Maude trans., *What Is Art?*, p. 174.

[24] Letter to A.A. Tolstaja, October 17-31, 1863. See *L.N. Tolstoj o literature*, pp. 95-6.

Chapter 3

[1] Ernest J. Simmons, *Leo Tolstoy*. p. 316.

[2] Aylmer Maude, trans., *A Confession and the Gospel in Brief by Leo Tolstoy*, p. 48.

[3] In *Confession* we read:
> It came to this that I, a healthy, fortunate man, felt I could no longer live... And it was then that I, a man favored by fortune, hid a cord from myself lest I should hang myself from the crosspiece of the partition in my room where I undressed alone every evening, and I ceased to go out shooting with a gun lest I be tempted by so easy a way of ending my life (*Confession*, p. 18), and in *Anna Karenina*:

> And though he was a happy and healthy family man, Levin was several times so near to suicide that he hid a cord he had lest he should hang himself, and he feared to carry a gun lest he should shoot himself.
> *Anna Karenina*, A Norton Critical Edition, New York, 1970, p. 714; *PSS, 19*, 371).

⁴ L. N. Tolstoj, *Tak čto že nam delat'?*, *PSS, 25*, 195.

⁵ As early as 1862 Tolstoy already expressed great skepticism concerning the notion that human experience accumulates in history and the weight of this accumulated cultural substance functions as a definition of civilization. In his article "Progress and the Definition of Education" he complained that, instead of giving him an ideal, a general law, a valid definition of progress, people simply speak of a "pile" of cultural experience that keeps growing, and say that this constitutes culture. His question: "Is it a good thing that this pile is growing? Why is it growing? No one will answer you these questions, and in fact, they will be astonished that you should worry about any answers to questions like that." See "Progress i opredelenie obrazovanija," in *PSS, 8*, 327.

⁶ Tolstoy here probably has in mind the so-called "lubočnye kartiny," cheap little drawings made by the common people and sold at country fairs and other such places, which were very popular among the peasants and workers in the old Russia.

⁷ See *What Is Art?*, Maude, 246.
> I must moreover mention that I consign my own artistic productions to the category of bad art, excepting the story *God Sees the Truth but Waits*, which seeks a place in the first [religious art] class, and *A Prisoner of the Caucasus*, which belongs to the second [good universal art] (*PSS, 30*, 163).

⁸ In his "Preface to the Critical Sketch by Carpenter," Birjukov, *Polnoe Sobranie sočinenij L'va Nikolaeviča Tolstogo*, Vol. 19, p. 239, Tolstoy makes an observation that has rather curious implications. He says:
> All those sciences which have it as their purpose to make human life better and happier: the religious, the moral and the social sciences are not even considered by the ruling science to be sciences at all and are left to priests, philosophers, jurists, historians and political economists...

One wonders, if it were not so, which "ruling" scientists would be studying all those subjects. It seems almost as if Tolstoy thought that there is a generic designation, "scientist," possibly describing a person who thinks according to a certain methodology, who should be applying his method to the moral sciences instead of letting all the "priests," etc. do it. In that sense, Tolstoy himself would be a "scientist" par excellence.

[9] "Pis'mo k N.A. Aleksandrovu," *PSS*, *30*, 210.

[10] In *What Then Must We Do?* it went: "If we take some repulsive thing, like naked women dancing, and describe that with the Greek term "choreography," and say that this is art, then it will also be art" (*PSS*, *25*, 364).

[11] One may remember here the naked arms and shoulders of the beautiful Countess Helen in *War and Peace*, at the ball, when, as Tolstoy put it, they "seemed, as it were, hardened by a varnish left by the thousands of looks that had scanned her person" (Book Six, Chapter nine), as compared to the gawky Natasha, a little funny in her new ballroom dress. In its ultimate implications, this contrast between Helen and Natasha is the same as the contrast between true and false art, restated years later and many times in the language of expository argument.

[12] "Predislovie k sborniku 'Cvetnik'," Birjukov, *Polnoe sobranie*," vol. 19, p. 189.

[13] Henri Frederick Amiel (1821-1881), a French aesthetician and philosopher of the idealist school.

[14] "O tom, čto est' i čto ne est' iskusstvo, i o tom, kogda iskusstvo est' delo važnoe i kogda ono est' delo pustoe," *PSS*, *30*, pp. 216-225. One sometimes gets the distinct impression that Tolstoy felt words should serve thought and not preen themselves before the mirror of style, like some spoiled household serfs.

[15] Given, of course, that to demand it exclusively is wrong and leads to false criticism.

[16] "Progress i opredelenie obrazovanija," *PSS*, *8*, 330.

[17] N.V. Gorbačev, "Istorija pisanija i pečatanja predislovija k sočinenijam Guy de Maupassant," *PSS*, *30*, 499.

[18] N. Afanasjeva "Problemy dramaturgii v èstetike L.N. Tolstogo. Aftoreferat dissertacii." Moscow, 1956, p. 1, quoted in E. Nuralov, *Èstetika L.N. Tolstogo v ocenke kritiki*, Erevan, 1979, p. 45.

[19] For instance, G.V. Kurjakova writes in "Mopassan v ocenke L.N. Tolstogo," *Učenye zapiski*, Sbornik trudov kafedr russkogo jazyka, literatury i pedagogiki. Vypusk V, Kemerovskij gosudarst-

vennyj pedagogičeskij institut. Kemerovo, 1962, p. 91: "And so, Tolstoy's interest in Maupassant, his efforts to acquaint the Russian reader with him, and finally, the introduction to the works of this French writer were not an incidental matter, but blended in logically with the general progress of the struggle for people's art."
[20] L. Tolstoy, "Introduction to the Works of Guy de Maupassant," Maude, 25-6; *PSS*, *30*, 7-8. Tolstoy's attachment to Maupassant continued throughout his life. Even as late as 1909, Tolstoy could read Maupassant with deep feeling. See *U Tolstogo. Jasnopoljanskie zapiski D.P. Makovickogo,* IV, *Literaturnoe nasledstvo* Vol. 90, 1979. pp. 32-3.
[21] All the quotes are from Maude, Maupassant, pp. 28-32; *PSS*, *30*, 3-24.

Chapter 4

[1] It seems easy to think of Tolstoy's arrogance during these "examination proceedings," but the point may be somewhere else, namely, in his ingrained independence of mind, his reluctance to accept anything that was thought through and formulated by someone else than himself. Quite early in his career, in 1857, for instance, Tolstoy noted in his diary: "The mind which I possess and which I like in others is such, that a person does not believe any theory; either he extends them on to their further consequences and thus destroys every single one or else, he drops them and starts constructing his own. For instance: the theory of the subjective and the objective in art is nothing but nonsense." See *L.N. Tolstoj o literature*, p. 42.
[2] In one French response to the essay, however, the legitimate point is made that Tolstoy failed to refer to those ideas of Guyau which come closer to Tolstoy's own:
> Tolstoï a cité et inexactement interpreté *les Problèmes de l'esthétique contemporaine* de Guyau (en ajoutant la date de la naissance et de la mort de l'auteur); pourquoi n'a-t-il pas également cité *l'Art au point de vue sociologique?*. Toujours est-il que cet ouvrage de Guyau renferme, avec les paradoxes en moins et les preuves en plus, la théorie fondamentale de Tolstoi". Signaller cette priorité, c'est faire oeuvre de simple justice."

See *La Grande Revue*, Tome premier, Paris, 1899, p. 278.

³ See Maude, 87, *PSS*, *30*, 38:
> In Russian, by the word *krasota* (beauty) we mean only that which pleases the sight, and though latterly people have begun to speak of "an ugly deed," or of "beautiful music," it is not good Russian.

⁴ Jan Mukařovsky, "Aesthetic Function Among Other Functions," in John Burbank and Peter Steiner, editors, *Structure, Sign and Function. Selected Essays by Jan Mukařovsky*, New Haven and London: Yale University Press, 1978, p. 46.

⁵ Eugene Veron, "General Definition of Art." Quoted from: Holley Gene Duffield and Manuel Bilsky, editors, *Tolstoy and the Critics: Literature and Aesthetics*. Chicago: Scott, Foresman and Company, 1965, p. 6.

⁶ F.D. Batjushkov, an acquaintance of Tolstoy, has left a record of Tolstoy's impassionate outburst during a conversation in 1897, a year before the essay was published, in which Tolstoy reached even deeper, beyond the mere issue of transmitting feelings, to insist that an artist must reveal the inner, invisible person in each one of us:

> "What do I call true art?", suddenly quickened Lev Nikolaevich. "Just this: I see you for the first time; you have a head, arms, legs, like everybody else; your face has features. This is what I and everybody else can see. But now, if I can manage to penetrate inside you, to enter here" (he laid one hand on my shoulder and pressed the other hand to my breast) "if I can call to the surface what is hidden there, if I know how to make you feel excitement, bring tears to your eyes, if I can stir all your feelings, show the invisible person inside this envelope that everyone can see, then I am a true artist."
>
> He was magnificent at that moment: his eyes were burning, his cheeks were flushed, he seemed somehow to stand taller, and then, after a brief silence, he added: "This must be felt and understood; who understands it is a critic, who creates it is an artist."

See F.D. Batjuškov, "Večer u L.N. Tolstogo (počti stenograma) v 1897 godu, na vtoroj den' Pasxi," quoted by P. Sirmakov in *Russkaja literatura*, Leningrad, Vol. 4, 1963, p. 221. This quote is particularly interesting because here Tolstoy seems to equate the process of transmitting feelings with that of removing outer layers from a person, as if the "addressee" of an artist were a piece of marble in which, inside, the artist sees the inner form, his work. In *Anna Karenina,* this is precisely how the artist Mixajlov felt about creating his picture of Christ before the Pilate. It seems almost as if the transmission of feelings is like the conception of new life: a penetration, a fertilization of the womb which is the human soul.

[7] Vladimir Weidlé notes that Tolstoy's definition of art as a process and an activity, not an entity is incomplete and one-sided, but that this is a good thing, because:

> It is not possible to approach any topic, especially one as complex as this, from all sides at once, and to begin with it is better to approach the issue of art from its aspect of movement, of becoming and not, as is usually done, from its aspect as a completed and self-enclosed work of art.

See V. Weidlé, "Tolstoj ob iskusstve," *Novyj žurnal,* 105 (1971), p. 94.

[8] These factors have been described by Jakobson by means of the following diagram:

$$\begin{array}{c} \text{context} \\ \text{message} \\ \text{addresser}\text{------------------}\text{addressee} \\ \text{contact} \\ \text{code} \end{array}$$

See, for example, Terence Hawkes, *Structuralism and Semiotics,* Los Angeles: University of California Press, 1977, p. 83.

[9] In his early article "Progress and the Definition of Education" 1862, Tolstoy expressed very similar views about history:

> If one but adds the word "historical" to any concept whatever, that concept loses its lifelike, true meaning in some sort of artificially made historical worldview. *PSS, 8,* 327.

[10] Art understood as its contemplation in history looks equally counterfeit to Tolstoy. What is called "progress," then, is precisely an accumulation of such abstract and artificial constructs. Nevertheless, Tolstoy did agree with Mathew Arnold that the task of criticism consists in finding good and true works of art and drawing attention to them, so that the working masses could read them with-

out first wading through mountains of worthless verbiage. See his "Predislovie k romanu Polenca 'Krestjanin'," (Von Polentz, "Der Bütnerbauer") *Polnoe sobranie,* ed. P. I. Birjukov, Vol. 19, pp. 245-6.

[11] A large reproduction in black and white of Raphael's Madonna still hangs in Tolstoy's study in Yasnaja Polyana and was there during most of Tolstoy's life. A Soviet author, I. Danilova, made the following comment on this seeming paradox:

> L.N. Tolstoy, having visited the [Dresden] gallery in 1857, noted in his diary: "the Madonna touched me strongly. I remained cold to everything except the Madonna." A year later, in one of his letters, [Tolstoy] writes: "'Madonna' is hanging on my wall and gives me joy..." In the 90s, in the article "What Is Art?," carried away by the pathos of struggle against classical art which seemed to him insufficiently effective, Tolstoy forgot his enthusiasm of the 50s and affirmed the opposite with merciless directness: "The Sistine Madonna ... does not evoke any feeling, but only a torturous uncertainty whether or not I am experiencing with regard to it the kind of feeling which is expected."

See I. Danilova, "Russkie pisateli i xudožniki XIX veka o Dresdenskoj galleree," in *Starye mastera v Dresdenskoj galleree,* Gosizdat "Iskusstvo", Moscow, 1959 (also Maude, 243-4; *PSS, 30,* 161). In 1909 Tolstoy was quite blunt about the Madonna: "Take the Madonna (Raphael) — it's so repulsive, in spite of the fact that I have it hanging on the wall."
See: *U Tolstogo. Jasnopoljanskie zapiski D.P. Makovickogo,* IV, 94.
This, of course, does not clear up the question of why Tolstoy kept the picture there in the first place, and for so many years.

[12] P. K. Engel'majer in *Kritika naučnyx i xudožestvennyx učenij Gr. L.N. Tolstogo,* Moscow, 1898, p. 56, answers Tolstoy
rather succinctly on this point:

> It says on the base of Pushkin's monument why it was built:
> "And long I'll be beloved by the people
> Because my lyre awakened goodness in their hearts".

These lines are from Pushkin's poem in imitation of Horace's "Exegi monumentum."

[13] L. William Flaccus, "Tolstoy," in *Artists and Thinkers*, New York, Longmans, Green and Co., 1916. Quoted from Holley Gene Duffield, editor, *Tolstoy and the Critics: Literature and Aesthetics*, Chicago, Scott, Foreman and Company, 1965, p. 88.

[14] Hugh I'Anson Fausset, however, takes the view that the particular works mentioned by Tolstoy are, in essence, but primitive expressions of consciousness and must stand as rudimentary in relation to the responsibilities of developing civilization:

> In writing this Tolstoy was as exclusive as those whom he attacked. The examples of 'good, supreme art' which he cited, were almost all expressions of a primitive consciousness. All great art is religious in this sense. But the purpose of the great artist is to discover new meaning and to advance and enrich the human consciousness within its comprehension. See Fausset, *Tolstoy. The Inner Drama*, New York, Russel and Russel, n.d., p. 283.

[15] At one point in his work, Tolstoy gave a quite succinct description of what at least the Russian common people, the peasants, were in his mind:

> the Russian people, the true peasant Russian people, not the people which conquered Napoleon, conquered and subjected to itself other peoples; not that which, unfortunately, learned so quickly to make machines and railroads, and revolutions, and parliaments with all possible subdivisions of parties and political trends, but that humble, working, Christian, unassuming, patient people which brought up and now bears on its shoulders all that which today tortures and corrupts it to such a great extent.

See "Preface to N. Orlov's Album 'Russian peasants'," P.I. Birjukov, ed., *Polnoe sobranie sočinenij*, Vol. 19, pp. 260-263.

[16] In *What Is Art?*, 9 *PSS*, *30*, 178; Maude, 266, Tolstoy says: "The art of our time and of our circle has become a prostitute. And this comparison holds good even in minute details. Like her, it is not limited to certain times, like her, it is always adorned, like her it is always salable and like her it is enticing and ruinous." Tolstoy's further statement: "real art, like the wife of an affectionate husband, needs no ornaments" (*ibid.*) can throw an interesting retro-

spective light on the final chapter of *War and Peace* where Natasha is depicted as "gone to seed," forgotten about jewelry and nice clothes, abandoned her singing, for it was no longer needed to attract Pierre who loved her irrevocably. If there are readers who think Tolstoy was inconsistent with his own early depictions of Natasha as a captivating creature of great vivacity and charm, this passage in *What Is Art?*, no matter how much later in time, does suggest that the less attractive (as this notion exists in society) Natasha became, the more positive was her image in Tolstoy's own mind.

[17] *The Columbia Encyclopedia*, New York: Columbia University Press, 1967, p. 1848.

[18] John Ruskin, *The Stones of Venice*, New York: John Wiley and Sons, 1890, Vol. III, p. 60.

[19] It is well to note, however, that P.A. Sergeenko, one of the people close to Tolstoy's inner circle, records Tolstoy as having said that the *Kreutzer Sonata* was written without any moralizing intent, just for the art of it (note of December 21, 1900):

> "I was walking along the Arbat recently and I saw in a bookshop window a dog-eared copy of "The Kreutzer Sonata." And it struck me that the "Kreutzer Sonata," "The Power of Darkness" and "[the living] Corpse" are my only works in which I did not place before myself any didactic or educational aims, but submitted myself to an exclusively artistic emotion. I wrote the "Kreutzer Sonata" for the actor Burlak to read; yet, I do have grounds for thinking that these works did pave a road to the hearts of the readers and did accomplish something in the moral sphere as well."

See "Tolstoj o literature i iskusstve," zapisi V. T. Čertkova i P.A. Sergeenko. Publikacija A. Sergeenko. *Literaturnoe nasledstvo*, No. 37-38. Moscow: the USSR Academy of Sciences, 1939, p. 547; note by Sergeenko.

[20] In 1898, the same year as *What Is Art?* was completed, Tolstoy also wrote a "Preface to the Novel 'Der Bůtnerbauer' by Von Polentz, in which he referred to Nietzsche's works in a brutally simple way as "the immoral, crude, blown-up and incoherent prattle of Nietzsche." See P.I. Birjukov, ed. *Polnoe sobranie*, vol. 19, p. 247.

[21] Gary Jahn in his lucid discussion "The Aesthetic theory of 'What

Is Art?'," *Journal of Aesthetics and Art Criticism*, XXXIV, I, Fall, 1975, pp. 60-61, does also note the difficulty (p. 61): "In explaining what he meant by *chuvstvo*, Tolstoy first distinguished it from the concept of thought (*mysl'*). Just what Tolstoy meant by thought is rather difficult to grasp."

[22] All the quotes are from Maude, 74-76; *PSS, 30*, 28-29. As if indeed to imply a reference to Dante, Tolstoy even mentions a "guide" leading him through all those dark and gloomy passages to the depths of that cavernous building with the stage at its center.

[23] This recalls the entire issue of education, which concerned Tolstoy all his life, but particularly in early 1860's, during the so-called Yasnaja Polyana period, when he established a school for his peasant children that antedated many features of modern progressive education. A large part of Tolstoy's educational method and philosophy at the Yasnaja Polyana school had to do with the subject of art.

Chapter 5

[1] Tolstoy, *The Resurrection*, trans. by Vera Traill. A Signet Classic, 1961, pp. 357-8.

[2] Aylmer Maude perceived this quality of Tolstoy's mind quite clearly in his comments on *What Is Art?* when he said:
"To fit him with this task [writing the essay on art] he possessed great knowledge of men and books a wide experience of life, a knowledge of languages, *and a freedom from bondage to any authority but that of reason and conscience* [my emphasis, R.Š.]. See: Aylmer Maude, *Tolstoy and His Problems*, p. 43. In order for the artist to express the innermost needs of his soul and thus to speak fully from the heart, he must, first of all, not waste his time on all sorts of trifles which get in the way of loving that which one should and, secondly, to love by himself, with one's own heart, not with that of another, and not to pretend to love something which others deem, or admit, to be worthy of love. And in order to achieve this, the artist must do as Valaam did when messengers came to him and he withdrew, waiting for God, so as to say only that which God shall command (*PSS, 30*, 213).

[3] *The Resurrection*, p. 406. When Tolstoy died at the railroad station in Astapovo, he was in effect just such a man, trying to travel incognito, without name, without home, alone, face to face with his

God.

⁴ Tolstoy's friend Romain Roland noted in his biography of Tolstoy that the late works, such as *Death of Ivan Ilyich*, *Power of Darkness*, and others, do reflect Tolstoy's efforts to practice his own precepts in the essay:

> La plus belle théorie n'a de prix que par les oeuvres ou elle s'accomplit. Chez Tolstoï, théorie et création sont toujours unies, comme foi et action. Dans le même temps ou il elaborait sa Critique de l'Art, il donnait des modèles de l'art nouveau qu'il voulait, — des deux formes de l'art, l'une plus haute, l'autre moins pure, mais toutes deux "religieuses", au sens le plus humain, — l'une, travaillant à l'union des hommes par l'amour, l'autre, en livrant combat au monde ennemi de l'amour.

See Romain Roland, *Vie de Tolstoï*, Paris: Librairie Hachette, 1921, p. 127.

⁵ Rosemary Edmonds, trans. *The Cossacks, Happy Ever After, The Death of Ivan Ilyich*, Penguin Books, 1978, p. 176.

⁶ We are using the term "estrangement" here in the sense in which the Russian Formalist critic Viktor Shklovsky used a propos of Tolstoy's artistic method: to de-automize our perceptions, so as to make it seem that all the rules have been forgotten and everything appears as if seen for the first time, without any assumptions about what it meant. The device, Shklovsky says, is to "make the stone stony again."

⁷ The diary of Druzhinin, a contemporary of Tolstoy, has a note to the effect that in 1855 Tolstoy said: "Only a person stuffed with pompous phrases can admire either Homer or Shakespeare." See *PSS*, 35, p. 680.

⁸ See *Tolstoy on Shakespeare*. New York & London: Funk & Wagnalls, 1907.

⁹ To be sure, in his essay on Shakespeare, Tolstoy found that scene itself to be rather nonsensical. See *Tolstoy on Shakespeare*, 1907, pp. 41, ff.

¹⁰ Richard Wagner, *Gesammelte Schriften und Dichtungen*, Leipzig: Verlag von E.H. Fritsch, n.d., Band 3-4, 7, pp. 232-3:

> Die Absicht der Oper lag also von je, und so auch heute, in der Musik, Bloss um der Wirksamkeit der Musik Anhalt zu irgendwie gerechtfertiger Ausbrei-

> tung zu verschaffen, wird die Absicht des Drama's *hergezogen*, — natürlich aber nicht um die Absicht der Musik zu verdrängen, sondern vielmehr ihr nur als Mittel zu dienen, ohne Anstand wird diess auch von allen Seiten annerkannt [except by Tolstoy!]; Niemand versucht es auch nur, die bezeichnete Stellung des Drama's zur Musik, des Dichters zum Tonkünstler, zu läugnen: nur im Hinblick auf die ungemeine Verbreitung und Wirkungsfähigkeit der Oper hat man geglaubt, mit einer monströsen Erscheinung sich befreunden zu müssen, ja ihr die Möglichkeit zuzusprechen, in ihrer unnatürlichen Wirksamkeit etwas Neues, ganz Unerhörtes, noch nie zuvor Geahntes zu leis ten, nämlich *auf der Basis der absoluten Musik das wirkliche Drama zu Stande zu bringen.*

[11] Norton, p. 620. In a footnote, the translator, Maude, provides the following information about that statue:
Tolstoy had in mind a work Antokolsky submitted to the academy of Art in 1875 in anticipation of the Pushkin celebration held in Moscow. He represented Pushkin sitting on a stone bench on a rock, and on ledges of the rock as on a ladder, fenced in by railings, figures of characters from Pushkin's works — Boris Godunov, the Miserly Knight, Tatyana, Mazeppa, Pugachev, and so on — are ascending, some of them actually holding on to the railings.
This sculpture could have been inspired by Pushkin's lines:
> I tut ko mne idet nezrimyj roj gostej,
> Znakomcy davnie, plody mečty moej
> (And here, they come to me, the unseen host of guests
> All old acquaintances, the fruit of mine own dreams)

from the poem "Autumn" (Osen'), written in 1833. Pushkin's poem "To the Sea," 1824, contains the line "Odna skala, grobnica slavy..." (A single rock, a tomb of glory), apparently referring to Napoleon's last days on St. Helen's island.

[12] Aylmer Maude, trans., *The Kreutzer Sonata* in *The Death of Ivan Ilyich and Other Stories*. A Signet Classic, 1964, p. 219.

[13] Tolstoy, *The Resurrection*, Signet, 1961, p. 142).

[14] Vronsky is portrayed by Tolstoy as an amateur artist.

[15] Second preface to *Childhood*, 1852, in: *L. N. Tolstoj o literature*, 1955, pp. 9-10.

[16] Tolstoy's son, Sergey L'vovich Tolstoy, notes in his memoirs that: At that time [when writing *Anna Karenina*] Lev Nikolaevich idealized family life and considered infidelity by either husband or wife an absolutely immoral act. This is what he wanted to show in his novel. At that time he read many English family novels and sometimes mocked at them, saying: "These novels all have endings where he puts his hand round her waist, marries her and obtains a baronetcy and an estate."
See "Ob otraženii žizni v *Anne Kareninoj*. Iz vospominanij S.L. Tolstogo." *Literaturnoe nasledstvo, 37-38,* 1939, p. 567. In other words, as Anna was reading her novel and experiencing everything its heroes went through, thus, ostensibly, fulfilling Tolstoy's later requirement of art, that it should infect with feeling, there was the narrator Tolstoy, from his mocking perspective, already condemning her in terms of the very same novels.

[17] In the essay (Maude, p. 152) Tolstoy said: "...in reality, almost all the feelings of people of our class amount to but three very insignificant and simple feelings — the feeling of pride, the feeling of sexual desire, and the feeling of weariness of life." Yet, in *Anna Karenina,* these very same feelings, infinitely varied and tragic in their intensity and profundity, constitute the basic texture of this great novel.

[18] Stiva misquotes Heinrich Heine, from "Heimkehr," 8:
>Himmlisch war's, wenn ich bezwang
>Meine sündige Begier,
>Aber wenn's mir nicht gelang,
>Hatt' ich doch ein gross Pläsier.

See Heinrich Heine, "Heimkehr," *Gesammelte Werke*, Erster Band, Gedichte, Berlin: Aufbau Verlag, 1956, 8, p. 350.

[19] One of Tolstoy's comments about his own *War and Peace* has a similar ring. In an early, unpublished foreword to the novel, he wrote:
>In my work, the heroes are only princes who speak and write in French, as if the whole Russian life of that time were focused upon these people. I agree that this is neither true nor liberal in attitude, and I can give only one, but irrefutable answer. The life of officials, merchants, students, and peasants does not interest me, and I only half comprehend it; the life of

> the aristocrats of that time, thanks to the monuments of the age, and for other reasons, I do understand, and it is interesting and dear to me. See *Literaturnoe nasledstvo*, No. 35-36, I, 288.

The implicit sharp criticism of aristocratic life of St. Petersburg that we find in the novel does not much support Tolstoy's claim that it was "dear" to him. At any rate, the later moral uneasiness with the aristocracy, in contrast to the proclaimed preference for it in Tolstoy's statement at the time, may help explain why at the end he did denounce his former works, including *War and Peace*.

[20] A French critic, Camille Mauclair, however, felt that there was a great deal more in common between Tolstoy and at least some of the French Symbolists than it may seem:

> Verlaine lui-même eut consenti — et il était plus prés de l'âme du maitre russe qui celui-ci ne le pourra jamais savoir. Verlaine disait presque les mêmes choses, et nous raillait aussi, et souvent avec moins de douceur. Même si des opinions, des heredités, des nuances les séparent, les grandes âmes sublimes s'apallent et fraternisent à travers le monde: il y a entre Baudelaire, Ibsen ou Villier, et Tolstoï, une solidarité que Tolstoï ne supprimera jamais.

See *La Grande Revue*, Tome premier, pp. 311-312.

[21] Valerij Brjusov, *Dnevniki 1891-1910*, published by M. and S. Sabašnikovs, 1927, p. 32. E. Nuralov (*Èstetika*, p. 170) notes that Brjusov did actually write to Tolstoy, claiming that he, Brjusov, should be among the first mentioned in the essay as among the predecessors of Tolstoy (apparently meaning that Tolśtoy should have referred to him among those authors on esthetics whose views came closer to Tolstoy's own). Tolstoy, however, never bothered to respond.

[22] This is not to say that his *characters* were never prone to such confusion. Here, for instance, is how Prince Andrey in *War and Peace* imposes his own feelings upon a tree in the forest that merely stood there minding its own business:

> "Spring, love, happiness!" this oak seemed to say. "Are you not weary of that stupid, meaningless, constantly repeated fraud? Always the same and always a fraud! There is no spring, no sun, no happiness! Look at those cramped dead firs, ever the same, and

at me too, sticking out my broken and barked fingers just where they have grown, whether from my back or my sides: as they have grown so I stand, and I do not believe in your hopes and your lies" (Norton, p. 459).

In view of what we know of Tolstoy's own attitude toward such fallacies, this passage becomes a way of describing and judging Andrey, a device to convey something about his personality that might explain his own ultimate irrelevance to, or perhaps freedom from, life, and thus his death. In this sense, the grotesque image of the oak as a "person, with bark-like fingers sticking out from the sides and back" may be, even if unconsciously, a self-portrait of Andrey's, as he was at that moment in the novel, painted upon the canvas of nature.

[23] It is difficult to say, but fascinating to speculate, what lessons about life and the importance of human doings would Prince Andrey have drawn from the lofty Austerlitz skies which taught him to think that our great battles and exploits are insignificant, like the running about of ants, if he could have been as curious about the busy microcosm of an anthill as Irtenyev was.

[24] Tolstoy, *Childhood*. Penguin, p. 40.

[25] Eleanore M. Zimmermann, *Magies de Verlaine*, Paris: Librairie Jose Corti, 1967, p. 298:

> Depuis longtemps déja les lignes et les couleurs n'avaient plus la valeur absolute que Verlaine leur conferait dans ses premiers vers. Mais dans l'ariette VIII on assiste au triomphe de l'incertitude.
> Pourtant le cadre est ferm et net. Verlaine a choisi pour son poème une forme de chanson, ou du moins une forme musicale: théme 1, théme 2, variation 1, théme 2, variation 2 théme 1; terre, ciel, terre-ciel, ciel- terre, terre. Mais paradoxalement, par cette forme stricte il met en question la realité même du tableau. Une description normale ne comprend pas ces retours.

[26] Incidentally, Tolstoy was quite capable of making similar destructive comments on writers not in any way connected with Decadence, and not even with Western literature. On one occasion, in 1890, he even took it upon himself to disparage Pushkin:

> Just think about that passage in his [Pushkin's] *Eu-*

> gene Onegin which is printed in all anthologies for children: "Winter. The peasant, celebrating ..." Every stanza is nonsense! /.../ Why "celebrating?" Maybe he is just going to town to buy salt or tobacco. "In a flat sledge inaugurates the track;" "his naggy, having sensed the snow..." How can you "sense" the snow!? If the sled is running on the snow, what point is there about "sensing" it? Further: "shambles at something like a trot." This "something like a..." historically speaking, is a stupid thing. It got in there only for the rhyme.

The verses referred to are part of the second stanza in Chapter Five of *Onegin*. The translation is by Vladimir Nabokov. See "Vstreči s Tolstym," the diary of A.V. Žirkevič, publication by E. Zajdenšnur, *Literaturnoe nasledstvo*, Nos. 37-8, p. 424. Tolstoy, then, did not like Pushkin's snow any better than Verlaine's, even if Pushkin could not be called either a "Symbolist" or "Decadent."

[27] In spite of many opinions to the contrary, such is the consistency of Tolstoy the artist with Tolstoy the thinker, that just this very act of listening to the sounds of nature participates in Tolstoy's dialogue of conscience with himself in *Confession,* where the issue in the moral dimension is that of the existence or non-existence of God:

> I remember, it was in early Spring, I was alone in the forest, listening to the sounds of the forest. I listened and thought always about one thing, as I always have thought of just one thing alone during these last three years. I was again searching for God.

See *Confession*, Chapter XII. *Ispoved'*, Bradda Books, 1962, p. 73.

[28] In all this discussion, we must, of course, keep it in mind that Verlaine was a poet, while Tolstoy works with a prose narrative that has movement and time and events, and space to permit juxtapositions of elements with the aim of evoking their potential symbolic dimensions. A poet must try to achieve this by means of imagery alone.

[29] See, for instance, Margaret F. Freeman, *The Unicorn Tapestries*, New York, E.P. Dutton, Inc., 1983.

[30] In his comments, Tolstoy says that there is not a single poem in Baudelaire "that would be simple and understandable without a

certain effort — an effort rarely rewarded, since the feelings transmitted by the poet are both mean and evil" (*PSS*, 30, 94; Maude 161).

[31] The critic Jean Prevost explains:
> Parmi les *Caprices*, il note, entre deux planches qui l'ont particulièrement frappé, "un paysage fantastique, un mélange de nuées et de rochers. Est-ce un coin de Sierra inconnue et infrequentée? Un échantilon du chaos? Deux monstres roulent à travers l'air tenebreux. Toute la hideur, toutes les saletés morales, tous les vices que l'esprit human peut concevoir sont écrits sur ces deux faces, qui tiennent le milieu entre l'hommme et la bête." Dans cet article, Baudelaire a indiqué le sujet réel: il s'agit de la bataille de deux sorcières. Mais sur la gravure le sexe de l'être qui se trouve roule sous l'autre n'est pas visible. Il est donc assez naturel que le poéte ait pu rever sur cette gravure en songeant à sa propre *sorcière*, car c'est ainsi qu'il appelait Jeanne Duval: l'oeuvre de Goya est devenue pour lui le symbole de ses disputes avec sa maitresse et de leur haine amoureuse. (Peut-être s'est-il inspiré plutot du dessin preparatoire, ou un chat-pard monstrueux hante le gouffre et semble guetter le resultat de la lutte.)

See, Jean Prevost, "Ce que Baudelaire doit a Goya" in: *Baudelaire*, Mercure de France, 1964, p. 121.

[32] One might perhaps say that Tolstoy's direct descriptions because of the associations they give rise to, function like metaphors, in a manner, however, which affects not only descriptions but also the plot. This point was already noted by Viktor Shklovsky: "Tolstoy's best metaphors are developed so thoroughly that one may not immediately recognize them as metaphors; they have, so to speak, a worldview-articulating, a plot-forming quality." See V. Šklovskij, *Xudožestvennaja proza. Razmyšlenija*, Moscow, Sovetskij pisatel', 1959, p. 128.

[33] See Tolstoy "Predislovie k romanu Polenca "Krestjanin" (Bütnerbauer)," *PSS 19*, 246.

[34] In *What Is Art?*, *PSS*, *30*, 178, Maude, p. 178, Tolstoy says: "The art of our time and of our circle has become a prostitute. And this comparison holds good even in minute details. Like her, it is not

limited to certain hours, like her, it is always adorned, like her it is always salable and like her it is enticing and ruinous."

35 "Vronsky followed the guard to the carriage, and had to stop at the entrance of the compartment to let a lady step out. The trained instinct of a society man enabled Vronsky with a single glance to decide that she belonged to the best Society. He apologized for being in her way and was about to enter the carriage, but felt compelled to have another look at her, not because she was very beautiful nor because of the elegance and modest grace of her whole figure, but because he saw in her sweet face as she passed him something specially tender and kind. When he looked round she too turned her head. Her bright gray eyes which seemed dark because of their black lashes rested for a moment on his face as if recognizing him, and then turned to the passing crowd evidently in search of some one. In that short look Vronsky had time to notice the subdued animation that enlivened her face and seemed to flutter between her bright eyes and a scarcely perceptible smile..." Norton, *Anna Karenina*, p. 56.

When we realize that it is Vronsky, not the narrator, who notices all these things, we can understand what a complex universe of inner events has been created in him, and by implication, in Anna during this brief encounter.

Chapter 6

[1] A significant exception to this general trend appears to be a book by N. Mikhailovsky, entitled *Desnica i šuica grafa Tolstogo*, where, according to E. Nuralov (*Èstetika Tolstogo*, 1979, p. 8) "Mikhxailovsky, in essence, was one of the first to note Tolstoyan contradictions, exposing them by juxtaposition of Tolstoy's philosophical, historical and pedagogical works with his novels *Anna Karenina*, *War and Peace*, and others."

[2] Tchaikovsky, for instance, who otherwise had a tremendous per-

sonal regard for Tolstoy, thought his opinions on art and music "amateurishly superficial" and was so embarrassed by them that he would avoid meeting Tolstoy on the street, lest their conversation should turn to the arts. This is attested to by another composer, Ippolitov-Ivanov, in his memoirs. See Vl. V. Protopopov, ed., *Vospominanija o P. I. Čajkovskom*, Gosmuzizdat, 1962, p. 250. Ivanov himself, overwhelmed by Tolstoy's personality to the point feeling like a nonentity in his presence, was also helpless to "reconcile Tolstoy the writer with his views on art." *ibid*., p. 251.

[3] For instance, a priest, S. Kuljukin, objected to Tolstoy's description of religious consciousness because "Good, or God, according to Tolstoy, is nothing more than a basic concept of our reasoning." See S. Kuljukin, "Otklik na nekotorye mysli grafa L.N. Tolstogo v ego proizvedenii 'Čto takoe iskusstvo'," *Xristianskoe čtenie*, June, 1902, p. 836.

[4] V. Zubov, "Tolstoj i russkaja èstetika 90-x godov ('Čto takoe iskusstvo' i ego kritiki)," *Èstetika L'va Tolstogo*. Sbornik statej pod redakciej P. N. Sakulina. Moscow, Gosudarstvennaja akademija xudožestvennyx nauk, 1929, p. 154.

[5] L. Tolstoy, *What Is Art? and Essays on Art*. Maude, p. 121.

[6] V.T. Val'ter. *V zaščitu iskusstva. Mysli muzikanta po povodu stat'i L.N. Tolstogo "Čto takoe iskusstvo?"* Saint Petersburg, 1899, p. 8.

[7] *Ibid*., p. 9. In a later day, one of the founders of Russian Formalism, Roman Jakobson, also noted the difference between mere emotional language, which indeed may communicate feeling without itself being art, and poetic language with its "orientation toward expression" which is "governed, so to speak by its own immanent laws; the communicative function which belongs both to practical and emotional language is here reduced to a minimum." See R. Jakobson, *Novejšaja russkaja poezija*. Nabrosok pervyj. Prague, 1921, p. 10. In this sense, Jakobson and the Formalists in effect maintained that art, being a matter of expression, is truly art precisely when it does not, in itself communicate or infect anyone with the feelings of the artist.

Maude, trans. A Signet Classic, 1984, p. 220.

[8] D.N. Certelev, "Po povodu poslednej stat'i gr. L.N. Tolstogo," *Russkij vestnik*, July, 1898, p. 5. V.T. Val'ter in *V zaščitu iskusstva*, p. 11, makes the same point with respect to Tolstoy's description of Kitty's birth pangs in *Anna Karenina*: "It can be said that the author vividly imagined and depicted these feelings, but we cannot

say that he experienced them himself."

[9] N.K. Mikhailovsky, a review of Tolstoy's *What is Art?* in *Russkoe bogatstvo*, No. 4, 1898, p. 143.

[10] D.S. Trizna, *Graf Tolstoj ob iskusstve i literature. Kritičeskij razbor.* Kiev, 1901, p. 22.

[11] V. Posse, review of *What is Art?* in *Obrazovanie. Pedagogičeskij i naučno-populjarnyj žurnal.* No. 3 (March, 1898), p. 88.

[12] Ja. Borisov, "Graf Tolstoj ob iskusstve," *Russkaja mysl'*, No. 4. 1898, p. 129.

[13] F.D. Batjuškov, "Utopija vsenarodnogo iskusstva," *Voprosy filosofii*, Book 46, Part I (January - February, 1899), p. 36.

[14] N. Mixajlovskij, "Ešče ob iskusstve i gr. Tolstom," *Russkoe bogatstvo*, No. 8 (August, 1902), p. 145.

[15] Batjuškov, "Utopia vsenarodnogo iskusstva,' pp. 3-31.

[16] V.T. Val'ter, *V zaščitu iskusstva*, p. 12.

[17]. D.N. Certelev, *Russkij vestnik*, July, 1898, p. 7.

[18] N.K. Mikhailovsky, a review of *What Is Art?* in *Russkoe bogatstvo*, April, 1898, p. 132. Mikhailovsky was referring to a book by Fechner, called *Vorschule der Aesthetic*.

[19] D.N. Certelev, *Russkij vestnik*, August, 1898, pp. 49-50.

[20] F.D. Batjuškov, "Utopija vsenarodnogo iskusstva," p. 13.

[21] This concept of goodness seems to have replaced in Tolstoy's mind an earlier, more conventional-abstract understanding of "truth." In 1886, in his introduction to the almanach "Cvetnik," Tolstoy already understood Godhead as a dynamic process, but called it "truth": "Truth will be known not by him who finds out only what has been, is and can be, but by him who finds out what must be according to the will of God. Truth is a path. Christ said: 'I am the path, and the truth, and the life.' And therefore truth is known not by him who looks under his own feet but by him who knows by the sun where he must go." See P.I. Birjukov, *Polnoe sobranie*, Vol. 19, p. 189. A couple of years later, in a diary note dated December 27, 1889, we can see Tolstoy already groping toward the rejection of the "Baumgartenian Trinity" of Truth, Beauty and Good; here also, the word "truth" stands where later Tolstoy placed the concept of goodness: "It is a crude philosophical error, this acknowledgment of three spiritual elements: 1) truth, 2) goodness, 3) beauty. There are no such elements. There is only that if a man's action is goodness (goodness for himself and others); and as for the manifestation of goodness, it is always beau-

tiful. So that goodness is the consequence of truth and beauty is the consequence of goodness." See *PSS, 50-51*, 195.

[22] V.N. Močul'skij, "N.G. Černyševskij i L.N. Tolstoj ob iskusstve." Otdel'nyj ottisk iz žurnala *Russkij filosofičeskij vestnik*. Warsaw, 1909, p. 15.

[23] Ja. Borisov, *Graf L. N. Tolstoj ob iskusstve*, p. 120.

[24] P.K. Engel'mejer, *Kritika naučnyx i xudožestvennyx učenij gr. L.N. Tolstogo*. Moscow, 1898, p. 18.

[25] N. Mixajlovskij, "Ešče ob iskusstve i gr. Tolstom," p. 144.

[26] Engel'mejer, "Kritika...", p. 66.

[27] Mixajlovskij, "Ešče ob iskusstve...," p. 145.

[28] In chapter XIV of his treatise Tolstoy writes:
> For a country peasant of unperverted taste this is as easy as it is for an animal of unspoilt scent to follow the trace he needs among a thousand others in wood or forest. The animal unerringly finds what he needs. So also the man, if only his natural qualities have not been perverted, will without fail select from among thousands of objects the real work of art he requires — that which infects him with the feeling experienced by the artist.

[29] Lev Šestov, *Dobro v učenii gr. Tolstogo i F. Nicše (Filosofija i propoved')* in Vol. II, 2nd edition of Šestov's collected works, St. Petersburg, šipovnik, 1900, p. 58.

E. Nuralov, 1979, pp. 156-7, notes Tolstoy's reaction to Šestov:
> L.N. Tolstoy, answering Chekhov, who did not like Šestov's book, noted with deadly sarcasm: "I, on the contrary, thought it amusing. Written with spunk. I do like cynics when they are sincere. Here, he says: 'There is no need for truth,' and really, 'What does he need truth for? He'll die anyway.'" In talking with Gorky, Tolstoy noted: "Now here is a bold pedant (*parikmakher*); he goes right ahead and says that I deceived myself, which means that I deceived others as well."

The term *Parikmakher*," borrowed from German, means "a barber," literally "wig-maker," and is used as a haughty aristocratic slur on city craftsmen as a "lower caste," sometimes also with anti-Semitic overtones. Here we see Tolstoy the Count amused at the antics of his underling. On another occasion, Tolstoy referred to

Chernyshevsky as "klopovonjajuščij gospodin" -- "the gentleman with the stink of bedbugs around him" -- again a slur mocking Chernyshevsky's insignificance and his presumption.

[30] Vernon Lee, "Tolstoi on Art," in *Gospels of Anarchy*. London: T. Fisher Unwin, 1908; Duffield, p. 57.

[31] R.F. Christian. *Tolstoy. A Critical Introduction*. Cambridge: at the University Press, 1969, p. 253.

[32] It is, however, precisely because of this religious consciousness that an early theoretician of Russian Marxism, G.B. Plekhanov, saw no compatibility whatsoever between Tolstoy and Marxism, calling Tolstoy a "metaphysician":

> Marx' world-view is dialectical materialism. On the contrary, Tolstoy is not only an idealist, but all his life he was also, in the devices of his thought, the most pure-blooded metaphysician.

See "Karl Marks i Lev Tolstoy," 1911, in: *G.B. Plexanov, Stat'i o Tolstom*, Moscow, n.d., p. 46.

[33] Hugh I'Anson Fausset, *Tolstoy. The Inner Drama*, p. 273.

[34] This, in effect, was the interpretation by the Soviet critic N.G. Kulikov who in 1955, spoke of "social consciousness, described by Tolstoy as religious consciousness." See p. 31, below.

[35] This similarity, and difference, between Tolstoy and Lenin was well noted by William B. Edgerton:

> Tolstoy's conception of the state and all its related institutions shows striking parallels with that of Lenin: they both saw the governments of their time as mechanisms resting on violence and serving for the exploitation of man by man. But the differences in their views are equally striking: whereas Lenin looked forward to the end of this exploitation through revolution and the establishment of a new form of government based on Marxist principles, Tolstoy viewed all forms of government as subject to the same corrupting influence of violence.

See William B. Edgerton, "The Artist Turned Prophet: Leo Tolstoy After 1880," *The American Contributions to the Sixth International Congress of Slavists*, Prague, 1968, p. 72.

[36] V. I. Lenin, "Lev Tolstoj kak zerkalo russkoj revoljucii," in: *V.I. Lenin o literature i iskusstve*, Moscow, 1960, p. 262.

[37] L.I. Aksel'rod (Ortodoks), "Metodičeskie problemy iskusstva

(Očerk tretij)", *Krasnaja nov'*, 1926, book 12, pp. 149-168.
[38] L. Ja. Zivel'činskaja, *Opyt marksistskogo analiza istorii èstetiki*, Kommunističeskaja akademija, sekcija literatury i iskusstv, Moskva, izdanie Kommunističeskoj Akademii, 1928.
[39] Tolstoy's argument in Chapter VLII of *What Is Art?* goes as follows:
> fine art can arise only on the slavery of the masses of the people, and can continue only as long as that slavery lasts; ... only under conditions of intense hardship for the workers can specialists -- writers, musicians, dancers, and actors -- arrive at that fine degree of perfection to which they do attain, or produce their refined works of art, and that only under the same conditions can there be a fine public to appreciate such productions. Free the slaves of capital, and it will be impossible to produce such refined art (Maude, p. 146; *PSS, 30,* 82).

[40] B. Bursov, "Èstetičeskaja sistema L. Tolstogo," *Zvezda*, Leningrad, kn. 11 (November), 1935, pp. 59-69.
[41] M. Rozental', "Vremennoe i 'bessmertnoe'," *Literaturnyj kritik*, book 11, 1935, pp. 649-651.
[42] *Èstetika L'va Tolstogo*. Sbornik statej pod redakciej Akademika P.N. Sakulina. Moskva, Gosudarstvennaja Akademija Xudožestvennyx Nauk, 1929.
[43] T. Rajnov, *Èstetika*, p. 33: "Although Tolstoy opposes feeling to thought, he always ascribes to feeling a certain rational content."
[44] For example, V. Asmus in "Voprosy realizma v èstetike Tolstogo," *Pod znamenem marksizma*, No. 1-2, 1943, p.97.
[45] N.K. Gudzij, "Tolstoj o russkoj literature," *Èstetika*, pp. 185-239.
[46] For a lucid, still standard description of the entire Formalist movement, see Victor Erlich, *Russian Formalism. History, Doctrine*. Mouton: 'S-Gravenhage, 1955.
[47] In addition to various articles, Eikhenbaum's largest work on Tolstoy consists of a three-volume study encompassing Tolstoy's life and work from the beginnings until the end of the 1870s. The first two volumes came out in 1928-1931, and the last, *Lev Tolstoj. Semidesjatye gody*, although completed in late 1930s, did not appear until 1960.
[48] B. Ejxenbaum, "Lev Tolstoj," 1919, in *Boris Ejxenbaum. Literatura. Teorija, kritika, polemika*, Leningrad, 1927; reprinted at: Chi-

cago, Russian Language Specialties, 1969, p. 19.
[49] Viktor Shklovsky, "Art as Technique" in: Lee T. Lemon and Marion J. Reis, editors, *Russian Formalist Criticism. Four Essays.* Lincoln: University of Nebraska Press, 1965, p. 12. Shklovsky also published a volume on Tolstoy in 1978.
[50] The term was used to refer to the more extreme leftists in the Soviet literary establishment who sought to establish a Marxist science of literature. The most prominent in the group was V. F. Pereverzev, a Dostoevsky critic, who developed his radical ideas as early as 1912. Cf. Victor Terras, editor, *Handbook of Russian Literature*, Yale University Press, 1985, p. 515.
[51] A. Mixajlov, "Èstetika L'va Tolstogo v osveščenii buržuaznyx iskusstvovedov" *Na literaturnom postu*, No. 33 (November), 1931, pp. 27-32.
[52] V.P. Malinovskij, "Paradoksy L'va Tolstogo ob iskusstve" in: *Istorija èstetičeskoj mysli i literaturovedenja, Voprosy russkoj literatury*, No. 12, 1969, p. 10.
[53] E. Nuralov, *Èstetika L.N. Tolstogo*
[54] Even before the revolution, there were observers who noted certain similarities between Tolstoy and Chernyshevsky. For instance, V.N. Mochul'sky wrote as early as 1909: "Chernyshevsky completely agrees with Tolstoy that art must pursue utilitarian purposes and must make a contribution to society." See V.N. Močul'skij, "N.G. Černyševskij i L.N. Tolstoj ob iskusstve," *Russkij Filologičeskij vestnik*, Warsaw, 1909, p. 2.
[55] Victor Terras, *Belinskij and Russian Literary Criticism. The Heritage of Organic Aesthetics*. The University of Wisconsin Press, 1974, p. 237.
[56] N.G. Černyševskij, "Kritičeskij vzgljad na sovremennye èstetičeskie ponjatija," in B.I. Bursov, editor, *N.G. Černyševskij. Èstetika i literaturnaja kritika*. Izbrannye stat'i, Moscow - Leningrad, 1951, pp. 78-9.
[57] G. Plekhanov, for one, drew a clear line of distinction between Chernyshevsky and Tolstoy on the grounds that Tolstoy was "metaphysical" through and through, while Chernyshevsky was concrete and dialectical -- a Marxist -- in his thinking: "those dialectical considerations with which Chernyshevsky reinforced his thinking remained forever inaccessible to the 'absolutely consistent' Tolstoy." See G. Plexanov, "Karl Marks i Lev Tolstoj," p. 84.
[58] James F. Scanlan, "Chernyshevsky and Rousseau." Anthony M.

Mlikotin, editor *Western Philosophical Systems in Russian Literature: A Collection of Critical Studies*. Los Angeles: University of Southern California Press, 1979, p. 117.

[59] For instance, K. Lomunov in his book *Èstetika L'va Tolstogo,* Moscow, 1972, remembers from time to time to point out similarities between Tolstoy's ideas and those of the "progressive critics" by saying such things as, on p. 49: "The thoughts of the young Tolstoy which were formed at the time when he wrote the story *The Childhood*, his first completed work, correspond astonishingly with the statements of Belinsky, Chernyshevsky and Dobrolyubov pertaining to the role of 'heart' and feeling in art."

[60] N.K. Lomunov, "Tolstoj v bor'be protiv dekadentskogo iskusstva," *Lev Nikoaevič Tolstoj*. Sbornik statej i materialov pod redakciej D.D. Blagogo, N.K. Lomunova, i I.N. Uspenskogo. Moskva, ANSSSR, Institut mirovoj literatury imeni A.N. Gor'kogo, 1951, pp. 22-97.

[61] N.K. Lomunov, "Lev Tolstoj v bor'be za realizm v iskusstve (k 125-letiju so dnja roždenija velikogo russkogo pisatelja)" *Voprosy filosofii*, No. 5, 1953, pp. 178-195.

[62] B. Bursov, "Èstetičeskaja sistema L. Tolstogo," p. 212.

[63] Tolstoy said: "No matter how unnatural the situations in which he places his characters, how alien to them is the language which he forces them to speak, how lacking in individuality they may be, the movement of feeling itself: its growing intensity, its changes, the combination of many contradictory feelings, are often truthfully and powerfully expressed in some of the scenes of Shakespeare, and, when played by good actors, evoke, even if only for a short time, a feeling of sympathy for the characters." "O Šekspire i o drame," *L.N. Tolstoj o literature*, Moscow, 1955, pp. 544.

[64] P. Solncev, "Literaturno-èstetičeskie vzgljady L.N. Tolstogo 90-godov XIX v." *Aftoreferat diskussii na soiskanie učenoj stepeni kandidata filologičeskix nauk*. Minsk. Belorusskij gosudarstvennyj universitet im. V.I. Lenina, 1953, p. 12.

[65] G.I. Kulikov, "Vzgljady L.N. Tolstogo na iskusstvo v 90-ie gody," *Aftoreferat dissertacii na soiskanie učenoj stepeni kandidata filologičeskix nauk*. Moskva, Moskovskij gosudarstvennyj universitet, 1955.

[66] G.I. Kulikov, "Bor'ba L.N. Tolstogo s dekadentskim iskusstvom," *Učenye zapiski*, Ural'skij pedagogičeskij institut im. A.S. Puškina, Tom. III, vypusk 10, Ural'sk, 1956, pp. 205-231.

[67] See E. Nuralov, *Ob Èstetičeskix vzgljadax L.N. Tolstogo.* Erevan, 1965, p. 4. Perhaps, for balance, it is worth quoting at this point from V. Lazursky's memoirs of his conversations with Tolstoy:
> "Here Lev Nikolaevich started to tear the Russian critics apart, mercilessly. Belinsky is a prattler; every thing he says is so immature. True, there are good passages in his works, he is a talented boy. But if Belinsky and other critics were translated into foreign languages, foreigners would not bother reading them, so elementary and dull is all that. In the West there are good, serious critics, for instance, Lessing, Sainte-Beuve, Carlyle and others. True, Carlyle keeps harping on this hero worship of his, whether anyone likes it or not, as if from sheer stubbornness, against both time and Christianity. But still, he is an educated man. As for our clumsy-pawed critics, they are trash, like everything Russian. Our poor young people are still being educated on Dobrolyubov, Chernyshevsky, Pisarev and never go beyond them. That Chernyshevsky who read up on smart books in his seminary then learned to read several foreign books, and can't keep his mouth together from the great joy that he knows them, reproaches Professor Yushkevich for not having read these books. Our literature was always ahead of our criticism. Take for example Pushkin: he was a man with a true European education."

V. Lazurskij, "Razgovory s L.N. Tolstym o pisateljax, russkix i innostrannyx." *Vospominanija o L.N. Tolstom,* Moscow, 1911, p. 37.

[68] Unfortunately, Nuralov's interpretations of Tolstoy's attitude to Wagner suffer from the typical Soviet "socialist-realist" cant that leads him into making silly political statements, such as the following, from another article:
> With an artist's intuition, he [Tolstoy] felt and understood, of course, the efforts of the German composer manifest in that in depicting the underground Nibelungenheim with its horrors, Wagner was alluding to the contemporary capitalist hell.

See E. A. Nuralov, "Critique of Bourgeois art in L.N. Tolstoy's Treatise "What Is Art?," in *Naučnye trudy* of the Erevan State

University, Vol. 70, issue 7, Erevan, 1960, p. 54.
[69] Indeed, the four Appendixes to *What Is Art?* consist of illustrative materials on the French symbolists and of a brief synopsis of Wagner's *Nibelungen Ring*.
[70] E. Nuralov, pp. 144-5.
[71] E. Nuralov, pp. 123-3.
[72] E. Nuralov, *Èstetika L.N. Tolstogo v ocenke kritiki*, Erevan, 1979, pp. 105-186.
[73] E.G. Babaev, *Tolstoj ob iskusstve*, Tula, 1966, p. 25.
[74] V.A. Asmus, "Mirovozzrenie Tolstogo," *Literaturnoe nasledstvo*, Vol. 69, book 1, 1961, p. 92.
[75] E.N. Kuprejanova, *Èstetika L.N. Tolstogo, op. cit.*
[76] This, happily, seems like a return to Rajnov's idea expressed back in 1929. See Sakulin, *Èstetika*, p. 27.
[77] D.N. Iščuk, *Problemy Èstetiki pozdnego L.N. Tolstogo.* Rostov-on-Don, 1967, p. 33.
[78] K. Lomunov in his 1972 *Èstetika L'va Tolstogo*, pp. 108-9 informs us that Tolstoy respected Ruskin very highly, but that in spite of his having freed himself from the heritage of dogmatic thought, "the opaque - ecclesiastic - Christian understanding of life which made it possible for him [Ruskin] to unite the ethic and the aesthetic ideals stayed with him to the end and weakened his teaching; it was also weakened by artificialities and therefore obscurities of poetic language" (*PSS*, 73, 111, quoted by Lomunov on p. 111 of *Èstetika*).

Chapter 7

[1] Aylmer Maude, *Tolstoy and His Problems*. Republication by Haskell House Publishers Ltd. New York, 1974, p. 43.
[2] "Count Leo Tolstoi," an editorial in *Literature*, The American Edition. Published by *The Times* and by Harper and Brothers, New York, No. 41, July 30, 1898, p. 73.
[3] *Pen Portraits and Reviews by Bernard Shaw*, p. 258.
[4] Shaw must surely have known more about the English aristocracy than about the Russian. At any rate, for Tolstoy the issue of art was not a just matter between gentlemen and gamekeepers.
[5] John Albert Macy, "Tolstoy's Moral Theory of Art," *Century Magazine*, No. 62, 1901; reprinted in Duffield, *Tolstoy and the Critics*.
[6] Arthur Symons, "Tolstoi on Art," in *Studies in Prose and Verse*,

New York: Dutton, 1904; Duffield, p. 83.

[7] Tolstoy becomes quite eloquent in his essay (Maude, p. 152) about the great variety of important human experiences which the life of the simple people contains and which, in consequence, provides many fitting themes and subjects for important art, the art which communicates religious consciousness.

[8] See Viktor Shklovsky, "Art as Technique" in Lee T. Lemon and Marion J. Reis, editors, *Russian Formalist Criticism,* p. 15:
> Tolstoy makes the familiar seem strange by not naming the familiar object. He describes an object as if he were seeing it for the first time, and event as if it were happening for the first time. In describing something he avoids the accepted names of its part and instead names corresponding parts of other objects.

[9] T.S. Knowlston "Art Criticism" in *Leo Tolstoy: a Biographical and Critical Study*. London and New York: Frederick Warne and Co., 1904; Duffield, p. 81.

[10] Romain Rolland, *Vie de Tolstoï*. Paris: Librairie Hachette, 1921, p. 114 [All translations from the French are my own R.Š.].

[11] E. Halperine-Kaminsky, editor,"Le rôle de l'Art. Réponses à Tolstoï. Introduction." *La Grande Revue,* Tome premier, 1899, p. 265.

[12] *La Grande Revue*, No.3, March 1, 1899, p. 671.

[13] *La Grande Revue*, Tome premier, p. 281.

[14] Doumic, *Mercure de France*, May, 1898, p. 451. Quoted in Thaïs S. Lindstrom, *Tolstoï en France*. Paris: Institut d'études slaves de l'Université de Paris, 1952, p. 77.

[15] René Doumic, "Les idées du comte Tolstoï sur l'art [1898] in: *Études sur la Littérature Française* Troisieme serie. Paris: Librairie académique, 1910, p. 196.

[16] Josephin Sar-Peladan, *La Décadence Esthétique. Réponse a Tolstoï*. Paris: Chamuel, Éditeur, 1898.

[17] In one of his essays, for instance, Orwell briskly dismissed Tolstoy as a critic of Shakespeare:
> Artistic theories such as Tolstoy's are quite worthless, because they not only start out with arbitrary assumptions, but depend on vague terms ("sincere", "important" and so forth) which can be interpreted in any way one chooses. Properly speaking, one cannot *answer* Tolstoy's attack.

"Lear, Tolstoy and the Fool," Sonia Orwell and Ian Angus, editors, *In Front of Your Nose. The collected Essays, Journalism and Letters of George Orwell*. IV, New York: Harcourt, Brace, Inc., 1968, p. 290.

[18] Israel Knox, "Tolstoy's Definition of Art." *The Journal of Philosophy,* Vol. XXVII, No. 3, 1930, p. 65.

[19] The notion of "infection" was even understood by H.W. Garrod to be literally a matter of disease:

> Using a metaphor not too happy, but selected with care, Tolstoi speaks of him [an artist] as "infecting" others with those feelings. I say "selected with care" because, behind Tolstoi's choice of this metaphor, lies his conviction that three-fourths of modern art is no better than a disease. He believes that, and he is unwilling to forget it or to allow us to forget it.

See H.W. Garrod, *Tolstoi's Theory of Art*, The Taylorian Lecture 20 Nov., 1935. Oxford: at the Clarendon Press, 1935, reprinted by Folcroft Library editions, 1974, p. 11.

[20] Gary R. Jahn, "The Aesthetic Theory of Leo Tolstoy's *What Is Art?*". *The Journal of Aesthetics and Art Criticism*, XXXIV, I, Fall, 1975, p. 60.

[21] Tolstoy was not altogether sure that forbidding all the arts would be such a bad idea, and there have been readers who clearly saw Tolstoy's affinity to Plato as, for instance, Harold Osborne in his *Aesthetics and Art Theory. An Historical Introduction*, New York: E.P. Dutton and Co., Inc., 1970, p. 240:

> Such composite theories, which predominated in antiquity and have been prominent at all periods in the West, may be termed "amelioration" theories because they tend to assess works of art not by aesthetic standards, or not by these standards alone, but by their effect upon persons exposed to them. The two outstanding names associated with theories of this kind are Plato and Tolstoy.

[22] Hugh I'Anson Fausset, *Tolstoj. The Inner Drama*, p. 2.

[23] William B. Edgerton, "The Critical Reception Abroad of Tolstoy's *What Is Art?*". Victor Terras, editor, *American Contributions to the Eighth International Congress of Slavists*, Vol. II, Literature. Columbus: Slavica, p. 160.

Chapter 8

[1] *Lev Tolstoj ob iskusstve i literature*, Vol. I, 1958, pp. 335-6.

[2] See, for instance, Andrey's moment of clarity just before the battle of Borodino, where the metaphor of light itself is used to convey the new insight that makes reality at once lucid, dreadful and strange:

> And from the height of this perception all that had previously tormented and preoccupied him suddenly became illumined by a cold white light without shadows, without perspective, and without distinction of outline. All life appeared to him like magic-lantern pictures at which he had long been gazing by artificial light through a glass. Now he suddenly saw those badly daubed pictures in clear daylight and without a glass. "Yes, yes! There they are, those false images that agitated, enraptured and tormented me," said he to himself, passing in review the principal pictures of the magic lantern of life and regarding them now in the cold white daylight of his clear perception of death"
> (*War and Peace*, Norton, p. 858).

Andrey's sentiments, incidentally, have something in common with those in verse 68 of Edward FitzGerald's *The Rubayat of Omar Khayyam*, where it says:

> We are no other than a moving row
> Of Magic Shadow-shapes that come and go
> Round with the Sun-illumined Lantern held
> In Midnight by the Master of the Show

[3] See E. N. Kuprejanova *Èstetika L.N. Tolstogo*. p. 140:

> In Tolstoy's landscapes (and not only in landscapes) the barrier between "depiction" of outside things and "expression" of inner life is taken away. It disappears to the extent in which the inner and the outer, the objective and the subjective become one in the act and process of direct contemplation and experience.

[4] The Mountains in *The Cossacks* and the Austerlitz sky in *War and Peace* share the same quality of being in themselves the measure of all values at the given moment of a character's experience.

[5] Compare Andrey's experience upon being wounded at Austerlitz:

> Above him there was now nothing but the sky — the lofty sky, not clear yet still immeasurably lofty, with

> gray clouds gliding slowly across it. "How quiet, peaceful, and solemn; not at all as I ran," thought Prince Andrew — "not as we ran, shouting and fighting, not at all as the gunner and the Frenchman with frightened and angry faces struggled for the mop: how differently do those clouds glide across that lofty infinite sky!" (*War and Peace*, Norton, p. 302)

with the moment of his death after Borodino:

> In his words, his tone, and especially in that calm, almost antagonistic look could be felt an estrangement from everything belonging to this world, terrible in one who is alive. Evidently only with an effort did he understand anything living; but it was obvious that he failed to understand, not because he lacked the power to do so but because he understood something else — something the living did not and could not understand — and which wholly occupied his mind (*ibid*, p. 1084-5).

[6] In *The Death of Ivan Ilyich*, with Tolstoy's vision darkened considerably, the sick Ilyich found out that the doctors denied him precisely this human comfort and confidence, just like he himself had denied it to the terrified people brought before him for judgment.

[7] Morson, *Hidden in Plain View. Narrative and Creative Potentials in "War and Peace,"* Stanford, 1987.

[8] In 1919, Maxim Gorkij wrote of Tolstoy:

> And he seemed to me like a living ancient stone which knows all the beginnings and all the ends and is thinking about when and how the end will come to all stones and all grass on the earth, to waters of the sea and to humanity, and the whole world, from a stone to the sun. And the sea seemed a part of his soul, and everything around — of him and from him. In the pensive immobility of this old man one could feel something all-knowing, something magic, dwelling deep down in the darkness below him and something that has searchingly driven its peak into the blue emptiness over the earth, as if it was he — his concentrated will — that was calling and sending forth the waves, was governing the movements of the clouds and shadows that seemed really to be moving the stones, awak-

>ening them. And suddenly, in some sort of a momentary madness, I felt that — quite possibly — he will stand up, wave his hand, and the sea will freeze solid, turn to glass, and the stones will move and give voice, and everything around will become alive, will sound out, will speak in tongues about themselves, about him, against him.

See Maksim Gorkij, *Sobranie sočinenij*, Vol. 18, Literary Portraits, 1963, p. 81

[9] One is reminded of what the critic Andonis Decavalles said in another context: "...when divine myths are lost, it is the ego of the poet which must shape the world." See *World Literature Today*, Spring, 1985, p. 227.

SELECTED BIBLIOGRAPHY

Works by Tolstoy

Polnoe sobranie sočinenij L.N. Tolstogo v 90 tomax. Moscow: Xudožestvennaja literatura, 1929-58.

P.I. Birjukov, editor, Polnoe sobranie sočinenij L'va Nikolaeviča Tolstogo. Moscow, 1913.

L.D. Gromova-Opul'skaja, et al., editors. L.N. Tolstoj o literature. Stat'i, pis'ma, dnevniki. Moscow, 1955.

K.N. Lomunov, ed. Lev Tolstoj ob iskusstve i literature. Vols. I & II. Moscow, 1958.

S. Rozanova, editor, L.N. Tolstoj, Perepiska s russkimi pisateljami. Moscow, 1962.

Aylmer Maude, trans. What Is Art? and Essays on Art. London: Oxford University Press, 1962.

------------ Confession and the Gospel in Brief, by Leo Tolstoy. London: Oxford University Press, 1933.

Articles by Tolstoy

"O narodnom obrazovanii," PSS, 8.
"Vospitanie i obrazovanie," PSS, 8.
"Progress i opredelenie obrazovanija," PSS, 8.
"Predislovie k sočineniju G.M. Bondareva," Birjukov, Vol. 19.
"Predislovie k dnevniku Amielja," Birjukov, 19.
"Komu u kogo učit'sja pisat': krestjanskim rebjatam u nas ili nam u krestjanskix rebjat?" PSS, 8.
"Tak čto že nam delat'?", PSS, 25.
"O tom, čto est' i čto ne est' iskusstvo, i o tom, kodga iskusstvo est' delo važnoe i kogda ono est' delo pustoe," PSS, 30.
"Predislovie k sočinenijam Gjui de Mopassana," PSS, 30.

"Predislovie k romanu Polenca 'Krestjanin'," Birjukov, 19.

"O Šekspire i o drame," PSS, 35.

Books on Tolstoy

Azarova, N. I. L. Tolstoj, iskusstvo, vremja. Moscow: "Sov. Rossija", 1981.

Babaev, E. G. Očerki èstetiki i tvorčestva L. N. Tolstogo. Moscow: Izd-vo Moskovskogo universiteta, 1981.

------------ Tolstoj ob iskusstve. Tula, 1966.

Brjusov, Valerij. Dnevniki 1891-1910. M. and S. Sabašnikov, publishers, 1927.

Bursov, B. Lev Tolstoj: idejnye iskanija i tvorčeskij metod, 1847-1862. Moscow, 1960.

Christian, R.F. Tolstoy. A Critical Introduction. Cambridge: at the University Press, 1969.

Duffield, Gene and Manuel Bilsky, editors. Tolstoy and the Critics: Literature and Aesthetics. Chicago: Scott, Foreman and Company, 1965.

Ejxenbaum, Boris Mixailovič. Tolstoy in the Seventies. Ann Arbor: Ardis, 1982.

------------ Tolstoy in the Sixties. Ann Arbor: Ardis, 1982.

------------ Literatura. Teorija, kritika, polemika. Moscow, 1927.

Engel'majer, P.K. Kritika naučnyx i xudožestvennyx učenij Gr. L.N. Tolstogo. Moscow, 1898.

Garrod, H.W. Tolstoi's Theory of Art. The Taylorian Lecture, 20 Nov., 1936. Oxford: at the Clarendon Press, 1936.

Gibian, G. Tolstoj and Shakespeare. 's Gravenhage: Mouton, 1957.

Gorning, B.V. L.N. Tolstoj i tradicija "novogo iskusstva." Moscow, 1929.

Gromov, Pavel. O stile L'va Tolstogo: stanovlenie dialektiki duši. Leningrad: Xudož. lit., 1971.

Fausset, Hugh, Tolstoy. The Inner Drama. New York: Russel and Russel, n.d.

Gustafson, Richard, Leo Tolstoy. Resident and Stranger. A Study in Fiction and Theology. Princeton University Press, 1986.

Iščuk, D.N.. Problemy èstetiki L'va Tolstogo. Rostov-on-Don, 1967.

Kulikov, G.I. Bor'ba L.N. Tolstogo s dekadentskim iskusstvom. Uralsk, 1956.

Kuprejanova, E.N. Èstetika L.N. Tolstogo. Moscow-Leningrad: "Nauka," 1966.

Lindstrom, Thaïs S. Tolstoï en France. Paris: Institut d'études slaves de l'Université de Paris, 1952.

L. N. Tolstoj i izobrazitel'noe iskusstvo. Moscow: Izobrazitelnoe iskusstvo, 1981.

Lomunov, K. Èstetika L'va Tolstogo. Moscow: Sovremennik, 1972.

Makovicky, Dušan. U Tolstogo. V.R. Ščerbina, et al., editors, Literaturnoe nasledstvo, Vol. 90, four books. Moscow: "Nauka,"1979.

Močul'skij, V.N. N.G. Černyševskij i L.N. Tolstoj ob iskusstve. Warsaw, 1929.

Mann, Thomas. Goethe and Tolstoy. University of Alabama Press, 1984.

Maude, Aylmer, trans. Confession and the Gospel in Brief by Leo Tolstoy. London: Oxford University Press, 1933.

------------, Leo Tolstoy. What Is Art? and Essays on Art. London: Oxford University Press, 1962.

------------, Tolstoy and His Problems. Republication by Haskell House Publishers, New York, 1898.

Morson, Saul. Hidden in Plain View. Narrative and Creative Potentials in "War and Peace." Stanford: University of California Press, 1987.

Nikolaev, M.P. L.N. Tolstoj i N.G. Černyševskij. Tula: Proškskoe knižnoe izd-vo., 1969.

Nuralov, E. Èstetika L. Tolstogo v ocenke kritiki. Erevan, 1979.

------------ Ob èstetičeskix vzgljadax L.N. Tolstogo. Erevan, 1965.

Plexanov, G.B. Stat'i o Tolstom. Moscow, n.d.

Roland, Romain. Vie de Tolstoi. Paris: Librairie Hachette, 1921.

Sakulin, P.N., editor. Èstetika L'va Tolstogo. Moscow: Gosudarstvennaja akademija xudožestvennyx nauk, 1929.

Steiner, George, Tolstoy or Dostoevsky. An Essay in the Old

Criticism. New York: Vintage Books, 1961.
E.J. Simmons, Leo Tolstoy. Boston: Little, Brown & Co., 1946.
Šestov, Lev. Dobro v učenii gr. Tolstogo i F. Nicše. St. Petersburg, 1900.
Šifman, A.N. Lev Tolstoj — obličitel' buržuaznoj kul'tury. Tula, 1969.
Trizna, D.S. Graf Tolstoj ob iskusstve i literature. Kritičeskij razbor. Kiev, 1901.
Troyat, Henri, Tolstoy. New York: Doubleday, 1967
U Tolstogo. Jasnopoljanskie zapiski D.P. Makovickogo. Literaturnoe nasledstvo. No. 90, 1979.
Val'ter, V.T. V zaščitu iskusstva. Mysli muzikanta po povodu stat'i L.N. Tolstogo" Čto takoe iskusstvo?" St. Petersburg, 1899.
Vinogradov, I. I. Kritičeskij analiz religiozno-filosofskix vzgljadov L.N. Tolstogo. Moskva: Izd-vo Znanie, 1981.
Wiener, Leo., trans. Tolstoy on Education. The University of Chicago Press, 1967.

Articles on Tolstoy

Ardens, N.N. "Lev Tolstoj o Šekspire i o drame." Učenye zapiski Moskovskogo pedagogičeskogo instituta, No. 405 (1970), pp. 247-275.
Asmus, V.F. "Mirovozzrenie Tolstogo." Literaturnoe Nasledstvo, Vol. 69, kn. 1 (1961), pp. 35-102.
------------ "Voprosy realizma v èstetike Tolstogo," Pod znamenem marksizma, No. 1-2, 1943.
Aksel'rod (Ortodoks), L.I., "Metodičeskie problemy iskusstva (Očerk tretij), Krasnaja nov', 1926, book 12
Babaev, E.G. "K voprosu o principe narodnosti v èstetike L.N. Tolstogo." Učenye zapiski Taškentskogo pedagogičeskogo instituta im. V.G. Belinskogo), No.4. (1957), pp. 103-140.
Baranov, Vadim, "Revolution and Art: Eighty Years Ago Lenin Published His Article 'Lev Tolstoy as the Mirror of the Russian Revolution'." Soviet Literature 11, 1988, pp. 125-127.
Batjuškov, F.D., "Utopija vsenarodnogo iskusstva," Voprosy filosofii, Book 46, Part I (January-February, 1899).
Borisov, Ja. "Graf Tolstoj ob iskusstve," Russkaja mysl', No. 4.

1898
Bursov, B. "Èstetičeskaja sistema L. Tolstogo." Zvezda, No. 11 (1935).
Carden, Patricia, "Tolstoj and the Plutarchan Tradition." In Jane Harris, ed., American Contributions to the Tenth International Congress of Slavists. Sofia: 1988; Slavica: 1988, pp. 83-95.
Černyševskij, N.G., "Kritičeskij vzgljad na sovremennye èstetičeskie ponjatija," in B.I. Bursov, editor, N.G. Černyševskij. Èstetika i literaturnaja kritika. Izbrannye stat'i, Moscow - Leningrad, 1951.
Certelev, D.N. "Po povodu poslednej stat'i gr. L.N. Tolstogo," Russkij vestnik, July, 1898.
Čičerin, Z.V., "Rabota L'va Tolstogo nad romanom o dekabristax," Učenye zapiski L'vovskogo Gosudarstvennogo Universiteta imeni Ivana Franko, Vol. xxiv, 1953, issue 2.
Danilova, I., "Russkie pisateli i xudožniki XIX veka o Dresdenskoj galleree," in Starye mastera v Dresdenskoj galleree, Moscow: Gosizdat "Iskusstvo," 1959.
Denisova, L.F. "Lenin o Tolstom (K voprosu o metode èstetičeskogo analiza)." Voprosy filosofii, No. 4 (1965) pp. 19-28.
Dosyčeva, E., "Pedagogika i poetika v statje L. N. Tolstogo 'Komu u kogo učitsja pisat': krestjanskim rebjatam u nas ili nam u krestjanskix rebjat?'" Prosveščenie, pedagogičeskij sbornik. Petrograd: Gosizdat, No. 2, 1922.
Doumic, René, "Les idées du comte Tolstoi sur l'art." études sur la littérature française. Troisième serie. Paris: librairie académique, 1910.
Edgerton, William B., "The Artist Turned Prophet: Leo Tolstoy After 1880," The American Contributions to the Sixth International Congress of Slavists, Prague, 1968.
------------ "The Critical Reception Abroad of Tolstoy's What Is Art?" American Contributions to the Eighth International Congress of Slavists. Columbus: Slavica, 1978.
Galagan, G. Ja. "Èstetičeskie i etičeskie iskanija molodogo Tolstogo." Russkaja literatura, No. 1 (1974), pp. 136-50.
Gavronskij, V. "Tolstoj o Šekspire." Novyj žurnal, No. 91 (1968), pp. 105-112.
Gej, N.K. "Tradicii romantizma i poetika L. Tolstogo." Russkaja literatura, No. 1 (1972), pp. 34-48.
Gornaja, V.Z. "Tolstoj-myslitel' v sovremennom buržuaznom

literaturovedenii i filosofii." Izv. AN SSSR. Serija literatury i jazyka. Vol. 27, vyp. 6 (1968), pp. 513-26.

Grineva, I.E. "Tema iskusstva v romane L.N. Tolstogo 'Vojna i mir'." Tolstovskij sbornik, No 3 (1967), pp. 34-50.

Gusev, T. "Tolstoj o xudožestvennom tvorčestve (Po neopublikovannym materialam i ličnym vospominaniam)." Oktjabr', No. 11 (1935), pp. 221-226.

Headings, Philip R. "The question of exclusive Art: Tolstoy and T.S. Eliot's The Waste Land." Revue des Langues Vivantes, XXII, pp. 82-95.

Heier, E. :Die Räuber in the Light of Tolstoy's Concept of Art." Canadian Review of Comparative Literature / Revue Canadienne de littérature Comparèe, Vol. 13, No. 4 (December) 1986, pp. 585-599.

Iščuk, G.N. "L.N. Tolstoj v spore s 'čistym iskusstvom' na stranicax "Al'berta i Ljucerna." Filologičeskie nauki, 5 (1972), pp.15-26.

------------ "Social'naja i èstetičeskaja problematika traktata L. N. Tolstogo 'Čto takoe iskusstvo?'" Učenye zapiski Marijskogo pedagogičeskogo instituta, Vol. XVIII vyp. 1 (1958), pp. 201-42.

Jackson. Robert, "The Archetypal Journey: Aesthetic and Ethical Imperative in the Art of Tolstoj; 'The Cossacks'." Russian Literature Vol. 11, No. 4, (May), 1982, pp. 389-410.

Jahn, Gary, "The Aesthetic theory of 'What Is Art?'," Journal of Aesthetics and Art Criticism, XXXIV, I, Fall, 1975

Karlova, T.S. "L.N. Tolstoj i problema naturalizma 80-90 gg." Učenye zapiski Kazanskogo instituta, Vol. CXVII, No. 9 (1957), pp. 76-81.

Kiraly, Gyula, "Tolstoy's Novel and Tolstoy's Thinking: Tolstoy and Shakespeare." Acta Litteraria Academiae Scientiarum Hungaricae, Vol. 23, No. 3-4, 1981, pp. 227-246.

Knox, Israel, "Tolstoy's Definition of Art." The Journal of Philosophy, Vol. XXVII, No. 3, 1930.

Kovalev, V.A. "L.N. Tolstoj o kriterijax xudožestvennoj literatury." L.N. Tolstoj. Materialy mežvuzovskoj naučnoj konferencii. Kustanaj, 1961, pp. 115-30.

Kulikov, G.I. "Bor'ba L.N. Tolstogo s dekadentskim iskusstvom." Učenye zapiski Ural'skogo pedagogičeskogo instituta., Vol. III, vyp. 10 (1956), pp. 205-31.

------------ "L.N. Tolstoj ob iskusstve buduščego." Učenye zapiski Ural'sk. pedagogičeskogo instituta im. A.S. Puškina), Vol. 4, vyp. 11 (1957), pp. 235-42.

Kuljukin, S., "Otklik na nekotorye mysli grafa L.N. Tolstogo v ego proizvedenii 'Čto takoe iskusstvo?'," Xristianskoe čtenie, June, 1902

Kuprejanova, E. "Prosvetitel'skie istoki filosofii i tvorčeskogo metoda L'va Tolstogo." Russkaja literatura, VII, ii, PP. 40-54.

------------ "Vyraženie èstetičeskix vozzrenij i nravstvennyx iskanij L. Tolstogo v romane 'Anna Karenina'." Russkaja literatura, No. 3 (1960), pp. 117-36.

Kurjakova. G.V. "Mopassan v ocenke L.N. Tolstogo," Učenye zapiski, Sbornik trudov kafedr russkogo jazyka, literatury i pedagogiki. Vypusk V, Kemerovskij gosudarstvennyj pedagogičeskij institut. Kemerovo, 1962

Lazurskij, V., "Razgovory s L.N. Tolstym o pisateljax, russkix i innostrannyx." Vospominanija o L.N. Tolstom, Moscow, 1911.

Lebedeva, L.A. "L.N. Tolstoj o tvorčeskom processe." Voprosy russkoj literatury, No. 3 (1970), pp. 58-66.

------------ "Lev Tolstoj o xudožestvennoj pravde." Problemy realizma i xudožestvennoj pravdy. L'vov gos. institut im. Franko, vyp.1 1961, pp. 20-42.

Lee, Vernon, "Tolstoi on Art," in Gospels of Anarchy. London: T. Fisher Unwin, 1908

Lenin, V.I. "Lev Tolstoj kak zerkalo russkoj revoljucii," V.I. Lenin o literature i iskusstve, Moscow, 1960.

Levin, Ju. "Lev Tolstoj, Šekspir, i russkaja literatura 60-x godov XIX veka." Voprosy literatury, No. 8 (1968), pp. 54-73.

Lomunov, K. "L. Tolstoj-kritik." Istorija russkoj kritiki, Vol. 2 (Moscow-Leningrad, 1958), pp. 337-401.

------------ "Lev Tolstoj ob iskusstve i literature." Lev Tolstoj ob iskusstve i literature. Vol. 1 Moscow, 1958, pp. 5-67.

------------ "Tolstoj v bor'be s dekadentskim iskusstvom." L.N. Tolstoj. Sbornik statej i materialov, Moscow, AN, SSSR, In-t. mirovoj lit-ry. gos. muzej Tolstogo. 1951, pp. 22-97.

------------ "Lev Tolstoj v bor'be za realizm v iskusstve." Nekotorye voprosy marksistsko-leninskoj èstetiki. Moscow, 1954.

------------ "Tolstoj v bor'be protiv dekadentskogo iskusstva," Lev Nikoaevič Tolstoj. Sborniki statej i materialov pod redakciej D.D. Blagogo, N.K. Lomunova, i I.N. Uspenskogo. Moscow: Institut mirovoj literatury imeni A.N. Gor'kogo, 1951.

Mal'cev, I.V. "Traktat L.N. Tolstogo 'Čto takoe iskusstvo?' i polemika po voprosam èstetiki pered revoluciej 1905 goda." Učenye zap. Doneckogo pedagogičeskogo instituta, vyp. 8 (1960), pp. 3-78.

Malinkovskij, V.P. "Èstetičeskie vzgljady L.N. Tolstogo i tradicii revoljucionno-demokratičeskoj kritiki (K postanovke voprosa)." Učenye zapiski (Vinnick. gos. pedagogičeskogo instituta. im. N. Ostrovskogo), Vol. 5, c. 2, 1957), pp. 3-31.

------------ "Paradoksy L'va Tolstogo ob iskusstve." Istorija èstetičeskoj mysli i literaturovedenja. Voprosy russkoj literatury, No. 12, 1969.

Mann, Thomas, "Goethe und Tolstoi. Fragment zum Problem der Humanität," in Thomas Mann, Adel des Geistes. Sechzehn Versuche zum Problem der Humanität, Stockholm: Berman-Fischer Verlag, 1945.

Mixajlov, A. "Èstetika L'va Tolstogo v osveščenii buržuaznyx iskusstvovedov." Na literaturnom postu, No. 33 (November), 1931.

Močul'skij, V.N., "N.G. Černyševskij i L.N. Tolstoj ob iskusstve." Otdel'nyj ottisk iz žurnala Russkij filosofičeskij vestnik. Warsaw, 1909.

Naumenko, T.K. "Voprosy iskusstva v rasskazax L.N. Tolstogo konca pjatidesjatyx godov XIX veka." Učenye zapiski Bijskogo pedagogičeskogo instituta., vyp. 6 (1963), pp. 22-32.

Nevler, V.E. "Lev Tolstoj i Džuzeppe Madzini (O vlijanii èstetičeskix i filosofičeskix vzgljadov ital. revoljucionera na tvorčestvo L. N. Tolstogo)." K 100-letiju so dnja smerti Madzini, Izv. AN SSSR. Serija liVol. i jaz., Vol. 31, vyp. 4, (1972), pp. 297-308.

Nuralov, E.L. "Èstetika L.N. Tolstogo i tradicii russkoj revoljucionno-demokratičeskoj mysli." Erevan: Molodoj nauč. rabotnik, No. 1 (1973), pp. 50-60.

------------ "Èstetika L.N. Tolstogo v ocenke sovetskogo literaturovedenija." Nauč. trudy Erevanskogo pedagogičeskogo instituta. russ. inostran. jaz., no 3 (1971), pp. 130-45.

------------ "Kritika russkogo dekadentstva v èstetike L.N. Tolstogo." Vestnik Moskovskogo instituta., serija VII, No. 5 (1962), pp. 31-42.

------------ "Voprosy muzyki v èstetike L.N. Tolstogo." Studenčeskij naučnyj sbornik Russ. pedagogičeskogo instituta., 5 (1957), pp. 67-85.

------------ "Kritika buržuaznogo iskusstva v traktate L.N. Tolstogo 'Čto takoe iskusstvo?'," Naučnye trudy Erevanskogo gosudarstvennogo universiteta, Vol. 70, issue 7, Erevan, 1960.

Opul'skaja, L.D. "Literaturno-èstetičeskie vzgljady L.N. Tolstogo." L.N. Tolstoj o literature. Moscow: Goslitizdat, 1955, pp. V-XL.

Osnovin, V.V. "K voprosu o tvorčeskix iskanijax L. Tolstogo poslednego perioda." Tolstovskij sbornik, No. 3 (1962), pp. 51-68.

Parkin, C.J.F. "Tolstoy's What is Art?" New Zealand Slavonic Journal, 4 (Sum. 1969), pp. 54-67.

Pomorska, Krystyna, "Tolstoy: Contra Semiosis." International Journal of Slavic Linguistics and Poetics, No. 25-6, 1982, pp. 383-390.

Ponomarev, G.I. "Izučenie èstetičeskogo nasledija L.N. Tolstogo v sovetskom literaturovedenji." Voprosy russkoj literatury, No. 3 (1967), pp. 53-63.

Rozental', M., "Vremennoe i 'bessmertnoe'," Literaturnyj kritik, book 11, 1935.

Scanlan, James F., "Chernyshevsky and Rousseau." Anthony M. Mlikotin, editor, Western Philosophical Systems in Russian Literature: A Collection of Critical Studies. Los Angeles: University of Southern California Press, 1979.

Schrader, Willi, "Shakespeare, Crosby und Graf Tolstoi," Shakespeare Jahrbuch, Band 112/1976. Weimar: Hermann Bühlaus Nachfolger, 1976.

Semenova, N.A. "Problema etičeskogo i èstetičeskogo v proizvedenijax L.N. Tolstogo," A.I. Ivanov, ed., Voprosy èstetiki. Sbornik statej. Izdatel'stvo Saratovskogo universiteta, 1963.

Sergeenko, A. "Tolstoj o literature i iskusstve," zapisi V. T. Čertkova i P.A. Sergeenko. Publikacija A. Sergeenko. Literaturnoe nasledstvo, No. 37-38. Moscow: the USSR Academy of Sciences, 1939

Shaw, G.B. "Tolstoy on Art." in Shaw, G.B., Selected Nondramatic Writings. pp. 427-32.

Šilbajoris, Rimvydas. "Lev Tolstoj: Esthetics and Art." Russian Literature, No. 1 (1971), pp. 58-72.

------------ "Tolstoy's Esthetics in Soviet Perspective," Bucknell Review, Winter, 1970, pp. 103-116.

------------ "Human Contact and Tolstoy's Esthetics." Papers in Comparative Studies. Columbus: The Ohio State University, No. 1, 1981.

----------- "Tolstoy's Humanism in His Critique of Shakespeare," American Contributions to the Tenth International Congress of Slavists. Columbus: Slavica, 1988, pp. 371-381.

Symons, Arthur, "Tolstoi on Art," Studies in Prose and Verse. New York: Dutton 1904.

Tolstoj, S.L. "Ob otraženii žizni v Anne Kareninoj. Iz vospominanij S.L. Tolstogo." Literaturnoe nasledstvo, 37-38, 1939.

Voinova, E.N. "Problema xudožestvennoj pravdy v èstetike L.N. Tolstogo." Voprosy teorii i istorii èstetiki, vyp. 7 (1972), pp. 118-130.

Weidlé, Wladimir. "Tolstoj ob iskusstve." Novyj Žurnal, (1971), pp. 76-113.

Whealy, Elizabeth. "What is Art?" Humanities Association Bulletin, 21, 1, pp. 14-26.

General literature

Hawkes, Terence, Structuralism and Semiotics. Los Angeles: University of California Press, 1977.

Mukařovsky, Jan. Structure, Sign and Function. New Haven and London: Yale University Press, 1965.

Mukařovsky, Jan, "Aesthetic Function Among Other Functions," in John Burbank and Peter Steiner, editors, Structure, Sign and Function. Selected Essays by Jan Mukarovsky, New Haven and London: Yale University Press, 1978

Orwell, Sonia and Ian Angus, editors. In Front of Your Nose. The Collected Essays, Journalism and Letters of George Orwell. New York: Harcourt, Brace, Inc. 1968.

Osborne, Harold. Aesthetics and Art Theory. A Historical Introduction. New York: E.P. Dutton and Co., 1979.

Protopopov, Vl., ed. Vospominanija o O.I. Čajkovskom. Gosmuzizdat, 1962.

Ruskin, John. The Stones of Venice. New York: John Wiley and Sons, 1890.

Sar-Peladan, Josephin. La Décadence Esthétique. Réponse a Tolstoï. Paris: Chamuel, éditeur, 1898.

Terras, Victor. Belinskij and Russian Literary Criticism. The

Heritage of Organic Aesthetics. Madison: The University of Wisconsin Press, 1974.

Šklovskij, Viktor. Xudožestvennaja proza. Razmyšlenija. Moscow: Sovetskij pisatel', 1959.

Wagner, Richard. Gesammelte Schriften und Dichtungen. Leipzig: Verlag von E.H. Fritsch, n.d.

Zivel'činskaja, L. Opyt marksistskogo analiza istorii èstetiki. Moscow: Kommunističeskaja akademija, 1928.

Other Books From Slavica

Ronelle Alexander: *The Structure of Vasko Popa's Poetry.*
American Contributions to the Tenth, Ninth, and Eighth International Congress of Slavists.
A. Barker: *The Mother Syndrome in the Russian Folk Imagination.*
R. P. Bartlett, A. G. Cross, and **Karen Rasmussen,** eds.: *Russia and the World of the Eighteenth Century.*
H. Birnbaum & T. Eekman, eds.: *Fiction and Drama in Eastern and Southeastern Europe.*
M. D. Birnbaum: *Humanists in a Shattered World: Croatian and Hungarian Latinity in the Sixteenth Century.*
K. Black, ed.: *A Biobibliographical Handbook of Bulgarian Authors.*
R. L. Busch: *Humor in the Major Novels of Dostoevsky.*
Jozef Cíger-Hronský: *Jozef Mak* (a novel), translated from Slovak.
J. Douglas Clayton, ed.: *Issues in Russian Literature before 1917.*
Gary Cox: *Tyrant and Victim in Dostoevsky.*
Carolina De Maegd-Soëp: *Chekhov and Women.*
Thomas Eekman and **Dean S. Worth,** eds.: *Russian Poetics.*
John M. Foley, ed.: *Oral Traditional Literature.*
Morris Halle, ed.: *Roman Jakobson: What He Taught Us.*
L. A. Johnson: *The Experience of Time in* <u>Crime and Punishment</u>.
Robert Mann: *Lances Sing: A Study of the Igor Tale.*
Vasa D. Mihailovich and **Mateja Matejic:** *A Comprehensive Bibliography of Yugoslav Literature in English, 1593-1980.*
E. Możejko, ed.: *V. P.Aksënov: A Writer in Quest of Himself.*
T. Pachmuss: *Russian Literature in the Baltic between the World Wars.*
Barry P. Scherr and **Dean S. Worth,** eds.: *Russian Verse Theory.*
P. Seyffert: *Soviet Literary Structuralism: Background Debate Issues.*
J. Thomas Shaw: *Pushkin A Concordance to the Poetry.*
Efraim Sicher: *Style and Structure in the Prose of Isaak Babel'.*
David A. Sloane: *Aleksandr Blok and the Dynamics of the Lyric Cycle.*
G. Slobin, ed.: *Aleksej Remizov: Approaches to a Protean Writer.*
J. Taubman: *A Life Through Poetry Marina Tsvetaeva's Lyric Diary.*
Janet G. Tucker: *Innokentij Annenskij and the Acmeist Doctrine.*
Vickery, ed.: *Aleksandr Blok Centennial Conference.*
J. Woodward: *The Symbolic Art of Gogol: Essays on His Short Fiction.*
Yordan Yovkov: *The Inn at Antimovo* and *Legends of Stara Planina,* translated from Bulgarian by John Burnip.

OHIO UNIVERSITY LIBRARY

se return this book as soon as